DISCARD

BEYOND MARRIAGE

BEYOND MARRIAGE

CONTINUING BATTLES FOR LGBT RIGHTS

Susan Gluck Mezey

ROWMAN & LITTLEFIELD
Lanham • Boulder • New York • London

Published by Rowman & Littlefield
A wholly owned subsidiary of The Rowman & Littlefield Publishing Group, Inc.
4501 Forbes Boulevard, Suite 200, Lanham, Maryland 20706
www.rowman.com

Unit A, Whitacre Mews, 26-34 Stannary Street, London SE11 4AB

Copyright © 2017 by Rowman & Littlefield

All rights reserved. No part of this book may be reproduced in any form or by any electronic or mechanical means, including information storage and retrieval systems, without written permission from the publisher, except by a reviewer who may quote passages in a review.

British Library Cataloguing in Publication Information Available

Library of Congress Cataloging-in-Publication Data

Names: Names: Mezey, Susan Gluck, 1944–
Title: Beyond marriage : continuing battles for LGBT rights / Susan Gluck Mezey.
Description: Lanham : Rowman & Littlefield, 2017. | Includes bibliographical references and index.
Identifiers: LCCN 2016052686 (print) | LCCN 2016059846 (ebook) | ISBN 9781442248625 (hardcover : alk. paper) | ISBN 9781442248649 (pbk. : alk. paper) | ISBN 9781442248632 (electronic)
Subjects: LCSH: Sexual minorities—Legal status, laws, etc.—United States.
Classification: LCC KF4754.5 .M489 2017 (print) | LCC KF4754.5 (ebook) | DDC 342.7308/7—dc23
LC record available at https://lccn.loc.gov/2016052686

∞™ The paper used in this publication meets the minimum requirements of American National Standard for Information Sciences Permanence of Paper for Printed Library Materials, ANSI/NISO Z39.48-1992.

Printed in the United States of America

CONTENTS

ACKNOWLEDGMENTS

As always, I owe a huge debt to my husband Michael for his encouragement and support of my research and writing, as well as my life as a whole. In addition to shouldering much of the burden of keeping our household afloat while I am chained to the computer, he is willing (usually) to listen to my explanations of the abstruse legal doctrines I come across in my research. He has heard this expression of my appreciation in the past, but I repeat it here to emphasize his importance to me.

The rest of the family, including my wonderful children and their loving spouses, and especially my grandchildren, Rebecca, Norah, Paul, Benjamin, and Daniel, have been most welcome distractions, and although they have not contributed to the research or writing of this book, they are a source of enormous pleasure in my life.

I want to thank Jon Sisk, vice president and senior executive editor at Rowman & Littlefield, who has supported my work for over a decade and has been willing (mostly) to acquiesce to my requests to be involved in all details of the book, including the cover design. Assistant editor Chris Utter was a pleasure to work with and very nice about granting my requests for favors. Production editor Andrew Yoder was very attentive to problems that arose during the production process and worked hard to fix them. Finally, I want to acknowledge David Patternotte and Manon Tremblay as friends and colleagues who played an important role in sparking my interest in the LGBT community as well as encouraging my work in this significant area of law and politics.

This book is the culmination of years of research and writings on the courts and LGBT policy making. Some of the material in chapters 3 and 5 is drawn from this previous work and included here with permission:

"Decisions in Search of a Doctrine: Marriage Equality in the Lower Federal Courts." 2015. *Journal of Civil and Human Rights* 1: 56–81.

"The Federal Courts and Marriage Equality: Who Decides?" 2015. *University of South Dakota Law Review* 6: 424–56.

"Gay Rights and the Courts." 2015. In *The Ashgate Research Companion to Lesbian and Gay Activism*, edited by David Paternotte and Manon Tremblay, 95–208 (Surrey, UK: Ashgate).

"Pursuing Marriage Equality in Four Democracies: Canada, the United States, Belgium, and Spain." 2013. *Global Journal of Human Social Science* 13: 1–11.

PREFACE

In focusing on the LGBT community's continuing struggle for equal rights, this book builds on my earlier publications, *Queers in Court* and *Gay Families and the Courts.* In the years since the latter was published, there has been significant progress toward egalitarianism in the public policy-making arena affecting LGBT rights. These advances include the demise of the military's Don't Ask, Don't Tell policy in 2011; the commitment to ending the exclusion of transgender service members; the US Supreme Court's historic ruling striking the Defense of Marriage Act in 2013 and its even more historic ruling in 2015, declaring marriage equality the law of the land; the opposition to religious liberty laws that shield offenders from the consequences of their discriminatory acts; and the Obama's administration commitment to promoting equal rights for the transgender community.

Outside the United States, there has been a plethora of international compacts and agreements, pledging to combat discrimination on the basis of sexual orientation and gender identity; increasing recognition of the legitimacy of same-sex relationships—ranging from civil unions and domestic partnerships to civil marriages—especially in western Europe and Latin America; greater acceptance of claims of discrimination on the basis of sexual orientation and gender identity by the European Court of Human Rights; and growing awareness of the medical, economic, and social needs of transgender people.

Despite these gains, there are critical problems that continue to confront members of the LGBT community all over the world, including in the United States: intransigence in granting basic human and civil rights, often resulting in violence and even death; unequal access to health care; restrictions on same-sex relationships in marriage and adoption laws; the role of religious institutions in countering equal rights claims; and the failure to acknowledge the importance of gender identity in individuals. Until these issues and others are resolved, members of the LGBT community will be forced to persist in their battles for equal rights.

This book examines the continuing struggles for LGBT rights over the past several decades, highlighting the role that courts have played in the policy-making process. Although its primary focus is on LGBT policy in the United States, it adds a comparative dimension by appraising selected issues affecting the LGBT community in other nations.

When first undertaking the research, I was chiefly interested in assessing the importance of litigation in furthering LGBT rights because it was clear that LGBT rights activists heavily relied on it to redress their grievances and, indeed, continue to view it as a potent weapon in their efforts to achieve equal treatment under the law. In courts around the world, LGBT litigants challenged policies restricting family relationships as well as laws they claimed discriminated against them on the basis of sexual orientation and gender identity in employment, education, health care, and criminal justice.

Because courts do not operate in a policy-making vacuum, the analysis also examines the interaction between the courts and other institutions in the rapidly changing policy arena of LGBT rights. In doing so, it seeks in part, to determine if the reliance on litigation in pursuing LGBT rights claims is justified. The book argues that although litigation is not the only path to equality of rights in all nations and across all policy areas, overall, the courts are the most effective institution in establishing equal treatment for members of the LGBT community. The argument stems from the premise that the courts' adjudicatory role frequently requires them to determine whether laws and policies adopted by representative institutions are consistent with the individual rights guarantees of their foundational national (or international) charters. Therefore, the success of the LGBT litigation strategy most often depends on the litigants' ability to persuade the courts that their obligation to protect minority rights outweighs their duty to defer to legislative or executive authority.

PLAN OF THE BOOK

Chapter 1 presents an overview of the employment status of the LGBT community in the public and private sectors, explaining discrimination on the basis of gender identity and sexual orientation and the efforts to remedy the discrimination.

Chapter 2 discusses issues affecting the transgender community, including discrimination because of gender identity in employment, prisoners' rights, and students' rights and the attempts to combat the discrimination.

Chapter 3 traces the battle for marriage equality in the United States by same-sex marriage activists, highlighting the role of the lower federal courts in adjudicating constitutional challenges to state and federal restrictions on same-sex marriage.

Chapter 4 discusses efforts to stem LGBT equality by opponents of same-sex marriage who defend themselves against charges of discrimination by claiming infringement on their religious liberty and state and local officials who seek to constrain transgender individuals from expressing their gender identity in meaningful ways.

Chapter 5 offers a global perspective on policies affecting the LGBT community, discussing the status of LGBT equality, especially with respect to relationship recognition, in many parts of the world, and focusing on the litigation over LGBT rights claims in the Canadian and South African courts, as well as the European Court of Human Rights.

1

EMPLOYMENT OPPORTUNITY

Because individuals are usually cautious about revealing their sexual orientation or gender identity in the workplace, it is difficult to present an accurate count of the number of LGBT employees in the nation (see Catalyst 2015; Human Rights Campaign Foundation 2009).[1] A 2013 report released by groups committed to advancing LGBT rights estimates that there are 5.4 million LGBT workers in the nation's workforce, out of almost 155 million (Movement Advancement Project, Center for American Progress, and Human Rights Campaign 2013). Underscoring the difficulty of obtaining consistent, reliable information, a 2009 study by the Williams Institute, based on government data—including the 2000 Census Bureau Report—revealed there were more than 1 million LGBT government employees (200,000 at the federal level; 418,000 at the state level; and 585,000 at the local level). The same analysis indicated there were slightly under 7 million LGBT employees working in the private sector (Williams Institute 2009).

Over the past several years, as the nation became more aware of employment discrimination on the basis of sexual orientation and gender identity, many public and private sector employers have attempted to alleviate workplace discrimination. Consequently, the LGBT community has achieved a number of victories in the battle against inequality in employment. An important indicator of progress is evident in a national survey showing growing public support for LGBT workers.[2] The survey showed that 65 percent of the respondents agreed that federal law should be expanded to prohibit job discrimination based on sexual orientation and gender identity; 44 percent indicated that they "strongly" favored such a law, with only 14 percent "strongly" opposing it (Harris Poll 2015).[3] Additionally, a survey conducted by Small Business Majority of 508 businesses found that more than two-thirds of them believed there should be state or federal laws to protect LGBT workers. Indeed, 81 percent thought that such a federal law existed (Movement Advancement Project, Center for American Progress, Human Rights Campaign 2013).

FEDERAL AGENCIES AND EMPLOYMENT DISCRIMINATION

Recently, federal agencies have taken leading roles in promoting equal employment opportunity for LGBT employees. The US Equal Employment Opportunity Commission (EEOC)—the key federal agency responsible for enforcing the nation's equal employment opportunity laws—ruled in *Macy v. Holder* (2012) that discrimination based on gender identity falls within Title VII's prohibition against sex discrimination. Attorney General Eric Holder later released a memorandum supporting the EEOC's position (Holder 2014).

In June 2015, four government agencies, including the EEOC, issued a jointly developed resource guide on employment discrimination for federal civilian employees. It explicitly states, "Title VII's prohibition on sex discrimination protects persons who have been discriminated against based on sexual orientation and gender identity. Further, civil service laws prohibit certain employment decisions or personnel actions when the decisions or actions are based on conduct that does not adversely affect job performance, including sexual orientation and gender identity" (Office of Personnel Management et al. 2015, 2). Soon after, supplementing its position on Title VII and gender identity announced in *Macy*, the EEOC held in *Baldwin v. Department of Transportation* (2015) that Title VII also applies to discrimination based on sexual orientation.

In other parts of the executive branch, President Barack Obama issued two executive orders extending job protection to the millions of LGBT workers employed by the federal government as well as by federal contractors.[4] Seeking to resolve a long-simmering dispute, the US

Occupational Safety and Health Administration (OSHA) issued a "Guide to Restroom Access for Transgender Employees." Designed to illustrate the best practices in allocating bathroom facilities, it began by stating, "[T]he core principle is that all employees, including transgender employees, should have access to restrooms that correspond to their gender identity" (US Department of Labor, Occupational Safety and Health Administration 2015).

On June 9, 2015, delivering the keynote address at the LGBT Pride Month ceremony, Defense Secretary Ashton Carter announced that the Pentagon's equal opportunity policy for active duty service members would extend to sexual orientation, protecting all gay, lesbian, and bisexual troops from discrimination. He confirmed that the Department of Defense (DOD) had "completed the process for updating its Military Equal Opportunity policy to include sexual orientation—ensuring that the department, like the rest of the federal government, treats sexual-orientation-based discrimination the same way it treats discrimination based on race, religion, color, sex, age, and national origin" (Carter 2015).[5]

There have been signs of improved conditions for LGBT workers at the state and local levels, as well. By early 2016, twenty states and the District of Columbia had laws prohibiting employment discrimination because of sexual orientation and gender identity, with two others prohibiting discrimination because of sexual orientation.[6] At the city and county levels, by 2015, 225 cities and counties had banned employment discrimination for LGBT workers (Human Rights Campaign 2015a).

By 2014, the vast majority of Fortune 500 companies (91 percent) had instituted job protection measures for individuals on the basis of sexual orientation—up from 61 percent in 2002. A smaller number (61 percent) had formulated a gender identity antidiscrimination policy—up from only 3 percent in 2002 (Fidas, Cooper, and Raspanti 2014). Another snapshot of the employment picture shows that forty-eight of the top fifty Fortune 500 companies (96 percent) prohibit discrimination because of sexual orientation, and thirty-five (70 percent) disallow it on the basis of gender identity (Williams Institute 2014a).

EQUAL EMPLOYMENT LAWS

Despite these gains, private sector employers are free to make adverse employment decisions based on sexual orientation and gender identity in twenty-eight states.[7] As recently as February 2016, more than half (52 percent) of the LGBT population were living in states with no statewide antidiscrimination laws (Movement Advancement Project 2016b).[8] Additionally, most states have at least some municipalities or counties that offer private sector job protection to LGBT workers, yet five states provide no protection to workers against discrimination on the basis of sexual orientation, and seven offer no protection to workers based on gender identity or sexual orientation (Movement Advancement Project 2016a).[9]

With no employment discrimination laws to guarantee the rights of LGBT employees in the majority of states, despite the public's support for LGBT workers manifested in public opinion polls, it is not surprising that studies have found that substantial numbers of LGBT employees report being subject to job discrimination. Although employees living in states without job protection suffer more discrimination, complaints of discrimination from employees living in protected states show that they are subject to it as well (Pizer et al. 2012). Additionally, because many employees hide their sexual orientation and gender identity on the job, they are forced to listen to demeaning jokes and comments from their coworkers. In short, the workplace remains a hostile environment for a substantial portion of the LGBT community.

Studies also found that the discrimination manifests in wage gaps between heterosexual men and gay and bisexual men, with the latter two groups earning from 10 to 32 percent less than the former; moreover, lesbian, gay, and bisexual (LGB) workers with same-sex partners or spouses received fewer workplace benefits, such as health insurance, than employees with different-sex spouses. Moreover, when compared to nontransgender workers, transgender employees had lower wages and higher rates of unemployment (Fidas, Cooper, and Raspanti 2014; Grant, Mottet, and Tanis 2011; Movement Advancement Project, Center for American Progress, and Human Rights Campaign 2013; Pizer et al. 2012; Sears and Mallory 2011; Williams Institute 2014a).

Numerous surveys of LGB workers conducted in the mid-1980s to the mid-1990s by researchers at the Williams Institute reveal that as many as 68 percent of LGB employees experience job discrimination at some time in their working lives. Later studies show that 15 to 43 percent of LGB employees are subject to discrimination, ranging from dismissals to refusals to hire, abuse, and inequities in pay.

When researchers asked heterosexual employees whether they were aware of job discrimination against LGB coworkers, 12 to 30 percent said they had witnessed discriminatory job actions. The authors conclude that "despite the variations in methodology, context, and time period in the studies . . . our review of the evidence demonstrates one disturbing and consistent pattern: sexual orientation-based and gender identity discrimination is a common occurrence in many workplaces across the country" (Badgett et al. 2007, 3).

Not surprisingly, an analysis of the experiences of transgender employees shows that 15 to 57 percent report also suffering from discrimination on the job (Badgett et al. 2007, 3). A more recent study of discrimination against transgender individuals conducted from September 2008 through February 2009 confirms that unemployment was twice as high among transgender individuals as the general population. Moreover, almost half of the transgender respondents (47 percent) reported negative experiences on the job, from being fired to being denied advances; one quarter (26 percent) reported being forced from their jobs because of their gender identity, and an overwhelming majority (78 percent) reported being discriminated against or otherwise mistreated on the job (Grant, Mottet, and Tanis 2011).[10] In May 2011, the Center for American Progress offered a more detailed analysis of job discrimination against LGBT employees. Its study of existing data shows that 8 to 17 percent of LGBT workers reported adverse job actions because of their sexual orientation or gender identity; another 10 to 28 percent claimed that they were not promoted or their work was negatively evaluated because of their status (Burns and Krehely 2011).

Scholars at the Williams Institute released an analysis in July 2011 summarizing the findings of numerous studies of workplace discrimination against LGBT employees, as well as the results of a 2008 General Social Survey.[11] They confirmed that many LGBT employees experience discrimination or harassment on the job—or at least are fearful of being subject to it. Moreover, in addition to finding evidence of sustained patterns of discrimination, they noted that an "emerging body of research shows that discrimination has negative impacts on LGBT employees both in terms of physical and emotional health, wages and opportunities, job satisfaction, and productivity" (Sears and Mallory 2011, 16).

The well-documented and widespread nature of job discrimination against LGBT employees, particularly the transgender or gender-nonconforming community, perhaps reflects the uneasiness that Americans feel about working alongside such workers. Surveys conducted in the United States in August and November 2014 show that almost one-third of the non-LGBT respondents indicated that they would be uncomfortable upon learning they have an LGBT coworker, with 23 percent "uncomfortable" and 7 percent "very uncomfortable" (Gay & Lesbian Alliance Against Defamation 2015).[12]

CONGRESS AND DISCRIMINATION IN EMPLOYMENT

In May 1974, Congresswoman Bella Abzug, Democrat from New York, sponsored legislation barring discrimination in employment on the basis of sexual orientation; her bill, entitled the Equality Act of 1974, would have banned discrimination because of sex, marital status, and sexual orientation by private employers as well as state governments and educational institutions (Feldblum 2000). Ahead of its time, the bill failed to clear the House Judiciary Committee, to which it was committed.

A year later, Abzug introduced the National Lesbian and Gay Civil Rights Bill in the 94th Congress. This bill, more narrowly written, would have added sexual orientation to the antidiscrimination language of Title VII.[13] When Abzug lost her seat in 1976, Ed Koch, also a Democrat from New York, introduced a version of the bill, and hearings were held in the House. Starting with about two dozen cosponsors when Abzug first brought it to the floor, the proposed bill gained an increasing number of sponsors in subsequent sessions. Despite widespread support, however, the bills were never debated or brought to the floor for a vote. A Senate version of the bill, first introduced in 1979, was no more successful (Endean 2006; Feldblum 2000).

Following Bill Clinton's election in 1992, there were renewed efforts to pass a civil rights measure, departing from its initial strategy of amending Title VII to add sexual orientation to the list of protected classes within the law. There was a good deal of debate over whether to continue to attempt to amend the 1964 Civil Rights Act, which would have extended civil rights protection more broadly to gay men and lesbians in employment, federally funded institutions, and public accommodations. Seen as a more ambitious goal, the gay and lesbian community perhaps felt disempowered by their defeat in the battle over Don't Ask, Don't Tell and believed it more realistic to enact a stand-alone law that would focus more narrowly on employment discrimination (Reed 2013; Reed 2014; see Feldblum 2000; Jasiunas 2000;).[14] In the end, borrowing from the language of Title VII and the Americans with Disabilities Act, the sponsors began drafting a stand-alone civil rights bill that banned discrimination because of sexual orientation in employment, housing, federally funded programs, and public facilities. Because some feared it would be more difficult to win approval for a broad-based bill, they stripped it of all but the employment discrimination provisions. For the same reason, they excluded discrimination on the basis of gender identity, a decision that became the subject of much controversy within the LGBT community over the next several years (see Frye 2003).

On June 23, 1994, in the second session of the 103d Congress, Massachusetts Democrats Gerry Studds and Barney Frank introduced H.R. 4636, the Employment Non-Discrimination Act (ENDA) of 1994, with a bipartisan group of more than one hundred cosponsors. The same day, Massachusetts Democrat Ted Kennedy and Vermont Republican John Chafee introduced its counterpart in the Senate as S. 2238. Kennedy optimistically described the proposed law as "another significant step on freedom's journey—another milestone in the civil rights march of our time . . . parallel[ing] protections against job discrimination already provided under title VII of the Civil Rights Act" (*Congressional Record* 1994, S7581). The bill was referred to the Labor and Human Resources Committee, yet despite committee hearings with testimony from members of the gay and lesbian community, civil rights, and labor leaders, no further action was taken on it.

The next year, another Vermont Republican, Jim Jeffords, introduced the 1995 ENDA as S. 932. He explained that the law would include sexual orientation as a prohibited basis of employment discrimination, saying, "[T]he time has come to extend this type of protection to the only group—millions of Americans—still subjected to legal discrimination on the job." He added,

> [T]he principles of equality and opportunity must apply to all Americans. Success at work should be directly related to one's ability to do the job, period. People who work hard and perform well should not be kept from leading productive and responsible lives—from paying their taxes, meeting their mortgage payments and otherwise contributing to the economic life of the nation—because of irrational, non-work-related prejudice. (*Congressional Record* 1995, S8502)

The Jeffords bill barred employers with fifteen or more employees from "subject[ing] an individual to a different standard or different treatment on the basis of sexual orientation"; it exempted religious organizations (except in their for-profit activities) and the military. Also committed to the Senate Labor and Human Resources Committee, it went no further; Studds's version, H.R. 1863, also died in committee.

In another effort to extend federal job protection to the LGB community, Kennedy, Jeffords, and Joseph Lieberman, Democrat from Connecticut, introduced S. 2056 on September 5, 1996. Kennedy promoted it as "predicated upon the American ideal of equal opportunity [and] it gives gays and lesbians a fair chance in the workplace" (*Congressional Record* 1996, S9986). Speaking in support of the bill, Virginia Democrat Chuck Robb stressed that the decision to end discrimination should not be a difficult one. He urged his colleagues to remember that "each American worker—whether they build houses, pave roads, serve meals in country diners, or manage corporations—deserves to be judged by their dedication to their job and the quality of their work. It is indefensible," he added, "that in a great nation like ours men and women can lose their jobs, be passed over for promotions, or suffer harassment because they have—or are perceived to have—a different sexual orientation than the rest of us" (*Congressional Record* 1996, S10131).

The opposition protested that the bill might force employers to document their employees' sexual orientation to defend themselves against the litigation they claimed would inevitably follow passage of the bill. Nancy Kassebaum, Republican from Kansas, stated that she did not believe that the law would end job discrimination but would instead "lead to more division in the workplace, not less" (*Congressional Record* 1996, S10130–31). Also expressing his opposition, Utah Republican Orrin Hatch called the bill a "litigation bonanza," characterizing it as a "massive increase in Federal power" and predicting that the "Federal bureaucracy will have a field day with this bill." To emphasize the harm that would follow from passage of the law, he cited letters from parents and school officials who believed the statute would prevent them from removing gay and lesbian teachers who were not "role models" for their children and warned of dire consequences if it were passed (*Congressional Record* 1996, S10132). Ironically, ENDA's opponents offered two contradictory arguments against the law. One side claimed that it would lead to a flood of litigation and hamper the courts' ability to deal with weightier matters. The other side contended that job discrimination because of sexual orientation was so rare that the law was unnecessary (see Rubenstein 2001).

After Kennedy threatened to introduce ENDA as an amendment to the 1996 Defense of Marriage Act (DOMA), he reached an agreement with Senate Majority Leader Trent Lott to bring both bills to the floor separately, with no amendments permitted on either. DOMA, voted on first, passed with an overwhelming bipartisan majority of 85–14. ENDA sponsors had hoped that pairing it with DOMA would allow senators to take the popular election-year position against same-sex marriage and then demonstrate their fairness with a positive vote on ENDA immediately after. Jeffords, who voted for both bills, said, "[P]eople don't want to go too far on changing marriage and traditional relationships. But the feeling is when someone wants to work someplace, they ought to be able to get a job" (*New York Times*, September 11, 1996).[15]

After a two-day debate, the Senate cast its vote on ENDA on September 10, 1996. Vice President Al Gore prepared himself to return to Washington, DC, to cast the deciding vote in case of a tie. As it turned out, his presence was not required; the vote was 50–49 against the bill. David Pryor, Democrat from Arkansas, who had indicated that he "probably" would support it, was in Little Rock at his ailing son's bedside during the vote. Forty-one Democrats and eight Republicans voted in favor of the bill; five Democrats and forty-five Republicans voted no (*Congressional Quarterly*, September 14, 1996, 2597). Although the vote was a setback, it represented the first successful effort in bringing the issue of equal employment opportunities for LGB workers to a congressional vote.[16]

Even if the bill passed the Senate, it was unlikely to be approved in the House. Nevertheless, Elizabeth Birch, executive director of the Human Rights Campaign (HRC), was upbeat after the Senate vote, saying, "[W]e came within a breath of victory today [and] we'll hit the ground running in the 105th Congress" (*New York Times*, September 11, 1996).[17] More broadly, she declared, "[W]e have witnessed gay civil rights in the 1990s completely embraced by the civil rights community in general [and] have firmly established that it is no longer a question of whether Congress will pass the employment non-discrimination act for gay Americans. It's a question of when." A leader of ACT-UP, a more radical LGB rights group, took exception to Birch's statement, saying, "[W]e just got beat up in the United States Senate and you're trying to sugarcoat it" (*Congressional Quarterly*, September 13, 1996, 2597).

Birch's optimism was indeed misplaced because, with the exception of the 109th Congress in 2005, ENDA was unsuccessfully introduced in every Congress thereafter. While gaining support over the years, the bills died in committee, never reaching the floor of either chamber for a vote. In 2007, with the Democrats in control of the House and the Senate following a strong showing in the 2006 election, ENDA became more viable in the 110th Congress, but the debate over including protection for transgender employees created discord within the ranks of ENDA supporters.

Introduced by Frank in the 110th Congress, H.R. 2015 prohibited employment discrimination on the basis of gender identity and gender expression. Most Democrats supported the transgender-inclusive language, but a few threatened to join Republicans to defeat the measure if it remained in the bill (Reed 2013). Amid rumblings from within the Democratic caucus about including gender identity as a protected category, it became clear to Frank and House leaders that there were not enough votes for passage. To the great disappointment of the transgender community, he introduced a second bill, H.R. 3685, stripped of the gender identity language.

H.R. 3685 succeeded in passing out of the Education and Labor Committee, and with the new Democratic House majority in place following the 2006 off-year election, the House approved it in a 235–184 vote; 35 Republicans joined the 200 Democrats.[18] Eleven years after the initial unsuccessful Senate vote, ENDA had finally come to the House chamber for a vote. To the dismay of its supporters, it proved to be a hollow victory, as the corresponding bill gained no momentum in the Senate.

There had been a great deal of controversy over the decision to go forward with the stripped-down version of the bill. Responding to intense criticism from the transgender community as well as several lesbian and gay rights groups for excluding transgender employees from the law, Frank said,

> I believe that it would be a grave error to let this opportunity to pass a sexual orientation nondiscrimination bill not go forward, not simply because it is one of the most important advances we'll have made in securing civil rights for Americans in decades, but because moving forward on this bill now will also better serve the ultimate goal of including people who are transgender than simply accepting total defeat today. (*The Advocate* 2007)

Frank said he was also convinced that if Congress had considered his original bill, there would have been enough votes to amend it to remove the gender identity provision (Reed 2013).

In addition to the controversy about its transgender inclusivity, opponents also charged that the proposed language in H.R. 2015 granting religious exemptions in hiring practices was too narrow.[19] They were able to amend the bill to mirror the more generous view of Title VII's religious exemption—as interpreted by the federal courts—that would permit religiously affiliated employers to claim the exemption more easily, even for employees more tenuously tied to the organization's religiously oriented positions (Thompson 2015).

In the following years, the LGBT community came together, and in June 2009, Frank proposed H.R. 3017 in the 111th Congress, with more than one hundred bipartisan cosponsors; the bill now included protections for transgender workers. Jeff Merkley, Oregon Democrat, assuming Kennedy's role, introduced S. 1584 in the Senate a few months later. The House Education and Labor Committee held a hearing on H.R. 3017 in September 2009; Merkley's bill was sent to the Senate Health, Education, Labor, and Pensions Committee, which held a hearing two months later. Despite Democratic majorities in both houses and the support of the newly elected Democratic president, neither bill advanced to the floor for a vote. Frank reintroduced the bill as H.R. 1397 in the 112th Congress, and Merkley introduced it as S. 811, but especially with the new Republican majorities in both houses after the 2010 off-year election, these bills fared no better than their predecessors.[20]

There was a breakthrough in the Senate in the 113th Congress, almost two decades after ENDA's near victory in 1996. In April 2013, Merkley introduced S. 815, the Employment Non-Discrimination Act of 2013; Representative Jared Polis, Democrat from Colorado, introduced an identical version in the House as H.R. 1755. After considering several amendments, the Senate Health, Education, Labor, and Pensions Committee approved the bill in a 15–7 vote on July 10, 2013. Committee Republicans complained that there were no hearings held on the bill, which had precluded them from raising questions about implementing the law. Most of their concerns focused on allowing transgender individuals to use restrooms in schools and workplaces that corresponded to their gender identity.[21] They also objected that the law did not exempt employers with deeply held religious beliefs about homosexuality; they saw no reason to distinguish their organizations from the religious institutions that were explicitly exempted under the law. Finally, they protested, the law was unnecessary, as a number of state and local governments as well as private companies had already enacted antidiscrimination laws and polling results indicated that more will do so in the future. Paradoxically, they also insisted, "in those States where the citizens do not see the need for such legislation, the Federal Government should not mandate it against their will" (US Senate 2013, 25–26).[22]

Prohibiting unfair treatment in hiring, firing, compensation, and other terms and conditions of employment, the law applied to employers with fifteen or more employees, employment agencies, labor organizations, Congress, the federal government, and state and local governments.[23] Borrowing from Title VII, the bill created a right of action in the federal courts for individuals claiming discrimination and granted enforcement authority to the attorney general and the EEOC, as well as other federal agencies.[24]

Most of the controversy over the bill centered on the breadth of the exemptions that would shield certain employers from complying with the law.[25] The bill's opponents were primarily concerned with its effects on religious liberty, which they claimed would be jeopardized if the bill were passed. Senator Dan Coats, Indiana Republican, warned, "[T]he so-called protections from religious liberty in this bill are vaguely defined and do not extend to all organizations that wish to adhere to their moral or religious beliefs in their hiring practices" (*New York Times*, November 7, 2013).

There were two floor amendments: The first, from Republican Senator Pat Toomey of Pennsylvania, seeking to expand the religious exemption to include religiously based employers performing primarily secular functions, was defeated. The second, sponsored by Republicans Rob Portman from Ohio and Kelly Ayotte from New Hampshire, to prevent government retaliation against religious institutions, was unanimously accepted.

Although a broad exemption counteracts the purposes of the law by undermining its antidiscrimination provisions, the committee report accompanying ENDA appeared to downplay the expansive nature of the religious exemption. It explained that, because ENDA mirrors Title VII, organizations would easily be able to determine whether they were eligible for exemption. Moreover, the report asserted that ENDA's nondiscrimination provisions would apply to organizations (that is, such organizations would not be exempt under the law) "that are not primarily religious in purpose and character" even if the "boss has a deeply held belief against homosexuality." Acknowledging that some believe the exemption did not go far enough to protect religious freedom, the report contended that such arguments had been raised in the context of other civil rights laws, saying, "[O]ur Nation's civil rights law rightly require non-religious organizations and entities, particularly those who participate in commercial activity, to adhere to broad principles of fairness and equality" (US Senate 2013, 8–9).

The final step toward Senate passage was the 61–30 vote for cloture on November 4, 2013, permitting the Senate to schedule a vote on the bill. Seven Republicans broke rank to join the fifty-two Democrats and two Independents to end the Republican filibuster and bring ENDA to the Senate floor. In the end, the Senate approved ENDA on November 7, 2013, in a strong bipartisan 64–32 vote, with ten Republicans joining fifty-four Democrats.

The House version of the bill did not fare as well. The Senate bill was sent to the House on November 12, 2013, and referred to committee, where its chances for passage were slim in the Republican-controlled House. Indeed, House Speaker John Boehner, Republican from Ohio, had repeatedly stated his opposition to the bill and promised he would not bring it to the House floor for a vote whatever the outcome in the Senate. Explaining his refusal to let the House consider the bill, Boehner said, “I am opposed to discrimination of any kind in the workplace or anyplace else, but I think this legislation . . . is unnecessary and would provide a basis for frivolous lawsuits,” adding, “[P]eople are already protected in the workplace” (Berman 2014).

In balancing the competing interests of religious liberty and the prohibition on employment discrimination in Title VII, the courts have permitted religiously based institutions to ground their employment decisions on religion in three circumstances: (1) the “bona fide occupational qualification” (BFOQ) or “ministerial” exception for individuals who publicly advance the organization’s religious beliefs, such as clergy; (2) the “curriculum” exception for teachers or religious leaders who promulgate the faith; and (3) the “religious organization” exception, allowing certain classes of employees—even those performing secular activities—to be exempt from the antidiscrimination law (Thompson 2015, 305; Dabrowski 2014). In *Hosanna-Tabor Evangelical Lutheran Church v. Equal Opportunity Employment Commission* (2012), the high court broadly held that the “ministerial” exception, arising from the First Amendment, exempts religious institutions from employment discrimination claims arising between the institution and and its ministers.

Notwithstanding their success in securing ENDA’s passage in the Senate, some scholars and LGBT rights organizations expressed concern that the religious exemption was too broad—exceeding the bounds of the First Amendment—and would fail to ensure equal employment opportunity for LGBT employees. In their view, the law would permit religious employers to discriminate on the basis of sexual orientation and gender identity without demonstrating a link between their religious precepts and the employees’ roles in the organization (see Dabrowski 2014; Thompson 2015).

Shortly after ENDA was introduced, several LGBT rights groups—the Transgender Law Center, the American Civil Liberties Union (ACLU), Lambda Legal, and the National Center for Lesbian Rights—wrote an open letter to Merkley, proclaiming their support for the proposed law and stressing its “vital importance to LGBT people across the country.” Nevertheless, the groups voiced their concern over the scope of the religious exemption in the law, citing the possibility that religiously affiliated hospitals and universities, for example, could discriminate against LGBT employees even if they did not perform the ministerial work related to carrying out the institution's religious functions. They declared that the law "gives a stamp of legitimacy to LGBT discrimination that our civil rights laws have never given to discrimination based on an individual's race, sex, national origin, age, or disability. This sweeping unprecedented exemption undermines the core goal of ENDA by leaving too many jobs, and LGBT workers, outside the scope of its protections" (Transgender Law Center 2013; *Washington Blade*, June 12, 2014; *Washington Blade*, June 5, 2014).

ENDA's religious exemption was broader than the exemption in Title VII because the latter prohibits organizations from discriminating on the basis of religion unless the employee's work relates to its religious mission; moreover, it does not excuse the organization from complying with the prohibition against discrimination based on race, sex, and national origin.[26] ENDA would have offered a safe harbor to institutions that would allow them to hire or fire LGBT employees as they wished, even if the employees were not engaged in furthering the organization's religious principles (see *ThinkProgress*, September 9, 2013).

On July 8, 2014, with ENDA still pending in the 113th Congress, the Transgender Law Center issued another statement on behalf of these groups as well as the Gay & Lesbian Advocates & Defenders (GLAD), announcing that they no longer supported ENDA with the provision for religious exemptions remaining in it (Transgender Law Center 2014).[27] Their decision to oppose the bill was prompted by the Supreme Court's opinion in *Burwell v. Hobby Lobby* (2014), a case indirectly related to religious exemptions in antidiscrimination policies. The owners of Hobby Lobby, a secular family-owned for-profit corporation, objected to an Affordable Care Act (ACA) regulation requiring them to provide employees with access to health insurance that covers contraceptive care. They argued that the 1993 Religious Freedom Restoration Act (RFRA) permitted them to exclude several types of contraception that they believed interfered with the exercise of their religious beliefs (see Dabrowski 2014; Samar 2015). The Court held that, as a privately held company, Hobby Lobby could fashion employee benefit packages around the owners' religious beliefs. LGBT rights groups feared that the preference shown for religion over equal rights would further embolden secular organizations to seek accommodation of the owners' religious beliefs in other arenas. The executive director of the National Gay and Lesbian Task Force expressed her concern, saying, "[I]f a private company can take its own religious beliefs and say you can't have access to certain health care, it's a hop, skip and a jump to an interpretation that a private company could have religious beliefs that LGBT people are not equal or somehow go against their beliefs and therefore fire them" (*Washington Post*, July 8, 2014).

In distancing themselves from ENDA, the groups represented in the Transgender Law Center's statement objected that tolerating discrimination as ENDA would do was "unprecedented in federal law [and] could provide religious affiliated organizations . . . a blank check to engage in workplace discrimination against LGBT people." Doing so, it said, would send a signal that "anti-LGBT discrimination is different—more acceptable and legitimate—than discrimination against individuals based on their race or sex." To illustrate the point, their statement recounted a narrative of a Massachusetts high school affiliated with the Catholic Church that hired a gay food service worker for a position entirely unrelated to promulgating religious doctrine. When he listed his husband on an employment form, the school withdrew the job offer, citing the Church's teachings on same-sex marriage (Transgender Law Center 2014).

When the proposed bill died at the end of the 113th Congress, it was replaced by the Equality Act of 2015 (H.R. 3185). Introduced by Representative David Cicilline, Democrat from Rhode Island, on July 23, 2015, the bill was launched less than a month after the Supreme Court's historic same-sex marriage decision. The Equality Act, amending the 1964 Civil Rights Act, equated discrimination based on sexual orientation, gender identity, and sex-based stereotypes to discrimination because of sex. In addition to these protections, it extended to rights not included within the 1964 act, such as jury duty, housing, and credit.[28] With these provisions, the bill would have become the most far-reaching civil rights law in the nation's history. It had wide approval in Cicilline's party: More than 80 percent of House Democrats and forty of the forty-five Democratic senators declared their support for it. The Senate version (S. 1858) was simultaneously introduced by Merkley (2015), but neither bill stood any chance of passage with Republican majorities in both chambers. Their lack of success in Congress underscored that the battle for equal rights for the LGBT community was far from over, despite the same-sex marriage victory in the high court (Berman 2015).

The new measure offered a more comprehensive approach to battling discrimination against the LGBT community than ENDA had; it would have guaranteed equality of treatment in public accommodations, jury service, consumer credit, public funding, housing, and education as well as employment by adding sexual orientation and gender identity as protected classes. Seeking to take advantage of the positive energy emanating from the nation's move toward marriage equality, when Cicilline introduced the bill, he said, "[O]ur country is in a different place today, and momentum is on our side. . . . partial equality is not acceptable. It's time for a comprehensive bill that protects LGBT Americans from discrimination in all aspects of everyday life" (*McClatchy DC*, July 23, 2015).[29] Merkley also noted that the fight against discrimination had reached a new level, saying, "Every person deserves to live free from fear of discrimination, regardless of who they are or who they love. Enacting the Equality Act will bring us another significant step forward in our nation's march towards inclusion and equality. It will extend the full promise of America to every American" (Merkley 2015).

EXECUTIVE ORDERS

On August 2, 1995, shortly after Don't Ask, Don't Tell was implemented, President Bill Clinton helped advance LGBT equality by ending the government's policy of arbitrarily denying security clearances to LGBT government workers on the basis of their sexual orientation. Although the primary purpose of Executive Order 12968 was to impose stricter financial disclosure requirements, most important for the LGBT community, it added sexual orientation to the list of prohibited classifications in determining an individual's access to secret information (Clinton 1995a).[30]

More broadly, Clinton spoke out for ENDA in 1995, writing to Kennedy on October 19, 1995, to condemn discrimination against LGBT employees. Such discrimination is "wrong," Clinton (1995b) said. He also sent his aide George Stephanopoulos to declare his support for ENDA at a meeting of the National Association of Gay and Lesbian

Journalists (*Boston Globe*, October 20, 1995; *New York Times*, October 20, 1995; *Washington Post*, October 20, 1995).

When asked about ENDA a year later during the second presidential debate, shortly after the vote was taken in the Senate, Clinton simply said, "I'm for it. That's my policy. I'm for it. I believe that any law-abiding, tax-paying citizen who shows up in the morning and doesn't break the law and doesn't interfere with his or her neighbors ought to have the ability to work in our country and shouldn't be subject to unfair discrimination. I'm for it" (Clinton 1996). In 1997, he proclaimed the "right of each individual in America to be judged on their merits and abilities and to be allowed to contribute to society without facing unfair discrimination on account of sexual orientation. It is about our ongoing fight against bigotry and intolerance, in our country and in our hearts" (Clinton 1997).

On May 28, 1998, with congressional action on the latest version of the antidiscrimination bill stalled, Clinton issued Executive Order 13087, banning discrimination against federal employees based on sexual orientation. Clinton expanded Executive Order 11478, issued by President Richard Nixon on August 8, 1969, by adding sexual orientation to the list of prohibited areas of discrimination by the federal government.[31] Observing that executive orders do not create rights in individuals that would allow them to file complaints with the EEOC or pursue litigation against offending employers, Clinton said that his order nevertheless "provides for a uniform policy for the Federal Government to prohibit discrimination based on sexual orientation in the Federal civilian workforce and states that policy for the first time in an Executive order of the President" (Clinton 1998).[32]

When Congress declines to act on civil rights legislation, administrative agencies may advance antidiscrimination policies in a number of ways. In the employment arena, for example, OSHA's announcement on access to restrooms for transgender employees and the EEOC's rulings on Title VII and discrimination because of sexual orientation and gender identity were attempts to fill some of the gaps left by the legislature's failure to pass ENDA.

Most important, as the Clinton presidency demonstrated, the White House has the authority to proclaim the federal government's commitment to fight employment discrimination through executive orders. Indeed, presidents have customarily issued executive orders to curb discriminatory employment practices by federal contractors, beginning with Franklin Roosevelt's 1941 order prohibiting discrimination against workers on the basis of their "race, creed, color or national origin" in companies granted defense contracts (*New York Times*, February 6, 2012).

Executive orders are limited in scope and enforcement power and may be reversed by the president's successors as well as challenged in court as exceeding the president's authority, yet advocates view them as useful vehicles for achieving their policy goals. In the months before the 2012 election, LGBT groups were vocal in their efforts to exert pressure on Obama to amend the existing antidiscrimination executive order to add gender identity and sexual orientation to the list of prohibited areas of discrimination. They attributed his failure to do so to avoid stirring up a controversy over a divisive issue before the election. Despite his success in passing the Matthew Shepard and James Byrd Jr. Hate Crimes Act, repealing Don't Ask, Don't Tell, and declining to defend DOMA against legal challenges as well as countless antidiscrimination policies that various executive branch agencies adopted, LGBT advocates expressed their disappointment in him. They pointed to a promise he made during the 2008 presidential campaign in which he committed his administration to issuing an executive order against workplace discrimination.

The administration's response, announced to LGBT organization leaders by aides in a private meeting, was to reassure them that Obama supported the principle of equal employment for LGBT employees and would continue to work for ENDA's passage, which, he said, would affect a larger number of workers than an executive order and could not be challenged as easily in court (*Washington Post*, April 16, 2012).[33]

In June 2014, when it became clear that the latest version of ENDA was doomed, the administration bowed to pressure from LGBT rights groups and announced that it would draft an executive order to advance equal rights for LGBT employees who worked directly or indirectly for the federal government. In issuing Executive Order 13672, on July 21, 2014, Obama expanded the rights of LGBT workers by amending two existing executive orders.[34] First, it amended Executive Order 11246 to make it illegal for the 24,000 companies doing business with the federal government to discriminate on the basis of gender identity and sexual orientation (Human Rights Campaign 2014b; Out & Equal 2014).[35]

Second, it expanded rights of transgender and gender-nonconforming federal employees by adding gender identity as a protected classification to Executive Order 11478, the order that Clinton had initially amended in 1998 to prohibit discrimination because of sexual orientation (see Obama 2014a).[36]

At the signing ceremony, Obama declared that he was fulfilling his campaign promise to protect LGBT workers, saying, "[I]t doesn't make much sense, but today in America, millions of our fellow citizens wake up and go to work with the awareness that they could lose their job, not because of anything they do or fail to do, but because of who they are—lesbian, gay, bisexual, transgender. And that's wrong. We're here to do what we can to make it right—to bend that arc of justice just a little bit in a better direction" (Obama 2014b).[37]

Encouraged by the *Hobby Lobby* ruling to press their claim for greater autonomy in determining their employee benefit policies, religious groups had lobbied Obama to weaken the executive order by including a religious exemption to allow federal contractors to hire or fire because of their opposition to homosexuality and transgender status. LGBT rights groups appreciated that Obama rejected the religious exemption yet were displeased by his refusal to rescind the existing Executive Order 13279, signed by President George W. Bush on December 12, 2002. Bush's order had fulfilled one of his long-standing aims of removing restrictions on federal funding for faith-based community groups. It amended Executive Order 11246 to specify, among other things, that religious social agencies serving as federal contractors may make hiring and firing decisions on the basis of their religious beliefs.[38] When Bush issued Executive Order 13279, Democrats accused him of using his executive powers to undermine civil rights laws by absolving religious organizations of the federal mandate not to discriminate simply by claiming that hiring certain employees would conflict with their religious beliefs.[39] In Congress, Kennedy charged, "[R]ather than use the faith-based initiative to undermine our national commitment to civil rights, the president's executive order should have made clear that no organization receiving taxpayer money can discriminate in its services or its employment practices (*New York Times*, December 13, 2002).

DISCRIMINATION AGAINST GOVERNMENT WORKERS

LGB federal civilian workers faced unique obstacles in challenging discrimination based on sexual orientation in employment.[40] Beginning in the early 1950s, they filed suit to ask the courts to reverse negative employment decisions on due process grounds. In *Norton v. Macy* (1969), a leading case addressing arbitrary dismissals of government employees, a divided Fifth Circuit panel held that discharging workers because of fear of embarrassment was arbitrary and capricious and violated their constitutional right of due process. It held the government may disapprove of their employees' activities but cannot simply fire them without showing that their conduct affected their job performance. In 1973, the Civil Service Commission (CSC) revised its personnel manual to put an end to discharging employees solely because of their sexual orientation. In 1975, it removed "immorality" as a justification for discharge unless it affects job performance.

The courts were not inclined to override the federal government's authority when it routinely denied security clearances to LGBT workers, citing their threat to national security. A series of cases beginning in the 1960s demonstrates the judiciary's initial reluctance to interfere with the government's determination that gay and lesbian employees posed threats to the national interest.[41] *Adams v. Laird* (1969), one of the first cases testing the linkage between homosexuality and security clearances, involved the revocation of a defense contractor's security clearance after he admitted to engaging in homosexual conduct. The District of Columbia Circuit Court panel rejected Robert Adams's due process claim, noting that the decision to grant or withhold a security clearance is within executive authority and judges should not "second-guess that choice unless the Constitution commands us to do so" (239).

Department of the Navy v. Egan (1988), viewed as the "seminal case on judicial review of security clearances," entirely precluded judicial review of security clearance decisions (Maravilla 2001, 786; Miller 2004). In restricting the courts' oversight of national security policy, the case had implications for gay and lesbian government employees. The Department of the Navy denied Thomas Egan a security clearance when an investigation revealed his felony convictions as well as treatment in an alcohol rehabilitation program. The Supreme Court ruled against Egan, holding that the Navy possesses the necessary expertise to judge suitability for security clearances and has broad discretionary authority to determine access to classified information. It held that, because the Navy gave Egan adequate notice of the reasons for the denial and sufficient opportunity for a hearing and an appeal, it had satisfied his right of due process.[42]

The Court again addressed the issue in *Webster v. Doe* (1988), a case exemplifying its deference to the executive branch in military and national security policy. The Central Intelligence Agency (CIA) removed John Doe, a covert agent, from his post after he voluntarily disclosed his homosexuality to a security officer. The agency told Doe told that "homosexuality was not a *per se* ground for dismissal" but that "it was a security concern which would be evaluated on a case-by-case basis" (*Doe v. Casey* 1985, 583, emphasis in the original). Shortly thereafter, without explanation, the CIA informed Doe that his homosexuality created a "security threat" and asked him to resign; when he refused, it fired him.

In a 6–2 majority, the Supreme Court held that, although Congress intended to shield the agency's decision to discharge an employee from judicial oversight, it had not "meant to preclude consideration of colorable constitutional claims arising out of the actions of the Director" (*Webster v. Doe* 1988, 603). The Court did not determine whether Doe had presented such a claim; it merely held that the district court had jurisdiction to make the determination. On remand, the lower court found the CIA policy rationally related to its interest in ensuring the nation's security because "homosexuals engaging in homosexual conduct pose a greater security risk than heterosexuals." The court stressed that "Doe may be particularly susceptible to blackmail and coercion by hostile intelligence agents to protect himself or his partners even if he has admitted his homosexuality to friends and family. The fact is that homosexual conduct is a characteristic that hostile intelligence services are likely to target, and at least some homosexuals may be coerced or manipulated" (*Doe v. Webster* 1991, 3).

A nationwide class action suit against the DOD challenged the classification of gay men and lesbians as bad security risks. The plaintiffs had applied for industrial security clearances in the early 1980s, claiming that the policy of subjecting them to expanded investigation procedures violated their right to equal protection as well as their speech and associational rights under the First Amendment. The government justified its policy by characterizing "homosexuality as 'sexual misconduct' and 'aberrant sexual behavior.'" It declared that participation in such "'deviant sexual activities' may tend to 'cast doubt on the individual's morality, emotional or mental stability and may raise questions as to his or her susceptibility to coercion or blackmail'" (*High Tech Gays v. Defense Industrial Security Office* 1987, 1364).

Addressing the plaintiffs' equal protection claim, California Federal District Court Judge Thelton Henderson held that, because classifications based on sexual orientation are analogous to classifications based on gender, courts should apply a stricter review of policies such as this. He decried the "wholly unfounded, degrading stereotypes about lesbians and gay men [that] abound in American society" and charged that "many people . . . have branded gay people as abominations to nature and considered lesbians and gay men mentally ill and psychologically unstable" (1369). In the end, Henderson declared that the level of review was irrelevant because there was no reasonable basis for treating gay people differently from other applicants. He dismissed the government's justification, declaring that it derived from outmoded thinking and stereotypical views and seemed to take special exception to its contention that gay men and lesbians are more susceptible to blackmail and coercion and thereby constitute a greater security risk.

The district court awarded the plaintiffs summary judgment; the Ninth Circuit reversed on appeal. The panel's unanimous decision announced by Judge Melvin Brunetti explained that the government's justification for the enhanced procedure was twofold: First, counterintelligence agencies "target homosexuals," and second, the enhanced procedures are necessary to determine if the applicant is susceptible to blackmail or other form of coercion (*High Tech Gays v. Defense Industry Security Clearance Office* 1990a, 576). Satisfied on both counts, the court concluded that subjecting gay men and lesbians to enhanced security measures reasonably related to the government's interest in protecting national security. It held that, because hostile intelligence agencies single gay people out, the government could proceed more cautiously to determine if they are likely to succumb to blackmail. Citing *Department of the Navy v. Egan* (1988), the court stressed that the judiciary must be especially deferential to executive branch agencies in areas affecting national security.

Several months later, the circuit court denied the plaintiffs' petition for a rehearing en banc (*High Tech Gays v. Defense Industry Security Clearance Office* 1990b). A sharp dissent from the denial by William Canby, joined by William Norris, charged that the court's "decision is wrong, and it will have tragic results" (376). Canby took issue with the panel's indifference to discrimination against gay men and lesbians, warning, "[T]his history of discrimination makes it far more likely that differential treatment is simply a resort to old prejudices" (376–77). He believed the government had not produced sufficient evidence to show that competing intelligence agencies target gay and lesbian employees. Instead, it had relied on old Soviet intelligence documents without questioning whether their assessment that gay men and lesbians were vulnerable to blackmail and coercion was itself rational. In his view, the government merely offered this evidence in a belated attempt to justify the bias against the plaintiffs. Canby agreed that protecting the nation's security is of paramount importance, but citing an amicus brief referring to the World War II Japanese exclusion policy, he charged, "[T]he last time we upheld class discrimination in the interest of national security, it took 42 years to remedy that wrong in the law of the circuit" (382). Clinton's 1995 executive order barring the government from discriminating on the basis of sexual orientation in access to classified information effectively removed the issue of security clearances from the courts' purview.

TITLE VII AND GENDER IDENTITY

The subject of litigation for more than fifty years, the "parameters of Title VII's prohibition against sex-based employment discrimination have [still] not been clearly established. The primary matter of interpretation with which courts must deal in sex-based Title VII cases is the statute's 'because of . . . sex' language" (Sachs 2004, 359).

Price Waterhouse v. Hopkins (1989) was an important milestone in clarifying the parameters of Title VII for LGBT plaintiffs; it changed the legal landscape for transgender plaintiffs by incorporating a more expansive reading of the statute's prohibition against discrimination. Before *Price Waterhouse*, three often-cited lower federal court decisions had held that discrimination against "transsexuals," even if proven, does not violate Title VII.

The Ninth Circuit was the first appellate court to rule in a Title VII case charging an employer with discrimination because of gender identity (*Holloway v. Arthur Andersen and Company* 1977). The plaintiff, a transgender woman, was fired from her position at Arthur Andersen after informing her supervisor that she was in treatment to prepare for sex reassignment surgery and would ask the company to change her name from Robert to Ramona. The lower court dismissed her complaint, holding that Title VII was not applicable to "transsexualism."[43]

She claimed that "'sex' . . . is synonymous with 'gender,' and that gender would encompass transsexuals" (662). Speaking for the 2–1 appellate panel, Judge Leland Nielsen's opinion displayed the court's ignorance of gender identity, including its reference to the plaintiff by the male pronoun. After a cursory review of Title VII's legislative history and language, the court concluded, "Congress had only the traditional notion of 'sex' in mind [and] later legislative history makes this narrow definition even more evident." Further, it added, "[S]everal bills have been introduced to *amend* the Civil Rights Act to prohibit discrimination against 'sexual preference' [and] none have been enacted into law" (662, emphasis in the original).

A few years later, the Eighth Circuit echoed the Ninth in *Sommers v. Budget Marketing Incorporated* (1982). In a per curiam opinion, the appeals court affirmed the lower court's dismissal of the case brought by the transgender female. Showing more understanding of the issue, the court referred to the plaintiff as "she" and seemed to recognize a distinction between "transsexualism" and "sexual preference." Acknowledging that Sommers's claim was not based on "sexual preference," it reasoned that Congress's rejection of legislation aimed at ending discrimination on the basis of "sexual preference" indicated the "word 'sex' in Title VII is to be given its traditional definition, rather than an expansive interpretation." Thus, the court concluded that because Congress had "not shown an intention to protect transsexuals," Title VII "does not encompass transsexualism" (750).

The last pre–*Price Waterhouse* appellate decision was the Seventh Circuit's ruling in *Ulane v. Eastern Airlines* (1984). Vietnam veteran Robert Ulane, a postoperative transgender woman, was hired as a pilot in 1968 and discharged as Karen Ulane in 1984; her suit alleged the airline violated Title VII by discriminating against her as a female and as a "transsexual." The lower court ruled in her favor on both counts and ordered her reinstated with back pay and full seniority.

Citing *Holloway* and *Sommers*, a unanimous panel reversed. Judge Diane Wood reiterated the court's responsibility to interpret the words of a statute by "their ordinary common meaning." In this case, she said, Congress intended Title VII to forbid discrimination "against women because they are women and against men because they are men" (1085). Moreover, there is no evidence in Title VII's sparse legislative history that would challenge this interpretation of the law. Last, the court pointed to Congress's continual refusal to amend Title VII to include "affectional or sexual orientation." This "strongly indicates that the phrase in the Civil Rights Act prohibiting discrimination on the basis of sex should be given a narrow, traditional interpretation, which would also exclude transsexuals" (1086).[44]

Price Waterhouse transformed the judiciary's rigid formulation of sex as a binary category and incorporated the concept of discrimination on the basis of gender into discrimination based on sex. Ann Hopkins, a senior manager in Price Waterhouse's Office of Government Services in the District of Columbia, applied for a partnership position in 1982. The firm placed her candidacy on hold, citing some of the partners' concerns about her interpersonal skills. They felt she lacked "femininity" and had an abrasive personality, characterizing her in stereotypical sex-based terms. Some described her as "macho" and believed she "overcompensated for being a woman"; another suggested she take a "course at charm school." In explaining to her why her candidacy was placed on hold, a partner counseled her that her professional problems would be solved if she would "walk more femininely, talk more femininely, dress more femininely, wear make-up, have her hair styled, and wear jewelry" (235).

Justice William Brennan announced the 6–3 ruling for himself, Byron White, and Sandra Day O'Connor, with Anthony Kennedy, Antonin Scalia, and Chief Justice William Rehnquist dissenting. Brennan devoted most of the opinion to the issue of proof in "mixed motive" cases, in which employment decisions are based on permissible and impermissible factors. Most relevant to future LGBT plaintiffs, the Court equated sex with gender, saying, "Congress' intent to forbid employers to take gender into account in making employment decisions appears on the face of the statute. . . . We take these words [because of sex] to mean that gender must be irrelevant to employment decisions" (239–40). The partners at Price Waterhouse denied Hopkins her partnership because she did not conform to their stereotypical image of a woman; by acting on the basis of her gender, they violated Tile VII. The Court left no doubt that, in enacting Title VII, "Congress intended to strike at the entire spectrum of disparate treatment of men and women resulting from sex stereotypes" (251).[45]

Although the high court recognized that sex stereotyping in the workplace has negative effects on employees, the "overwhelming trend among lower courts is to recognize a claim of sex discrimination based on a lack of conformity to gender norms, such as a male plaintiff's effeminacy or a female's tomboyish appearance, [yet] . . . remain largely confused about where to draw the line between claims based on orientation and those based on gender nonconformity" (Peebles 2015, 920).

Nine years later, the Supreme Court decided *Oncale v. Sundowner Offshore Services Inc.* (1998), another case exploring the implications of the ban on sex discrimination (and sexual harassment) in Title VII. The question for the Court was whether the statute provided a cause of action for Joseph Oncale, an employee of a Louisiana offshore oil-drilling company, who claimed he had been abused by other male employees who insulted him with derogatory references to his manhood, physically assaulted him, and even threatened to rape him.

Sexual orientation was not at issue in the case as neither Oncale nor his tormentors were gay (Barker 2009). In a brief unanimous opinion by Scalia, the Court expanded the definition of sex in Title VII, affirming that the law does not rule out same-sex harassment as long as it is of a sexual nature. The key to the outcome of the case, said the Court, is that there must be discrimination because of sex.[46] Moreover, although there may be cases in which same-sex harassment stems from sexual desire (which the court nearly always assumes it does when the harasser is gay), the plaintiff is not required to prove it (Clancy 2011). Acknowledging that Congress had not intended the law to apply to such plaintiffs as Oncale, Scalia broadly proclaimed, "[S]tatutory prohibitions often go beyond the principal evil to cover reasonably comparable evils, and it is ultimately the provisions of our laws rather than the principal concerns of our legislators by which we are governed. Title VII prohibits 'discrimination . . . because of . . . sex' in the 'terms' or 'conditions' of employment. Our holding that this includes sexual harassment must extend to sexual harassment of any kind that meets the statutory requirements" (*Oncale v. Sundowner Offshore Services Inc.* 1998, 79–80). Sung (2011) optimistically argues that these two cases

> laid down the doctrinal foundation for later courts and plaintiffs to drive Title VII's jurisprudence from a narrow prohibition of discrimination based on one's biological sex toward a broader prohibition on discrimination based on gender nonconformity. And because . . . effeminate men and masculine women, gay men and lesbian women, and transgender individuals are by definition gender nonconformists, discrimination against or harassment of them because they defy conventional gender expectations is discrimination on the basis of sex. (518)

Price Waterhouse proved crucial to transgender plaintiffs by "initiat[ing] a sea change in this Title VII jurisprudence, holding that discrimination against an employee due to his or her failure to adhere to traditional gender stereotypes constitutes impermissible sex discrimination" (Lee 2012, 427–28). Because "transgender persons are largely defined by their failure to conform to conventional gender norms, it would appear self-evident that the sex-stereotyping theory in *Price Waterhouse* would place them squarely under the protection of Title VII" (Reed 2013, 852; see Havlik 2012). Despite the logic of this position, lower federal courts initially dismissed Title VII suits brought by transgender plaintiffs, holding that gender identity was not within the meaning of sex in Title VII.[47]

The difficulty arose, in part, because courts required the plaintiffs to point to specific evidence of sex-stereotyping language by the employers (Koch and Bales 2008). Eventually, courts began to view these claims more favorably, adopting two theories related to Title VII: First, they relied on *Price Waterhouse*'s prohibition on discrimination based on sex stereotyping, known as the "gender-nonconformity approach"; second, they applied a per se approach, pointing to the text of Title VII and holding that discrimination against transgender workers constitutes sex discrimination under the statute (Lee 2012; Reed 2013; see Malloy 2011; Raflo 2010; Rao 2013).[48]

The first case to illustrate the effect of the gender nonconformity approach on transgender plaintiffs was the Ninth Circuit's ruling in

Schwenk v. Hartford (2000). The suit was brought by a preoperative transgender woman prisoner under the Gender Motivated Violence Act (GMVA). Judge Stephen Reinhardt analogized the prohibition on sex discrimination in the GMVA to the one in Title VII, declaring that the "initial judicial approach taken in cases such as *Holloway* has been overruled by the logic and language of *Price Waterhouse*" (*Schwenk v. Hartford* 2000, 1201).[49] Reinhardt explained that the high court's opinion had established that an employer's Title VII liability extends to gender when the discrimination is based on an employee's failure "to act in the way *expected* of a man or a woman" (1202, emphasis added).[50]

The Sixth Circuit opinion in *Smith v. City of Salem* (2004) exemplifies the gender-nonconformity approach in a transgender plaintiff's employment discrimination lawsuit. Lieutenant Jimmie Smith, a firefighter for the city of Salem, Ohio, was forced to resign from the force after he changed his appearance to adopt a "more feminine" manner following a diagnosis of gender dysphoria. The lower court dismissed his suit.

Turning to the heart of his Title VII action, Judge Ransey Guy Cole Jr. framed the key questions as whether Smith properly stated a "claim of sex stereotyping" and whether "Title VII protection is unavailable to transsexuals" (569). He explained that the district court had dismissed Smith's complaint because it believed his real claim was discrimination because of gender identity and that he merely used *Price Waterhouse*'s "sex stereotyping" theory as a pretext to avoid the fact that Title VII does not apply to gender identity. In rejecting the lower court's analysis, the appellate panel agreed that Smith satisfied the pleading requirements of Title VII by alleging that his employer discharged him because it thought him insufficiently "masculine" and failed to "look and behave" as a man is expected to behave (572). It faulted the district court for relying on cases prior to 1989, namely *Holloway*, *Sommers*, and *Ulane*, which had interpreted Title VII narrowly, an approach, it said, that was "eviscerated by *Price Waterhouse*" (*Smith v. City of Salem* 2004, 573).[51] The appeals court stressed that discrimination against a "transsexual" plaintiff is indistinguishable from the discrimination Ann Hopkins faced for her failure to act the way the partners expected a woman to act. It concluded that "sex stereotyping based on a person's gender non-conforming behavior is impermissible discrimination, irrespective of the cause of that behavior; a label such as 'transsexual,' is not fatal to a sex discrimination claim where the victim has suffered discrimination because of his or her gender non-conformity" (575). Henceforth, if it violates Title VII to discriminate against women because they lack charm and do not wear makeup, then it violates Title VII to discriminate against men because they do.[52]

In 2007, the Tenth Circuit aligned itself with the rulings in the Seventh, Eighth, and Ninth Circuits (*Etsitty v. Utah Transit Authority* (2007). Krystal Etsitty, a bus operator with the Utah Transit Authority, was diagnosed with gender dysphoria and prescribed hormone therapy in preparation for sex reassignment surgery. Four years into her course of therapy, the bus company hired her when she presented as a male. When she confided in her supervisor that she would begin to appear as a female on the job and eventually undergo sex reassignment surgery, he expressed no concern. Soon after, when other employees raised questions about her use of the women's restroom in the bus facility and in public spaces, the agency discharged her. Officials cited difficulties related to her restroom use during her transitional phase as the reason for the discharge; they did offer to rehire her after her transition was complete.

Etsitty argued both theories: First, under the per se approach, she claimed that "because a person's identity as a transsexual is directly connected to the sex organs she possesses, discrimination on this basis must constitute discrimination because of sex" (1221). In the alternative, she cited the gender-nonconformity theory, arguing that the company violated Title VII by discharging her for failing to conform to "stereotypical male behavior" (1220). The district court rejected both claims.

Citing circuit opinions preceding *Price Waterhouse* as well as the text in Title VII, a unanimous Tenth Circuit panel ruled that she had erred in asserting that Title VII protects "transsexuals" as a group. Speaking for the court, Judge Michael Murphy stated that Title VII only applies if the plaintiffs can show that the discrimination against them stemmed from their status as men or women. The court refrained from addressing her *Price Waterhouse* sex-stereotyping claim, saying even if she did state a valid claim under this theory, then the company's reason for discharging her because of its concern about her use of an inappropriate restroom was legitimate.[53]

In 2008, the District of Columbia District Court was the first court to formally adopt the per se approach, explicitly holding that discrimination based on the plaintiff's transgender status is sex discrimination. Diane, formerly known as David, Schroer filed suit against the Library of Congress for withdrawing its job offer after she revealed to the hiring official that she would transition to a woman prior to undergoing sex reassignment surgery a year later and would assume the name Diane when she began work. The lower court concluded in *Schroer v. Billington* (2008) that Schroer stated a valid Title VII claim under both theories: first, that she was discriminated against because she did not conform to gender stereotypes, and second, that she was discriminated against on the basis of her gender identity, which, according to the court, constituted discrimination based on sex.

Examining the first theory, District of Columbia District Court Judge James Robertson found that Schroer had clearly showed that the library withdrew its job offer because of her gender nonconformity, adding that it was irrelevant whether it found her "to be an insufficiently masculine man, an insufficiently feminine woman, or an inherently gender-nonconforming transsexual." In any event, he continued, she is "entitled to judgment based on a *Price-Waterhouse*-type claim for sex stereotyping" (305).

Second, going beyond the *Price Waterhouse* gender-nonconformity approach, Robertson formally adopted the per se approach, holding that principles of statutory construction require courts to apply the plain language of Title VII. In doing so, he held that the library's refusal to hire her after she informed its officials that she intended to alter her biological sex through surgery and begin presenting as a woman was "*literally* discrimination 'because of . . . sex'" (308).[54]

In *Glenn v. Brumby* (2011), the Eleventh Circuit ruled on a suit brought by Vandiver Elizabeth Glenn, a transgender woman who presented as a man when she was hired in 2005 by Georgia's Office of Legislative Counsel (OLC). In 2006, she informed her direct supervisor that she was transgender and would be transitioning to a woman, including legally changing her name and appearing at work in women's clothes; the supervisor subsequently relayed the information to the head of personnel. The OLC terminated Glenn on the grounds that her transition was "inappropriate" and "disruptive" and would make her "coworkers uncomfortable" (1314).

Her suit claimed the state violated her Fourteenth Amendment right of equal protection by discriminating against her because of sex and her unwillingness to conform to sex stereotypes. The district court upheld her claim and the circuit court agreed. The unanimous circuit panel recognized that transgender persons by definition contradict sex stereotypes, adding, "[T]here is thus a congruence between discriminating against transgender and transsexual individuals and discrimination on the basis of gender-based behavioral norms. Accordingly," the court continued, "discrimination against a transgender individual because of her gender non-conformity is sex discrimination, whether it's described as being on the basis of sex or gender" (1316–17). It ended by concluding it saw no reason to exclude transgender persons from the constitutional right of all individuals to be free from discrimination for failure to conform to gender stereotypes.[55]

Transgender workers scored an impressive legal victory when the EEOC announced its position on gender identity and Title VII in *Macy v. Holder* (2012).[56] Mia Macy, a transgender woman, filed a complaint against the Bureau of Alcohol, Firearms, and Tobacco for refusing to hire her after she told the director that she was in the process of transitioning to a female. After initially declining to process her claim of gender identity discrimination, the agency ultimately concluded that her "complaint of discrimination based on gender identity, change of sex, and/or transgender status is cognizable under Title VII" (at 1). The EEOC categorically stated that "intentional discrimination against a transgender individual because that person is transgender is, by definition, discrimination 'based on . . . sex,' and such discrimination therefore violates Title VII" (at 11).

Citing *Price Waterhouse* as well as *Schwenk*, *Smith*, *Glenn*, and *Schroer*, the EEOC's path-breaking decision melded the two theories of discrimination by broadly stating that the ban on sex discrimination in Title VII includes discrimination because of gender, defining it as the "cultural and social aspects of masculinity and femininity" (*Macy* v. Holder 2012, at 7). Therefore, it continued, discrimination against a transgender individual is discrimination based on the person's sex,

> regardless of whether an employer discriminates against an employee because the individual has expressed his or her gender in a non-stereotypical fashion, because the employer is uncomfortable with the fact that the person has transitioned or is in the process of transi-

> tioning from one gender to another, or because the employer simply does not like that the person is identifying as a transgender person. In each of these circumstances, the employer is making a gender-based evaluation, thus violating the Supreme Court's admonition that "an employer may not take gender into account in making an employment decision." (*Macy v. Holder* 2012, at 7–8, quoting *Price Waterhouse* 1989, 244; see Ellis 2014)

Acknowledging that most courts have relied on the gender-stereotyping theory to place transgender employees under the Title VII umbrella, the EEOC said that "evidence of gender stereotyping is simply one means [but not the only one] of proving sex discrimination" (*Macy v. Holder* 2012, at 12). Building on the court's interpretation in *Price Waterhouse* that sex encompasses gender, *Macy* extended the definition of gender to include gender identity, thus placing transgender plaintiffs within Title VII's protection (see Ellis 2014).

In a memorandum issued December 14, 2014, Holder echoed the EEOC's position in *Macy*, stating,

> [A]fter considering the text of Title VII, the relevant Supreme Court case law interpreting the statute, and the developing jurisprudence in this area, I have determined that the best reading of Title VII's prohibition of sex discrimination is that it encompasses discrimination based on gender identity, including transgender status. The most straightforward reading of Title VII is that discrimination "because of . . . sex" includes discrimination because an employee's gender identification is as a member of a particular sex, or because the employee is transitioning, or has transitioned, to another sex.

He ended by saying that the Justice Department will no longer argue that Title VII's ban on sex discrimination does not apply to discrimination based on gender identity (Holder 2014).

The effect of the EEOC's ruling in *Macy* was soon apparent when the agency made history by filing suit against a Garden City, Michigan, funeral home for discharging a transgender woman when she revealed that she was undergoing a gender transition. In *Equal Employment Opportunity Commission v. R.G. & G.R. Harris Funeral Homes Inc.* (2015), Michigan Federal District Court Judge Sean Cox denied the funeral home's motion to dismiss. He stated that, if Amiee Stephans had based her claim solely on her transgender status, then he would have dismissed her case for failure to state a valid Title VII claim. He allowed it to proceed because her complaint also alleged she was fired for not conforming to sex stereotypes under a *Price Waterhouse* theory.

On August 18, 2016, Cox granted the defendant's motion for summary judgment. Citing *Hobby Lobby*, he held that, as a "for-profit closely-held corporation," the funeral home is protected by the federal RFRA (*Equal Employment Opportunity Commission v. R.G. & G.R. Harris Funeral Homes Inc.* (2016, at 28). Cox found that requiring the funeral home to "allow an employee born a biological male to wear a skirt at work would impose a substantial burden on the ability of Rost [the owner] to conduct his business in accordance with his sincerely-held religious beliefs" (at 31). The judge said he presumed that the government's interest was compelling but that it did not satisfy the RFRA test because the plaintiff could have worn a pants suit instead of a skirt.

TITLE VII AND SEXUAL ORIENTATION

LGB plaintiffs had hoped that the lower courts would interpret *Price Waterhouse* and *Oncale* broadly and apply Title VII to their claims of employment discrimination, but most refused to do so. The problem largely stemmed from the Supreme Court's failure in *Price Waterhouse* to address the question of "whether gender nonconformity extends to conduct perceived to be or actually related with same-sex sexual attraction" (Peebles 2015, 913). In the absence of guidance from the high court, most lower federal courts have answered the question with a resounding "no."

Title VII "encompasses outward manifestations of gender nonconformity" (Peebles 2015, 213–14). But despite their acceptance of the *Price Waterhouse* theory of sex stereotyping for discrimination based on gender identity, most courts do not believe that the theory extends to employees who do not conform to sex-stereotypical behavior because of their sexual orientation (Case 2014; Gay 2015; see Reed 2014).

Because they object to including sexual orientation within the ambit of Title VII, they carefully parse the complaint to ensure that the discriminatory conduct arises from sex stereotyping rather than sexual orientation. If they believe it is the latter, they dismiss it for failure to state a valid claim. Indeed, because they deny that Title VII applies to discrimination based on sexual orientation, they often require gay and lesbian plaintiffs to prove that the conduct they complain of does not stem from their sexual orientation before allowing them to proceed with their sex-stereotyping claim (Szwalbnest 2010).[57]

In *DeSantis v. Pacific Telephone and Telegraph* (1979), the Ninth Circuit laid down a marker that has lasted more than three decades in denying Title VII protection to victims of discrimination based on their sexual orientation.[58] Robert DeSantis was one of six gay and lesbian plaintiffs who complained of discrimination because of sexual orientation. The lower courts dismissed their cases for failure to state a valid claim under Title VII.

Citing *Holloway*, the Ninth Circuit rejected the plaintiffs' argument that Congress intended to include discrimination on the basis of sexual orientation within Title VII. Speaking for the three-judge panel, Judge Herbert Choy explained that Congress clearly only had men and women in mind in 1964, a view bolstered by the fact that subsequent attempts to amend the law to add sexual orientation as a prohibited category had failed. In light of this, the court held that the prohibition against sex discrimination in Title VII "should not be judicially extended to include sexual preference such as homosexuality" (*DeSantis v. Pacific Telephone and Telegraph* 1979, 330). In what would become familiar language, the court rejected the plaintiffs' attempt to "bootstrap Title VII protection for homosexuals." Because the employer treated men and women alike by refusing to hire a person "who prefers sexual partners of the same sex," the court found the policy did not abridge Title VII (331). It would appear that bootstrapping has essentially become code language for a court to reject a plaintiff's sex-stereotyping claim (see Szwalbnest 2010).

Expressing concerns about judicial expansion of Title VII's traditional definition of sex, other federal courts follow the Ninth Circuit's lead in rejecting claims of discrimination on the basis of sexual orientation, most warning of the danger of conflating them with claims based on sex stereotyping. "Nearly all employment discrimination claims with a *hint* of sexual orientation are thrown out of federal courts"—even if the plaintiffs also present evidence of discrimination because of their race or religion (Barker 2009, 112, emphasis in the original). Thus, even if the plaintiffs incorporate the *Price Waterhouse* theory and argue that they are harassed because they deviate from sex-stereotypical norms, their cases are on much shakier ground if they cite sexual orientation as one of the reasons for the hostility toward them. In any event, with the exception of a 2014 district court decision, no court has accepted a discrimination claim based on sexual orientation alone. Thus, unless a complaint "include[s] gender-specific verbal harassment or sexualized touching, the plaintiff loses" (Rotondo 2014, 114).

In *Spearman v. Ford Motor Company* (2000), the Seventh Circuit devoted much of its opinion to attempting to read the minds of the plaintiff's tormentors to determine why they harassed him. Edison Spearman complained of a hostile work environment, claiming his co-workers harassed him because of his sexual orientation. The lower court granted Ford's motion for summary judgment. On appeal, Judge Daniel Manion reiterated the circuit's position "that the phrase in Title VII prohibiting 'discrimination based on sex' means that 'it is unlawful to discriminate against women because they are women and against men because they are men'" (1084, quoting *Ulane v. Eastern Airlines* 1984, 1085). Congress, he continued, viewed sex in biological terms only, excluding discrimination based on sexual orientation from the protection of Title VII. Manion acknowledged that the plaintiff's coworkers used sexually explicit language and insults and attacked him as being too "feminine" to work in the Ford plant but held that he had failed to show that the basis for the harassment was his sex. Analyzing the specific language directed against him, the court concluded that his coworkers were hostile to him because of his perceived sexual orientation, not because he was a man.

The Second Circuit also ruled against the plaintiff in *Simonton v. Runyon* (2000). Dwayne Simonton, a postal worker for twelve years, sued the US Postal Service for sex discrimination, complaining that he worked in a hostile environment. The district court dismissed his complaint because Title VII does not recognize discrimination based on sexual orientation. Admitting that Simonton had presented copious amounts of evidence of the abuse he suffered from name-calling and other verbal attacks—language that the court was hesitant to repeat in its entirety—Judge John Walker Jr. announced the opinion for the circuit panel. He rejected Simonton's reliance on *Oncale*, saying that the Supreme Court had merely held that same-sex harassment may fall within Title VII but not that it necessarily does. Because the plaintiff did not provide sufficient evidence to show that his treatment was based on sex, the court inferred that he was harassed because of his sexual orientation, which is legal under Title VII. The court appeared willing to accept a sex-stereotyping theory but held that Simonton had not provided evidence to show that he "behaved in a stereotypically feminine manner and that the harassment he endured was, in fact, based on his non-conformity with gender norms instead of his sexual orientation" (*Simonton v. Runyon* 2000, 38). The appeals court affirmed the court below.

An anomalous Ninth Circuit opinion in 2002 seemed to depart from the judiciary's rigid interpretation of Title VII when the court allowed a plaintiff to proceed under a Title VII suit without showing that he was a victim of sex stereotyping (*Rene v. MGM Grand Hotel, Inc.* 2002). Medina Rene, who was "openly gay," worked as a butler on the elite twenty-ninth floor of the MGM Grand Hotel in Las Vegas, Nevada, from 1993 to 1996. During this time, his coworkers and a supervisor physically assaulted and verbally harassed him in a clearly sexual manner. After the hotel fired him, he sued in federal district court, claiming that the harassment created a hostile environment that violated Title VII. His complaint to the Nevada Equal Rights Commission indicated that he believed that they tormented him because of his "sex, male." The district court granted the hotel's motion for summary judgment, holding that Title VII does not apply to claims of discrimination on the basis of sexual orientation. A three-judge panel of the Ninth Circuit affirmed.

Following a rehearing en banc, the circuit court reversed the lower court's grant of summary judgment for the employer. Speaking for a plurality of the court, Judge William Fletcher held that Rene's sexual orientation was irrelevant to the case (as were the harassers' sexual orientations and their motives), even if the harassment stemmed from hostility to his sexual orientation. The key, he said, was their behavior. Fletcher reviewed the Supreme Court's definition of sexual harassment under Title VII and found that Rene had satisfied the statute's requirements by "alleg[ing] physical conduct that was so severe and pervasive as to constitute an objectively abusive working environment. It is equally clear," he continued, that the tormentors' focus on certain parts of Rene's body was evidence that the "conduct was of 'a sexual nature'" (1065).

Fletcher cited more than a dozen cases in which courts held that physical sexual assaults constituted sexual harassment and criticized the district court judge who acknowledged that Rene worked in a hostile environment yet dismissed the case because he believed his coworkers were hostile to him because of his sexual orientation. Moreover, Fletcher added, there were numerous cases in which lesbian plaintiffs complained about sexual assault, and the courts had not considered their sexual orientation a material factor. "If sexual orientation is irrelevant for a female victim, we see no reason why it is also not irrelevant for a male victim," he said (1066).

In the end, the court viewed Rene's complaint "as a fairly straightforward sexual harassment claim" (1068), which, like Oncale's, alleged physical attacks of a sexual nature as well as verbal taunts by male coworkers. Unlike Oncale, Medina Rene was gay, yet the court held that Title VII applies whenever employees are subject to such treatment, regardless of their sexual orientation.

Rene could have broken new ground, but it proved to have limited utility for LGB Title VII plaintiffs for several reasons (Clark 2003, 320). First, because the physical nature of the discrimination was crucial to the outcome of the case, the court's approach would not apply to discrimination claims (such as hiring or firing decisions) where there were no allegations of physical contact. Second, because the physical contact was aimed at the plaintiff's sex organs, the court's approach would not apply to situations where other body parts were targeted by the harassers. Third, despite the fact that the court held that the plaintiff's sexual orientation was irrelevant to his claim, most courts have simply refused to accept the legitimacy of claims brought by gay and lesbian plaintiffs under Title VII (Clark 2003).

Another Second Circuit opinion, *Dawson v. Bumble and Bumble* (2005), was also based on the plaintiff's failure to provide the details necessary to state a valid Title VII claim. Dawn Dawson, a hairdresser, was enrolled in the salon's training program. When the salon terminated her, she filed a Title VII suit, claiming that it discriminated against her because of sex, sexual orientation, and sex stereotyping. The district court dismissed her complaint, holding that the statute does not prohibit discrimination based on sexual orientation.

Speaking for the Second Circuit panel, Judge Rosemary Pooler also warned of bootstrapping, saying that a court must be cautious about accepting a sex-stereotyping claim from an "avowedly homosexual plaintiff" to avoid allowing it to be "used to 'bootstrap protection for sexual orientation into Title VII'" (218, quoting *Simonton v. Runyon* 2000, 38). Because Dawson had not presented evidence that her termination stemmed from her failure to conform to sex stereotypes rather than her sexual orientation, the court affirmed the court below.

In these cases as well as cases in the First, Third, Fourth, Sixth, and Eighth Circuits, the courts rejected claims of sexual orientation discrimination, ruling that, however odious it may be, Title VII does not make such discrimination illegal.[59] The Third Circuit provided an opening for gay and lesbian plaintiffs in *Prowel v. Wise Business Forms, Inc.* (2009). After thirteen years at Wise Business Forms, Brian Prowel was terminated for "lack of work." His complaint stated that he was harassed because he was "effeminate" and did not conform to his coworkers' sex-role norms. Moreover, he said, after he was "outed" at work, he was verbally attacked and threatened as well as publicly accused of having AIDS.

The lower court granted the employer summary judgment, holding that Prowel's reliance on *Price Waterhouse*'s sex-stereotyping theory was merely a subterfuge for a sexual orientation claim. Speaking for the Third Circuit panel, Judge Thomas Hardiman reiterated that, although Title VII does not remedy discrimination based on sexual orientation, "this does not mean that, however, that a homosexual individual is barred from bringing a *sex discrimination* claim under Title VII" (*Prowel v. Wise Business Forms, Inc* 2009, 289, emphasis in the original).

Conceding the difficulty of drawing a line between a claim based on sexual orientation and one on sex stereotyping, Hardiman said the case is not appropriate for summary judgment and must be decided on whether Prowel was harassed because of his "homosexuality, his effeminacy, or both." Considering the facts of the case, the court concluded that the "record is ambiguous on this dispositive question [and] accordingly Powel's gender stereotyping claim must be submitted to a jury" (291).

A breakthrough for gay and lesbian employees finally came in 2014, when a District of Columbia District Court became the first court to permit a Title VII claim based on sexual orientation to go forward; shortly thereafter, the EEOC agreed that plaintiffs who complain of discrimination on the basis of sexual orientation state a valid claim under Title VII.

In *TerVeer v. Billington* (2014), the court departed from the conventional approach to Title VII in Peter TerVeer's suit against the Library of Congress. The suit claimed that, among other things, he was subject to a hostile work environment because of his sexual orientation; he contended that his supervisor treated him unfairly after discovering his sexual orientation because it was antithetical to the supervisor's religious beliefs.

TerVeer began working for the library in 2008. He filed suit in 2013, alleging that he received bad performance evaluations and was threatened with termination and his supervisors "continued to 'harass, intimidate, and retaliate'" against him and constructively discharged him while he was on medical leave (107).

In discussing TerVeer's Title VII actions for discrimination based on sex, religion, and retaliation, District of Columbia District Court Judge Colleen Kollar-Kotelly rejected the library's argument that she should dismiss his sex discrimination claim because he failed to specify how he deviated from sex stereotypes and how his gender nonconformity motivated the employer to treat him unfairly. She held that, in the District of Columbia Circuit, it is "sufficient to establish a viable sex discrimination claim" if the complaint states that an "employer is discriminating against an employee based on the employee's non-conformity with sex stereotypes" (116). Because TerVeer "alleged that he is 'a homosexual male whose sexual orientation is not consistent with the Defendant's perception of acceptable gender roles . . . [and] that his 'status as a homosexual male did not conform to the Defendant's gender stereotypes associated with men' . . . and that 'his orientation as homosexual had removed him from [the Defendant's] preconceived definition of male,'" she held that he satisfied the pleading requirement of a Title VII claim to survive a motion to dismiss (116). In the end, she ruled that TerVeer had met the standard for a sex-stereotyping claim under *Price Waterhouse* and allowed his case to go to trial.[60]

On July 15, 2015, the EEOC formally ruled that sexual orientation is within the purview of Title VII in *Baldwin v. Department of Transportation* (2015). David Baldwin, a temporary supervisory air traffic specialist at the Miami International Airport, claimed that the Federal Aviation Administration (FAA) did not select him for a permanent position because of his sexual orientation. He cited as evidence a number of derogatory remarks about his sexuality from one of the managers with a role in the hiring process. For example, he said his supervisor reacted to his comment that he was going to Mardi Gras with his partner by saying, "[W]e don't need to hear about that gay stuff." He also told Baldwin that he was a "distraction in the radar room" when he talked about his partner" (at 2).

The EEOC opinion dismissed as irrelevant whether sexual orientation was explicitly included as a protected category in Title VII. The key question, it said, was whether the FAA had relied on gender or "sex-based considerations" in making its employment decision, both of which are forbidden by Title VII. The agency stressed that sexual orientation is a "sex-based consideration" that is "premised on sex-based preferences, assumptions, expectations, stereotypes, or norms." Indeed, it added, "'sexual orientation' as a concept cannot be defined or understood without reference to sex." Citing the gender-stereotyping cases, the agency concluded, "[A]n allegation of discrimination based on sexual orientation is necessarily an allegation of sex discrimination under Title VII" (at 5–6).

Reacting to the EEOC's revised position on sexual orientation, HRC president Chad Griffin pronounced himself pleased but qualified it with a caveat reiterating the need for federal legislation: "This historic ruling by the EEOC makes clear they agree workplace discrimination on the basis of sexual orientation, much like gender identity, is illegal. While an important step, it also highlights the need for a comprehensive federal law permanently and clearly banning LGBT discrimination beyond employment to all areas of American life. Such a law would send a clear and permanent signal that discrimination against LGBT people will not be tolerated under any circumstances in this country, and we remain fully committed to making that happen" (*Washington Blade*, July 16, 2015).

In another dramatic advance for LGB rights, rather than moving to dismiss the case, the Department of Justice (DOJ) answered the complaint (*Baldwin v. Foxx* 2016). It could have argued that the law does not encompass discrimination based on sexual orientation; rather, it chose to litigate it on the merits, thus implicitly agreeing with the EEOC's position that Title VII applies to sexual orientation. A civil rights attorney underscored the importance of DOJ's action, saying that it "made the correct call by defending this case on the facts rather than making the outdated and conservative legal argument that the Civil Rights Act does not protect gays and lesbians from workplace discrimination" (*BuzzFeed*, January 28, 2016; Miller 2016).

Demonstrating the effect of *Baldwin* on agency policy, on March 1, 2016, the EEOC filed its first two cases against employers for sexual harassment based on sexual orientation. In *EEOC v. Scott Medical Health Center* (2016), the agency alleged that the gay employee's manager sexually harassed him by making offensive comments about his sexuality. In *EEOC v. Pallet Companies d/b/a/ IFCO Systems N.A., Inc.* (2016), the agency charged that the supervisor in the defendant's company sexually harassed a lesbian employee. In each case, the agency alleged that the employees were harassed "because of their sexual orientation and/or their non-conformity with the employer's gender-based expectations, preferences, or stereotypes." The outcome of these cases (and the likelihood that the EEOC will prevail) will depend on the courts' receptivity to the *Price Waterhouse* sex-stereotyping theory in cases based on discrimination because of sexual orientation and their willingness to accept the District of Columbia District Court's per se approach to sexual orientation and Title VII.

NOTES

1. Consistent with common usage, LGBT refers to lesbians, gay men, bisexual persons, and transgender persons as a whole. At times, it is necessary to differentiate among these types of individuals.

2. The survey was conducted online between September 9 and 17, 2015, by Harris, Witeck Communications, and Out & Equal Workplace Advocates. The results were based on responses of 2,368 adults, of whom 304 identified themselves as lesbian, gay, bisexual, and/or transgender.

3. According to a Harris Poll (2015) almost one-quarter of the respondents (21 percent) believed that all fifty states and the District of Columbia have laws preventing employers from firing LGBT employees because of their sexual orientation or gender identity.

4. Federal contractors employ 28 million workers, more than 20 percent of the nation's workforce (Human Rights Campaign 2014a).

5. The prohibition against transgender service members continued, with Carter admitting that there was no specific time set for a formal review of the regulations affecting transgender troops (Brydum 2015).

6. As of February 2, 2016, twenty states (plus the District of Columbia) prohibit employment discrimination because of sexual orientation and gender identity: California, Colorado, Connecticut, Delaware, Hawaii, Illinois, Iowa, Maine, Maryland, Massachusetts, Minnesota, Nevada, New Jersey, New Mexico, New York, Oregon, Rhode Island, Utah, Vermont, and Washington State. Two states: New Hampshire and Wisconsin prohibit discrimination because of sexual orientation only, bringing the number of states barring discrimination on the basis of sexual orientation to twenty-two, plus the District of Columbia (Movement Advancement Project 2016b; see Fidas, Cooper, and Raspanti 2014, 6). On October 22, 2015, because the Gender Expression Nondiscrimination Act (GENDA) failed to pass in the state legislature, New York Governor Andrew Cuomo relied on his executive power to direct the state's Division of Human Rights to promulgate regulations to make it illegal to discriminate on the basis of gender identity, transgender status, and gender dysphoria in public and private employment, housing, and public accommodations (New York State 2015). The state Human Rights Law already included sexual orientation as a prohibited category of discrimination, but even with Cuomo's action, gender identity was less securely protected because it was not included in the Human Rights Law.

7. Five states prohibit discrimination against public employees because of sexual orientation: Alaska, Arizona, Missouri, Montana, and Ohio; six states prohibit discrimination against public employees based on sexual orientation and gender identity: Indiana, Kentucky, Michigan, New York, Pennsylvania, Virginia (Human Rights Campaign 2016). North Carolina also added protections for state workers on the basis of gender identity and sexual orientation.

8. Twenty-eight states have no job protection measures in private employment: Alabama, Alaska, Arkansas, Arizona, Florida, Georgia, Idaho, Indiana, Kansas, Kentucky, Louisiana, Michigan, Mississippi, Missouri, Montana, Nebraska, North Carolina, North Dakota, Ohio, Oklahoma, Pennsylvania, South Carolina, South Dakota, Tennessee, Texas, Virginia, West Virginia, and Wyoming. Two of these: Arkansas and Tennessee bar local governments from enacting antidiscrimination laws (Movement Advancement Project 2016b).

9. Workers have no protection against discrimination based on gender identity in Alabama, Mississippi, New Hampshire, North Carolina, North Dakota, South Dakota, and Virginia. States that offer no protection against discrimination on the basis of sexual orientation are Alabama, Mississippi, North Carolina, North Dakota, and South Dakota (Movement Advancement Project 2016a).

10. In one of the most recent analyses of transgender employees, a 2014 Williams Institute study found that transgender and gender-nonconforming workers reported being discriminated against in myriad ways (see Williams Institute 2014a).

11. The General Social Survey is conducted by the National Opinion Research Center of the University of Chicago.

12. On behalf the Gay & Lesbian Alliance Against Defamation (its name changed to GLAAD in 2013), a Harris Poll measured attitudes toward the LGBT population in the United States in two surveys of a national representative sample of adults in 2014. These online surveys were conducted between August 21 and 25, 2014, with 2,014 adults aged eighteen and over; of these, 1,754 did not identify as LGBT. Another survey conducted from November 10 to 12, 2014, had 2,010 adult respondents; of these, 1,821 did not identify as LGBT (GLAAD 2015).

13. There were also attempts to amend the Fair Housing Act to ban discrimination based on sexual orientation in housing.

14. Reed (2014) agrees that it would be preferable to amend Title VII to include sexual orientation and gender identity.

15. Thirty-five senators voted for both measures.

16. The 1996 bill offered no protections for transgender workers.

17. The Human Rights Campaign is one of the nation's leading organizations working to achieve equal rights for the LGBT community.

18. Some Democrats voted against the final bill because it did not go far enough in protecting against discrimination because of gender identity; some Republicans argued to include gender identity provisions, likely as a way of undercutting support for the bill (Schwin 2009).

19. Section 6 of H.R. 2015 provides,

> (a) In General.—This Act shall not apply to any of the employment practices of a religious corporation, association, educational institution, or society which has as its primary purpose religious ritual or worship or the teaching or spreading of religious doctrine or belief.
> (b) Certain Employees.—For any religious corporation, association, educational institution, or society that is not wholly exempt under subsection (a), this Act shall not apply with respect to the employment of individuals whose primary duties consist of teaching or spreading religious doctrine or belief, religious governance, supervision of a religious order, supervision of persons teaching or spreading religious doctrine or belief, or supervision or participation in religious ritual or worship.

20. ENDA was introduced almost every year after its narrow loss in 1996. It was introduced in 1997 in the 105th Congress as S. 869 and H.R. 1858; in 1999, it was introduced in the 106th Congress as S. 1276 and H.R. 2355. ENDA of 2001 was introduced in the 107th Congress as S. 1284 and H.R. 2692; ENDA of 2003 was brought out in the 108th Congress as S. 1705 and H.R. 3285. The two House versions of the 2007 ENDA that were introduced in the 110th Congress were H.R. 2015 and H.R. 3685. The ENDA of 2009 was introduced in the 111th Congress as S. 1584 and H.R. 3017; the 2011 ENDA in the 112th Congress was introduced as S. 811 and H.R. 1397. In 2013, ENDA was introduced in the 113th Congress as H.R. 1755 and S. 815. In 2015, when the title was changed to the Equality Act, the bill was introduced as H.R. 3185 and S. 1858 (Human Rights Campaign 2015d; see US Senate 2013).

21. This was a constant refrain from those who opposed equal rights for transgender students and workers.

22. ENDA's opponents also claimed the law was unnecessary because the federal courts had expanded their interpretation of Title VII to include a ban on discrimination against transgender and gender-nonconforming individuals and could continue to do so in the future. They failed to mention that there was still opposition to including gender identity within Title VII and that the courts consistently refused to apply Title VII to discrimination because of sexual orientation.

23. Section 4 of the Employment Non-Discrimination Act of 2013 provides,

> It shall be an unlawful employment practice for an employer—(1) to fail or refuse to hire or to discharge any individual, or otherwise discriminate against any individual with respect to the compensation, terms, conditions, or privileges of employment of the individual, because of such individual's actual or perceived sexual orientation or gender identity; or (2) to limit, segregate, or classify the employees or applicants for employment of the employer in any way that would deprive or tend to deprive any individual of employment or otherwise adversely affect the status of the individual as an employee, because of such individual's actual or perceived sexual orientation or gender identity.

24. Unlike the case law that evolved from Title VII over time, ENDA would have excluded causes of action based on disparate impact claims; that is, when employers adopt neutral policies that have a disproportionate impact on protected groups. Title VII allows voluntary affirmative action plans under some circumstances; ENDA categorically excluded them. Title VII allows employers

to discriminate on the basis of religion but not on sex, race, national origin, or color. ENDA included a broader religious exemption than Title VII (see Reed 2015). The 1991 Civil Rights Act amended Title VII to provide that an "unlawful employment practice is established when the complaining party demonstrates that race, color, religion, sex, or national origin was a motivating factor for any employment practice, even though other factors also motivated the practice." ENDA likewise specified that an employer is liable if a plaintiff can demonstrate that gender identity or sexual orientation was a "motivating factor" behind the adverse job action—even if there were other permissible reasons for the action.

25. Section 6 of the Employment Non-Discrimination Act of 2013 provides,

> This Act shall not apply to a corporation, association, educational institution or institution of learning, or society that is exempt from the religious discrimination provisions of title VII of the Civil Rights Act of 1964 . . . pursuant to section 702(a) or 703(e)(2) of such Act . . . (referred to in this section as a "religious employer"). (b) A religious employer's exemption under this section shall not result in any action by a Federal agency, or any State or local agency that receives Federal funding or financial assistance, to penalize or withhold licenses, permits, certifications, accreditation, contracts, grants, guarantees, tax-exempt status, or any benefits or exemptions from that employer, or to prohibit the employer's participation in programs or activities sponsored by that Federal, State, or local agency. Nothing in this subsection shall be construed to invalidate any other Federal, State, or local law (including a regulation) that otherwise applies to a religious employer exempt under this section.

26. Section 702(a) of the 1964 Civil Rights Act provides, "This subchapter shall not apply to . . . a religious corporation, association, educational institution, or society with respect to the employment of individuals of a particular religion to perform work connected with the carrying on by such corporation, association, educational institution, or society of its activities." Section 703(e)(2) provides,

> It shall not be an unlawful employment practice for a school, college, university, or other educational institution or institution of learning to hire and employ employees of a particular religion if such school, college, university, or other educational institution or institution of learning is, in whole or in substantial part, owned, supported, controlled, or managed by a particular religion or by a particular relig-

> ious corporation, association, or society, or if the curriculum of such school, college, university, or other educational institution or institution of learning is directed toward the propagation of a particular religion.

Although the original version of Title VII restricts the exemption to employees who carry out the work linked to its religious activities, in 1972, believing the exemption too narrow, Congress broadened it by amending the statute to delete the term religious before the word activities.

27. In 2016, the organization, still known as GLAD, became known as the GLBTQ Legal Advocates & Defenders.

28. The Equality Act would also have extended the 1964 act's prohibition against discrimination in public accommodations to sex for the first time.

29. In an effort to forestall reliance on religious beliefs as a defense to discrimination, section 1107 of the Equality Act states, "The Religious Freedom Restoration Act of 1993 . . . shall not provide a claim concerning, or a defense to a claim under, a covered title, or provide a basis for challenging the application or enforcement of a covered title." On the other side of the aisle, seeking to halt the effect of the Supreme Court's ruling on marriage equality, Republicans introduced the First Amendment Defense Act, a bill intended to prevent the federal government from taking legal measures against individuals who act on the basis of their religious beliefs that marriage should be between a man and a woman (*McClatchy DC*, July 23, 2015).

30. Executive Order 12968 of August 2, 1995, Access to Classified Information, provides,

> Section 3.1(c) The United States Government does not discriminate on the basis of race, color, religion, sex, national origin, disability, or sexual orientation in granting access to classified information. (d) In determining eligibility for access under this order, agencies may investigate and consider any matter that relates to the determination of whether access is clearly consistent with the interests of national security. No inference concerning the standards in this section may be raised solely on the basis of the sexual orientation of the employee. (Clinton 1995a)

31. Executive Order 11478, Equal employment opportunity in the Federal Government, provides,

> Section 1. It is the policy of the Government of the United States to provide equal opportunity in Federal employment for all persons, to

> prohibit discrimination in employment because of race, color, religion, sex, national origin, handicap, or age, and to promote the full realization of equal employment opportunity through a continuing affirmative program in each executive department and agency. This policy of equal opportunity applies to and must be an integral part of every aspect of personnel policy and practice in the employment, development, advancement, and treatment of civilian employees of the Federal Government.

32. Executive Order 13087, Further Amendment to Executive Order 11478, Equal Employment Opportunity in the Federal Government, provides, "Section 1. The first sentence of section 1 is amended by substituting 'age, or sexual orientation' for 'or age.'

33. Among federal contractors, 61 percent of employees were protected by antidiscrimination laws or policies on the basis of sexual orientation, compared to 51 percent of noncontractor employees; 41 percent of employees were protected by antidiscrimination laws based on gender identity, compared to only 28 percent of noncontractor employees (Badgett 2012). A 2014 study found that 86 percent of the top fifty federal contractors prohibited discrimination based on sexual orientation, and 61 percent prohibited it because of gender identity (Williams Institute 2014b).

34. Obama's strategy in amending the existing executive order applying to federal contractors rather than issue a separate one was to make it more difficult for his successors to undo it (Human Rights Campaign 2014b). After the 2016 election, LGBT groups expressed concern, however, that the new administration would nullify it (*New York Times*, November 10, 2016). Moreover, Executive Order 13672 did not prohibit discrimination against LGBT-owned businesses. The National Gay and Lesbian Chamber of Commerce urged Obama to end discrimination against LGBT Business Enterprises before he left office (*Washington Blade*, October 25, 2016).

35. Executive Order 11246, as signed by President Lyndon Johnson on September 24, 1965, prohibits employment discrimination on the basis of race, color, religion, and national origin. Two years later (on October 13, 1967), Johnson signed Executive Order 11375, amending the previous one to include sex as a protected class.

36. Executive Order 13672, Further Amendments to Executive Order 11478, Equal Employment Opportunity in the Federal Government, and Executive Order 11246, Equal Employment Opportunity, provide,

> Section 1. Amending Executive Order 11478. The first sentence of section 1 of Executive Order 11478 of August 8, 1969, as amended, is

revised by substituting "sexual orientation, gender identity" for "sexual orientation." Sec. 2. Amending Executive Order 11246. Executive Order 11246 of September 24, 1965, as amended, is hereby further amended as follows: (a) The first sentence of numbered paragraph (1) of section 202 is revised by substituting "sex, sexual orientation, gender identity, or national origin" for "sex, or national origin."(Obama 2014a)

37. Following from Executive Order 13672, Secretary of Labor Thomas Perez (2014) issued a directive aimed at federal contractors "to clarify that existing agency guidance on discrimination on the basis of sex under Executive Order 11246, as amended, includes discrimination on the bases of gender identity and transgender status."

38. Section 4(c) of Executive Order 13279 of December 12, 2002, Equal Protection of the Laws for Faith-Based and Community Organizations, provides, "This Order shall not apply to a Government contractor or subcontractor that is a religious corporation, association, educational institution, or society, with respect to the employment of individuals of a particular religion to perform work connected with the carrying on by such corporation, association, educational institution, or society of its activities."

39. Bush claimed that his executive order was intended to prevent the federal government from discriminating against faith-based charities in awarding federal funds.

40. Federal workers were dismissed for homosexuality as early as the 1880s, when the civil service system was established (Cain 1993).

41. Executive Order 10865 of February 1960 "gave rise to the catchall phrase that security clearances could be denied if they would not be 'clearly consistent with the national interest'" (Lewis 1990, 140).

42. In *Carlucci v. Doe* (1988), the Supreme Court similarly upheld the National Security Agency's authority to deny a security clearance to one of its civilian employees.

43. The firm did not admit that she was discharged for "transsexualism" but because her dress and manner made her coworkers uncomfortable.

44. Although the lower court also held that she was discriminated against because of sex, the appeals court said that this was simply based on her "transsexual" status.

45. *Price Waterhouse* (1989, 258) held that "when a plaintiff in a Title VII case proves that her gender played a motivating part in an employment decision, the defendant may avoid a finding of liability only by proving by a preponderance of the evidence that it would have made the same decision even if it had not taken the plaintiff's gender into account." Because the lower court had

erred in holding the defendant to the higher standard of "clear and convincing evidence," the high court reversed and remanded the case to allow the lower court to use the proper legal standard.

46. The Court identified three types of evidence to prove that harassment is based on sex in same-sex harassment cases: first, if it is motivated by sexual desire; second, if the insulting language containing sexual terms stems from hostility to the presence of persons of that sex in the workplace; and third, if there is evidence that the harasser treats members of the opposite sex differently. None of these factual situations is likely to occur when the victims of same-sex harassment are gay or lesbian (Clark 2003).

47. The courts rejected claims by transgender plaintiffs in *Dobre v. National Railroad Passenger Corp*. (1993); *James v. Ranch Mart Hardware, Inc*. (1994); *Broadus v. State Farm Insurance* (2000); and *Oiler v. Winn-Dixie Louisiana Inc.* (2002). They were hospitable to claims only if they believed the plaintiffs had experienced adverse employment actions, including sexual harassment, because they strayed from gender-stereotypical norms. In *Nichols v. Azteca Restaurant Enterprises, Inc.* (2001), the court cited *Price Waterhouse*, ruling that the plaintiff had a valid claim under a sex-stereotyping theory because he stated that he was harassed because he was "too feminine." In *Lewis v. Heartland Inns of America* (2010), the court also upheld the claim of a woman who wore no makeup, had short hair, favored men's button-down shirts, and was described as looking "too boyish."

48. In addition to these two approaches, Lee (2012) identifies a "constructionist approach," a little-used theory based on the principle that sex and gender are socially constructed.

49. The court rejected the defendant's argument that the GMVA is only intended to protect women, not men, from violence, explaining that its legislative history shows that Congress intended it to also protect men, especially from prison assaults.

50. In *Rosa v. Park West Bank & Trust Co.* (2000), the First Circuit reversed the lower court's dismissal of a claim against the bank under the Equal Credit Opportunity Act (ECOA). Also analogizing the ECOA to Title VII, the appeals court agreed that the bank discriminated against the transgender woman plaintiff because it viewed her women's clothing as inconsistent with her biological sex.

51. Consistent with *Ulane,* a Seventh Circuit panel narrowly construed the word "sex" in Title VII in *Hively v. Ivy Tech Community College* (2016a). On October 11, 2016, the full circuit vacated the ruling and granted a rehearing en banc (*Hively v. Ivy Tech Community College* 2016b). The circuit's action suggests it may no longer be committed to its position in *Ulane*.

52. In *Barnes v. City of Cincinnati* (2005, 739), the Sixth Circuit upheld a lower court's ruling against the city for demoting a preoperative transgender woman police officer. Citing *Smith,* the appeals court ruled that the plaintiff is a "member of a protected class as defined in Title VII."

53. In *Kastl v. Maricopa County Community College* (2009), the Ninth Circuit recognized that Rebecca Kastl filed a valid complaint for discrimination under Title VII but held that the employer's reason for discharging her was based on a legitimate concern over safe use of the women's restroom and was not motivated by gender.

54. DOJ decided not to appeal (*Trans Policy News* 2009).

55. The court applied the heightened-scrutiny approach used in classifications based on gender, saying that "ever since the Supreme Court began to apply heightened scrutiny to sex-based classifications, its consistent purpose has been to eliminate discrimination on the basis of gender stereotypes" (*Glenn v. Brumby* 2011, 1319). Because Brumby was unable to offer an "important" reason for firing her, he violated her equal protection rights.

56. Although not binding on the courts, EEOC rulings are considered persuasive authority.

57. In cases of same-sex harassment with a heterosexual plaintiff and a gay defendant, the courts most often rule for the plaintiff, presuming that the defendant is motivated by sexual desire (see Sachs 2004).

58. In *Smith v. Liberty Mutual Insurance Co.* (1978), decided a little over a year before *DeSantis*, the Fifth Circuit affirmed a lower court ruling dismissing a case in which the plaintiff alleged that he was not hired because his interviewer thought him "effeminate." Citing the language in Title VII, the court simply held that the statute did not apply to such a "questionable" claim.

59. See, for example, *Williamson v. A. G. Edwards and Sons, Inc.* (1989); *Hopkins v. Baltimore Gas & Electric Company* (1996); *Higgins v. New Balance Athletic Shoe, Inc.* (1999); *Bibby v. Philadelphia Coca-Cola Bottling Company* (2001); *Vickers v. Fairfield Medical Center* (2006); *Gilbert v. Country Music Association, Inc.* (2011); *Pagan v. Gonzalez* (2011); and *Dingle v. Bimbo Bakeries* (2015).

60. TerVeer entered into a forty-five-day mediation period with his employer to explore whether a settlement of the case was possible. Because the parties continued the discovery process after the forty-five days were up, it appeared that the parties had not agreed on a settlement (*Washington Blade*, February 9, 2015). There has been no reported opinion on the outcome of the suit (see *Slate*, February 19, 2016).

2

TRANSGENDER RIGHTS

The nation's awareness of gender identity was heightened on April 24, 2015, when Bruce Jenner, the 1976 Olympic gold medalist, told Diane Sawyer on ABC's *20/20* that he transitioned to a woman (*Variety*, April 24, 2015).[1] Jenner's appearance as Caitlyn Marie Jenner on the cover of *Vanity Fair* a few months later caused an additional stir (Bissinger 2015).

As early as 2012, Vice President Joe Biden pronounced transgender discrimination as the "civil rights issue of our time" (Transgender Law Center 2012). Claims of discrimination because of gender identity have become commonplace in the nation, with federal agencies (the Department of Education [DOE], DOJ, and the EEOC) playing significant roles in advancing rights of transgender persons. In 2013, a California school district entered into an agreement with the federal government following a complaint of discrimination by a transgender boy in middle school, with the district promising to adopt individual and district-wide measures to end discriminatory policies. In 2014, Medicare included coverage of sex reassignment surgery, and Secretary of Defense Chuck Hagel suggested a review of the military's ban on transgender service members.[2]

The next year, Obama issued an executive order barring federal contractors from discriminating because of gender identity and sexual orientation. Also in 2015, the Department of Health and Human Services (HHS) drafted a rule to end discrimination based on gender identity by health care providers, insurance companies, and health care facilities receiving federal funds; the Department of Veterans Affairs also committed itself to providing necessary medical care to transgender veterans.[3]

In February 2015, reporters at an event in Kandahar, Afghanistan, asked the newly appointed Carter about transgender troops.[4] He admitted that he had not "studied" the matter "a lot" yet but was "very open-minded about [it]," adding that he did not "think anything but their suitability for service should matter" (US Department of Defense 2015; see *The Advocate*, February 23, 2015).

Later that year, Carter said the regulations barring transgender service members were "outdated" and ordered a Pentagon study on eliminating the ban (Lederman 2015). A Pentagon draft memo soon circulated among top officials detailing a plan for ending it by 2016 (Miller 2015).[5] Soon after, speaking at an HRC dinner, Biden affirmed, "[N]o longer is there any question transgender people are able to serve in the United States military" (*Huffington Post*, October 4, 2015).[6]

True to his word, on June 30, 2016, Carter announced that transgender individuals would now be able to "openly serve" without fearing discharge or other disciplinary action: "'This is the right thing to do for our people and for the force,' Carter said. 'We're talking about talented Americans who are serving with distinction or who want the opportunity to serve. We can't allow barriers unrelated to a person's qualifications prevent us from recruiting and retaining those who can best accomplish the mission.'" He indicated that questions about transitioning and medical care, among other things, would be resolved within the year (US Department of Defense 2016).[7]

The nation's widely publicized controversy over transgender service members had surfaced two years before Carter issued his statement. On August 21, 2013, Private First Class Bradley Manning was sentenced to thirty-five years in Fort Leavenworth, Kansas, for violating the Espionage Act, among other offenses, by leaking classified military documents to *WikiLeaks*, an online organization that publishes secret information. Upon conviction, Manning announced she was a transgender woman and requested that the army provide her with medically necessary hormone therapy treatment and psychotherapy. Her demands rejected, Manning (who would remain in the army while incarcerated) filed suit in 2014, charging the government with violating her Eighth Amendment right against cruel and unusual punishment. In

March 2015, the government acceded to her requests for hormone therapy and permitted her to change her name to Chelsea Elizabeth Manning. The army also agreed to refer to her in gender-neutral terms as "Private Manning" or use a female pronoun (*Christian Science Monitor*, February 14, 2015; *The Guardian*, March 5, 2015). On January 17, 2017, Obama commuted the rest of her sentence (*New York Times*, January 17, 2017; *Washington Post*, January 18, 2017).

In another advance for the transgender community in November 2015, the Equality Caucus of the House of Representatives announced the formation of a Transgender Equality Task Force. The caucus's first event was a congressional forum focusing on violence against transgender people (Bailey 2015). Caucus chair Mike Honda, Democrat from California, introduced the event saying, "[T]his week as we seek to raise awareness of the issues facing the trans community, it is important to renew our commitment to help trans individuals be free of the fear of violence or bullying just for being who they are" (*Washington Post*, November 13, 2015).

As 2015 drew to a close, the Obama administration announced its support for the Equality Act, a law to amend the Civil Rights Act of 1964 to prohibit discrimination based on gender identity and sexual orientation in employment, public accommodations, education, credit, and housing (Badash 2015; *New York Times*, May 5, 2014; *New York Times*, June 10, 2014; *New York Times*, April 10, 2015; *New York Times*, September 4, 2015).

The next year, the controversy over transgender persons reached new heights, with DOJ and DOE sending a joint guidance to the nation's school districts, outlining their position on equal rights for the transgender community (*New York Times*, May 13, 2016; *Washington Post*, May 13, 2016). In the same month, the rule barring insurers from routinely denying coverage on the basis of gender identity or sexual orientation became final (*Washington Post*, May 14, 2016).

At the subnational level, by 2014, eighteen states and the District of Columbia had laws banning discrimination because of gender identity and sexual orientation (National LGBTQ Task Force 2014).[8] At the local level, more than 225 cities and counties prohibited employment discrimination on the basis of gender identity (Human Rights Campaign 2015d). Some states and municipalities allowed transgender men and women to update their names and genders on birth certificates and other identity documents, but some required individuals to undergo sex reassignment surgery before issuing the new papers.[9] Some states also began to require private insurers to cover the costs of medically necessary procedures, such as hormone therapy and sex reassignment surgery.[10] In the private sector, a number of companies extended insurance coverage to gender transition services (*Hartford Register Citizen*, March 29, 2015; Human Rights Campaign 2015c; *New York Times*, June 10, 2014; *New York Times*, October 7, 2014).

In October 2015, pursuant to a settlement agreement in a federal lawsuit, California agreed to provide sex reassignment surgery for qualified transgender prisoners (*Los Angeles Times*, August 10, 2015). In the same month, in the face of the legislature's continued refusal to pass antidiscrimination legislation, New York Governor Andrew Cuomo issued an unprecedented executive action barring discrimination against transgender individuals in housing, employment, public accommodations, and financial services (*New York Times*, October 23, 2015).[11]

GENDER IDENTITY AND SEXUAL ORIENTATION

Despite the advances, the persons who do not conform to the expected manifestations of a binary gender identity are often treated badly. Most transgender persons do not live in jurisdictions where it is illegal to discriminate on the basis of gender identity and gender nonconformity (Tarzwell 2006).

Although the terms are often used interchangeably, it is important to understand the complex way in which sex and gender differ yet are intertwined.[12] Sex is a biological status assigned at birth—based on hormones, chromosomes, and reproductive organs—that manifests in physical attributes. Gender is socially constructed, expressing itself in roles, attitudes, and behavior that society considers appropriate for females and males. Gender identity refers to one's perception of one's own gender; gender expression indicates the way in which individuals signal their gender identity in typically "feminine" or "masculine" ways by their choices in grooming, dressing, walking, and speaking (see Givens 2013).

The term transgender refers to a continuum of nonconforming gender attitudes and behaviors.[13] There are complex reasons individuals may be dissatisfied with their assigned sex at birth and the gender norms to which society expects them to adhere (American Psychological Association 2015). The transgender community broadly includes individuals whose gender identity differs from the one associated with their sex at birth. Individuals within it may seek to alter their biological sex manifestations through hormone therapy as well as sex reassignment surgery; individuals who have altered their bodies through hormone therapy or surgeries to conform to their gender identity have been known as transsexuals in the past (American Psychological Association 2015).[14]

Gender dysphoria is a medical condition in which an individual's gender identity does not conform to his or her physical sex characteristics at birth. Formerly known as gender identity disorder, the American Psychiatric Association substituted the term gender dysphoria for gender identity disorder in 2013.[15] The revised *Diagnostic and Statistical Manual of Mental Disorders* (*DSM-V*), released in May 2013, cautions,

> [G]ender nonconformity is not in itself a mental disorder. The critical element of gender dysphoria is the presence of clinically significant distress associated with the condition. For a person to be diagnosed with gender dysphoria, there must be a marked difference between the individual's expressed/experienced gender and the gender others would assign him or her, and it must continue for at least six months. (American Psychiatric Association 2013; see American Psychological Association 2015)

Some argue against employing a medical model for gender nonconformity (World Professional Association for Transgender Health [WPATH] 2011; see Peek 2004).[16] Others claim that eschewing the medical model could undermine arguments for appropriate treatment of a serious medical condition (Bendlin 2013; Lee 2008).

According to the National Center for Transgender Equality, there is a scarcity of information about the transgender population in the United States, largely because questions related to gender nonconformity are rarely included in surveys, especially population-based surveys (Tobin, Freedman-Gurspan, and Mottet 2015, 46). More generally, surveys are often imprecise because many LGBT individuals do not publicly identify themselves and the responses are often dependent on the form of the questions (Bialik 2011).

To shed light on the myriad ways that discrimination because of gender identity manifests itself in the United States, the National Center for Transgender Equality and the National Gay and Lesbian Task Force launched a study of transgender and gender-nonconforming respondents in 2008.[17] Their 2011 report indicates that, of the 6,450 transgender and gender-nonconforming respondents in the national survey, 63 percent "experienced a serious act of discrimination—events that would have a major impact on a person's quality of life and ability to sustain themselves financially or emotionally." The discrimination was pervasive, manifesting as job bias, sexual violence, sexual harassment, physical assault, and lower levels of education and economic status; moreover, in all areas of investigation, transgender people of color fared worse than their white counterparts.

Perhaps even more disturbing, the rate of suicide and attempted suicide is much higher in the transgender population. The survey found that 41 percent of the respondents reported attempting suicide, compared to 1.6 percent in the general population. Moreover, the rates were even higher for those suffering job loss or harassment or physical or sexual assault (Grant, Mottet, and Tanis 2011, 10). A later study of violence against members of the LGBT community showed an 11 percent increase in homicides from 2013 to 2014, with transgender women especially likely to be victims (National Coalition of Anti-Violence Programs 2015).

A Pew Research Center survey on social acceptance of groups within the LGBT population reflected the disparate treatment of transgender persons. The responses showed that the vast majority of the LGBT respondents believe American society is much less accepting of transgender Americans than of other members of the LGBT community: 80 percent of them said that there is "only a little or no social acceptance of this group." In contrast, 27 percent of the respondents said that there is "only a little or no acceptance" of gay men, and 14 percent said the same about lesbians (Pew Research Center 2014).[18]

In an effort to determine the number of individuals who identify as LGBT, a study by Gary Gates of the Williams Institute on Sexual Orientation and Gender Identity Law and Public Policy averaged the results of surveys conducted between 2004 and 2011 in the United States and elsewhere.[19] Based on this, he estimates that nine million people (3.5 percent of adults) in the United States describe themselves as lesbian, gay, or bisexual. With his analysis of a 2007 study in California and a 2009 Massachusetts study, as well as federal data, Gates estimates that about 700,000 people (0.3 percent of adults) in the nation identify as transgender (Gates 2011).[20]

A year later, Gallup reported the results of a 2012 poll, in which 3.4 percent of respondents answered affirmatively when asked if they "personally identify as lesbian, gay, bisexual or transgender" (Gallup 2012).[21] More recently, Williams Institute researchers, who assessed more detailed state-level surveys, concluded that the number of transgender adults in the United States is higher than originally believed. Their 2016 report estimates that 1.4 million adults (0.6 percent of those eighteen and over) classify themselves as transgender. The authors attribute the higher numbers to respondents' greater willingness to be open about their gender identity on government surveys and a larger data set drawn from more than a dozen state surveys on which to base the new figures (Flores et al. 2016).[22]

THE EIGHTH AMENDMENT AND GENDER IDENTITY

A 2005 study found that transgender people are two to three times more likely to be imprisoned than nontransgender persons (Faithful 2009, 3). Not surprisingly, studies have shown that the larger states, such as California, New York, Florida, and Texas, have the highest number of transgender prisoners. It is difficult to obtain precise numbers, but based on information gathered in 2007 and 2008, it is estimated that there were between 500 and 750 transgender prisoners in state prisons and between 50 and 100 in federal prisons. To place these numbers in context, in December 2005, there were more than two million (2,193,798) prisoners in custody in the United States (Brown and McDuffie 2009, 281–82). A study released in June 2015 by the National Center for Transgender Equality reports that almost one in six transgender people (16 percent) have been imprisoned at some time in their lives, a higher rate than the general population. It concludes, "[T]hese high rates of incarceration are driven by pervasive discrimination, disproportionate poverty, homelessness, participation in street economies, and bias and abuse by law enforcement officers" (Tobin, Freedman-Gurspan, and Mottet 2015, 46).

Transgender people also face a disproportionate risk of harm in prison. A 2011–2012 survey of state and federal prisons by the Bureau of Justice Statistics found that 39.9 percent of transgender prison inmates and 26.8 percent of transgender jail inmates reported being sexually victimized (Beck 2014).

The Eighth Amendment prohibits "cruel and unusual punishment." Transgender persons—chiefly transgender women—are at risk of violations of the Eighth Amendment protection against cruel and unusual punishment in at least two ways. First, they may become prey to sexual victimization and harassment by their fellow inmates as well as prison guards and placed in solitary confinement (also known as administrative segregation), ostensibly for their own protection. Second, they may not get medically necessary health care, even if they had access to it prior to their imprisonment (Faithful 2009; Givens 2013; see Fleischaker 2014).

Most Eighth Amendment jurisprudence revolves around issues of punishment and sentencing rather than prison conditions. The Supreme Court first addressed judicial oversight of prison conditions under the Eighth Amendment in *Estelle v. Gamble* (1976), in which inmate J. W. Gamble injured himself doing a prison work assignment. Arguing that he received inadequate medical care for his severe back pain, he filed suit against prison authorities. In an 8–1 ruling, the high court held the government must "provide medical care for those whom it is punishing by incarceration . . . [and] that deliberate indifference to serious medical needs of prisoners constitutes the 'unnecessary and wanton infliction of pain . . . proscribed by the Eighth Amendment" (103–4). Because prisoners are unable to provide for their own medical needs, the state must assume the burden of delivering the necessary care. The Court broadly proclaimed it irrelevant "whether the indifference is manifested by prison doctors in their response to the prisoner's needs or by prison guards in intentionally denying or delaying access to medical care or intentionally interfering with the treatment once prescribed. Regardless of how evidenced," it concluded, "deliberate indifference to a prisoner's serious illness or injury states a cause of action" (104–5).[23]

The Court assessed the proper interpretation of the deliberate indifference standard in *Farmer v. Brennan* (1994). The case was brought by a transgender inmate, claiming federal prison officials violated her constitutional rights by showing deliberate indifference to the likelihood that she would be assaulted in the maximum-security prison to which she was assigned. Before she was imprisoned on charges of credit card fraud, Dee Farmer, a twenty-one-year-old with "feminine characteristics," had received hormone therapy and undergone a type of sex reassignment surgery. The prison followed the standard policy of placing preoperative transgender prisoners with members of their biological sex, an especially problematic arrangement for transgender women.[24] It assigned her to the general male prison population, often in solitary confinement, purportedly for her own protection.[25] Two weeks after a transfer from a state prison to a federal penitentiary, she was brutally beaten and raped. She filed suit, claiming that the prison authorities were aware that the inmate population was especially violent—with assaults a common practice—and knew that she, typically dressed "in a feminine manner," was likely to be attacked.

The district court rejected her claim, finding no evidence that the prison authorities were deliberately indifferent to her safety. The appeals court affirmed, and the Supreme Court accepted the case to flesh out the meaning of deliberate indifference. Refining the deliberate indifference standard adopted in *Estelle*, the unanimous Court adopted a two-part test. Inmates must meet an objective standard and show that they have a serious medical need; that is, they are "incarcerated under conditions showing a substantial risk of serious harm" to their health or safety. Second, they must satisfy a subjective standard and prove that prison officials are deliberately indifferent to their "health or safety" (*Farmer v. Brennan* 1994, 834).[26] Thus, although plaintiffs do not have to show officials intended to harm them, negligence or mere "lack of care" is insufficient to prove an Eighth Amendment violation. In refusing to adopt the objective test alone for the deliberate indifference standard, the Court sided with the government. Its ruling constrained the prison's liability, holding that a "prison official may be held liable under the Eighth Amendment for denying humane conditions of confinement only if he knows that inmates face a substantial risk of serious harm and disregards that risk by failing to take reasonable actions to abate it" (847).

Transgender inmates are usually able to demonstrate a serious medical need (Tarzwell 2006).[27] They have greater difficulty in showing an official was "aware of facts from which the inference" could be drawn (837). Some courts allow the prison to prevail despite a prisoner's showing of deliberate indifference by agreeing that safety concerns justify the authority's refusal to fulfill the prisoner's demands (Tieger 2014).

The Court further insulated prisons from liability by stating, "[T]he Eighth Amendment does not outlaw cruel and unusual 'conditions'; it outlaws cruel and unusual 'punishments.' . . . An official's failure to alleviate a significant risk that he should have perceived but did not, while no cause for commendation, cannot under our cases be condemned as the infliction of punishment" (837–38). Adopting a subjective standard advantages prison officials, permitting them to avoid responsibility by claiming that they are unaware of the risk of harm (Faithful 2009). This may serve as an incentive to officials to avoid keeping the records that would require them to draw the necessary inferences (Tarzwell 2006).[28]

In the end, the Court remanded the case because it believed that the courts below had dismissed the case too readily, allowing prison authorities to escape liability simply because the inmate had not notified them of the danger he was in. Ironically, although *Farmer* involved a transgender prisoner, the Court did not address the issue of gender nonconformity as a serious medical condition.

Citing the Supreme Court holding in *Farmer* and the overwhelming evidence of widespread violence and sexual assault in prisons, Congress enacted the 2003 Prison Rape Elimination Act (PREA) to "develop and implement national standards for the detection, prevention, reduction, and punishment of prison rape."[29] It established a bipartisan National Prison Rape Reduction Commission to study the causes and effects of prison rape. The commission was charged with reporting the results of its study and given responsibility for "provid[ing] the Attorney General and the Secretary of Health and Human Services with recommended National Standards for enhancing the detection, prevention, reduction, and punishment of prison rape." It finally proposed standards in 2009, but it took another three years before DOJ issued final regulations. Moreover, most states have half-heartedly complied with the law, with some opting out entirely and incurring only a minimal penalty. Thus, sexual assault and sexual harassment in prisons are still common occurrences in most states, making sexual victimization of gay and transgender inmates even more likely (Faithful 2009; Grant, Mottet, and Tanis 2011; *New York Times*, May 12, 2015).[30]

Despite the prevalence of sexual violence in prisons, most of the transgender prisoner litigation revolves around claims that correctional facilities have a constitutional mandate to provide necessary medical care for transgender or gender-nonconforming prisoners. Until recently, the plaintiffs chiefly sought hormone therapy for gender dysphoria, but they are now making claims for sex reassignment surgery as well.[31] When courts apply *Estelle* and *Farmer* to cases alleging denial of health care, inmates must demonstrate that they have a serious medical need and that prison officials knew of it and failed to deliver the care (Givens 2013). Interpreting *Estelle*, the lower courts have held that a prisoner is not entitled to the "'best" or "ideal" care and certainly not the "care of his choice" (*Kosilek v. Maloney* 2002). Rather, they are entitled to adequate care, with prison officials determining the adequacy of the treatment based on the advice of medical professionals.[32]

The circuits do not agree whether gender dysphoria is a serious medical need; some have not explicitly ruled on the matter, and some have accepted that certain manifestations of it, such as genital self-mutilation, are within the meaning of *Estelle*. The Seventh Circuit took a forthright stand in *Fields v. Smith* (2011), striking the Inmate Sex Change Prevention Act, a 2006 Wisconsin statute prohibiting the use of state and federal funds for prisoners' gender-related health care, including hormone therapy and sex reassignment surgery. Relying on the Eighth Amendment, the court held that inmates with gender dysphoria have serious medical needs and may require hormone therapy or sex reassignment surgery. Similarly, in *Battista v. Clark* (2011), the First Circuit viewed the inmate's gender dysphoria as a serious medical need and ordered the state to provide hormone therapy (see Bendlin 2013).

In 2015, the transgender community awaited the Supreme Court's decision to review the Eighth Amendment claim of Michelle Kosilek, a transgender woman. Michelle, known as Robert while on trial for the 1990 murder of his wife, was convicted of first-degree murder in 1992; the state supreme court upheld the conviction in 1996.

Kosilek, who legally changed her name to Michelle, was serving a life sentence with no possibility of parole in a medium-security male prison. She filed her first complaint against Massachusetts Department of Corrections (DOC) officials in 1999, claiming that the state had violated her Eighth Amendment right by refusing her request to treat her gender dysphoria (*Kosilek v. Maloney* 2002).[33] She did not specify the treatment she sought, merely asking the court to order DOC to allow a specialist to evaluate her, prescribe treatment, and provide the prescribed treatment. Reacting to her complaint, Commissioner Michael Maloney, who had taken charge of her medical decisions, adopted a "freeze-frame" policy for transgender inmates. This approach prohibits new treatments for inmates with gender dysphoria, absolving prisons of supplying hormones to inmates unless they were taking them prior to their incarceration; Maloney also categorically ruled out sex reassignment surgery. Because Kosilek had never been prescribed hormone therapy, the prison determined she was not entitled to it.[34]

Massachusetts Federal District Court Judge Mark Wolf discussed Kosilek's Eighth Amendment claim in two parts. He agreed that she had satisfied the objective standard by showing that she had a serious medical need that had gone untreated.[35] Demonstrating the difficulty of proving deliberate indifference under a subjective standard, the court delved into Maloney's state of mind in refusing her treatment and ruled that Kosilek had failed to prove deliberate indifference.

Wolf found that, even though Maloney had enough information to infer that Kosilek was substantially at risk by withholding treatment, he had not actually drawn the inference; that is, he was unaware that denying treatment to Kosilek would lead to serious injury. He believed that Maloney "did not adopt his policy with the intent to inflict pain on Kosilek or as a result of deliberate indifference." Rather, Wolf felt Maloney was reluctant to provide hormones or sex reassignment surgery unless compelled to do so because he had "sincere security concerns." Moreover, it was not the cost that troubled him but "fear of public and political criticism" that expenditures for hormone treatment or sex reassignment surgery would be viewed an "inappropriate use of taxpayers' money" (162).[36]

Wolf held that DOC was not liable under the Eighth Amendment, but because it was now aware of Kosilek's medical need, it was obliged to treat him for it. He stated that he expected Maloney to fulfill this obligation, but that he would be justified in balancing the prison's security needs against Kosilek's Eighth Amendment claim.

Kosilek returned to court in 2006 with a second pro se complaint, asking DOC to provide sex reassignment surgery. In recounting the history of the case, Wolf noted that, prior to his first decision, a specialist retained by DOC had concluded that Kosilek suffered severe gender dysphoria and recommended that DOC provide her with hormone therapy and, after a year, evaluate her for possible sex reassignment surgery. DOC replaced this specialist with a Canadian doctor who believed that prisoners who had not been treated with hormone therapy prior to their imprisonment should not receive it during the time they spend in jail.[37] Maloney had apparently heeded the court's warning and ended the "freeze-frame" policy in December 2002.[38] Before the new approach was implemented, the prison reevaluated Kosilek, beginning her hormone therapy treatments in August 2003 and scheduling her for possible sex reassignment surgery a year later.[39]

Maloney was replaced as commissioner by Kathleen Dennehy in December 2003.[40] According to the court, she "engaged in a pattern of pretense, pretext, and prevarication" to deny Kosilek the surgery that the DOC doctors prescribed. Wolf was unusually explicit in characterizing Dennehy's pretrial statements and trial testimony as untruthful. He said that she had "long falsely claimed" that she did not know whether the prescribed sex reassignment surgery was medically necessary and that she had testified untruthfully at trial that she denied the treatment entirely for security reasons. In the end, Wolf declared that her many falsehoods led "to the conclusion that her stated reasons for refusing to allow Kosilek to receive the surgery were pretextual" (202). He believed that she was motivated by politics, fearing that acceding to Kosilek's request would subject her to criticism from other public officials as well as the media for misuse of taxpayer dollars.

The court held that, by failing to treat Kosilek's serious medical condition, Dennehy subjected her to cruel and unusual punishment forbidden by the Eighth Amendment. It also ruled that, despite the hormone therapy, she remained at substantial risk of severe harm, including serious contemplation of suicide. Citing the urgency, Wolf ordered DOC to provide the surgery as soon as possible.[41]

On January 17, 2014—more than twenty years after Kosilek asked prison authorities to treat her gender dysphoria—a three-judge panel of the First Circuit Court announced its 2–1 decision.[42] Based on the medical testimony at trial, the panel agreed with the lower court's finding that the surgery was medically necessary to treat Kosilek's condition and affirmed that DOC officials were not motivated by valid concerns but were largely responding to external negative cues. The panel concluded,

> [T]he judge was well-placed to make the factual findings he made, and there is certainly evidentiary support for those findings. Those findings—thatKosilek has a serious medical need for the surgery and that DOC refuses to meet that need for pretextual reasons unsupported by legitimate penological considerations—mean that the DOC has violatedKosilek's Eighth Amendment rights." (*Kosilek v. Spencer* 2014a, 772–73)

The lower court had correctly granted her injunction.

The saga continued, as a month later, on February 12, 2014, the panel's decision was withdrawn, and the en banc court agreed to the rehearing sought by DOC (*Kosilek v. Spencer* 2014b). Judge Juan Torruella, who had dissented in the three-judge panel opinion, announced the 3–2 en banc ruling.[43] The outcome of the case became clear when he began by stating, "[W]e are faced with the question whether the DOC's choice of a particular medical treatment is constitutionally inadequate, such that the district court acts within its power to issue an injunction requiring provision of an alternative treatment—a treatment which would give rise to new concerns related to safety and prison security" (68).

In discussing the facts, Torruella conveyed sympathy for DOC's efforts to satisfy Kosilek's health care needs, emphasizing the difficulties it encountered determining whether the surgery was necessary and weighing the security issues. He noted the parties' agreement on the severity of Kosilek's gender dysphoria but underscored their disagreement "over whether SRS [sex reassignment surgery] is a medically necessary component of Kosilek's care, such that any course of treatment not including surgery is constitutionally inadequate" (86). The en banc court held that the lower court had erroneously concluded that the treatment plan was inadequate, as there was evidence that her mental condition had improved with the treatment she received and her suicidal tendencies could be addressed with standard psychotherapy. This attention to her mental state and the treatment it provided showed that DOC was not deliberately indifferent to her needs and could reasonably conclude that security issues would create difficulties in housing her after the surgery. Given the deference it should have accorded to the expertise of the prison authorities, the appellate court found that the district court had inappropriately denigrated their security concerns and attributed improper motives to them.

Based on these factors, the First Circuit concluded that Kosilek failed to prove that her Eighth Amendment rights were violated and reversed the lower court's ruling (*Kosilek v. Spencer* 2014c). After more than two decades of litigation, contrary to prevailing medical opinion that sex reassignment surgery was medically necessary to treat Kosilek's gender dysphoria, the circuit court upheld DOC's decision to withhold the treatment, and the US Supreme Court declined Kosilek's petition for review.

Meanwhile, events in California offered hope to transgender inmates. The story revolved around Michelle-Lael Norsworthy, a fifty-one-year-old transgender woman who was serving a sentence of seventeen years to life for a murder committed in 1987.[44] Housed in Mule Creek State Prison, a California men's prison, she was diagnosed with gender dysphoria in 1999. The prison began treating her with hormone therapy and injections for chemical castration in 2000 but denied her sex reassignment surgery and did not permit her to change her name legally. Because of her hormone levels and appearance, she was identified as a biological woman in prison records and was repeatedly raped, including a gang rape by nine inmates in 2009 that led to a hepatitis C infection. For more than two years, her treating psychologist had continually recommended the surgery as a medical necessity for her physical and mental well-being.[45] On September 16, 2012, after hearing about the first ruling in *Kosilek*, she filed a health care appeal with prison authorities, seeking sex reassignment surgery. They rejected it on the grounds that it was medically unnecessary.

She filed suit against the California Department of Corrections and Rehabilitation (CDCR) on February 14, 2014, charging it with violating her Eighth Amendment rights in refusing her medically necessary health care in the form of sex reassignment surgery for her gender dysphoria and denying her the right to change her name legally.[46]

The state relied on the expert testimony presented by Dr. Stephen Levine, an opponent of sex reassignment surgery for inmates who, among other things, evidently mischaracterized the requisites for the surgery under the WPATH Standards of Care. He depicted it as "always an elective procedure . . . [with] no immediacy to it" (*Norsworthy v. Beard* 2015a, 1179). California Federal District Court Judge Jon Tigar devoted much of his opinion to the reports of the dueling medical experts. Refusing to strike portions of Levine's testimony—as Norsworthy had asked—he gave it little weight, adding that, because Levine believes no prisoner should be allowed sex reassignment surgery, "his conclusions are unhelpful in assessing whether she has established a serious medical need for SRS [sex reassignment surgery]."

In determining whether to grant Norsworthy's request for a preliminary injunction, Tigar held that she presented sufficient evidence that she had a serious medical need and the surgery is medically necessary. He rejected the state's arguments that the hormone therapy treatment had obviated the necessity of performing the surgery and that she had not shown that she would suffer severe harm if denied. "Defendants," he said, "have provided no credible support for the idea that Norsworthy must demonstrate that she is likely to commit suicide or attempt auto-castration in order to demonstrate a serious medical need, or that her claim fails because she has survived for decades without SRS [sex reassignment surgery]." Citing *Estelle*, he continued, "[A] plaintiff demonstrates a 'serious medical need' when she establishes that failure to treat her condition could result in further significant injury or the unnecessary and wanton infliction of pain" (*Norsworthy v. Beard* 2015a, 1187–88).

Tigar also ruled that Norsworthy would likely prevail on the deliberate indifference standard. By failing to recognize the well-established standards of care and ignoring the recommendations of her treating psychologist, he believed that CDCR demonstrated deliberate indifference to her dysphoria. Moreover, he distinguished the First Circuit en banc ruling in *Kosilek* because, unlike the Massachusetts DOC, California prisons had a blanket policy of refusing surgery for all transgender inmates.

On April 2, 2015, the court issued a preliminary injunction, ordering the state agency to provide her with adequate health care "as promptly as possible" (*Norsworthy v. Beard* 2015a, 1195). On May 21, 2015—the day the appellate court stayed the lower court order—the parole board found that Norsworthy was suitable for parole, sending the case to the governor for review. On August 7, 2015, the governor's office announced that it would take no action on the board's decision, allowing her release to go forward. She was freed on August 12, 2015.[47]

The surgery was scheduled for July, but the Ninth Circuit stayed the injunction to allow CDCR to appeal. The state argued that the court should vacate the district court's preliminary injunction because her release mooted the case. On October 5, 2015, the circuit court agreed and dismissed the case but remanded it to the district court to determine if it should vacate the injunction because the parole board had acted independently of CDCR (*Norsworthy v. Beard* 2015b).

As the *Norsworthy* litigation proceeded, on August 7, 2015, California entered into a settlement agreement with fifty-six-year-old Shiloh (born Rodney) Heavenly Quine, who was serving a life sentence without parole for murder, kidnapping, and robbery. Without admitting fault in the lawsuit, the state agreed to pay for her sex reassignment surgery and transfer her to a woman's prison after the surgery. While nearly four hundred transgender state prisoners were receiving hormone treatment at the time, Quine's case represents the first instance of a state agreeing to pay for surgery to treat gender dysphoria (*Los Angeles Times*, August 10, 2015; Transgender Law Center 2015).

While the transgender community awaited developments in California, on the other side of the country, Ashley Diamond's lawsuit against the Georgia Department of Corrections (GDOC), filed on February 19, 2015, transformed prison litigation. Diamond, a thirty-six-year-old nonviolent offender, was imprisoned in 2012 for violating the terms of her probation after her theft conviction. Following a suicide attempt at fifteen, she was diagnosed with gender dysphoria. For an unknown reason, despite Diamond loudly proclaiming her status and announcing that she had been receiving hormone therapy for seventeen years, the prison did not identify her as transgender during processing. The authorities denied her request for hormone therapy because Georgia's version of the "freeze-frame" policy prohibited starting or expanding treatments for transgender inmates with gender dysphoria or providing treatment to those who were not identified as transgender (even erroneously) and referred to treatment during the intake process. Instead, GDOC assigned her to Macon State Prison, a men's maximum-security prison with a record of gang activity and brutality. Shortly after her arrival in March 2012, she was violently assaulted and, when transferred to another facility, was repeatedly attacked there as well. She attempted suicide and self-castration.

Diamond's suit claimed GDOC violated her Eighth Amendment right to be free from cruel and unusual punishment by failing to provide her with appropriate medical care and refusing to transfer to a medium-security facility as well as refusing to allow her to express her gender identity. She sought two preliminary injunctions: first, to order the state to provide her with medically necessary treatment for her gender dysphoria and permit her to express herself with her choice of clothing and grooming; and second, to end the state's "freeze-frame" policy (*Diamond v. Owens* 2015).[48] The prison psychologists found that she clearly suffered from gender dysphoria and expressed concern for her physical and mental health without the hormone therapy. Nevertheless, prison authorities refused to accommodate her medical needs.[49]

In a dramatic turn of events, while her suit was pending, DOJ filed a Statement of Interest on her behalf with the court. It argued that the state's policy denied individualized consideration of inmates' medical conditions, violating their Eighth Amendment protection against cruel and unusual punishment (US Department of Justice 2015a).[50] Shortly after the federal government filed the statement, the state announced that it had "rescinded" its policy and would provide appropriate evaluation and treatment for transgender inmates. On May 8, GDOC transferred Diamond to a medium-security prison and, on August 31, unexpectedly released her from custody despite the fact that she was ineligible for parole.

On September 14, 2015, Georgia Federal District Court Judge Marc Treadwell stated held that he "assume[d]" that the US government's interest was satisfied with her release and that the state's action also resolved her claims.[51] He largely devoted his opinion to determining if the prison officials were entitled to qualified immunity, measured by whether they knew their action (or inaction) violated a clearly established constitutional right. Citing numerous cases, he denied them immunity, concluding that they knew that deliberate indifference to her serious necessary medical needs and protection from violence violated a clearly established constitutional right. In February 2016, the state agreed to a settlement of more than $250,000 (Gay & Lesbian Advocates & Defenders 2011; *New York Times*, February 13, 2016).

The few victories achieved by these transgender individuals have not translated to revisions in correctional policy. Except for California, the prison systems essentially swept the problems under the rug by releasing the transgender prisoners. The PREA helped to focus attention on the treatment of transgender and gender-nonconforming persons in state and federal prisons and underscored the lack of meaningful enforcement mechanisms. The courts' reluctance to interfere with correctional policies—especially when prison officials raise security concerns—means that safety and health care needs of transgender prisoners are frequently overlooked.

TITLE IX AND GENDER IDENTITY

It is very difficult to determine the number of transgender children; surveys rarely ask, and respondents may be unsure or unwilling to reveal it.[52] Basing their numbers on local probability and national convenience sample surveys, Wilson and his colleagues (2014, 36–37) determined that transgender youth comprise between 1.3 and 3.2 percent of the American youth population.[53]

It is well documented that transgender youth are subjected to bullying, harassment, and other forms of victimization—in and out of school (see Kosciw, Bartkiewicz, and Greytak 2012). Indeed, LGBT young people manifest higher levels of emotional distress than their non-LGBT counterparts (Almeida et al. 2009).

The Gay, Lesbian and Straight Education Network's (GLSEN) National School Climate Surveys offer a comprehensive view of issues facing LGBT young people in schools (Kosciw et al. 2014).[54] The 2013 survey shows that, while conditions improved since GLSEN began appraising them, more than half the respondents reported that they feared for their safety in school; almost three-quarters of them heard derogatory comments, and nearly all said that they were victims of verbal and/or physical harassment.[55] The report also found that the LGBT students reacted to the hostile climate with frequent absences and lower grade point averages as well as lower feelings of self-esteem and greater feelings of depression. Summarizing its findings, the report warns that "schools nationwide are hostile environments for a distressing number of LGBT students, the overwhelming majority of whom routinely hear anti-LGBT language and experience victimization and discrimination at school" (xvi).

Over time, GLSEN's biennial national climate surveys document the problems LGBT students face over issues of physical safety, biased language, and lack of support from school authorities. Based on its findings over the years that transgender students suffer greater hardship in school than their nontransgender lesbian, gay, and bisexual classmates, GLSEN devoted an entire survey solely to the experiences of transgender students.[56] It found that almost all the transgender respondents hear derogatory comments directed at them by their fellow students and sometimes even by staff members, are frequent victims of harassment and assault, and feel unsafe in school.[57] The analysis revealed that, compared to their nontransgender lesbian, gay, and bisexual counterparts, their absentee rates are higher, their grades are lower, and they have diminished educational aspirations. The study underscored that transgender youth

> often face extremely hostile school environments . . . [and] compared to their non-transgender peers, transgender students consistently reported higher levels of harassment and assault, were less likely to feel like a part of their school community, and had poorer educational outcomes. [Moreover, they] . . . are faced with unique challenges in school, such as accessing gender-segregated facilities and being addressed by their preferred names and pronouns. (Greytak, Kosciw, and Diaz 2009)

As the surveys indicate, transgender youth must overcome myriad obstacles in navigating the nation's educational system, ranging from verbal and physical harassment to bullying and sexual violence.[58] A number of states have recognized the difficulties they face by enacting legislation to protect them in public schools from bullying and harassment.[59] For the most part, transgender students rely on Title IX of the Education Amendments of 1972, the federal law barring discrimination because of sex in federally funded educational institutions.[60] The statute broadly applies to "any public or private preschool, elementary, or secondary school, or any institution of vocational, professional, or higher education."[61] In some instances, students also allege violations of their rights under the Fourteenth Amendment's equal protection clause.[62]

Title IX has played an important role in furthering equality in education, beginning with the Supreme Court's decision to allow private individuals to sue educational institutions for sex discrimination.[63] Over the next two decades, the Court expanded the reach of the law to encompass sexual harassment as a form of sex discrimination.[64] The most contentious issue (and most relevant to transgender students) in these lawsuits was whether schools are liable when students harass other students, known as peer harassment. In *Davis v. Monroe* (1998), the Court refused to dismiss a fifth-grader's suit that claimed that she was sexually harassed over many months by another fifth-grader and that the school knew about it and did not act. The Court held that school districts might be liable for sexual harassment that is so severe, pervasive, and objectively offensive that it deprives victims of access to the educational opportunities or benefits the school provides. Rejecting the school district's argument that allowing such suits will require schools to punish mere acts of teasing or name-calling, the Court ruled schools could be held liable for peer harassment.[65]

In the 1980s, the courts began to expand Title IX's prohibition against sex discrimination to sexual harassment. In their efforts to battle discrimination against transgender students, advocates argue that Title IX bars unequal treatment because of gender nonconformity. As a result, "since 2009, the nation's schools have become gender-identity battle grounds, [with] the battle rag[ing] on two fronts: between students themselves on the one hand, and between students and school officials on the other" (McKay 2011, 494).

The first victory for transgender students arose from a complaint against the Arcadia Unified School District in California brought by the National Center for Lesbian Rights (NCLR) to DOE and DOJ on October 10, 2011. It claimed that the school discriminated against the twelve-year-old transgender boy on the basis of sex by denying him equal access to the school's programs and activities.

Presenting as a girl in elementary school, the child began to transition to a boy, including a legal name change, before entering middle school and was looking forward to attending the new school as a boy. His middle school banned him from boys' bathrooms and locker rooms and required him to use a private bathroom and change for gym class in the nurse's office. Because the office was far from the gymnasium, he was frequently late for class and teased by classmates who did not know why he changed clothes there. In the seventh grade, the school refused to allow him to share a cabin with other boys on an overnight field trip, forcing him to stay in a separate cabin with his father as chaperone.

The complaint charged that the district "violates Title IX under two distinct theories: (1) gender stereotyping; and (2) change of sex" (National Center for Lesbian Rights 2013, 4).

The district cited the portion of the California Education Code that mirrored Title IX by permitting schools to provide sex-segregated bathroom and locker facilities.

In July 2015, the Arcadia School District signed a resolution agreement with the two federal agencies, ending their investigation into the student's complaint (National Center for Lesbian Rights 2015). The agreement began by defining gender-based discrimination as a

> form of sex discrimination [that] . . . refers to differential treatment or harassment of a student based on the student's sex, including gender identity, gender expression, and nonconformity with gender stereotypes, that results in the denial or limitation of education services, benefits, or opportunities. Conduct may constitute gender-based discrimination regardless of the actual or perceived sex, gender identity, or sexual orientation of the persons experiencing or engaging in the conduct.

Without admitting fault, the district committed itself to treating him the "same as others in all respects," including in sex-specific facilities. It also pledged to revise its policies and practices to "specifically include gender-based discrimination as a form of discrimination based on sex" and to specify that it "includes discrimination based on a student's gender identity, gender expression, gender transition, transgender status, or gender nonconformity," as well as to ensure that transgender and gender-nonconforming students have equal access to all school facilities, programs, and activities. (US Department of Justice 2013)[66]

Less than a month after the Arcadia agreement was filed, on August 12, 2013, California Governor Jerry Brown signed the School Success and Opportunity Act (AB 1266), mandating that schools allow students access to sex-segregated facilities (restrooms and locker rooms) and activities (sports teams) based on the gender with which they identify rather than their gender at birth. The California law was the first in the nation to require school districts to accommodate the needs of gender-nonconforming students.[67] Reacting to it, a spokesperson for the Capital Resources Institute voiced what became the rallying cry for groups opposing the policy: "Most Californians don't want their daughters showering or going to the restroom with boys" (*Reuters*, August 12, 2013).

FEDERAL AGENCIES AND GENDER IDENTITY

In October 2010, DOE's Office for Civil Rights (OCR) issued a "Dear Colleague Letter" (DCL), explaining that Title IX's ban on sex discrimination encompasses harassment of any student who presents as gender nonconforming.[68] The letter stated that Title IX

> prohibits gender-based harassment, which may include acts of verbal, nonverbal, or physical aggression, intimidation, or hostility based on sex or sex-stereotyping. It can be sex discrimination if students are harassed either for exhibiting what is perceived as a stereotypical characteristic for their sex, or for failing to conform to stereotypical notions of masculinity and femininity. Title IX also prohibits sexual harassment and gender-based harassment of all students, regardless of the actual or perceived sexual orientation or gender identity of the harasser or target. (Ali 2010)

The next year, DOE released another DCL on Title IX and sexual violence in schools and school-sponsored activities. The 2011 DCL made it clear that "Title IX also prohibits gender-based harassment, which may include acts of verbal, nonverbal, or physical aggression, intimidation, or hostility based on sex or sex-stereotyping, even if those acts do not involve conduct of a sexual nature." (Ali 2011)[69]

On April 29, 2014, DOE's assistant secretary issued a document entitled "Questions and Answers on Title IX and Sexual Violence," emphasizing OCR's jurisdiction over complaints of sexual violence related to gender nonconformity as well as to gender identity (US Department of Education, Office for Civil Rights 2014). It states,

> Title IX's sex discrimination prohibition extends to claims of discrimination based on gender identity or failure to conform to stereotypical notions of masculinity or femininity and OCR accepts such complaints for investigation. Similarly, the actual or perceived sexual orientation or gender identity of the parties does not change a school's obligations. Indeed, lesbian, gay, bisexual, and transgender (LGBT) youth report high rates of sexual harassment and sexual violence. A school should investigate and resolve allegations of sexual violence regarding LGBT students using the same procedures and standards that it uses in all complaints involving sexual violence. The fact that incidents of sexual violence may be accompanied by anti-gay com-

> ments or be partly based on a student's actual or perceived sexual orientation does not relieve a school of its obligation under Title IX to investigate and remedy those instances of sexual violence. (US Department of Education, Office for Civil Rights 2014)

THE COURTS AND GENDER IDENTITY

Because of the similarity between the two statutes, courts have looked for guidance in adjudicating Title IX suits to the case law developed in Title VII, and it is well established that the "Title IX term 'on the basis of sex' is interpreted in the same manner as similar language in Title VII" (*Miles v. New York University* 1997).[70] In bringing Title IX claims of discrimination against educational institutions, transgender students cite *Price Waterhouse* and extrapolate from it and lower court Title VII rulings, arguing that, like Title VII, Title IX forbids discrimination and harassment of students whose behavior or appearance does not conform to gender stereotypes, categorizing both under the rubric of sex discrimination prohibited by the statute (see McKay 2011; Skinner-Thompson and Turner 2013).

In *Montgomery v. Independent School District* (2000) and *Theno v. Tonganoxie Unified School District No. 464* (2005), for example, high school boys claimed that they were harassed by their male classmates who believed that they exhibited feminine behavior traits. Citing *Price Waterhouse*, the courts ruled that schools could be liable for peer harassment based on gender nonconformity and sex stereotyping. While reiterating that Title IX does not apply to harassment based on sexual orientation or perceived sexual orientation, they held that the schools may be liable if they fail to stop the harassment of students whose behavior diverges from gender norms.

The proposed Student Non-Discrimination Act of 2015 (SNDA), introduced in both houses of Congress, would supplant the protection offered by Title IX by barring "discrimination based on actual or perceived sexual orientation or gender identity in public schools or for other purposes." The purpose of the bill is to protect K–12 LGBT youth from "discrimination, including harassment, bullying, intimidation, and violence," as existing federal civil rights laws do not include gender identity or sexual orientation as prohibited categories. Following Title

IX case law, the law would apply the deliberate indifference standard, requiring school officials to act if they are aware of banned activities and making schools liable for failure to act.[71]

Its passage is unlikely—identical bills were unsuccessfully introduced for several years—but its best chance was in 2015, when its sponsor, Senator Al Franken, Democrat of Minnesota, attempted to attach it as an amendment to the bipartisan Every Child Achieves Act, revising the now-reviled No Child Left Behind. Even though his amendment received fifty-two votes (forty-five Democrats and seven Republicans), it fell short of the sixty required to defeat the opponents' filibuster.[72] Acknowledging "bullying or harassment of children based on actual or perceived sexual orientation or gender identity is a terrible problem," Senator Lamar Alexander, Republican from Tennessee, urged his colleagues to vote against the amendment, saying, "[T]he question is, is this best addressed by the local school board or the national school board in Washington, D.C." (*Washington Post*, July 14, 2015).

PUBLIC FACILITIES AND TRANSGENDER STUDENTS

> "The issue of transgender bathroom access was heralded as the 'next frontier of civil rights' as early as six years ago [in 2008]. But just recently transgender students' right to access the restroom that corresponds with their gender identity in public schools has taken center stage." (Hart 2014, 317)

Most courts have sided with plaintiffs who argue that the law protects them from harassment because of their gender identity—either through a broad reading of the word sex in Title IX, interpretation of the Fourteenth Amendment's equal protection clause, an analogy with Title VII case law, or application of state or local law. Unlike those cases, in which the courts sympathize with the victims, the controversies over shared school bathrooms and locker rooms are proving to be more difficult, forcing courts to balance competing interests of transgender and nontransgender students.[73] Some courts have drawn the line at requiring schools to allocate such facilities on the basis of the transgender student's gender identity, allowing them to separate students on the basis of their anatomical sex or, more commonly, on the sex shown on their birth certificates.[74]

In states and municipalities with nondiscrimination laws, transgender students are able to secure access to bathroom and locker room facilities based on their gender identity more easily (Tobin and Levi 2013).[75] Given the indeterminate status of Title IX case law and the absence of a national antidiscrimination law that expressly includes gender identity as a protected classification, the status of the law at the national level remains unclear.

Over the last few years, transgender students in Virginia, Illinois, Colorado, and Maine filed suit against their school districts. At the college level, a transgender University of Pittsburgh student who was expelled and criminally charged for indecent exposure asserted equal protection and Title IX claims in his suit against the university. In these cases, the students claim that refusing to allow them to use the facilities that match their gender identities denies them an equal opportunity to learn and is emotionally and psychologically harmful. The schools cite Title IX and its implementing regulations that allow segregation of bathroom and locker room facilities on the basis of physical sex characteristics.[76] They argue that allowing transgender students to use staff restrooms meets their obligation under Title IX. The plaintiffs counter that

> denying access to school facilities for transgender students effectively singles them out, apart from all others in the community, with a stigmatizing message that a transgender boy is not a normal or real boy, or a transgender girl is not a normal or real girl. This message, which coincides precisely with the cultural messages that drive bullying of transgender youth, is reinforced on a daily basis when students are treated differently from other boys and girls. (Tobin and Levi 2013, 309)

A Colorado transgender student prevailed in *Mathis v. Fountain-Fort Carson School District 8* (2013) when the Colorado Division of Human Rights ruled in favor of first-grader Coy Mathis, who identified and presented as a girl. Coy's parents sued the school district, claiming that it discriminated against the first-grader by refusing to allow her to use the girl's bathroom and instead only allowing her to use the boys' bathroom or an adult private bathroom in the health office or staff room.

In his probable cause determination, Stephen Chavez, director of the Civil Rights Division, considered her original birth certificate showing her as a boy against the more recent documents indicating that she was a girl and concluded that she was female. Because the school denied her the opportunity to use the bathroom of her choice—though the other students were permitted to do so—Chavez found sufficient evidence of discrimination because of sex or sexual orientation in violation of the state public accommodations law.[77] He ordered the parties to resolve the conflict through conciliation.

The next victory for a transgender plaintiff, in Maine, marked the first time a state high court ruled that a transgender student diagnosed with gender dysphoria could use the bathroom of the gender with which she identified. The Does, parents of a transgender elementary school child and the Maine Human Rights Commission (MHRC) filed suit in 2009, charging the Orono, Maine School Department with violating the Maine Human Rights Act by requiring her to use a staff restroom instead of the girls' restroom that she had been using through the fourth grade.[78] School officials had intervened to restrict her access to the girls' bathroom in 2007 when the grandfather of a fifth-grade boy, who had followed her into the girls' bathroom twice, complained about her.[79] In April 2010, the girl and her parents filed a complaint with the MHRC, which found reasonable grounds to believe that the school had discriminated against her, violating the state education and public accommodations laws.[80]

On April 1, 2011, the superior court held that the school does not have a duty to accommodate her transgender status as it must accommodate a student with a physical or mental disability (*Doe v. Clenchy* 2011). The state supreme court weighed the two conflicting state laws: the first, requiring sex-segregated toilet facilities in school buildings, and the second, barring discrimination on sexual orientation in public accommodations.[81] Announcing the opinion for the 5–1 majority on January 30, 2014, Judge Warren Silver found the two laws were not "irreconcilable." Acknowledging that schools must have separate bathrooms for each sex, he held that the law cannot "dictate the use of the bathrooms in a way that discriminates against students in violation of the Human Rights Act (*Doe v. Regional School Unit 26* 2014, 606).

Silver observed that the school had considered her a girl and treated her as a girl, including letting her use the girls' restroom, until the publicity about her case and opposition from the community caused officials to change the policy. He concluded that Susan Doe was treated differently from other students solely because of her transgender status and ended by saying, "[W]here, as here it has been clearly established that a student's psychological well-being and educational success depend upon being permitted to use the communal bathroom consistent with her gender identity, denying access to the appropriate bathroom constitutes sexual orientation discrimination in violation of the MHRA" (607).

Shortly after the court ruled in Doe's favor, a federal court announced its opinion in Seamus Johnston's suit against the University of Pittsburgh for discrimination based on sex and transgender status (*Johnston v. University of Pittsburgh* 2015). Johnston, a transgender man with gender dysphoria, began to transition in 2009 and to undergo hormone therapy as part of the process. He claimed that the university's refusal to allow him to access the bathroom and locker room consistent with his gender identity violated his rights under Title IX and the equal protection clause.

Johnston had marked female on his application form but presented as male when entering school in September 2009, using the men's restroom and locker room without incident and even enrolling in a men's training class. In September 2011, a university official informed him that he would have to stop using the men's locker room, and he agreed to use a private one. The school told him that he would be permitted to use the men's locker room if he officially changed his sex on his student records, requiring either a court order or a new birth certificate. [82] He nevertheless continued to use it until he was evicted and charged with disorderly conduct.

Over the next months, there was an ongoing battle over his use of the locker room until campus officials denied him access to all male locker rooms and restrooms on campus. Eventually, after a number of confrontations, the university expelled him and filed a criminal complaint against him. Johnston responded by suing on the basis of Title IX and the Fourteenth Amendment as well as state antidiscrimination laws. The crux of his constitutional argument was that the university "treated him differently from other similarly situated students on the basis of his sex, including his transgender status and perceived failure to conform to gender stereotypes" (667–68).

Pennsylvania Federal District Court Judge Kim Gibson noted two competing interests at stake: Johnston's interest in using the facilities that accord with his gender identity and the university's interest in maintaining traditional sex-segregated bathroom facilities. He found that the latter outweighed the former, adding that the school was justified in treating him as a female and disregarding his gender identity.

The judge displayed ignorance of the meaning of transgender, saying,

> [W]hile Plaintiff alleges that he is a 'male,' the complaint also alleges that Plaintiff was assigned the sex of 'female' at birth. Importantly, Plaintiff has not alleged that he has undergone a sex change. Thus, while Plaintiff might identify his gender as male, his birth sex is female. It is this fact—that Plaintiff was born a biological female, as alleged in the complaint—that is fatal to Plaintiff's sex discrimination claim. Regardless of how gender and gender identity are defined, the law recognizes certain distinctions between male and female on the basis of birth sex. Thus, even though Plaintiff is a transgender male, his sex is female. (671)

Therefore, being treated as a woman (and assigned to a women's restroom) cannot be considered sex discrimination.

Turning to the Title IX claim, the court simply found that its "plain language" indicates that it does not protect against discrimination on the basis of gender identity but only on the basis of sex. And requiring him to use facilities based on his sex rather than on his gender identity does not infringe on Title IX's ban on sex discrimination. Noting that this was a case of first impression in the Third Circuit and that no federal circuit had squarely decided the issue of transgender status in educational institutions, Gibson looked to Title VII case law and, ignoring recent developments, found that it does not encompass discrimination on the basis of gender identity in the workplace. Johnston withdrew his appeal of Gibson's ruling after entering into a settlement in which the university agreed to adopt policies to accommodate transgender students (*BuzzFeed*, March 29, 2016).

In Virginia, a transgender high school boy's request to use the bathroom that conformed to his gender identity led to a lawsuit that would have vital implications for the nation's transgender community and the status of Title IX law. G.G., born a biological female, began identifying as male when he was very young.[83] Shortly after entering high school, he informed his parents that he was transgender. His treating psychologist diagnosed him with gender dysphoria and recommended that he begin hormone therapy and be treated as a boy—including being allowed to use the boys' bathroom at school.

G.G. successfully petitioned for a legal name change, his school records reflected his new name, and school officials referred to him as a boy.

When G.G. met with the school principal at the start of his sophomore year, he agreed to use the bathroom in the nurse's office but soon became uncomfortable with the arrangement and asked to use the boys' bathroom instead. The principal agreed, but members of the community soon raised an outcry. As a result, the school board met to consider the following resolution at its November board meeting:

> Whereas the [Gloucester County Public Schools] recognizes that some students question their gender identities, . . . [and] the [Gloucester County Public Schools] seeks to provide a safe learning environment for all students and to protect the privacy of all students, therefore It shall be the practice of the [Gloucester County Public Schools] to provide male and female restroom and locker room facilities in its schools, and the use of said facilities shall be limited to the corresponding biological genders, and students with gender identity issues shall be provided an alternative appropriate private facility. (*G.G. v. Gloucester County School Board* 2015, 740)[84]

The majority of community members attending the meeting who spoke approved the proposed policy, expressing concern about privacy issues and fearing that unless the resolution were accepted, "'it might lead to sexual assault in the bathrooms'" (740). They voiced their concerns that nontransgender boys would dress as girls and enter girls' bathrooms to carry out sexual assaults.

The board postponed a decision at its November meeting. On December 9, 2014, with widespread support from community members attending the meeting, it voted 6–1 to restrict his use of the boy's bathroom and locker room. The principal subsequently informed him of this and warned him of the consequences if he continued to do so.[85]

As the year progressed, with G.G. receiving hormone treatment and acquiring more masculine features, it became impossible for him to enter a girls' bathroom without incident. He refused to use the private facilities, finding them stigmatizing and humiliating because everyone knew they had been constructed for him; when necessary, he used the nurse's bathroom but largely refrained from using the facilities at all, often leading to discomfort and infections.

On June 11, 2015, G.G. and his mother filed suit, claiming that the policy violated Title IX and the equal protection clause of the Fourteenth Amendment; they sought a preliminary injunction against the school's policy of barring him from the boys' bathroom. The district pointed to the DOE regulation, 34 C.F.R., section 106.33, that permitted sex-separated "toilet, locker room, and shower facilities" and cited *Johnston*, stressing that it was the only ruling on discrimination on the basis of gender identity and transgender status under the equal protection clause and Title IX. The district argued that its claim was even stronger than the university's in *Johnston* because that had involved adults and this one hinged on the district's responsibility to keep children safe by using the facilities consistent with the societal tradition of sex-separate spaces. Additionally, it raised the likelihood that a ruling for G.G. could lead to a situation in which anatomical male students who identified as female might seek to use the girls' bathrooms in the future.

The federal government submitted a Statement of Interest on G.G.'s behalf, weighing in on the likelihood of success of his case on the merits. It began by asserting that, under Title IX, "discrimination based on a person's gender identity, a person's transgender status, or a person's nonconformity to sex stereotypes constitutes discrimination based on sex" (US Department of Justice 2015b, at 1).[86] The government also pointed to the April 29, 2014 document entitled "Questions and Answers on Title IX and Sexual Violence," in which OCR clarified its position that Title IX's ban on sex discrimination applies to transgender students. The brief also included an opinion letter dated January 7, 2015, from James A. Ferg-Cadima of OCR. Responding to a request for guidance about policy relating to transgender students and restrooms, he reiterated OCR's position that, although the regulations allow a school to provide separate bathroom facilities, it "generally must treat transgender students consistent with their gender identity" (US Department of Education, Office for Civil Rights 2015). Ferg-Cadima noted that it has become more commonplace to permit transgender persons at work and school to access facilities based on their gender identity and that allowing negative community reaction to thwart such policies is contrary to the public interest.

On July 27, 2015, Virginia Federal District Court Judge Robert Doumar held a hearing on G.G.'s motion for a preliminary injunction and the board's motion to dismiss. At the hearing, he verbally granted the school board's request to dismiss the Title IX claim and denied G.G.'s motion for a preliminary injunction without ruling on his equal protection claim. On September 4, 2015, the court issued a written order denying the preliminary injunction; in a subsequent written order dated September 17, 2015, it dismissed G.G.'s Title IX claim and more fully explained its reason for denying the injunction (*G.G. v. Gloucester County School Board* 2016a).

In his September 17 ruling, Doumar cited the Title IX regulations permitting the use of sex-segregated bathroom and locker room facilities and concluded that the school did not discriminate by assigning G.G. to a bathroom based on his anatomical sex rather than his gender identity. He found the federal government's Statement of Interest unpersuasive, noting that DOE guidance documents and letters are not entitled to the same weight as regulations.

Doumar concluded that G.G. would not prevail on the merits of the case and had failed to present sufficient evidence that he would be harmed if the school continued to deny him access to the boys' restroom during the litigation. On the contrary, he stated, granting the injunction would undermine the school's "strong interest in protecting student privacy" and safety and "overturn a long tradition of segregating bathrooms based on biological differences between the sexes" (*G.G. v. Gloucester County School Board* 2015, 752–53). He did not address G.G.'s constitutional claim, saying that he needed more information, but added that, even if G.G. had stated a valid claim, he did not satisfy the standard for a preliminary injunction on equal protection grounds either.

Halfway across the country, another skirmish over facilities between the United States and Township High School District 211 in Palatine, Illinois—the largest district in the state—was erupting over locker rooms. This was the first instance in which a transgender student sought access to a locker room corresponding to her gender identity. The student, born male, had presented as female for many years. Diagnosed with gender dysphoria and undergoing hormone therapy, she changed her name legally and obtained a passport in her new identity. Her Title IX complaint, filed in December 2013, charged that the district denied her access to the girls' locker room because of her gender identity and gender nonconformity. In a meeting with high school officials just before the school year began, she asked to change clothes in a private bathroom stall within one of the girls' locker rooms, but the officials said it was too crowded, with too few stalls available. She next offered to use a privacy curtain in the girls' locker room if the school would install it. The district instead offered to allow her to change in a private restroom, one that required staff personnel to open. During OCR's investigation, it learned that the district had installed curtained areas in one of the locker rooms but refused to allow her entrance to it. The school argued that it wanted to protect the other students' privacy and avoid female students seeing an unclothed biological male and a biological male seeing unclothed female students.

After many months, the district offered her the option of either using the private room or the boys' locker room. A school official defended its decision, saying, "[A]t some point, we have to balance the privacy rights of 12,000 students with other particular, individual needs of another group of students." The student's ACLU attorney called the district's stance "blatant discrimination, no matter how the district tries to couch it" (*Chicago Tribune*, October 13, 2015). The student, who played on a girls' sports team and was referred to as she in school, said she would probably use a privacy curtain in the locker room if allowed (*New York Times*, November 2, 2015). The district continued to require her to use the private changing room for gym class and sports activities.

Following a two-year investigation, on November 2, 2015, OCR's regional director Adele Rapport wrote to district superintendent Dr. Daniel Cates, stating that, after extensive interviews and review of documents, OCR concluded that the district abridged the student's rights under Title IX. Rapport declared that the "evidence shows that, as a result of the District's denial of access to the girls' locker rooms, Student A has not only received an unequal opportunity to benefit from the District's educational program, but has also experienced an ongoing sense of isolation and ostracism throughout her high school enrollment at the School" (Rapport 2015, 10). The letter ended by warning that, unless an agreement were reached within thirty days, OCR would take the next step of issuing a letter of impending enforcement action, possibly leading to the loss of federal funding and a DOJ lawsuit.

Not surprisingly, the controversy grew more heated when parents and advocacy groups became involved in the standoff between the district and the federal government. About a dozen formed a group called District 211 Parents for Privacy and urged the board to reject any settlement agreement with the federal government. The parents were aligned with the Alliance Defending Freedom (ADF) and the Thomas More Society, two conservative Christian groups that opposed any accommodation of transgender students, insisting that they use locker room and restroom facilities that correspond with their biological sex.

One day before the deadline, after a rancorous school board meeting, the district voted to enter into a resolution agreement with OCR, stating that

> based on her representation that she will change in private changing stations in the girls' locker rooms, the District agrees to provide Student A access to locker room facilities designated for female students at school and to take steps to protect the privacy of its students by installing and maintaining sufficient privacy curtains (private changing stations) within the girls' locker rooms to accommodate Student A and any students who wish to be assured of privacy while changing. (Rapport 2015; US Department of Education 2015; see *Chicago Tribune*, December 2, 2015; *Chicago Tribune*, December 8, 2015)

The new district policy attempted to accommodate the privacy needs of all students, including the transgender student, by constructing several private restroom and locker room stalls. Despite this commonsense resolution of the matter, on May 4, 2016, fifty-one Palatine families filed suit in federal district court, naming Secretary of Education John King Jr., DOJ, and Attorney General Loretta Lynch as defendants. Represented by the Thomas More Society and the ADF, the plaintiffs claimed the district's new approach disregarded the students' "privacy and safety" and asked the court to order it to return to the policy of segregating locker room and bathroom facilities on the basis of biological sex. They also sought to enjoin the DOE rule requiring the nation's schools to allow students to use facilities consistent with their gender identities (*Students and Parents for Privacy v. United States Department of Education* 2016a).

On October 18, 2016, US Magistrate Judge Jeffrey Gilbert recommended that Illinois Federal District Court Judge Jorge Alonso deny the plaintiffs' motion for a preliminary injunction. He ruled that, among other things, they failed to show they would likely be able to prove that the definition of sex in Title IX is entirely limited to biological sex. On the contrary, he said, "it appears the law in the Seventh Circuit concerning the interpretation of the term 'sex' in Title VII, as relevant to the almost identically worded Title IX, may be in flux" (*Students and Parents for Privacy v. United States Department of Education* 2016b, 43).

In the battle over their rights, transgender children have had a powerful ally in DOJ. On April 19, 2016, the effect of its support became clear when the Fourth Circuit ruled on G.G.'s appeal of Doumar's decision in *G.G. v. Gloucester County School Board* (2016a). G.G. had asked the appellate court to reverse the dismissal of his Title IX claim and grant his motion for a preliminary injunction. He also requested the circuit court to assign his case to a different judge, arguing that Doumar's preconceived notions about gender and sexuality would interfere with his consideration of the scientific principles involved in gender identity. The board had asked the appeals court to uphold the lower court Title IX rulings and dismiss the equal protection claim as well.[87] The federal government filed an amicus brief to support its position that Title IX requires schools to allow transgender students to utilize restrooms consistent with their gender identity.

The Fourth Circuit was the first circuit to rule on the question of a transgender student's access to a public school restroom. In a 2–1 opinion announced by Judge Henry Floyd, the panel sided with the administration's position on the role of Title IX in combatting discrimination based on gender identity.[88] It held that the lower court judge should have deferred to DOE's interpretation of the statute and regulations, and because he did not, he erroneously dismissed G.G.'s Title IX claim. Further, because the appeals court found that Doumar abused his discretion in refusing to grant G.G. a preliminary injunction, it remanded the case and ordered him to use the correct standard.

The controversy revolved around the deference owed to DOE's interpretation of 34 C.F.R., section 106.33. Doumar had rejected DOE's construction of the regulation, finding that it lacked controlling weight. After an extensive analysis of administrative law principles, the three-judge panel held that he had erred by not according "appropriate deference to the relevant Department of Education regulations" (715). It noted that it did not find *Johnston* persuasive because the judge in that case had not weighed the importance of DOE's interpretation of its regulation.

Acknowledging that Title IX allowed sex-segregated facilities, the appeals court cited DOE's construction of 34 C.F.R., section 106.33, presented in Ferg-Cadima's opinion letter of January 7, 2015. The letter reflected the agency's 2014 document, "Questions and Answers," that had been designated a "significant guidance document." The panel recognized that the regulation encompassed a binary vision of sex but found it ambiguous with respect to transgender students. Because of this, it found DOE's opinion that schools must treat transgender students on the basis of their gender identity, not on their anatomical sex at birth, "reasonable" and therefore entitled to controlling weight. In reaching this conclusion, the court relied on *Auer v. Robbins* (1997), in which the US Supreme Court deferred to the Secretary of Labor's interpretation of the Fair Labor Standards Act of 1938, saying, "[B]ecause Congress 'has not spoken directly to the precise question at issue,' we must sustain the Secretary's approach so long as it is 'based on a permissible construction of the statute'" (457, quoting *Chevron v. Natural Resources Defense Council, Inc.* 1984, 842–43).

Intent on avoiding accusations of engaging in judicial activism, the circuit court added that "courts must, in some cases, reconcile competing political interests, but not on the basis of the judges' personal policy preferences. In contrast, an agency to which Congress has delegated policy-making responsibilities may, within the limits of that delegation, properly rely upon the incumbent administration's views of wise policy to inform its judgments" (*G.G. v. Gloucester County School Board* 2016a, 724, quoting *Chevron v. Natural Resources Defense Council, Inc.* 1984, 865–66).

The court criticized the lower court judge for improperly analyzing G.G.'s request for a preliminary injunction, first, by limiting himself to the issue of the balance of harms only, and second, by dismissing the expert medical testimony showing that G.G. would be irreparably harmed. By imposing a more rigorous evidentiary standard in deciding on a motion for injunctive relief and rejecting G.G.'s proffered evidence, the appeals court found that the lower court abused its discretion in denying his motion for a preliminary injunction. It vacated Doumar's ruling on the motion and remanded the case to allow him to assess the evidence properly.

In deciding whether to remand to another judge, the court considered G.G.'s contention that he manifested "pre-existing views which it would be unwilling to put aside in the face of contrary evidence about medical science generally and about 'gender and sexuality in particular'" (*G.G. v. Gloucester County School Board* 2016a, 726). Paradoxically, admitting that the judge's comments demonstrated a lack of understanding about transgender individuals, the appellate court held that, because his written opinions did not include such statements and G.G. had not presented specific evidence of his bias, it was unwilling to take the unusual step of reassigning the case to another court.

Concurring in the opinion, Judge Andre Davis added that he believed that G.G. had satisfied the standard for a preliminary injunction and that the appeals court had enough evidence to grant it while awaiting the lower court ruling on the merits. Nevertheless, he ended by agreeing that the court should defer to the lower court but that he hoped it would grant an injunction quickly before G.G. suffered more harm.

The dissenting judge, Paul Niemeyer, believed the majority erroneously interpreted the word sex in the Title IX regulation to mean gender identity, not anatomical sex. He accused the majority of failing to cite any case law and instead relying only on the 2015 DOE letter that required schools to treat transgender students according to their gender identity. Niemeyer declared,

> Accepting that new definition of the statutory term "sex," the majority's opinion, for the first time ever, holds that a public high school may not provide separate restrooms and locker rooms on the basis of biological sex. Rather, it must now allow a biological male student who identifies as female to use the girls' restrooms and locker rooms and, likewise, must allow a biological female student who identifies as male to use the boys' restrooms and locker rooms. This holding completely tramples on all universally accepted protections of priva-

> cy and safety that are based on the anatomical differences between the sexes. (731)

On May 31, 2016, with Niemeyer dissenting, the Fourth Circuit denied the district's petition for a rehearing en banc and entered judgment for G.G. (*G.G. v. Gloucester County School Board* 2016b). As is customary, the full court was polled about the rehearing, and no judge asked for a vote. Niemeyer briefly restated his reasons for his dissent in the case, explaining that he had not voted for the poll because he believed that the "momentous nature of the issue deserves an open road to the Supreme Court to seek the Court's controlling construction of Title IX for national application" (at 1). Given the court's unwillingness to be polled about a rehearing, he nevertheless voted for it, understanding that it was a futile gesture.

A few weeks later—on June 23, 2016—Doumar cited the appellate court's position on G.G.'s Title IX claim, granting the preliminary injunction and ordering the Gloucester County School Board to allow him to use the boys' restroom in Gloucester High School (*G.G. v. Gloucester County School Board* 2016c).[89] Unwilling to permit G.G. to begin the school year with this order in effect, the school board returned to the three-judge panel, seeking a stay of the ruling while it prepared a petition for a writ of certiorari to the high court. On July 12, 2016, in the same 2–1 vote, the panel denied the motion. Davis concurred but wrote separately to note that four circuits (the First, Sixth, Ninth, and Eleventh) "all recognized that discrimination against a transgender individual based on that person's transgender status is discrimination because of sex under federal civil rights statutes and the Equal Protection Clause" (*G.G. v. Gloucester County School Board* 2016d, 607).[90]

Niemeyer dissented from the denial of the stay pending appeal, criticizing Doumar's analysis in granting the injunction. He also accused the majority of ignoring the language of Title IX that allows separate facilities based on sex, deferring to DOE simply on the basis of a letter and intruding on the students' "bodily privacy . . . to the dismay of the students and their parents," likely disrupting the school. Declaring that he was sensitive to G.G.'s gender transition, he believed it "unlikely" that he would "suffer substantial injury" if the court granted the stay. He urged that the court return to the status quo ante because, prior to making the "changes the injunction would require—and that the Department of Justice and Department of Education now seek to impose nationwide on the basis of our earlier decision," it would be beneficial to receive guidance from the high court or Congress "before having to undertake these sweeping reforms" (at 607).[91]

The school board's last hope to prevent the injunction from taking effect was to ask the Supreme Court for a stay while it reviewed the board's petition for certiorari.[92] On August 3, 2016, Kennedy with Chief Justice John Roberts and Justices Samuel Alito, and Clarence Thomas voted to grant the stay, joined by Stephen Breyer. Breyer explained that his vote was a "courtesy" to the other justices to "preserve the status quo (as of the time the Court of Appeals made its decision)." Ruth Bader Ginsburg, Sonia Sotomayor, and Elena Kagan voted to deny the stay (*Gloucester County School Board v. G.G.* 2016a).

The school board filed its petition for certiorari on August 29, 2016, presenting three questions: "1. Should this Court retain the *Auer* doctrine despite the objections of multiple Justices who have recently urged that it be reconsidered and overruled? 2. If *Auer* is retained, should deference extend to an unpublished agency letter that, among other things, does not carry the force of law and was adopted in the context of the very dispute in which deference is sought? 3. With or without deference to the agency, should the Department's specific interpretation of Title IX and 34 C.F.R. § 106.33 be given effect?" (*Gloucester County School Board v. G.G* 2016b, at 1).[93]

The Supreme Court listed the case for discussion at its October 14 conference, but reached no decision that day (*Daily Press*, October 17, 2016). Two weeks later, on October 28, 2016, it granted certiorari, limiting its review to Questions 2 and 3 of the board's petition. In agreeing to hear the case, the Court continued the board's policy of denying G.G. access to the restroom corresponding to his gender identity (*Gloucester County School Board* v. G.G. 2016c). G.G. expressed disappointment in the Court's action, saying, "While I'm disappointed that that I will have to spend my final school year being singled out and treated differently from every other guy, I will do everything I can to make sure that other transgender students don't have to go through the same experience" (*BuzzFeed*, October 28, 2016). Critics argue the Court was precipitous in taking the case because transgender equality would have benefited from having more time to gain societal understanding and acceptance (*Bloomberg*, October 31, 2016).

NOTES

1. Although transgender persons most often prefer to be known by the gender with which they identify, Jenner used the male pronoun during the interview with Sawyer.

2. Also known as gender confirmation surgery, the courts use the term sex reassignment surgery more frequently. The executive director of the National Center for Transgender Equality explains that

> transitioning is first and foremost not about surgery but about gender identity and living and expressing that identity. For some people surgery is desired or necessary, for others it is not. For some there are medical contraindications that preclude surgery. And many, if not most, trans people just can't afford it and many others don't feel surgery is necessary for them to live consistently with their gender identity. In fact, most transpeople do not have any kind of surgery. (Keisling 2016)

3. In 2008, the American Medical Association (AMA) House of Delegates approved two resolutions: "Resolved, That the AMA support public and private health insurance coverage for treatment of gender identity disorder" and "Resolved, That the AMA oppose categorical exclusions of coverage for treatment of gender identity disorder when prescribed by a physician" (American Medical Association House of Delegates 2008).

4. On December 22, 2010, Obama signed legislation to begin the process of repealing Don't Ask, Don't Tell. On July 22, 2011, the president, defense secretary, and chair of the joint chiefs of staff "certif[ied] to Congress that the Armed Forces are prepared to implement repeal in a manner that is consistent with the standards of military readiness, military effectiveness, unit cohesion, and recruiting and retention of the Armed Forces" (US Department of Defense 2011). The policy officially ended on September 20, 2011.

5. The Williams Institute (Gates and Herman 2014) and the Palm Center (Elders and Steinman 2014) estimate that in 2014, roughly 15,000 transgender individuals served in the armed forces, including active duty, the National Guard, and the reserves.

6. *USA Today* was the first newspaper to report that the ban on transgender service members would end before July 4, 2016 (*USA Today*, June 24, 2016).

7. On June 24, 2016, the Rand Corporation issued the results of a study in which it concluded that there would only be a minor impact if transgender persons openly served in the military (Schaefer et al. 2016).

8. California, Colorado, Connecticut, Delaware, the District of Columbia, Hawaii, Illinois, Iowa, Maine, Maryland, Massachusetts, Minnesota, Nevada, New Jersey, New Mexico, Oregon, Rhode Island, Vermont, and Washington prohibit discrimination based on gender identity; the protections in these laws vary.

9. One of the thornier issues in the courts revolved around the validity of a marriage between a man and a transgender woman in states that prohibited same-sex marriage. *In the Matter of the Estate of Marshall G. Gardiner* (2002) illustrates the difficulty that arises when one state allows a transgender person to amend his or her birth certificate and another refuses to accord it full faith and credit. In a dispute over probate, the Kansas Supreme Court invalidated the Kansas marriage between Marshall Gardiner and J'Noel Gardiner, a transgender woman who had undergone sex reassignment surgery. Their Kansas marriage relied on J'Noel's birth certificate, amended to show her as a female according to Wisconsin law. The court held that, despite the amended birth certificate, the full faith and credit clause does not require Kansas to accept Wisconsin's determination of her legal sex and ruled that she was a male under Kansas law. With the Kansas ban on same-sex marriage, their marriage was not recognized. Similarly, in *Littleton v. Prange* (1999), the court ruled that Christie Lee Littleton (a transgender woman) could not sue a physician for malpractice following the death of her husband. The court held that, despite her sex reassignment surgery, she was a man under state law, and her marriage was therefore invalid because of the state's ban on same-sex marriage.

10. Sex reassignment surgery, encompassing a number of procedures, alters an individual's primary or secondary sex characteristics. Most transgender people do not undergo it, in part because it is expensive and outside the coverage of most insurance policies (Tarzwell 2006). The hormone treatments that precede surgery alter secondary sex characteristics but leave the individual's sex-linked chromosome unchanged.

11. A bill, known as the Gender Equality Non-Discrimination Act (GENDA), that would have prohibited discrimination in housing, employment, and other services passed the New York State Assembly seven times but never reached the Senate floor (*New York Times*, December 12, 2014).

12. Sexual orientation and gender identity are two analytically distinct concepts; the former refers to a person's romantic attachment to another person,

the latter to internal feelings of maleness or femaleness. Both transgender and nontransgender people may have romantic feelings for persons of either sex. For example, if a transgender woman—a male at birth who has transitioned to a female—were attracted to a woman, she would likely consider herself a lesbian. Similarly, if a transgender man—a female at birth who has transitioned to a male—is attracted to a man, he would likely identify as a gay man (American Psychological Association 2015). A transgender woman—born with male secondary sex characteristics—who is attracted to men would likely identify as a straight woman (GLAAD 2014).

13. The term cisgender identifies a nontransgender person.

14. Transgender is the more inclusive term, encompassing a range of nonconforming gender identities and gender expressions; the two are often conflated (see Peek 2004; Simopoulos and Khin Khin 2014).

15. For the sake of consistency, gender dysphoria is used throughout.

16. The WPATH standards are internationally recognized as the gold standard in treating gender dysphoria (Rezabek 2014).

17. The survey, conducted online and on paper, was based on the responses of 6,450 transgender and gender-nonconforming participants aged eighteen to eighty-nine, from all fifty states, the District of Columbia, Guam, Puerto Rico, and the US Virgin Islands.

18. Pew surveyed 1,504 LGBT adults nationwide from May 1 to 5, 2013; of these, 1,197 responded (Pew Research Center 2014).

19. The Williams Institute, founded in 2011, is at the University of California at Los Angeles Law School.

20. A method of identifying likely transgender persons involves analysis of alterations to Social Security Administration records for name changes and sex coding (see Harris 2015).

21. Gallup conducted the poll from June 1 to September 30, 2012. Other surveys reported slightly higher numbers. An online Indiana University study found that 5.6 percent of respondents identified themselves as LGBT. Gallup reports that Americans perceive that more than one in five Americans are gay or lesbian, larger by far than the actual number reported in Gallup Daily tracking polls (Gallup 2015).

22. Witeck-Combs Communication, a Washington, DC marketing and public relations firm that has surveyed gay men and lesbians in partnership with Harris Interactive since 2000, estimates that 6.7 percent of American adults are gay, lesbian, bisexual, or transgender (Bialik 2011).

23. The complaint was based on 42 U.S.C., section 1983, an 1871 law that authorizes individuals to seek a federal remedy when deprived of federal constitutional and statutory rights by a defendant acting under color of state law. The Court found insufficient evidence of the medical personnel's indifference;

it remanded the case to allow the appellate court to consider whether the head of the state corrections department and prison warden showed deliberate indifference.

24. Prisons typically base their decisions on whether a prisoner belongs in a male or female population on genital surgery, making preoperative transgender women more vulnerable to physical and sexual assault (Peek 2004).

25. In California jails, preoperative transgender women are placed in male units and classified as "total separation" (T-sep) inmates; gang members are also classified as "T-sep" inmates. Thus, transgender prisoners suffer conditions typically considered punishment for misbehavior (Smith 2009, 689).

26. The Court also clarified that the deliberate indifference standard is inappropriate when prison officials are charged with causing the harm.

27. The Seventh Circuit noted in *Meriwether v. Faulkner* (1987, 413) that courts have acknowledged that a "psychiatric or psychological condition may present a 'serious medical need' under the *Estelle* formulation . . . [and] there is no need to treat transsexualism differently than any other psychiatric disorder." In *Torraco v. Maloney* (1991, 234), it stated that there is "no underlying distinction between the right to medical care for physical ills and its psychological or psychiatric counterpart."

28. Tarzwell (2006) and Peek (2004) discuss administrative and evidentiary problems that transgender inmates face in attempting to validate their Eighth Amendment rights after *Farmer*.

29. Public L. No. 108-79, 117 Stat. 972 (September 4, 2003).

30. In August 2015, Administrative Law Judge Denise Oakes Shaffer held that the harassment of a Maryland transgender prisoner violated the PREA. Shaffer ruled that the state failed to train its employees to deal with transgender prisoners (*Guardian*, September 24, 2015).

31. In North America, sex reassignment surgery began as early as the 1950s. It is estimated that by January 2006, 30,000 surgeries were performed in the United States (*Kosilek v. Spencer* 2014a).

32. In *De'Lonta v. Johnson* (2013, 526), the Fourth Circuit held that, although the state had provided the prisoner with "*some* treatment . . . it does not follow that they have necessarily provided her with *constitutionally adequate* treatment" (emphasis in the original). The state paroled her while it was considering her request for sex reassignment surgery (*New York Times*, August 31, 2015).

33. The court dismissed Kosilek's first complaint against Maloney and former Sheriff David Nelson on grounds of qualified immunity (*Kosilek v. Nelson* 2000).

34. From 1992 to 1994, while imprisoned in the county jail and awaiting trial, Kosilek had taken birth control pills that she obtained illegally from a jail guard.

35. Kosilek was in serious danger of harm, having tried to commit suicide twice as well as trying to castrate herself.

36. The court noted that cost is not a relevant consideration in determining whether to provide treatment, but security concerns could be valid reasons to deny treatment.

37. This was the policy that led to Kosilek's first suit (*Kosilek v. Spencer* 2012).

38. As the name indicates, the policy freezes the treatment of transgender inmates with gender dysphoria at the level provided at the time they entered the prison system.

39. Under the new policy, a private health care provider, under contract to DOC, would recommend whether additional care was required, and DOC would assess whether security concerns would be implicated in the recommended care.

40. Dennehy stepped down as commissioner in April 30, 2007, and was replaced by Harold Clarke in November 2007. Clarke served until Luis Spencer became commissioner in May 2011; Spencer's name was substituted as the defendant in the second district court opinion and thereafter.

41. This appeared to be the first time a federal court judge ordered a state to provide sex reassignment surgery to an inmate (*New York Times*, September 5, 2012).

42. At the time of the appellate court's ruling, Kosilek was sixty-four years old and had still not undergone the surgery.

43. The author of the panel opinion, Judge Ojetta Rogeriee Thompson, dissented from the 3–2 en banc ruling, as did Judge William Kayatta.

44. Although she began to call herself Michelle-Lael, CDCR did not allow her to legally change her name and referred to her in prison records as Jeffrey, her birth name.

45. In California, both Medicaid and private health insurers cover treatment for gender transitions, including sex reassignment surgery (*Norsworthy v. Beard* 2014, 1104–5).

46. The court had dismissed Norsworthy's complaint to seek a legal name change in *Norsworthy v. Beard* (2014).

47. Unlike California, Georgia's Medicaid program does not pay for gender-affirming care for transgender persons.

48. In September 2011, GLAD announced that its 2009 suit against the Federal Bureau of Prisons on behalf of Vanessa Adams was settled, ending the

federal government's "freeze-frame" policy (Gay & Lesbian Advocates & Defenders 2011.)

49. Presumably in response to her lawsuit, they provided her with a hormone patch, but the dosage was too low to meet her needs (*New York Times*, April 5, 2015).

50. The US attorney general has the authority to file a Statement of Interest "to attend to the Interests of the United States" in any suit pending in state or federal court (28 U.S.C. §517).

51. Following a hearing in April 2015 to consider her request for an immediate transfer to a less dangerous facility, Treadwell denied her request, saying that the federal courts have been cautioned about interfering with prison authorities (*New York Times*, April 20, 2015).

52. A 2006 Boston youth survey of 1,032 public high school students found that 1.6 percent of respondents reported being transgender (Almeida et al. 2009, table 1); a 2011 study of 2,730 San Francisco Unified School District middle school students (grades 6 to 8) found that 1.3 percent identify as transgender (Shields et al. 2013, 249); a 2015 Dane County (Wisconsin) survey of 18,494 students found that 1.5 percent of the high school students surveyed viewed themselves as transgender (Dane County Youth Commission 2015, 5).

53. According to the US Census Bureau, based on national projections, there were 74 million youth under eighteen in 2014 (Colby and Ortman 2015).

54. GLSEN, which celebrated twenty-five years in 2015, began assessing the climate for LGBT youth in schools in 1999; its national school climate surveys, conducted every two years, provide the most comprehensive information about the environment for LGBT students in the nation's education system.

55. The GLSEN survey was conducted online, with a national sample of 7,898 LGBT students aged thirteen to twenty-one from all fifty states and the District of Columbia.

56. The sample included 295 transgender students, selected from the larger sample of 6,209 LGBT students in the national school climate study conducted during the 2006–2007 academic year.

57. Grant, Mottet, and Tanis (2011, 33) found that transgender students of color were subjected to more instances of harassment and violence.

58. The difficulties are enhanced for transgender student athletes (see Buzuvis 2011; Skinner-Thompson and Turner 2013).

59. As of January 30, 2015, only fifteen states and the District of Columbia have "Safe School Nondiscrimination Laws" in place that include protection on the basis of gender identity and sexual orientation in education; Wisconsin prohibits discrimination on the basis of sexual orientation only; the remainder

of the states cover only sex discrimination (American Civil Liberties Union 2015; National Center for Transgender Equality 2015).

60. 20 U.S.C., section 1681, provides, "No person in the United States shall, on the basis of sex, be excluded from participation in, be denied the benefits of, or be subjected to discrimination under any education program or activity receiving Federal financial assistance."

61. There are a number of exceptions to Title IX; among other things, it does not apply to admissions policies of private undergraduate schools (see Buzuvis 2013).

62. McKay (2011) argues that the courts should apply the same standard of review in Fourteenth Amendment claims of discrimination on the basis of gender identity or expression as it applies to sex (gender) and nonmarital children. Under this standard, known as heightened or intermediate review, the school must show that it has an important goal and that its policy is substantially related to achieving that goal.

63. Title IX does not expressly include a private right of action; that is, it does not specify that individuals may sue educational institutions for sex discrimination. By its language, it only provides termination of federal funding to the offending institution as the remedy for sex discrimination. In *Cannon v. University of Chicago* (1979), the Supreme Court explained that Title IX had two purposes: to prevent institutions from using federal funds for discriminatory practices and to protect individuals from sex discrimination. Reasoning that although cutting off federal funds to a guilty institution would aid in the first goal, it would not further the statute's second aim of promoting individual rights. Therefore, the Court allowed Geraldine Cannon's suit against the University of Chicago Medical School to proceed.

64. In *Franklin v. Gwinnett County Public Schools* (1992), the high court held that schools could be liable for money damages in Title IX suits. In *Gebser v .Lago Vista Independent School District* (1998), the Court adopted the deliberate indifference test for sexual harassment in schools, requiring plaintiffs to prove that school officials with responsibility to correct the harassing behavior knew of it and deliberately failed to act.

65. The fifth-grader was harassed by name-calling and offensive contact of a sexual nature.

66. In 2014, Atherton High School in Jefferson County, Kentucky, approved extending the county's nondiscrimination policy to include gender identity, allowing students to use the restroom and locker room of their gender identity. The issue arose when a first-year high school student, a transgender girl, received the principal's permission to use the girls' bathroom and locker room facilities. After a short debate, the school council supported his decision

in an 8–1 vote. The policy was modeled on the Los Angeles one (*Courier-Journal*, May 16, 2014; *Courier-Journal*, June 6, 2014).

67. AB 1266 took effect on January 1, 2014. The opposition, led by the Privacy for All Alliance, unsuccessfully attempted to gather the necessary signatures to place an initiative on the November 2014 ballot that would have effectively repealed the law. When that attempt failed, they geared up to try again for the November 2016 ballot (*Huffington Post*, February 25, 2014; *Sacramento Bee*, April 20, 2015).

68. A DCL is a "significant guidance document" that provides "recipients with information to assist them in meeting their obligations, and . . . members of the public with information about their rights, under the civil rights laws and implementing regulations that we enforce" (US Department of Education, Office for Civil Rights 2011). A DCL must meet the standards set by the Office of Management and Budget (US Office of Management and Budget 2007).

69. The 2011 DCL also expanded on a 2001 Guidance on the duty of federally funded educational institutions to combat sexual harassment by school employees, students, and third parties under Title IX (US Department of Education, Office for Civil Rights 2001).

70. The high court applied Title VII case law in *Davis* and *Franklin,* indicating the linkage between the two statutes.

71. Borrowing the language of Title IX, the bill states, "No student shall, on the basis of actual or perceived sexual orientation or gender identity of such individual or of a person with whom the student associates or has associated, be excluded from participation in, be denied the benefits of, or be subjected to discrimination under any program or activity receiving Federal financial assistance."

72. Senator Al Franken, Democrat of Minnesota, introduced S. 439 on February 10, 2015, and Colorado Democrat Jared Polis introduced H.R. 486 the same day.

73. Some suggest that different standards might be applied to bathrooms and locker rooms; others argue that this distinction has no basis in law (see Tobin and Levi 2013).

74. Although young children may discover that their gender identity differs from their anatomical sex, they are too young to undergo sex reassignment surgery.

75. Some transgender students, claiming discrimination on the basis of gender dysphoria, cite Section 504 of the 1973 Rehabilitation Act, the Americans with Disabilities Act (ADA), or the First Amendment right to freedom of expression. Section 504 and the ADA, however, explicitly exclude transgender status as a disability (Harris 2010; Jones 2010).

76. 34 C.F.R., section 106.33, states, "[A] recipient may provide separate toilet, locker room, and shower facilities on the basis of sex, but such facilities provided for students of one sex shall be comparable to such facilities provided for students of the other sex."

77. According to the commission, sexual orientation includes transgender status.

78. The superior court allowed the parents to use the pseudonym Susan Doe in court documents.

79. The boy was apparently directed to do so by his grandfather, who had objected to the school's decision to allow her to use the girls' bathroom. When the boy was disciplined, he argued that he was also entitled to use the girls' bathroom.

80. The state human rights law broadly defines sexual orientation as a "person's actual or perceived heterosexuality, bisexuality, homosexuality, or gender identity or expression."

81. Before fifth grade, students use single-stall bathrooms separated by sex; beginning in the fifth grade, students use a communal sex-segregated bathroom with individual stalls.

82. In Pennsylvania, a revised birth certificate requires a doctor to confirm that the individual has undergone sex reassignment surgery (*ThinkProgress*, April 2, 2015).

83. The plaintiff, Gavin Grimm, is referred to as G.G. in court papers.

84. G.G. never sought to use locker rooms designated for either sex.

85. The school added three single-stall unisex bathrooms for all students to use.

86. Earlier in the year, the federal government submitted a Statement of Interest in a Michigan federal court case filed by the ACLU in 2014 on behalf of a fourteen-year-old middle school transgender boy who claimed discrimination on the basis of Title IX and the equal protection clause of the Fourteen Amendment. School officials had rejected his request to use the boys' restroom, instructing him to use a "staff ladies' room" or a unisex restroom, even though it was rarely available. The other students harassed him, using sexual terms, and school officials continued to call him a girl, despite his requests to refer to him as a boy. The school argued that a transgender Title IX plaintiff can only claim discrimination because of sex stereotyping, not discrimination based on gender identity or transgender status, and that he had not stated sufficient facts for a valid sex-stereotyping claim. The Statement of Interest cited relevant Title VII cases showing that sex encompasses gender identity and argued that it is also cognizable under Title IX. Moreover, it said, courts have recognized claims of harassment and discrimination based on an individual's failure to conform to sex stereotypes (US Department of Justice 2015c).

87. Because the lower court had not ruled on the equal protection issue, the appeals court declined to discuss it.

88. In *Miles v. New York University* (1997), the court denied the university's motion to dismiss the transgender student's Title IX claim for sexual harassment, adding that it wondered why the harassment was not actionable merely because the victim is not a "biological female" as everyone, including the harasser, believed. The court did not expressly hold that discriminating because of gender identity violates Title IX (see Rao 2013).

89. A few days after he granted the injunction, Doumar denied the school board's motion for a stay (*Richmond Times-Dispatch*, August 3, 2016).

90. In his concurring opinion in *G.G. v. Gloucester County School Board* (2016d, at 1), Davis cited *Glenn v. Brumby* (2011: equal protection); *Rosa v. Park West Bank & Trust Co.* (2000: Equal Credit Opportunity Act); *Schwenk v. Hartford* (2000: Gender Motivated Violence Act); and *Smith v. City of Salem* (2004: Title VII).

91. On July 19, 2016, a fourteen-year-old transgender boy named M. A. B. filed suit against the Board of Education of Talbot County in St. Michaels, Maryland, which had barred him from using the restroom or locker room facilities corresponding to his gender identity. After the Fourth Circuit's ruling in G.G.'s case, the school board informed M. A. B. that he would be allowed to use the boys' restroom. Because G.G.'s case had not involved locker rooms, the board continued to restrict his access to the boys' locker room (*Baltimore Sun*, July 19, 2016).

92. The school constructed three single-user restrooms to which all students have access. G.G.'s lawyers argued that the school is still violating his rights under Title IX because he would still be "isolated from his peers and stigmatized" (*Los Angeles Times*, August 3, 2016).

93. In May 2016, the Supreme Court denied certiorari in *United States Student Aid Funds, Inc. v. Bryana Bible* (2016), a case in which it was asked to overrule *Auer v. Robbins* (1997). With only Thomas dissenting, seven justices declined to hear a challenge to DOE's interpretation of its regulation affecting college loan repayments. Roberts and Alito, who had also urged reconsidering *Auer*, nevertheless voted against taking the case.

3

MARRIAGE EQUALITY

The modern struggle over marriage equality in the United States began with a short-lived victory by gay men and lesbians in Hawaii, with the state supreme court declaring in *Baehr v. Lewin* (1993) that the same-sex marriage restriction might conflict with the state constitution's ban on sex discrimination.[1] The state high court remanded the case to the lower court, ordering the state to prove that the ban on same-sex marriage furthered a compelling interest.

THE ASCENT OF MARRIAGE EQUALITY

A decade later, state supreme courts began to rule that prohibiting same-sex marriage violated the equality principles of their state constitutions.[2] In *Goodridge v. Department of Public Health* (2003), the Massachusetts high court declared the state's restrictions on same-sex marriage unconstitutional.[3] Over the next decade, citing state constitutional guarantees, plaintiffs successfully mounted challenges to restrictions on same-sex marriage in Connecticut (*Kerrigan v. Commissioner of Public Health* 2008), California (*In re Marriage Cases* 2008), Iowa (*Varnum v. Brien* 2009), New Jersey (*Garden State Equality v. Dow* 2013), and New Mexico (*Griego v. Oliver* 2013).[4]

In these cases, same-sex marriage advocates relied on state constitutional principles to challenge marriage inequality in the courts. They were secure in the knowledge that the US Supreme Court would not reverse a ruling in their favor, for in *Michigan v. Long* (1983), the Court ruled that principles of federalism preclude it from reviewing state supreme court decisions interpreting their state constitutions.

By the end of 2013, in addition to the six states in which the litigation ended marriage inequality, twelve other jurisdictions eased marriage restrictions, allowing same-sex couples to wed. [5] The remaining states continued to ban same-sex marriage, by statute or constitutional amendment or, in some states, both (Berg 2012). While continuing to prohibit same-sex marriage, a number of states recognized lesser forms of same-sex relationships, such as domestic partnerships or civil unions; Pinello (2009) characterized states that barred legal recognition of all same-sex relationships as "super-DOMA" states.

THE FEDERAL GOVERNMENT AND MARRIAGE EQUALITY

Prior to 1996, the federal government played virtually no role in marriage policy-making; in that year, concerned that states would legalize same-sex marriage, Congress created a federal definition of marriage by enacting the Defense of Marriage Act (DOMA). Its main purpose was to prevent couples from marrying in marriage equality states and demand recognition of their marriages in their home states under the full faith and credit clause of the US Constitution (Koppelman 1996; see Shuki-Kunze 1998).[6]

Leaving no doubt about their motives, DOMA's sponsors stated that the law registers "both moral disapproval of homosexuality, and a moral conviction that heterosexuality better comports with traditional (especially Judeo-Christian) morality" (US House Committee on the Judiciary 1996, 16). In urging its passage, supporters painted a dire picture of the future without the law. A House member warned during floor debate, "[T]he very foundations of our society are in danger of being burned. The flames of hedonism, the flames of narcissism, the flames of self-centered morality are licking at the very foundations of our society: the family unit" (*Congressional Record* 1996, H7482). Both chambers overwhelmingly approved the bill, and Clinton signed it on September 21, 1996.[7] DOMA allowed states to refuse to recognize same-sex marriages performed in other states (section 2) and specified that only different-sex marriages were valid under federal law (section 3).[8]

Same-sex couples soon raised legal challenges, arguing that the law violated the rights of legally wed same-sex couples and contravened federalist principles by encroaching on state authority over marriage. Courts in California, Florida, and Oklahoma dismissed their suits, holding that only couples married in the United States and denied federal benefits could claim injury under the act and therefore had standing to sue.[9]

In *Gill v. Office of Personnel Management* (2010), the plaintiffs, a group of legally married couples and surviving spouses, were the first to have standing to argue that section 3 unconstitutionally deprived them of the federal benefits to which they were entitled.[10] Massachusetts Federal District Court Judge Joseph Tauro agreed, holding that DOMA transgressed "core constitutional principles of equal protection" (*Gill v. Office of Personnel Management* 2010, 387).[11]

In a surprising move, despite defending it in Tauro's court and appealing his ruling, Holder advised House Speaker John Boehner, an Ohio Republican, that the administration now believed that section 3 was unconstitutional, and while it would continue to enforce DOMA, it would no longer defend it in court.[12] Holder's letter states,

> [T]he President has instructed Executive agencies to continue to comply with Section 3 of DOMA, consistent with the Executive's obligation to take care to that the laws be faithfully executed, unless and until Congress repeals Section 3 or the judicial branch renders a definitive verdict against the law's constitutionality. This course of action respects the actions of the prior Congress that enacted DOMA, and it recognizes the judiciary as the final arbiter of the constitutional claims raised. (US Department of Justice 2011)[13]

Signaling a major shift in its approach to discrimination against gay men and lesbians, DOJ filed a revised brief in the First Circuit Court of Appeals, urging the court to consider the purpose and effect of the law carefully as well as the nature of the individuals affected by it. In the language of equal protection jurisprudence, it asked the court to treat gay men and lesbians as a protected class and subject laws affecting them to a more rigorous review; that is, to a higher level of scrutiny. (Kaplan and Fink 2012)

THE SCRUTINY DOCTRINE

Scrutiny is a shorthand term depicting the extent to which courts defer to majoritarian decision-making in adjudicating constitutional claims. The same-sex marriage litigants frequently raised the scrutiny issue in the lower courts, reflecting their understanding that a ruling on the matter was integral to the outcome of the case. They also knew that raising the level of scrutiny would mean a "gigantic leap forward for the principle of equal protection of the laws for gay men and lesbians" (Kaplan and Fink 2012, 204).

The scrutiny doctrine encompasses the relationship between courts and legislatures, and by applying a higher level of scrutiny, the courts signal that they are less inclined to defer to policies emanating from representative bodies or the ballot box. In addition to determining the likely outcome of the case, a court's decision about the proper level of scrutiny has important implications for the judiciary's role in policy-making. Applying a lower level of scrutiny indicates a greater willingness to accept policies arising from the majoritarian policy-making process; a higher level demonstrates the court's concern that the democratic process may be detrimental to the interests of vulnerable minority groups and it must help insulate them from its effects.

One of the first obstacles for the marriage equality litigants was to persuade the courts to scrutinize the challenged laws more rigorously; that is, to apply a higher level of scrutiny than is customary in evaluating social or economic legislation. A court's determination of the appropriate level of scrutiny, crucial to the outcome of the case, primarily depends on its view of the class of people challenging the law; the scrutiny is higher when reviewing laws affecting groups with insufficient political influence to prevent legislation that infringes on their rights (Mezey 2007; Mezey 2011).

The courts apply strict scrutiny, the highest level, to laws affecting groups whose members are historically subject to discrimination, possess immutable and innate characteristics, and lack political power.[14] To survive strict scrutiny—an almost herculean task—the government must prove that it has a compelling justification for the challenged law and the means are narrowly tailored to achieve the asserted objective. Limited to laws implicating race, ethnicity, and national origin, strict scrutiny almost invariably results in declarations of unconstitutionality, as the government is unable to satisfy this standard. Using the same approach, the courts apply this level of scrutiny to laws affecting fundamental rights protected by the due process clause of the Fourteenth Amendment and require the defendants to offer a compelling reason for the law.

When applying the lowest level, minimal scrutiny—also known as rational basis review—the courts invariably defer to the legislature's judgment by presuming such laws are constitutional and almost reflexively upholding them, merely asking whether they are rationally related to a legitimate goal. Minimal scrutiny means virtually no scrutiny, as courts "will make no effort to determine the government's actual ends, will accept as true unsupported factual assertions for which the government has no evidence, and will, if necessary, assist the government with the defense of its case by inventing 'conceivable' justifications for the challenged law or policy" (Neily 2012, 1059).

A middle tier, intermediate or heightened scrutiny—formulated in 1976—is almost exclusively reserved for laws based on sex; to survive this standard, the government must show that the law furthers an important objective and is substantially related to the goal. Because this is a difficult but not impossible standard to meet, the government frequently loses such cases.

The high court's rulings in its prior gay and lesbian rights cases illustrate the vagueness of its approach to the scrutiny doctrine when reviewing laws challenged as equal protection or due process violations. In *Romer v. Evans* (1996), it held that a Colorado constitutional amendment violated the Fourteenth Amendment's equal protection clause by preventing local communities from adopting ordinances against discrimination on the basis of sexual orientation. Without explicitly raising the level of scrutiny, the majority based its opinion largely on its belief that the policy stemmed from animus toward the gay and lesbian community. In *Lawrence v. Texas* (2003), the Court ruled that Texas antisodomy law—aimed at same-sex couples only—abridged the due process clause of the Fourteenth Amendment. Again, without clarifying its position on the appropriate level of scrutiny for laws affecting lesbians and gay men, the majority encompassed same-sex sexual relationships within the right to privacy protected by the due process clause and stressed that the state cannot impose majoritarian principles of morality on society.[15]

With the administration's refusal to defend DOMA, Boehner convened a Bipartisan Legal Advisory Group (BLAG) in the House. With three Republicans and two Democrats on it, it voted 3–2 to defend the law on appeal. In arguing for heightened scrutiny, the administration was asking the courts to extend *Romer* and *Lawrence* and declare that DOMA abridged rights guaranteed by the equal protection clause as well as the fundamental right to marry under the due process clause.

The appeals court affirmed Tauro's opinion in *Commonwealth of Massachusetts v. United States Department of Health and Human Services* (2012).[16] Declining to raise the level of scrutiny, the appeals court observed that the high court had established precedent for a more careful review of laws when the "protesting group was historically disadvantaged or unpopular" (10). Weaving states' rights and equal rights discourse, the unanimous three-judge panel announced that it would apply a "closer than usual review based in part on discrepant impact among married couples and in part on the importance of state interests in regulating marriage" (8).

In what would become familiar arguments, BLAG claimed that DOMA was intended to preserve traditional marriage, promote morality, and conserve government resources. The court questioned the logic of BLAG's contention that the law promoted stable families with children raised in two-parent heterosexual families because it does not preclude same-sex couples from adopting. Moreover, there was no evidence, it said, that denying benefits to same-sex couples strengthens the marital bonds of different-sex couples. It also dismissed Congress's justification that DOMA was intended to "preserve traditional notions of morality," emphasizing that *Lawrence* undermined the legislature's ability to enact laws reflecting the majority's beliefs about morality. Conceding that Congress might have reasonably believed that expanding the definition of marriage would lead to lower tax revenues and higher entitlement payments, it stressed that, even if true, the government cannot target a politically vulnerable group for this purpose. In the end, without formally raising the level of scrutiny, the First Circuit found that section 3 had no rational basis and declared it unconstitutional.

DOMA LITIGATION

Rapidly following the First Circuit's ruling, in *Windsor v. United States* (2012a), New York Federal District Court Judge Barbara Jones believed she was unable to apply a higher level of scrutiny to the challenged law but also rejected minimal scrutiny.[17] Instead, like the First Circuit, she opted for a more rigorous review because the law appeared to reflect a desire to harm a politically powerless group. In assessing the government's justifications for DOMA, she conceded that "promoting family values and responsible parenting and nurturing the foundational institution of marriage" may be legitimate, but she did not see how DOMA reasonably furthered those objectives (403–4). Her ruling ultimately bypassed the scrutiny issue entirely because she found that DOMA failed to satisfy even minimal scrutiny.

In *Pedersen v. Office of Personnel Management* (2013), departing from her New York colleague, Connecticut Federal District Court Judge Vanessa Bryant believed intermediate scrutiny was appropriate but decided not to apply it because she found DOMA unconstitutional "even under the most deferential level of judicial scrutiny" (333).

Differing in their approach to the scrutiny doctrine, these judges found DOMA unconstitutional because, even if its goals were legitimate, the law was not a reasonable method of achieving those goals. In its appeal of the lower court's ruling in *Windsor*, BLAG argued against raising the level of scrutiny, denying that sexual orientation is an immutable characteristic or that lesbians and gay men are an unpopular minority who are victims of discrimination. In a 2–1 decision, the Second Circuit panel disagreed. Characterizing gay men and lesbians as a "politically weakened minority" that has "historically endured persecution and discrimination," the appeals court adopted the higher level of scrutiny, becoming the first appellate court in the nation to do so (*Windsor v. United States* 2012b, 181–82).

Applying heightened scrutiny, the court appraised BLAG's claims that DOMA promotes the "unique federal interests" of maintaining a consistent federal definition of marriage, conserves public money, and "encourag[es] responsible procreation" (185). In what would become a familiar reaction to the defendants' arguments in marriage equality litigation, the appeals court noted that history and tradition are insufficient justifications to infringe on the rights of same-sex couples. The government may have an important interest in responsible procreation, but the court believed that DOMA did nothing to further it because it provided no incentives for different-sex couples to marry and procreate. The Second Circuit formally adopted heightened scrutiny review yet also applied minimal scrutiny in evaluating DOMA's constitutionality and concluded that it was not rationally related to the government's asserted interest in promoting procreation and child welfare.

In oral arguments before the high court on BLAG's appeal of the Second Circuit ruling in *Windsor*, same-sex marriage advocates again sought to persuade the Court to apply heightened scrutiny to DOMA and declare it unconstitutional. BLAG urged it to retain the minimal scrutiny standard and uphold the law because the ban on same-sex marriage was reasonably related to the government's interest in preserving the family and traditional marriage.

The US Supreme Court delivered its ruling in *United States v. Windsor* (2013) on June 26, the last day of the 2012–2013 term. Announcing the decision for himself and Ginsburg, Breyer, Sotomayor, and Kagan, Kennedy's opinion reflected a mix of federalist principles and equal rights discourse, primarily the latter. He initially framed the issue as a dispute over federalism's boundaries and emphasized the federal government's limited authority over domestic affairs. Citing the few exceptions in which the federal government was involved in marriage policy—chiefly in immigration and social security—Kennedy explained that these were narrowly focused laws with discrete purposes that advanced specific federal policy concerns. In contrast, he stressed, DOMA has a far broader impact, extending to more than one thousand federal statutes and regulations.[18] Moreover, he added, it is directed at individuals, such as Windsor, who had been assured of equal marital rights under state law.

After an extended discussion of marriage policy within the context of federal–state relations, the Court refrained from basing its ruling on federalism principles, saying that it was unnecessary to decide whether DOMA transgressed the constitutional boundaries between the state and federal governments. Instead, shifting to equal rights jurisprudence, Kennedy emphasized DOMA's far-reaching impact that negated the state's decision to accord same-sex couples a "dignity and status of immense import" (2692). Echoing *Lawrence*'s focus on individual autonomy for lesbians and gay men, Kennedy charged that, by creating a two-tiered marriage policy within the state, DOMA "demeans the couple, whose moral and sexual choices the Constitution protects" (*United States v. Windsor* 2013, 2694).

Without commenting on the lower courts' approach to scrutiny, the Court seemed to employ a more robust form of review than minimal scrutiny, delving into the intent behind the law to assess whether it is inspired by an "improper animus or purpose" (2693). Kennedy's approach, known as "rational basis with bite review" (Strasser 2012, 623) or "rigorous rational basis scrutiny" (McGowan 2012, 382), reflected the Court's methodology in similar cases. Without formally adopting a higher level of scrutiny, it examined laws more carefully than typical in minimal scrutiny review if it believed that they are enacted to harm targeted groups.

Kennedy compared DOMA to a provision of the federal Food Stamp Act that denied eligibility to selected groups. In striking that portion of the law in *Department of Agriculture v. Moreno* (1973, 534–35), the Court characterized it as motivated by a "bare congressional desire to harm a politically unpopular group" (*United States v. Windsor* 2013, 2693, quoting *Department of Agriculture v. Moreno* 1973, 534). Analogizing DOMA to Colorado's Amendment 2 struck in *Romer*, he depicted both as laws based on "discriminations of an unusual character [that] especially require careful consideration to determine whether they are obnoxious to the constitutional provision" (*United States v. Windsor* 2013, 2693, quoting *Romer v. Evans* 1996, 633).[19]

Assessing whether DOMA was motivated by an improper purpose, the Court concluded that interfering with the state's domain over marriage and denying same-sex couples the benefits of their lawful marital status was "strong evidence" that the law has the "purpose and effect" of denigrating same-sex couples by "impos[ing] a disadvantage, a separate status, and so a stigma upon all who enter into same-sex marriages made lawful by the unquestioned authority of the States" (*United States v. Windsor* 2013, 2693).

In dissent, Roberts argued that there was insufficient evidence showing that DOMA was motivated by hostility toward gay men and lesbians. Looking ahead to the marriage equality litigation that was sure to follow, he said that he hoped that the majority's commitment to federalism principles would "come into play on the other side of the board in future cases about the constitutionality of state marriage definitions" and that its "concerns for state diversity and sovereignty" would play a role in adjudicating state prohibitions on same-sex marriage (2697).

Scalia's biting dissent, laying the groundwork for future challenges to state marriage restrictions, described the majority's opinion as "rootless" and "shifting" (2705), characterizing it as "legalistic argle-bargle" (2709). In addition to his critique that the Court wrongly usurped legislative authority, he attacked the majority for abandoning federalism principles and adopting equal rights jurisprudence without explanation. Moreover, he said, after doing so, it inconsistently continued to refer to the "usual tradition of recognizing and accepting state definitions of marriage" (2705). The only justification for this, he said, was that the Court was pretending "that today's prohibition of laws excluding same-sex marriage is confined to the Federal Government, leaving the second, state-law shoe to be dropped later" (2705).

Scalia also condemned the opinion for departing from the longstanding practice in constitutional rights adjudication of deciding the crucial matter of scrutiny, "the issue," he declared, "that divided the parties and the courts below" (2706). Perhaps even worse, he charged that the majority used minimal scrutiny language, but it did "not *apply* anything that resembles that deferential framework" (2706, emphasis in the original).

He accused his colleagues of ignoring valid reasons for DOMA's passage, pointing out that Congress was merely trying to stabilize conditions so that state experiments with marriage policies did not lead to an uneven operation of federal law. Instead, he said that the majority focused on unfounded accusations against DOMA supporters, charging them with acting "with malice," intending to "disparage and to injure same-sex couples," "demean" them, and "humiliate" their children (2708).

Scalia ended by prophesizing that, despite Kennedy's assurance that the opinion was confined to legally married couples, the ruling would inevitably lead to successful challenges against state bans on same-sex marriage in the state and federal courts. He demonstrated this point by substituting "state law" for "DOMA" in the following passages:

> ~~DOMA's~~ *This state law's* principal effect is to identify a subset of ~~state-sanctioned marriages~~ *constitutionally protected sexual relation-*

> *ships* . . . and make them unequal. The principal purpose is to impose inequality, not for other reasons like governmental efficiency. Responsibilities, as well as rights, enhance the dignity and integrity of the person. And ~~DOMA~~ *this state law* contrives to deprive some couples ~~married under the laws of their State~~ enjoying *constitutionally protected sexual relationships*, but not other couples, of both rights and responsibilities.
>
> ~~[DOMA]~~ *This state law* tells those couples, and all the world, that their otherwise valid ~~marriages~~ *relationships* are unworthy of ~~federal~~ *state* recognition. This places same-sex couples in an unstable position of being in a second-tier ~~marriage~~ *relationship*. The differentiation demeans the couple, whose moral and sexual choices the Constitution protects.
>
> And it humiliates ~~tens of~~ thousands of children now being raised by same-sex couples. The law in question makes it even more difficult for the children to understand the integrity and closeness of their own family and its concord with other families in their community and in their daily lives (2710, emphasis in the original).

Scalia's words had a familiar ring. Ten years earlier, he predicted that *Lawrence* would be the basis for successful claims against restrictions on same-sex marriage. Undoubtedly, to his displeasure, the lower courts would frequently cite his dissents in *Lawrence* and *Windsor* for his prophesies about the successful outcomes in the ensuing marriage equality litigation.

Alito's dissent emphasized the need for judicial restraint when a court uses minimal scrutiny review; he argued against the Court's intrusion into a policy that should be decided by the people and their elected representatives. Reiterating Roberts's support for state control over marriage policy, he declared that, "to the extent that the Court takes the position that the question of same-sex marriage should be resolved primarily at the state level, I wholeheartedly agree [and] I hope that the Court will ultimately permit the people of each State to decide this question for themselves" (2720).

Despite the favorable outcome for the plaintiff, the majority opinion sent mixed signals about the Court's approach to marriage equality. By initially framing the issue as a conflict over federalism and emphasizing that states retained virtually unlimited control over marriage policy inside their borders, the Court appeared to doom future challenges to state laws against same-sex marriage. Advantageous for the litigants in this case, the state sovereignty approach might harm future plaintiffs; in stressing the state's preeminent authority over marriage policy, the majority laid the groundwork for states to assert their power to prohibit same-sex marriage.

THE RIGHT TO MARRY

Kennedy limited *Windsor* only to couples in "lawful [same-sex] marriages" (2695). One of the first Supreme Court cases dealing with marriage, *Loving v. Virginia* (1967), the Court declared that the antimiscegenation 1924 Racial Integrity Act infringed on the constitutional right to marry.[20] Speaking for a unanimous Court in *Loving*, Chief Justice Earl Warren stated that the law's only purpose was "invidious racial discrimination" (11). Applying strict scrutiny to it because it was a racial classification, the Court declared that it violated the Lovings' right under the Fourteenth Amendment's equal protection clause by discriminating against them on the basis of race.

The heart of the ruling was the Court's vehement attack on the racist nature of the Virginia law. Crucially important to litigants in future marriage cases was its linkage of the two Fourteenth Amendment clauses (see Wardle 1998). By depriving the Lovings of equal protection with its discriminatory racial classification, the state also deprived them of the liberty inherent in the amendment's due process clause. The Court explained that denying the Lovings a "fundamental freedom on so unsupportable a basis as the racial classifications embodied in these statutes, classifications so directly subversive of the principle of equality at the heart of the Fourteenth Amendment, is surely to deprive all the State's citizens of liberty without due process of law" (12).

Solidly placing the right to marry within the due process clause, Warren noted, "[T]he freedom to marry has long been recognized as one of the vital personal rights essential to the orderly pursuit of happiness by free men. Marriage is one of the 'basic civil rights of man' fundamental to our very existence and survival" (12, quoting *Skinner v. Oklahoma* 1942, 541–42).

For decades to follow, *Loving* was viewed as the "most important, most coherent, clearest, most frequently cited case explaining the constitutional right to marry" (Wardle 1998, 347). The Court looked to it in *Zablocki v. Redhail* (1978) in striking a Wisconsin law requiring residents with an obligation of child support for noncustodial children to obtain a court order before marrying. In doing so, it formally declared the right to marry as a fundamental right. Almost a decade later, the Court reaffirmed the importance of marriage in *Safley v. Turner* (1987), a case challenging a Missouri policy that prevented inmates from marrying without permission from the prison superintendent—permission that was rarely granted. Citing *Zablocki*, the Court held that the regulation infringes on the constitutional right of prisoners to marry. Predating the arguments of same-sex marriage proponents, it portrayed marriages as "expressions of emotional support and public commitment" (*Safley v. Turner* 1987, 95).

Despite its strong support for the right to marry in *Loving* and its continued reliance on the principles it articulated there, the Court has never defined the scope of the right. Ironically, after *Windsor*, each side of the same-sex marriage litigation argued that, because the Court did not specify whether the right to marry a partner of the same sex was subsumed within the fundamental right to marry, *Loving* supported its position (see Koppelman 1996). Because *Windsor* refused to declare that same-sex marriage is a constitutionally protected fundamental right lying within the parameters of the right to marry, the high court seemed to imply that states could argue that the fundamental right to marry only pertains to different-sex couples and insist that the lower courts apply minimal scrutiny to the challenged laws rather than the strict scrutiny used when fundamental rights are at stake.

The same-sex marriage advocates contended that the Court did not define the right to marry as narrowly as the states proclaimed. They denied that they were asking the courts to create a new fundamental right, emphasizing that the high court had not created a new right of interracial marriage in *Loving*. Rather it had simply incorporated the Lovings' claim into an already-existing right to marry. They insisted that they merely wished to include same-sex marriage within the well-accepted fundamental right of individuals "to select the partners of their choosing" (*De Leon v. Perry* 2014, 58).

Well before the marriage equality litigation, the Supreme Court had instructed lower courts on the proper way of determining whether an asserted due process right is fundamental. In *Washington v. Glucksberg* (1997), it reviewed a challenge to a Washington State statute that made it a felony to "promote a suicide attempt." The plaintiffs argued that the law infringed on the "liberty interest" of the Fourteenth Amendment's due process clause and that assisted suicide was comparable to other rights declared fundamental by the Court, requiring the state to have a compelling reason to invade it.

In response, the Court reviewed the rights included in the liberty guarantees of the Fourteenth Amendment: the right to marry, the right to raise and educate one's children, the right to marital privacy, the right to use contraception, and the right to terminate a pregnancy. The majority pointed out that the principle of judicial restraint hinders courts from readily accepting new rights as fundamental because it allows judges to impose their own values on the policy-making process. *Glucksberg* established a two-part test to determine when a right not specified in the Constitution should be viewed as fundamental. First, the Court declared that the right at issue must be "rooted in the traditions and conscience of our people" and "implicit in the concept of ordered liberty" so that "neither liberty nor justice would exist if they were sacrificed"; second, there must be a "careful description" of the claimed liberty interest at stake (721).

In addition to the uncertainty about whether the right to same-sex marriage satisfied the *Glucksberg* standard for a fundamental right under the due process clause, *Windsor* also failed to address the scrutiny doctrine, the issue Scalia declared was the "central question in the litigation" and about which both sides submitted voluminous amicus curiae briefs (*United States v. Windsor* 2013, 2706).

Although Kennedy pointedly included gay and lesbian couples within the class of persons the "state sought to protect," he did not characterize them as vulnerable minorities in need of judicial protection from hostile policy-makers—the chief indicia of heightened scrutiny. In cases following *Windsor* therefore, the lower courts could apply minimal scrutiny to state marriage policies and uphold them if they believe them reasonable.

Moreover, as in *Romer*, the Court demonstrated its willingness to override majoritarian policies that stemmed from a motivation to harm.

Delving into DOMA's legislative history, it cited "at least two dozen pejorative terms describing the Act and the intents, purposes, and motives of the members of Congress" (Wardle 2014, 419). But although Congress's intent in enacting DOMA was readily apparent, the Court's approach could prompt lower courts to require plaintiffs to present evidence that state marriage bans were prompted by hostility toward gay men and lesbians.

MARRIAGE EQUALITY IN THE DISTRICT COURTS

Because *Windsor* left a number of questions unanswered, some scholars predicted that it would have only a "limited impact . . . due in part to the doctrinal obscurity of the opinion" and that, "because Justice Kennedy avoided a more sweeping and clearer doctrinal ruling, the opinion will not control in subsequent cases involving the constitutionality of marriage inequality laws" (Myers 2014, 331). Even supporters of marriage equality criticized *Windsor* for its "thinly reasoned analysis," with "ambiguous levels of scrutiny and lack of doctrinal rigor" (Sanders 2014, 12–13).

Despite the dire predictions, *Windsor* sparked a flood of litigation as same-sex marriage advocates responded to it by challenging state restrictions on the right to marry all over the nation but especially in the southern states, where same-sex marriage bans had remained in place. By November 2013, twenty-nine lawsuits were filed in twenty-three states (Pierceson 2014, 247).

As a preliminary matter, the lower courts had to decide whether they were constrained by *Baker v. Nelson* (1972), in which the high court summarily dismissed an appeal of a 1971 Minnesota Supreme Court decision "for want of a substantial federal question."[21] Most courts rejected the states' arguments that *Baker* required them to dismiss Fifth and Fourteenth Amendment challenges to marriage restrictions. Citing *Romer*, *Lawrence*, and *Windsor*, they held that the high court would now take a different view of same-sex marriage and that *Baker* was no longer binding on the lower courts.[22]

Because *Windsor* had left the matter open, the courts were unclear about the appropriate level of scrutiny to use in ruling on state bans on same-sex marriage. Unlike the *Windsor* majority, most lower courts addressed the question of scrutiny at great length, but given the lack of direction from the high court, they often reached different conclusions. For the most part, the courts acknowledged *Windsor*'s departure from traditional minimal scrutiny analysis and delved more deeply into the states' justifications for the laws, engaging in a more searching appraisal than is common in minimal scrutiny review. Some courts explicitly raised the level of scrutiny, citing longstanding discrimination against gay men and lesbians and their political powerlessness, but most felt constrained to apply minimal scrutiny. In the end, whatever the level of scrutiny the courts applied, virtually all refuted the rationality of the states' exclusionary policies.[23]

Not surprisingly, given the key role that legislative intent played in *Romer* and *Windsor*, most plaintiffs maintained that the policies stemmed from hostility toward them. However, the courts generally found insufficient evidence to support their claim. The states offered both procedural and substantive grounds for rejecting marriage equality: First, they claimed that their autonomy over marriage policy as well as judicial restraint obliged the courts to defer to state policy-makers; second, they argued that their interests in the family and welfare of children superseded the plaintiffs' desire to marry.

An Ohio ruling, *Obergefell v. Kasich* (2013), presented the first opportunity to assess *Windsor*'s impact on the lower courts. Ohio resident James Obergefell challenged Ohio's nonrecognition policy, seeking to have his Maryland marriage recognized by Ohio before his partner's imminent death so that his name would appear on the death certificate as the surviving spouse. Ohio Federal District Court Judge Timothy Black recognized that *Windsor* was distinguishable but characterized the case as another "shoe" dropping, just as Scalia predicted. Black concluded that sexual orientation met the criteria for heightened-scrutiny review, but without deciding whether the policy met the heightened standard, he found that the state law failed even minimal scrutiny, for it had no legitimate purpose in creating the two classes of legally married couples merely distinguished by their sexual orientation. Like DOMA, he believed the purpose of the law was to denigrate same-sex couples.

Several months later, in *Obergefell v. Wymyslo* (2013), Black granted Obergefell's motion for a permanent injunction, acknowledging that neither the Supreme Court nor the Sixth Circuit recognized a fundamental right to marry a same-sex partner. Nevertheless, he found that same-sex couples have a "significant liberty interest" in the recognition of their existing marriages. Conceding that the high court had not declared this right fundamental, he noted that it applies heightened scrutiny to laws affecting marriage and families. In his view, the state's justifications for the policy, including its argument that states have dominant authority over marriage policy, failed to satisfy this heightened standard of review.

Turning to the equal protection claim, Black concluded that sexual orientation satisfies the test for heightened scrutiny, and because the Sixth Circuit had not definitively ruled on the matter, he believed it appropriate to apply it to Ohio's nonrecognition policy. Without determining whether it passed heightened scrutiny, he held that it would not satisfy minimal scrutiny because, even under the most deferential form of review, courts must ensure that a challenged law is not merely a subterfuge for intentional discrimination against a vulnerable group.

Comparing the nonrecognition policy to DOMA, Black found that the state's "sweeping marriage bans likewise exclude same-sex couples and their children system-wide from the protections and benefits afforded married couples and their families under the law" (993n17). Just as DOMA diverged from the norm by interfering with the state's definition of marriage, the Ohio policy deviated from the customary practice of accepting valid out-of-state marriages, even if they did not conform to Ohio law. By singling out same-sex couples and refusing to recognize their marriages, Black concluded that Ohio had engaged in an "unusual discrimination" that merited more careful scrutiny.

Black weighed the state's familiar justifications—preserving traditional marriage, promoting the stability of the family, and fostering children's welfare by helping to ensure that they grow up with different-sex parents—and found them all lacking. Taking issue with the last especially, he pointedly stated that, even if the assumption that children are better off with a mother and a father is correct, there is no connection between this objective and the nonrecognition policy because the law does not prevent gay men and lesbians from having or adopting children. Its real effect, he insisted, is to deprive children of the "protection and stability of having parents who are legally married" (995).

Because he found that the nonrecognition policy was not rationally related to the state's purported goal, he believed it unnecessary to determine whether it stemmed from a discriminatory purpose. With the state unable to satisfy even rational basis review, Black's inclination to apply a higher level of scrutiny was no longer pertinent to the outcome of the case. His final order was narrow, limited to requiring the state to "recognize valid out-of-state marriages between same-sex couples on Ohio death certificates" (973).[24]

He ended by speculating about the constitutionality of the state's prohibition on same-sex marriage, noting that he did not have to address this question, but the "logical conclusion to be drawn from the evidence, arguments, and law presented here is that Ohio's violation of the constitutional rights of its gay citizens extends beyond the bounds of this lawsuit" (995n22).

Shortly after Black issued his decision, Kentucky District Court Judge John Heyburn II ruled on the Kentucky nonrecognition policy in *Bourke v. Beshear* (2014). He criticized the high court's failure to provide the lower courts with the proper approach to scrutiny, saying that its application of scrutiny in *Windsor* left the lower courts "without a clear answer" (558). Paradoxically, he echoed Scalia's criticism of the majority opinion, noting that "some of Justice Kennedy's language corresponded to rational basis review, [but] . . . the scrutiny that the Court actually applied does not so much resemble it" (548).

Heyburn indicated that he was disposed to apply a higher form of scrutiny but refrained from doing so because neither the Sixth Circuit nor the Supreme Court had paved the way for imposing a higher level of scrutiny on laws based on sexual orientation nor for viewing the right to marry a partner of the same sex as fundamental. Frequently evoking *Windsor*, Heyburn called Kennedy's skepticism about the legitimacy of laws barring recognition of same-sex marriage "instructive." Like DOMA, he found that the Kentucky policy had the purpose and effect of discriminating against same-sex couples. Whether intentional or not, it debased them and their children by denying them rights other families easily acquired. Whatever the motivation, he said, even under minimal scrutiny, a policy must be rationally related to a legitimate goal. Preserving the institution of marriage in its current form might be legitimate, he said, but it did not justify infringing on the plaintiffs' constitutional rights; moreover, he stressed, tradition is an insufficient justification for subverting individual liberties. Like Black, Heyburn declared that the broader question of the state's ban on same-sex marriage was not before him. He added, "[T]here is no doubt that *Windsor* and this

Court's analysis suggest a possible result to that question" (*Bourke v. Beshear* 2014, 555).

In another Kentucky action, two couples sought to intervene in *Bourke*, attacking Kentucky's prohibition against same-sex marriage. After the *Bourke* order became final, Heyburn granted them permission to intervene but denied their motion for a preliminary injunction, saying that the issues in their case were separable from Bourke's and that they had to pursue their own legal remedy (*Love v. Beshear* 2014).

Heyburn was unwilling to declare same-sex marriage a fundamental right but held that the characteristics of the class of persons affected by the policy fell within the parameters of heightened scrutiny. This time the state offered a different justification, arguing that "traditional marriages contribute to a stable birth rate which, in turn, ensures the state's long-term economic stability" (548). Calling this a "disingenuous twist" to the standard claim, Heyburn derisively stated, "[T]hese arguments are not those of serious people" (548). He ultimately concluded that the level of scrutiny was not germane, as there was no conceivably reasonable relationship between the policy and the state's purported goal. Thus, he held that it failed even under the deferential standard; on July 1, 2014, recapping *Bourke*, Heyburn declared Kentucky's marriage ban unconstitutional.

In mid-March, Tennessee District Court Judge Aleta Trauger announced her decision in *Tanco v. Haslam* (2014), a case brought by three married couples asking the state to recognize their out-of-state marriages. Trauger granted their motion for a preliminary injunction, devoting most of her opinion to assessing the likelihood that they would prevail in a final ruling on the merits. She discussed the expansiveness of the post-*Windsor* rulings, in which courts struck nonrecognition laws on due process or equal protection grounds or both, stating, "[I]n light of this rising tide of persuasive post-*Windsor* federal case law, it is no leap to conclude that the plaintiffs here are likely to succeed in their challenge to Tennessee's Anti-Recognition Laws" (768).

Trauger declared that marriage equality was on the nation's horizon, for "all signs indicate that the plaintiffs' marriages will be placed on an equal footing with those of heterosexual couples and that proscriptions against same-sex marriage will soon become a footnote in the annals of American history" (768).[25] She briefly dismissed the state's contention that the policy furthers its interest in responsible procreation and is consistent with *Windsor*'s commitment to federalism, noting that courts had held such policies unconstitutional—even under a deferential rational basis standard. Because she believed that the plaintiffs would prevail on their equal protection claim, she saw no need to address the matter of the appropriate level of scrutiny nor the due process arguments.

The cases challenging state nonrecognition policies, although undoubtedly important to the plaintiffs, were not the chief focus of attention in the nation's ongoing battle over marriage equality. The first opportunity for a court to rule on an overall marriage ban arose in Utah when a group of same-sex couples charged that the state violated their rights to due process and equal protection (*Kitchen v. Herbert* 2013a).

Utah Federal District Court Judge Robert Shelby began by noting that both sides relied on *Windsor* for support. Associating itself with the arguments in the Roberts and Alito dissents, the state contended that *Windsor* underscored the fact that marriage policy is within the state's regulatory domain. Therefore, it maintained, if federalism principles prevent DOMA from overriding a state's decision to allow same-sex marriages, they also preclude the federal government from interfering in a state's decision to ban same-sex marriage.

The plaintiffs responded that the Court did not decide *Windsor* on federalism principles but instead grounded it on the theory of individual liberty protected by the Fifth Amendment. They asserted that the majority had rejected DOMA because it demeaned a way of life protected by the Constitution and treated same-sex couples as second-class citizens. Turning the state's argument on its side, they insisted that, if the federal government cannot distinguish among couples because of their sexual orientation, then neither can the state.

Shelby conceded that both sides presented compelling arguments, noting that the high court was not obliged to resolve the conflict between the two in *Windsor* because DOMA had infringed on both individual liberties and states' rights. When the Court had to reconcile these opposing interests, as in *Loving*, it favored individual rights over state authority and struck the Virginia antimiscegenation law. Shelby acknowledged the federalism concerns at stake but emphasized that *Windsor* had cited *Loving* to show that the state's authority over domestic affairs may be constrained by constitutional principles. The state cannot simply assert federalism principles to justify infringements on individual rights. He considered it irrelevant that the *Windsor* plaintiffs had asked the high court to defer to the state marriage policy and these plaintiffs asked the court to annul one.

Extrapolating from the majority opinion in *Windsor*, Shelby was the first federal court judge to declare that the longstanding fundamental right to marry encompassed same-sex marriage and that the couples were not seeking to establish a new right but merely to prevent the state from depriving them of an existing one. Applying strict scrutiny, he held that, with no compelling—or even rational—reason for the state's policy, it violated the plaintiffs' rights of due process.

Shelby believed that *Windsor* left the issue of scrutiny open but considered himself bound by *Price-Cornelison v. Brooks* (2008), a Tenth Circuit decision that applied minimal scrutiny to a classification based on sexual orientation. Moreover, despite the heightened form of minimal scrutiny suggested in *Romer* and *Windsor*, he decided not to apply that either because the high court had not sufficiently defined the parameters of the type of "unusual discrimination" that would trigger that higher level of review (*Kitchen v. Herbert* 2013a, 1208).

The judge conceded that the principle of judicial restraint placed him in an awkward position because two-thirds of Utah voters had supported the prohibition against same-sex marriage in a 2004 constitutional amendment that restricted marriage to a man and a woman. He cautioned that courts may negate the results of the democratic process only under "exceptional circumstances" (1188).

Recognizing his obligation to defer to the legislature and uphold a challenged law under minimal scrutiny review, Shelby insisted that a court must still inquire into the relationship between the law and the state's goal to determine its reasonableness. In his view, the ban on same-sex marriage did not reasonably relate to the state's objectives of furthering procreation, child-rearing, and preserving traditional marriage. On the contrary, like Kennedy, he found that the restriction on same-sex marriage harmed and humiliated the thousands of children living with same-sex parents and declared it unconstitutional.

Paradoxically, in a later proceeding, Shelby approvingly referred to Scalia's *Windsor* dissent. Recognizing it as a minority view, he characterized its assessment of the majority opinion and its effect on future cases as "perceptive and compelling" and said that he viewed it "not as binding precedent, but as persuasive authority" (*Kitchen v. Herbert* 2013b, at 6).

Shelby refused to stay his ruling, and when the Tenth Circuit also declined to do so, the state turned to the Supreme Court. On January 6, 2014, without explanation, the high court stayed the order, pending a decision by the Tenth Circuit (*Herbert v. Kitchen* 2014). The Court did not comment on the validity of the numerous Utah same-sex marriages that occurred during the seventeen days Shelby's order was in effect.

Events in Utah became chaotic, with couples uncertain about the legality of their marriages and receiving mixed signals from state officials. Governor Gary Herbert announced that the state government would not recognize the marriages as valid but that it would not revoke any benefits they had gained (such as spousal health benefits). In an odd turn of events, the state mailed marriage certificates to the newly married couples.

The federal government also weighed in, with Holder announcing that, despite Utah's refusal to recognize their marriages, the couples were eligible for federal benefits. He stated that he believed it unfair for these families to "endure uncertainty regarding their status as the litigation unfolds" (US Department of Justice 2014b).

While Utah's appeal awaited a decision by the Tenth Circuit, on January 14, 2014, Oklahoma Federal District Court Judge Terence Kern announced his opinion in *Bishop v. United States* (2014), a case challenging state and federal marriage policies. The case had lingered in the courts for more than a decade, with multiple rulings prior to Kern's. After disposing of the procedural arguments, Kern addressed the unconstitutionality of the Oklahoma policy, recognizing that both sides could credibly cite *Windsor* for support.

In an effort to reconcile these positions, he reduced *Windsor* to two legal principles: First, a law restricting same-sex marriage does not upset the federal–state balance to such an extent that it demonstrates that the state has an improper purpose; second, courts must inquire into any marriage policy, whether state or federal, to ensure that the goal of preserving a traditional understanding of marriage is not a pretext for discrimination.

Kern agreed with Shelby that the Tenth Circuit had not authorized district courts to apply heightened scrutiny to laws based on sexual orientation. In applying minimal scrutiny, he evaluated the state's oft-cited justifications for banning same-sex marriage: morality, child-rearing, procreation, and conserving traditional marriage. Even if these interests were legitimate, he held, the marriage policy was not rationally related to them and was instead an "arbitrary and irrational exclusion of just one class of Oklahoma citizens from a governmental benefit" (*Bishop v. United States* 2014, 1296).

The judge ended by saying that he was persuaded that, while not formally altering its stance about classifications based on sexual orientations, the Supreme Court had undergone a "rhetorical shift" since 1996. Conceding that the marriage restrictions reflected popular opinion, he believed that this did not outweigh the Constitution's command to protect equal rights. He enjoined the state from carrying out its ban on same-sex marriage but also granted a stay that prevented Oklahoma couples from marrying while the state's appeal was before the Tenth Circuit.

With the Utah and the Oklahoma district court opinions on appeal in the Tenth Circuit, the Ninth Circuit followed the Second Circuit in adopting heightened scrutiny for claims of discrimination based on sexual orientation. In *Smithkline Beecham v. Abbott Laboratories* (2014), the court upheld a challenge to the California jury selection process that allowed a potential juror to be dismissed because of his sexual orientation. A unanimous Ninth Circuit opinion concluded that, despite its adherence to minimal scrutiny, "in its words and its deed, *Windsor* established a level of scrutiny for classifications based on sexual orientation that is unquestionably higher than rational basis review" (*Smithkline Beecham v. Abbott Laboratories* 2014, 481).

Speaking for himself and Judges Mary Schroeder and Marsha Berzon, Reinhardt pointed to Kennedy's inquiry into DOMA's purpose and effect as well as the majority's refusal to defer to Congress; he held that *Windsor* authorized lower courts to apply heightened scrutiny to claims of discrimination based on sexual orientation.

The Ninth Circuit's endorsement of heightened scrutiny in equal protection cases was perhaps not surprising, given its stance in a 2008 ruling in a challenge to the Air Force's Don't Ask, Don't Tell policy. In *Witt v. Department of the Air Force* (2008), the appeals court held that, despite Kennedy's use of traditional minimal scrutiny language in *Lawrence*, the high court had abandoned minimal scrutiny in striking the Texas antisodomy law as a violation of the due process clause (Bartrum

2014; Shay 2014). Because *Lawrence* had not formally adopted it, the Ninth Circuit hesitated to apply strict scrutiny in *Witt*, suggesting, however, that the law warranted some form of heightened scrutiny.

Smithkline had a far-reaching impact on same-sex marriage within the circuit. Among other things, it precipitated a change in Nevada's position on its marriage restrictions. After a lower court ruling in the state's favor in *Sevcik v. Sandoval* (2012), Attorney General Catherine Cortez Masto submitted a brief, asking the appeals court to affirm it. On February 10, 2014, she announced (with Governor Brian Sandoval's approval) that the state was withdrawing its brief. She pointed to the circuit's new position on heightened scrutiny in equal protection cases for classifications based on sexual orientation and said, "[A]fter thoughtful review and analysis, the state has determined that its arguments grounded upon equal protection and due process are no longer sustainable" (*Las Vegas World News*, February 10, 2014).

Another "shoe" fell in a Virginia federal courthouse on February 13, 2014, when Virginia Federal District Court Judge Arenda Wright Allen handed down her opinion in *Bostic v. Rainey* (2014). She signaled the likely outcome of her ruling by beginning with a lengthy quote from Mildred Loving's 2007 address commemorating the fortieth anniversary of the high court's opinion striking Virginia's ban on interracial marriage.

The plaintiffs argued that Virginia's restrictions on same-sex marriage violated their fundamental right to marriage under the due process clause. Allen equated the right to same-sex marriage with the right to interracial marriage, affirmed by the Supreme Court in *Loving*. She agreed with the plaintiffs that same-sex marriage was an integral part of the fundamental right to marry, a right enjoyed by Virginia citizens. Because it was a fundamental right, she applied strict scrutiny to the Virginia policy. Frequently citing *Loving* and *Windsor*, Allen rejected the state's arguments that its interests in protecting traditional marriage, responsible child-rearing, and federalism were compelling and outweighed the plaintiffs' right to marry. Like Shelby, she also pointed to Scalia's prediction on the inevitability of courts declaring state restrictions on same-sex marriage unconstitutional. Because the policy failed minimal scrutiny, she saw no need to address plaintiffs' arguments for using heightened scrutiny but characterized them as compelling, adding in a footnote that she "would be inclined to so find" (*Bostic v. Rainey*, 2014, 482n16). Finally, pointing to recent policies aimed at gay men and lesbians, Allen believed that there were "reasonable grounds to suspect" that animus was a motivating factor in the state's ban on same-sex marriage.

She ended by quoting from a letter by Abraham Lincoln: "It can not have failed to strike you that these men ask for just . . . the same thing—fairness, and fairness only. This, so far as in my power, they, and all others, shall have." She added in her own voice, "[T]he men and women, and the children too, whose voices join in noble harmony with Plaintiffs today, also ask for fairness, and fairness only. This, so far as it is in this Court's power, they and all others shall have" (484).

In a sudden shift in the state's legal posture, a week before the argument in Allen's courtroom, Mark Herring, the state attorney general, followed the Obama administration's approach and refused to defend the legal challenges to DOMA. He announced that he disagreed with the state's legal position on same-sex marriage and would not represent it in court. In explaining his decision at a news conference, Herring attributed it to his refusal to contribute to Virginia's long history of taking the wrong side in legal battles, such as interracial marriage, school integration, and women's admission into military academies (*Richmond Times Dispatch*, January 23, 2014).

Not the first attorney general to take this step, Herring explained why Virginia's marriage ban was unconstitutional. He noted that Kennedy had relied on federalism and equal rights in *Windsor* but that these rationales led to inconsistent results in the Virginia case, and the court must choose between them. Herring believed equality trumped federalism for three reasons: First, the high court did not base *Windsor* on federalism; second, as *Loving* demonstrated, it has overridden federalism principles in the past, relying on equal rights rationales; and third, even though the majority had not explicitly ruled on it, the equal rights rationale had controlled in *Windsor*.

Shortly thereafter, in a speech to the National Association of Attorneys General on February 25, 2014, Holder advised state attorneys general that they were not obligated to defend state laws they believed unconstitutional and compared the ban on same-sex marriage to the "separate but equal" school segregation laws of the 1950s (*New York Times*, February 25, 2014).

The next "shoe" to fall was in Texas, when Texas Federal District Court Judge Orlando Garcia announced his ruling in *De Leon v. Perry* (2014). The plaintiffs challenged the Texas marriage policy, stemming from a 2005 constitutional amendment, for depriving them of their right to marry. Closely adhering to the prior federal court rulings, Garcia said that he found the plaintiffs' arguments for heightened scrutiny "compelling," but that it was unnecessary to apply it because the state marriage policy failed even under minimal scrutiny. In his equal protection analysis, Garcia found that the state's asserted goals of promoting responsible procreation and child-rearing were not rationally related to its same-sex marriage policy. He added that no court had found that a same-sex marriage ban was rationally related to any of the state's objectives.

Addressing the due process challenge, Garcia pondered the uncertainties of the Supreme Court's approach to fundamental rights. The state had argued that the plaintiffs were asking the court to create a new fundamental right, but he countered this by pointing to *Loving* and emphasizing that the high court had not created a right of interracial marriage in *Loving* but had subsumed the Lovings' claim into the already-existing right to marry. Similarly, the plaintiffs before him merely wished to include same-sex marriage within the well-accepted fundamental right of individuals "to select the partners of their choosing" (*De Leon v. Perry* 2014, 659).

Another case arose in Michigan, when two same-sex couples challenged the 2004 state constitutional amendment prohibiting same-sex marriage (*DeBoer v. Snyder* 2014a). They originally had filed suit in 2012, contending that the state adoption law preventing second-parent adoptions violated their right to equal protection. Michigan Federal District Court Judge Bernard Friedman ruled that the plaintiffs lacked standing to challenge the law because their injury stemmed from the state's marriage policy, not its adoption law. He permitted them to amend their complaint (indeed, he even suggested it to them) and attempt to prove their challenge to the marriage law at trial. The amended complaint charged that the state's marriage policy violated their right to due process and equal protection.

Friedman delayed his ruling on the state's motion to dismiss until the Supreme Court decided *Windsor* and, in the meantime, set a date for trial. He asked the parties to address the narrow question of whether the state marriage prohibition "proscribes conduct in a manner that is rationally related to the achievement of a legitimate governmental purpose"; in other words, whether the marriage policy satisfies minimal scrutiny (*DeBoer v. Snyder* 2014a, 769). He noted that other circuits had adopted heightened scrutiny when reviewing similar marriage policies but conceded that, because the Sixth Circuit had not, he was compelled to use minimal scrutiny.

The state argued that its exclusive domain over marriage gave it the authority to determine that banning same-sex marriage produced the optimum environment for raising children, furthered its interest in upholding tradition and morality, and avoided the negative consequences of redefining marriage. At trial (the only same-sex marriage case in the nation to go to trial), he heard testimony from social scientists, legal experts, and historians who testified about differences in the quality of parenting by both sets of parents and whether children living with their biological different-sex married parents are psychologically healthier.

Friedman found that the evidence presented by the plaintiffs' witnesses was "highly credible," in contrast to the testimony of the state's witnesses, which he held was "entirely unbelievable and not worthy of serious consideration." He characterized these witnesses as ideologically driven by a "fringe viewpoint that is rejected by the vast majority of their colleagues across a [wide] variety of social science fields" (766). In the end, he ruled that the state had not presented sufficient evidence to show that children living in households headed by same-sex parents were worse off than those in families with different-sex parents.

Armed with these facts, the judge considered whether the Michigan policy violated the plaintiffs' constitutional rights. Recognizing that other federal courts adopted heightened scrutiny for classifications based on sexual orientation, he acknowledged that the Sixth Circuit had not. In the end, he believed it unnecessary to depart from circuit precedent because the marriage policy was unable to satisfy even minimal scrutiny. He found that the marriage policy did not logically relate to any of the state's asserted objectives; as the evidence at trial showed, children fared just as well in households headed by same-sex couples. Indeed, he said, echoing Kennedy, the state policy had the opposite effect of undermining the ability of same-sex parents to raise their children in a stable environment.

In addressing the state's federalism argument, Friedman admitted that *Windsor* had affirmed the state's supremacy over marriage policy but that the Court had relied on *Loving* to underscore that the Constitution constrains state power. As in *Loving*, he ruled that the state cannot exercise its authority over marriage at the expense of protected family relationships, and because it furthers no legitimate state interest, the policy violates equal protection. In light of this finding, Friedman avoided having to decide whether the marriage code infringed on a fundamental due process right, simply noting that the high court had long held that the right to marry is fundamental. Because the electorate approved the policy, Friedman said that he was unable to discern whether it was motivated by animus toward same-sex couples; he added that, in any event, voter approval of a policy does not insulate it from constitutional review. On the contrary, he said, "[T]he very purpose of a Bill of Rights was to withdraw certain subjects from the vicissitudes of political controversy, to place them beyond the reach of majorities and officials and to establish them as legal principles to be applied by the courts." He added that "fundamental rights may not be submitted to vote; they depend on the outcome of no elections" (*DeBoer v. Snyder* 2014a, 774–75, quoting *West Virginia Board of Education v. Barnette* 1943, 638).

The Sixth Circuit stayed Friedman's ruling, but as in Utah, sufficient time had elapsed between the trial court ruling and the issuance of the stay. The delay allowed hundreds of couples to marry, leading to uncertainty about the validity of their marriages. Michigan Governor Rick Snyder declared that the state would not recognize their marriages, but a few days later, Holder again announced that these "families will be eligible for all relevant federal benefits on the same terms as other same-sex marriages" (US Department of Justice 2014a).

Some months later, on June 6, 2014, Wisconsin Federal District Court Judge Barbara Crabb announced her decision in *Wolf v. Walker* (2014) on Wisconsin's ban on same-sex marriage. In her view, the case did not revolve around principles of religious beliefs, morality, or even child welfare but only about "liberty and equality, the two cornerstones of the rights protected by the United States Constitution"; she believed her role was to ensure that the government did "not intrude without adequate justification on certain fundamental decisions made by individuals" (987). Crabb acknowledged that federalism principles allow states to experiment with social policy-making but maintained that they do not outweigh a court's mandate to ensure that its policies are consistent with constitutional rights, adding that the courts must fulfill this responsibility even when the policies reflect the will of the majority.

The judge agreed with the plaintiffs that, because the well-established right to marry subsumes same-sex marriages, they were not asking the court to create a new fundamental right. Because the state's ban on same-sex marriage interfered with the plaintiffs' fundamental rights, she held that the state must demonstrate an important interest in it.[26]

On the more difficult question of the level of scrutiny, she determined that, in the absence of clear guidance from the Supreme Court and the Seventh Circuit about the proper level of scrutiny in equal protection cases, it was appropriate to apply a higher standard of scrutiny to classifications based on sexual orientation. After reviewing the standards for heightened scrutiny (political powerlessness, immutability, and discrimination), she concluded that, because sexual orientation is most similar to sex among the classifications that receive a higher level of scrutiny, she would also apply heightened scrutiny. Noting that the state asserted most of the same interests as other states of promoting responsible procreation, preserving the family, and proceeding cautiously in uncertain policy areas, she found the reasons unpersuasive. She ended by saying, "[B]ecause my review of that law convinces me that plaintiffs are entitled to the same treatment as any heterosexual couple, I conclude that the Wisconsin laws banning marriage between same-sex couples are unconstitutional" (1028).

Her opinion confounded both sides. Because Crabb did not order county clerks to issue marriage licenses nor issue a stay of her decision, some counties complied with the ruling, and others did not, leading to confusion and uncertainty for Wisconsin same-sex couples. The state reacted by announcing that it still considered the ban on same-sex marriage in place and refused to accept marriages certificates issued in some counties. It soon reversed course and announced that it would accept the certificates but that the legality of the marriages would be unknown until the Seventh Circuit ruled.

Indiana Federal District Court Judge Richard Young followed the same approach in *Baskin v. Bogan* (2014a), decided on June 25, 2014.[27] Beginning with the due process claim, he rejected the state's narrow interpretation of the right to marry. Young agreed with the plaintiffs that they were not proposing a new fundamental right but were merely asking the court to recognize that the right to marry a person of the same sex was within the scope of the well-recognized fundamental right to marry.

Drawing on the rulings from the Virginia and Utah courts, he said that the plaintiffs were merely seeking to exercise the "same right that is currently enjoyed by heterosexual individuals: the right to make a public commitment to form an exclusive relationship and create a family with a partner with whom the person shares an intimate and sustaining emotional bond" (1157, quoting *Bostic v. Rainey* 2014, 472, quoting *Kitchen v. Herbert* 2013a, 1202–3).

Because the law significantly interfered with the plaintiffs' fundamental right to marry, Young applied strict scrutiny, saying that even the defendants admitted that it would be appropriate if the right to marry subsumes the right to marry a partner of the same sex. He assumed without analysis that the state's objective of encouraging unmarried different-sex parents to marry to care for any unintended children was legitimate. But aside from the fact that the state did not base its marriage policies on procreation, "excluding same-sex couples from marriage has absolutely no effect on opposite-sex couples, whether they will procreate, and whether such couples will stay together if they do procreate" (*Baskin v. Bogan* 2014a, 1158). Because of this, he found that the law was not closely tailored to meet its purported goal and did not satisfy strict scrutiny.

In determining the proper level of scrutiny to apply under equal protection analysis, Young considered himself bound by a 2002 Seventh Circuit decision, *Schroeder v. Hamilton School District* (2002), in which the court applied minimal scrutiny to a classification based on sexual orientation. But even under minimal scrutiny, he found that, because same-sex and different-sex couples have comparable commitments and relationships, the state unreasonably prohibited same-sex marriages.

With the Indiana policy against same-sex marriage declared unconstitutional, clearly the nonrecognition policy must also fall. Young suggested that there were separate grounds for finding it unconstitutional. As is common in most states, with the exception of same-sex couples, Indiana recognizes all valid out-of-state marriages—even marriages that would be illegal in Indiana. By singling out same-sex couples, the state relegated them to second-class citizenship, demonstrating the type of animus that the court found violated the equal protection clause in *Windsor*. Whatever its motivation, though, he said, it was irrational to refuse to recognize the marriages of same-sex couples because the policy had no relationship to the state's articulated goal of encouraging different-sex couples to stay together for the sake of their unintended children.

MARRIAGE EQUALITY IN THE CIRCUIT COURTS

The lower courts upheld marriage equality in virtually every state, vindicating the judgment of gay rights advocates to litigate the same-sex marriage restrictions. They succeeded for several reasons. First, retaining minimal scrutiny language, *Windsor* departed from the traditional minimal scrutiny approach of presuming challenged laws constitutional and accepting almost any justification for them. The ambiguity in Kennedy's opinion allowed lower courts to speculate about its intended meaning and application. Thus, despite the high court's unwillingness to formally adopt either a heightened or a minimal-plus approach in sexual orientation cases, the lower courts could replicate *Windsor* and conduct a more searching appraisal of the purpose and effect of a state ban on same-sex marriage to justify striking it.

Additionally, by frankly criticizing Congress's motives in enacting DOMA, the Court also gave the lower courts permission to question the states' justifications for restricting same-sex marriage. Despite their dutiful efforts to interpret the high court's approach to scrutiny, *Windsor*'s lack of clarity presented them with the opportunity to arrive at their own decisions about the proper level of scrutiny to apply. Using the standard indicia of heightened scrutiny, a number of lower courts reviewed the historical evidence and, not surprisingly, found that gay men and lesbians constituted a minority group that lacked political power and was subject to discrimination. Consequently, using the high court's own criteria, they were able to apply a higher level of scrutiny (or at least express their inclination to do so) without openly flouting Supreme Court precedent.

Even when interpreting *Windsor* as a signal to continue to use the lowest level of scrutiny, the courts concluded that the same-sex marriage restrictions unconstitutionally infringed on the plaintiffs' rights and that history and tradition were often merely subterfuges for discrimination. Moreover, acknowledging that the states' objectives of responsible procreation and promoting stability in the family were legitimate, they did not believe the objectives rationally related to the state's marriage policies.

Thus, the courts found bans on same-sex marriage indefensible under any level of scrutiny. Frequently citing *Loving*, most courts compared the plaintiffs in the cases before them to the *Loving* plaintiffs and held that the principles articulated there controlled. In the end, the courts were more inclined to follow *Windsor*'s approach to same-sex marriage (accepting the plaintiffs' intimate choices and honoring their family relationships) than its jurisprudential guidance. The lower courts all expressed concern about the uncertainty following *Windsor*, particularly with regard to scrutiny, but their opinions demonstrated that they were more influenced by *Windsor*'s language than its legal analysis. They extensively quoted Kennedy's stirring phrases about the intent of the restrictive marriage policies and their destructive effect on same-sex couples and their children. Ironically, they also frequently cited Scalia's prediction about the likely outcome of future litigation. Like Scalia, they appeared to believe that *Windsor* inexorably paved the way for a national marriage equality policy and did not view the state's dominion over marriage policy an insurmountable obstacle.

When the litigation moved to the circuit courts, the appeals courts devoted much of their attention to the theoretical discussion of judicial restraint, focusing their attention on the question of the proper role of the federal courts in the political system. Aware of their duty to defer to the democratic decision-making process, they also recognized their responsibility to adjudicate claims of rights guaranteed by the Fourteenth Amendment.

As in the lower courts, this issue was encapsulated in their discussions of the scrutiny doctrine, with the debate centered on the degree to which courts may override the state's determination that same-sex marriage was detrimental to society by applying a higher level of scrutiny. Few judges, even those who voted in favor of state restrictions on marriage, explicitly argued for the merits of the policies, largely confining themselves to urging their colleagues to refrain from imposing their views of marriage on the states. Thus, the appellate court opinions demonstrated a greater concern with the legitimacy of the courts' decision-making posture than with the legitimacy of same-sex marriage.

A divided Tenth Circuit panel announced its opinion in *Kitchen v. Herbert* (2014) on June 25, 2014. The panel voted 2–1, with Jerome Holmes and Carlos Lucero in the majority and Paul Kelly concurring in part and dissenting in part. Lucero said that he agreed with Shelby that the fundamental right to marry included same-sex marriage and the state must offer a compelling reason to infringe on it. In assessing the state's four (well-worn) arguments under strict scrutiny, the court held that the three relating to marriage and the family may be compelling, but by singling out same-sex marriage, the law assumes a nexus between procreation and marriage that fails to satisfy the narrowly tailored prong of strict scrutiny (1218–28). Indeed, the state even conceded that its arguments fell short of the strict scrutiny test. Lucero simply dismissed the last argument, that the marriage policy protects religious liberty and reduces civil unrest, as not compelling; he cited the Supreme Court's comment that the public disapproval of a practice does not justify a violation of fundamental rights. Lucero also rejected the state's argument that courts should affirm policies enacted through the democratic decision-making process, saying that they cannot "defer to majority will in dealing with matters so central to personal autonomy. The protection and exercise of fundamental rights are not matters for opinion polls or the ballot box" (1228).

Kelly reproved the majority for using strict scrutiny and not adhering to the principle of judicial restraint. He said that the Supreme Court had only extended the fundamental right to marry to different-sex couples and the majority erred in including it within the right to marry. Its recent appearance on the nation's political agenda, he insisted, indicated that it was a newly formulated right. In his view, the court should refrain from removing the decision about same-sex marriage from the legislature and electorate, where it properly belonged, allowing the political branch to determine whether same-sex marriage furthers the state's goals.

In using minimal scrutiny, a court must uphold a policy as long as the government has a reasonable belief in its effectiveness. Kelly believed the Utah law constitutional because it was rationally related to the state's goals of promoting the welfare of children and the family as well as its legitimate "desire to proceed cautiously in this evolving area"

(1230). Although others may disagree, the courts should not take the leading role in deciding how to further the state's legitimate interest in marriage. Absent an encroachment on a fundamental right or the appropriate use of heightened scrutiny, policy decisions such as these should be left to the people and their elected representatives.

Shortly after *Kitchen*, on July 18, 2014, the same members of the Tenth Circuit panel announced their ruling in *Bishop v. Smith* (2014), echoing *Kitchen* and addressing the state's child welfare argument in greater depth. Even if children do better living with their biological parents, Lucero said, Oklahoma does not advance that goal and indeed enacts adoption laws that specifically defeat it. Moreover, the state allows different-sex couples to marry without inquiring into their procreative capacities or wishes. He ended by finding that, even if the child welfare objective is compelling, the marriage policy is not narrowly tailored to it.

Holmes briefly concurred, pleased that Kern did not base his ruling on a finding of animosity toward gay men and lesbians because, in his view, the Oklahoma policy did not reflect the type of hostility that the Court found in *Romer* and *Windsor*.

Kelly reprised his dissent in *Kitchen*, again charging the majority with exceeding judicial boundaries and infringing on the state's domain. He argued,

> [S]ame-gender marriage is a public policy choice for the states and should not be driven by a uniform, judge-made fundamental rights analysis. At a time when vigorous public debate is defining policies concerning sexual orientation, this court has intervened with a view of marriage ostensibly driven by the Constitution. Unfortunately, this approach short-circuits the healthy political processes leading to a rough consensus on matters of sexual autonomy, and marginalizes those of good faith who draw the line short of same-gender marriage. (*Bishop v. Smith* 2014, 1112)

The Fourth Circuit soon added its voice to the increasing number of circuit opinions on marriage equality in *Bostic v. Schaefer* (2014). Speaking for Roger Gregory and himself, Henry Floyd rejected the states' arguments that the high court would not view same-sex marriage as a fundamental right because *Lawrence* and *Windsor* demonstrated that it extended the right to choose partners of the same sex for intimate relationships. Citing *Loving*, he said, "[O]ver the decades, the Supreme Court has demonstrated that the right to marry is an expansive liberty interest that may stretch to accommodate changing societal norms" (*Bostic v. Schaefer* 2014, 376). Moreover, the Supreme Court did not establish a right to interracial marriage in *Loving*; rather, it included the right to marry a person of another race within the right to marry. Similarly, this court was simply following *Loving*'s approach by including the right to marry a person of the same sex within the longstanding right to marry.

Because the plaintiffs challenged the law as an infringement on their fundamental rights, the court applied the highest level of scrutiny. Floyd evaluated the state's argument that the policy survived strict scrutiny because it resulted from a ballot measure and reflected the electorate's will. Acknowledging that "Americans' ability to speak with their votes is essential to our democracy," he cautioned that the "people's will is not an independent compelling interest that warrants depriving same-sex couples of their fundamental right to marry" (*Bostic v. Schaefer* 2014, 379).

Paul Niemeyer's dissent denied that he was averse to marriage equality; rather, he said he was concerned that the court was acting as a constitutional umpire charged with approving or disapproving same-sex marriage. He objected to the majority's premise that the right to same-sex marriage is simply a variant of the long-recognized fundamental right to marry, maintaining that plaintiffs were seeking a new constitutional right.

Under these circumstances, he argued, strict scrutiny was inappropriate. He believed that the policy met the standard for minimal scrutiny because a state may withhold a benefit from some people if it does not serve its interests to extend such benefits. Because the state can reasonably believe that allowing same-sex marriage would not further its goal of encouraging stable families, the marriage policy does not violate due process.

Noting that the majority had not addressed the equal protection claim, Niemeyer cited both Supreme Court and circuit cases supporting the use of minimal scrutiny in classifications based on sexual orientation. He maintained that the Court chose not to raise the level of scrutiny in *Romer*, and with the exception of the Second and Ninth Circuits, no other circuit had done so. Finally, reiterating his call for judicial restraint, he rebuked the majority for removing the decision from the people. Claiming that he was agnostic about the future of same-sex marriage, Niemeyer closed by urging the courts to "allow the States to enact legislation on the subject in accordance with their political processes. . . . The U.S. Constitution does not, in my judgment, restrict the States' policy choices on this issue. If given the choice, some States will surely recognize same-sex marriage and some will surely not. But that is, to be sure, the beauty of federalism" (*Bostic v. Schaefer* 2014, 398).

On September 4, 2014, less than two months after the Fourth Circuit announced its decision, the Seventh Circuit was next to weigh in on marriage equality in *Baskin v. Bogan* (2014b), ruling on the cases appealed from Indiana and Wisconsin. A unanimous panel, with Richard Posner announcing the decision for himself, Ann Williams, and David Hamilton, began by noting that the court is "mindful of the Supreme Court's insistence that . . . equal protection is not a license for courts to judge the wisdom, fairness, or logic of legislative choices" (654). But although judicial restraint should inhibit courts from imposing their views on reasonable government policies, it should not prevail when such policies breach fundamental rights or follow along "suspect lines" (654). Moreover, even when adhering to principles of restraint, courts must ensure that states have a reasonable basis for their policies. The focus of the cases before him, he said, was to determine whether the governments of Indiana and Wisconsin have a reasonable basis for prohibiting same-sex marriage.

Posner identified four questions on which the court would base its ruling, explaining that, because these included a cost-benefit analysis, they were slightly different from questions asked in standard equal protection cases.[28] First, does the policy reflect a pattern of discrimination, reflecting prejudice, against an identifiable group; second, is it based on an innate or immutable trait that is irrelevant to a person's abilities; third, is the discrimination against the targeted group outweighed by a benefit to society as a whole; and fourth, could the benefit to society be achieved with a different policy?

He dismissed the claim that the states most strenuously argued, that same-sex couples do not need to marry because they cannot procreate, characterizing it as "so full of holes that it cannot be taken seriously" (656). Because it is "irrational," it is unconstitutional—even without a heightened scrutiny analysis. Simply put, he said, this finding allows the court to avoid deciding the thorny questions of fundamental rights and levels of scrutiny.

Turning to a more detailed review of equal protection, Posner concluded that the marriage restrictions discriminate on the basis of innate and immutable characteristics and cause significant tangible and intangible harm to a vulnerable minority. Because of its " *groundless* rejection of same-sex marriage," the state must offer a "clearly offsetting governmental interest" to prevail (659, emphasis in the original). Evaluating Indiana's government interest, he turned to its sole argument that restricting same-sex marriage promotes child welfare by encouraging a father to marry the mother of his child in the event of an unintended pregnancy. Because same-sex couples cannot have unintentional children, the state contended that it has no reason to encourage their marriage.

Following a lengthy discussion on the relationship between fertility and marriage, Posner ridiculed the state for basing its policies on the belief that

> straight couples tend to be sexually irresponsible, producing unwanted children by the carload, and so must be pressured (in the form of governmental encouragement of marriage through a combination of sticks and carrots) to marry, but that gay couples, unable as they are to produce children wanted or unwanted, are model parents—model citizens really—so have no need for marriage. Heterosexuals get drunk and pregnant, producing unwanted children; their reward is to be allowed to marry. Homosexual couples do not produce unwanted children; their reward is to be denied the right to marry. Go figure. (662)

He ended his analysis of the Indiana case by reiterating that even discriminatory laws must be rational and the state's justification for its law does not even rise above this bar. Turning to the Wisconsin case, he reported that the state had advanced four reasons to justify its same-sex marriage policy: to maintain traditional heterosexual marriage; to proceed cautiously in an uncertain policy terrain; to avoid undermining the institution of marriage; and to abide by policies created by democratic decision-making. Persuaded by the other circuits, he easily disposed of the first three arguments. With respect to the last, he noted acerbically that the state argues that the policy arose as a result of a "democratic process—the enactment of a constitutional ban by popular vote. But homosexuals are only a small part of the state's population—2.8 percent, we said, grouping transgendered and bisexual persons with homosexuals. Minorities trampled on by the democratic process have recourse to the courts; the recourse is called constitutional law." (671)

Posner's views on the wisdom of the courts entering into the same-sex marriage policy arena represented a shift in his opinion on the importance of judicial restraint in marriage equality cases. In a 1997 article, he wrote that a Supreme Court decision declaring that same-sex couples had a right to wed would be an

> unprecedented example of judicial immodesty [and] that well-worn epithet "usurpative" would finally fit. . . . This is not to say, that courts should refuse to recognize a constitutional right merely because to do so would make them unpopular. Constitutional rights are, after all, rights against the democratic majority. But public opinion is not irrelevant to the task of deciding whether a constitutional right exists. When judges are asked to recognize a new constitutional right, they have to do a lot more than simply consult the text of the Constitution and the cases dealing with analogous constitutional issues. (Posner 1997, 1585)

By October 1, 2014, marriage equality advocates had scored impressive victories in the federal courts. Despite the virtual unanimity of opinions in the district and appeals courts, some states nevertheless sought Supreme Court review, asking the high court to focus on the federalism aspect of the *Windsor* ruling and support their claim that marriage policy-making was within their purview. Expectations were high that the Court would put their cases on its docket during the October 2014 term. On October 6, 2014, however, without explanation, it denied petitions for certiorari from the Fourth, Seventh, and Tenth Circuits (arising from Utah, Virginia, Oklahoma, Wisconsin, and Indiana). In declining to review these cases, the appellate court rulings in favor of marriage equality remained in effect.[29]

A day after the high court denied certiorari in these cases, the Ninth Circuit disposed of the appeals from lower court rulings in Nevada (*Sevcik v. Sandoval* 2012), in which Nevada Federal District Court Judge Robert Jones ruled in favor of the state, and Idaho (*Latta v. Otter*

2014a), in which Chief US Magistrate Judge Candy Wagahoff Dale had decided for the plaintiffs.

Idaho presented the novel argument that the marriage restriction was not based on sexual orientation but on the ability to procreate. Consequently, it maintained, because the law did not implicate sexual orientation, *SmithKline* was distinguishable, and it was inappropriate to use heightened scrutiny. Reinhardt announced the opinion for himself, Berzon, and Ronald Gould. He rejected the state's attempt to justify the marriage restriction by pointing to procreative differences between same-sex and different-sex couples because it was clear that the legal distinction was based on sexual orientation (*Latta v. Otter* 2014b).

With the court committed to heightened scrutiny, the state argued that the marriage restrictions furthered its important interest of ensuring that children are raised by their biological parents. To allow same-sex marriage, it contended, would undercut this goal. Additionally, because mothers and fathers have "complementary" perspectives on child-rearing, the policy would help to ensure that children would be raised by different-sex parents and would have a "better upbringing" (469).

Reinhardt pointed out that the state legislature had not established a factual basis for these arguments and failed to produce any evidence to bolster its claim that permitting same-sex couples to marry would send a message to society that marriage is no longer valued and lead to diminished support among the population for traditional marriage. In a footnote, he added that Governor C. L. "Butch" Otter had made the rather startling claim that "allowing same-sex marriage will lead opposite-sex couples to abuse alcohol and drugs, engage in extramarital affairs, take on demanding work schedules, and participate in time-consuming hobbies" (471n12). Reinhardt's rejoinder was, "[W]e seriously doubt that allowing committed same-sex couples to settle down in legally recognized marriages will drive opposite-sex couples to sex, drugs, and rock-and-roll" (471n12).[30]

The court found the states' arguments unpersuasive because they had not shown that restricting same-sex marriage led to the responsible procreation that promoted the welfare of children. Indeed, it noted, if the states were serious about ensuring that children lived with their married biological parents, then they would repeal no-fault divorce and adoption laws and outlaw surrogacy as well as sperm and egg donations.

On a more serious note, echoing *Windsor*, the court concluded that denying same-sex couples the right to marry caused numerous harms to same-sex couples and their children.

Reinhardt quickly disposed of the remaining arguments that principles of federalism and judicial restraint required the court to uphold the laws. As *Windsor* demonstrated, he said, federalism principles alone cannot justify state laws that infringe on individuals' constitutional rights. Moreover, with respect to judicial restraint, he declared that a "primary purpose of the Constitution is to protect minorities from oppression by majorities." In the end, because it found that their arguments were grounded neither in fact nor in reason, the court declared that they did not survive heightened scrutiny and struck the bans on same-sex marriage in both states.

With *Latta*, the Ninth Circuit joined the growing number of appellate courts that ruled in favor of marriage equality. Some states refused to acquiesce in the circuit rulings; Alaska, for example, which prohibited same-sex marriage since 1998, did not immediately reverse its same-sex marriage policy. Indeed, when Alaska Federal District Court Judge Timothy Burgess struck the state's prohibition on same-sex marriage in *Hamby v. Parnell* (2014), Governor Sean Parnell promised to appeal, citing his "duty [as governor] to defend and uphold the law and the Alaska Constitution." He justified his decision, saying, "[A]lthough the district court today may have been bound by the recent Ninth Circuit panel opinion, the status of that opinion and the law in general in this area is in flux. I will defend our constitution" (*Alaska Dispatch News*, October 12, 2014).[31]

The pace of one circuit at a time likely seemed slow to some, but the nation was clearly moving toward a national consensus on marriage equality. Indeed, it appeared to many that the nation's debate over same-sex marriage had essentially ended by 2014. The Court's denial of the petitions for certiorari from the Fourth, Seventh, and Tenth Circuit Courts of Appeals in October of that year and the Ninth Circuit's ruling immediately thereafter removed the final obstacles to same-sex marriage in more than half the states, encompassing the majority of the nation's population.[32]

Public opinion polls also demonstrated that support for same-sex marriage had markedly increased by 2014. In a *Washington Post*/ABC national poll taken in March 2014, 59 percent of respondents said that they supported "allowing gays and lesbians to marry legally," with only 34 percent opposing it (*Washington Post*, March 5, 2014). Surveying the results of several national polls, Daniel Cox of *FiveThirtyEight*—a website that analyzes polling data—reports that the percentage of respondents who thought gay and lesbian relations were morally acceptable rose from 40 percent in 2001 to 63 percent by 2015. Indeed, by 2013, one poll showed that 72 percent of the American public saw same-sex marriage as "inevitable." Cox (2016) asserts that "on no other issue have public sentiment and politics been transformed so quickly and completely."

On November 6, 2014, the Sixth Circuit Court of Appeals ended the spirit of optimism among advocates of marriage equality by announcing its decision in the appeals from the Michigan, Ohio, Kentucky, and Tennessee federal courts (*DeBoer v. Snyder* 2014b). Judge Jeffrey Sutton delivered the 2–1 opinion, joined by Judge Deborah Cook; Judge Martha Craig Daughtrey dissented.

The ruling was the mirror image of those in the other appellate courts, with the majority applying minimal scrutiny and accepting the states' justifications for their policies and the dissent making a case for applying heightened scrutiny and subjecting the states' reasoning to meaningful review.

The outcome of the case seemed evident at the outset, when Sutton framed the question as whether to allow the democratic decision-making process to resolve the national debate over same-sex marriage. Ironically, borrowing Posner's phrase, he asked, "Who decides?" The federal courts or the "less expedient, but usually reliable, work of the state democratic processes?" (396) Sutton identified several theories plaintiffs relied on but insisted that none of them "makes the case for constitutionalizing the definition of marriage and for removing the issue from the place it has been since the founding: in the hands of state voters" (402–3).

With this introduction, not surprisingly, Sutton declared minimal scrutiny the appropriate standard to use, specifying that it requires a court to uphold a law if there is even a conceivable reason for the state's action. And it would be implausible, he said, if the courts did not view the states as having an acceptable reason for a policy that has persisted for thousands of years—marriage between a man and a woman. He identified the primary goals of the state's marriage restrictions: regulating procreation and advancing the interests of children. Surely, he contended, the government may take reasonable steps to encourage stable relationships between men and women that redound to a child's benefit. Moreover, under minimal scrutiny, the courts should not preempt states that want to take a "wait and see" attitude toward such an enormous social change. Conceding that the plaintiffs were being harmed by the slow pace of the change, he agreed that it was a subject for discussion but that the discussion should not take place within the courts, for their role does not permit them to weigh such arguments.

According to the majority, cases in which courts struck laws based on animus were distinguishable because the courts only declared such laws unconstitutional when they were novel and targeted a single group for disadvantage. Marriage laws hardly fall into this category, and if anything, these laws were motivated by the reasonable desire to take the decision away from the courts, not to harm the gay and lesbian community and their children. Because it is difficult to ascertain the motives of citizens voting on ballot measures, those earlier rulings did not depend on discovering the voters' motivations; rather, they were based on the Court's belief that the challenged laws could only be explained by prejudice.

Sutton rejected the plaintiffs' claims that same-sex marriage satisfied the fundamental rights standard formulated in *Glucksberg*. Because it only became legal in 2003, it was neither "deeply rooted" nor "implicit in ordered liberty." Moreover, he said, these plaintiffs are different from those in *Loving*, for unlike the Lovings, they sought to create a new definition of marriage. The court denied that classifications based on sexual orientation merited a higher level of review. Although it agreed that the plaintiffs were victims of discrimination, unlike other minority groups, it believed gay men and lesbians were not subject to the type of debilitating prejudice that requires judicial intervention to insulate them from a majority seeking to harm them; indeed, it added, society has begun to accept them and will likely to continue to do so. Returning to the theme of restraint, the court reiterated that federal judges should not impose their values on the people, for they do not have superior wisdom and knowledge, and ultimately, it is preferable that acceptance comes about gradually rather than having it imposed from above. It asked,

> [I]sn't the goal to create a culture in which a majority of citizens dignify and respect the rights of minority groups through majoritarian laws rather than through decisions issued by a majority of Supreme Court Justices? It is dangerous and demeaning to the citizenry to assume that we, and only we, can fairly understand the arguments for and against gay marriage. (*DeBoer v. Snyder* 2014b, 418)

Concluding, Sutton returned to his initial question of the proper decision-maker. He admitted that the courts would be able to impose social change more quickly but that it will be accomplished by depriving the people of the opportunity to proceed at a more gradual pace and resolve the debate over marriage among themselves in a more constructive manner. He maintained,

> When the courts do not let the people resolve new social issues like this one, they perpetuate the idea that the heroes in these change events are judges and lawyers. Better in this instance, we think, to allow change through the customary political processes, in which the people, gay and straight alike, become the heroes of their own stories by meeting each other not as adversaries in a court system but as fellow citizens seeking to resolve a new social issue in a fair-minded way. (421)

In a vigorous dissent, Daughtrey accused the court of obfuscating the constitutional issues in the case with a lengthy, largely irrelevant, discourse on federalism and democracy and undermining the court's role of protecting minority rights. She criticized the majority for thoughtlessly ignoring the injuries the marriage restrictions impose on the plaintiffs and their families: "Instead of recognizing the plaintiffs as persons, suffering actual harm . . . my colleagues view the plaintiffs as social activists who have somehow stumbled into federal court, inadvisably, when they should be out campaigning to win 'the hearts and minds' of Michigan, Ohio, Kentucky, and Tennessee voters to their cause" (421).

Daughtrey complained that the majority opinion applauded marriage for its beneficial effect on children, ignoring the damage it inflicted on the tens of thousands of children in such families as the plaintiffs'. Like Posner, she was baffled by the states' assertion that its legitimate goal of encouraging different-sex couples to marry to care for the "unintended children" they may produce (the responsible procreation argument) would be thwarted by allowing same-sex couples to wed. She questioned the states' assumptions that permitting same-sex couples to join the ranks of married couples would diminish support for the institution among different-sex couples and decrease their desire to marry. Moreover, it defies reason, she charged, that same-sex couples, who are unable to have children spontaneously and will have no unintended children, should be penalized for their thoughtfulness in family planning by being denied the benefits of marriage. Echoing Posner, she ending saying, "Go Figure" (422, quoting *Baskin v. Bogan* 2014b, 662). Even more baffling, she said, was the fact that many of these unintended and unwanted children who were born to different-sex couples would be adopted into same-sex households. Surely, they would benefit from a legal system in which their parents were allowed to marry. She underscored her point by describing at great length the heartbreaking story of the Michigan couple with their three adopted children, two with special needs, who were seeking the legal benefits and security for their family that marriage provides.

She reviewed the most recent decisions of the four other circuits and found that, together, they convincingly rebutted the states' justifications for the marriage restrictions. She speculated that perhaps the majority's reason for its ruling was to create a split among the circuits that would encourage the Supreme Court to review the case. Perhaps it believed that the high court would be persuaded to rein in *Windsor* and uphold state restrictions on same-sex marriage on the dual grounds of judicial restraint and federalism.

Like her colleagues in most circuits, Daughtrey rejected the state's argument that social policy-making should be exclusively reserved to the people and their representatives and that courts should permit societal changes to evolve over time. On the contrary, she insisted, "under our constitutional system, the courts are assigned the responsibility of determining individual rights under the Fourteenth Amendment, regardless of popular opinion or even a plebiscite" (*DeBoer v. Snyder* 2014b, 434–35).

Moreover, even under rational basis review, she said, the court should not simply dismiss the role that animus may have played in formulating a state's same-sex marriage policy. She stressed that the Supreme Court has not required plaintiffs to demonstrate that laws arise from feelings of animosity by individuals. The litigants may prove that animus was a factor by pointing to general feelings of societal disapproval, and the majority itself acknowledged those feelings in discussing the history of prejudice against gay men and lesbians. She ended by charging the majority with "demonizing" the courts, adding that, "if we in the judiciary do not have the authority, and indeed the responsibility, to right fundamental wrongs left excused by a majority of the electorate, our whole intricate, constitutional system of checks and balances, as well as the oaths to which we swore, prove to be nothing but shams" (436–37).

On January 16, 2015, the Supreme Court entered the marriage policy-making arena by agreeing to review the Sixth Circuit ruling.[33] It was a late entry in the debate over marriage equality; when it agreed to take the case, only thirteen states still prohibited same-sex marriage.[34] In granting the petitions for certiorari, the Court limited its consideration to the following questions: "1) Does the Fourteenth Amendment require a state to license a marriage between two people of the same sex? 2) Does the Fourteenth Amendment require a state to recognize a marriage between two people of the same sex when their marriage was lawfully licensed and performed out-of-state" (*Obergefell v. Hodges* 2015a, 1040).

NOTES

1. With the litigation in progress, in 1988, the electorate approved a state constitutional amendment granting the legislature the power to restrict marriage to different-sex couples.

2. In *Baker v. Vermont* (1999), the Vermont Supreme Court ordered the state to extend the civil benefits of marriage to all couples. In response, the legislature created the civil union, a legal status granting same-sex partners most of the rights and privileges of marriage without designating it as such.

3. Prior to November 2003, when *Goodridge* was decided, same-sex marriage had become legal in Belgium, the Netherlands, and the Canadian province of Ontario. Soon after, it became legal in the rest of Canada, Portugal, South Africa, and Spain (see chapter 5).

4. The California Supreme Court's ruling in favor of marriage equality was overturned by Proposition 8, which was eventually declared unconstitutional by a federal district court in *Perry v. Schwarzenegger* (2010) and the Ninth Circuit Court of Appeals in *Perry v. Brown* (2012). The Supreme Court

reached no decision on the merits of the case, declaring in *Hollingsworth v. Perry* (2013) that the Proposition 8 proponents were not proper parties to appeal the district court's ruling to the appellate court, thus once again legalizing same-sex marriage in the state.

5. Same-sex marriage became legal through legislative acts or popular votes in: Delaware, the District of Columbia, Hawaii, Illinois, Maine, Maryland, Minnesota, New Hampshire, New York, Rhode Island, Vermont, and Washington State.

6. Article IV of the US Constitution, the full faith and credit clause, provides, "Full Faith and Credit shall be given in each State to the public Acts, Records, and judicial Proceedings of every other State. And the Congress may by general Laws prescribe the Manner in which such Acts, Records and Proceedings shall be proved, and the Effect thereof." Scholars argued that DOMA was superfluous because the judicially derived "public policy exception" arising out of the clause would have allowed states to reject same-sex marriages solemnized in other states because they conflicted with the state's public policy. The committee report acknowledged that Congress was aware of the "public policy exception," but it was unwilling to leave it to chance (Bossin 2005, 387).

7. A few years later, the proposed Marriage Protection Act would have denied the federal courts jurisdiction to adjudicate challenges to DOMA's nonrecognition provision. Approved by the House, it died in the Senate. Republicans also attempted to prevent state recognition of same-sex marriages with the Federal Marriage Amendment and the Marriage Protection Amendment.

8. Section 2, codified at 28 U.S.C., section 1738C, provides,

> No State, territory, or possession of the United States, or Indian tribe, shall be required to give effect to any public act, record, or judicial proceeding of any other State, territory, possession, or tribe respecting a relationship between persons of the same sex that is treated as a marriage under the laws of such other State, territory, possession, or tribe, or a right or claim arising from such relationship.

Section 3, codified at 1 U.S.C., section 7, provides,

> In determining the meaning of any Act of Congress, or of any ruling, regulation, or interpretation of the various administrative bureaus and agencies of the United States, the word "marriage" means only a legal union between one man and one woman as husband and wife, and the word "spouse" refers only to a person of the opposite sex who is a husband or a wife.

9. *Bishop v. Oklahoma* (2006); *Smelt v. County of Orange* (2005); *Wilson v. Ake* (2005).

10. The plaintiffs were encouraged by recent legal challenges to DOMA in the Ninth Circuit. The judges, acting in their capacity to resolve employment disputes, upheld challenges from federal employees whose spouses were denied benefits (*In re Golinski* 2009; *In the Matter of Brad Levenson* 2009).

11. Massachusetts Attorney General Martha Coakley brought a companion case, claiming that DOMA violated the Tenth Amendment as well as the taxing and spending clause. Tauro relied on his finding of the equal protection violation in *Gill v. Office of Personnel Management* (2010) to hold that Congress exceeded its authority under the taxing and spending clause and the Tenth Amendment by interfering with the state's power to define marriage and requiring it to illegally discriminate among its citizens (*Commonwealth of Massachusetts v. United States Department of Health and Human Services* 2010).

12. Obama announced in March 2009 that he favored repealing DOMA; in June, he ordered agency heads to determine which benefits could be extended to domestic partners of federal employees and, in some cases, their children. A year later, he made long-term care insurance available to same-sex partners of federal employees, broadened the interpretation of the Family and Medical Leave Act to allow same-sex domestic partners to care for the children of their partners, and required hospitals receiving Medicare or Medicaid to allow visitation between gay men and lesbians and their families. He formally announced his support for marriage equality in July 2012.

13. The federal government elected not to defend a federal statute in court in at least a dozen cases during the Bush and Obama administrations (see Hansen 2013; Pepper 2013).

14. The Supreme Court developed the concept of scrutiny in equal protection jurisprudence in *Korematsu v. U.S.* (1944), in which it upheld the World War II–era Japanese Exclusion Order. Emphasizing that its decision was not based on ethnicity, the Court declared that "all legal restrictions which curtail the civil rights of a single racial group are immediately suspect . . . [and that] courts must subject them to the *most rigid scrutiny*" (216, emphasis added).

15. *Lawrence* was decided on due process grounds; only O'Connor's concurring opinion discussed equal protection analysis, pointing to the statute's sole focus on male sexual conduct.

16. The appellate court consolidated *Gill v. Office of Personnel Management* (2010) with *Commonwealth of Massachusetts v. United States Department of Health and Human Services* (2010), in which the state challenged DOMA on federalism grounds.

17. Edith Windsor was the executor of the estate of her deceased spouse. Residents of New York, the couple married in Ontario in 2007. Although same-

sex marriage was illegal in New York at the time, the state recognized valid same-sex marriages performed elsewhere. When her spouse died in 2009, the government denied her a spousal exemption and required her to pay more than $360,000 in federal taxes. She filed suit in November 2010.

18. The US General Accounting Office (2004) identified 1,138 financial benefits associated with marriage.

19. The Supreme Court first suggested this implicit heightened scrutiny approach in *Louisville Gas & Electric Company v. Coleman* (1928).

20. The Lovings, an interracial couple, were married in Washington, DC, in 1958. After returning to their home state, Virginia, they were arrested and charged with violating the state's law against interracial marriage. They pleaded guilty and were sentenced to a year in jail unless they left the state and remained away for twenty-five years. Upon their return to Washington, DC, they continued to petition the Virginia courts to have their conviction set aside and their case ultimately reached the high court.

21. The US Supreme Court's summary disposition left standing the Minnesota Supreme Court's holding in *Baker v. Nelson* (1971) that the restrictions on same-sex marriage did not infringe on the Fourteenth Amendment's equal protection or due process clauses.

22. At the time, the Supreme Court was required to accept appeals of state cases that involved federal constitutional challenges to state laws; it used summary affirmances and dismissals that required no explanation as a convenient way to reduce the number of cases to which it would give full consideration. As the Court later declared in *Hicks v. Miranda* (1975), summary affirmances and dismissals are considered precedent, and if the "Court has branded a question as unsubstantial, it remains so except when doctrinal developments indicate otherwise" (344–45). Litigants argued over whether *Romer, Lawrence*, and *Windsor* represented the kind of doctrinal developments that indicated that the Court would likely take a different view of the matter.

23. Ironically, despite the judges' careful attention to scrutiny in their decisions, the rulings cast doubt on the continued validity of the doctrine in equal protection cases or at least in classifications based on sexual orientation.

24. In *Henry v. Himes* (2014), a case brought by adoptive parents challenging the nonrecognition policy more generally, the court again ordered the state to refrain from enforcing it. It emphatically declared that the "record before the Court . . . is staggeringly devoid of any legitimate justification for the State's ongoing arbitrary discrimination on the basis of sexual orientation, and, therefore, Ohio's marriage recognition bans are facially unconstitutional and unenforceable under any circumstances" (1039).

25. Plaintiffs also mounted challenges to nonrecognition policies in Alabama, Louisiana, and Missouri.

26. Her opinion discussed the state's reasons in the equal protection portion.

27. Young ruled on three consolidated cases in which the plaintiffs were four unmarried couples and one couple married in Massachusetts who challenged Indiana's nonrecognition policy.

28. Posner compared his analysis to the Ninth Circuit's in *SmithKline Beecham v. Abbott Laboratories* (2014), in which the latter had used the conventional approach to scrutiny in determining whether a peremptory challenge based on sexual orientation violated equal protection. He later admitted that the differences between the two approaches were "semantic rather than substantive" (*Baskin v. Bogan* 2014b, 656).

29. Even as the circuit courts issued rulings in favor of same-sex marriage, some states within the circuits initially refused to recognize the legitimacy of same-sex marriage, forcing couples living in those states to return to the district court to seek rulings striking down the states' same-sex marriage bans.

30. The court noted that some of these arguments were offered by the governor and the interveners, not by attorneys for the state.

31. The state was eventually forced to acquiesce after the Supreme Court denied its attempts to stay Burgess's order pending its appeal to the Ninth Circuit less than a week after he issued his opinion.

32. The only post-*Windsor* rulings to uphold bans on same-sex marriage were *Ada Conde-Vidal v. Alejandro Garcia-Padilla* (2014) and *Robicheaux v. Caldwell* (2014).

33. There were thirty litigants in these cases: fourteen same-sex couples and two men whose same-sex partners were deceased.

34. In addition to the four Sixth Circuit states, nine other states, mostly in the South, banned same-sex marriage: Arkansas, Georgia, Louisiana, Mississippi, Missouri, Nebraska, North Dakota, South Dakota, and Texas (Karimi and Pearson 2016).

4

CONTINUING STRUGGLES

On June 26, 2015, three years after its historic *Windsor* ruling, the Supreme Court addressed one of the most hotly debated issues in the nation's culture war by ruling on the legality of same-sex marriage (*Obergefell v. Hodges* 2015b). In a 5–4 vote, with Kennedy announcing the opinion for the same majority as in *Windsor*, the Court continued on the path it had first embarked on in *Romer* and followed in *Lawrence* and *Windsor*. The outcome was not surprising, with the opinions of the justices essentially unchanged from those they expressed in *Windsor*.

Echoing his paean to marriage voiced in *Windsor*, Kennedy extolled its importance, describing it as "essential to our most profound hopes and aspirations" (*Obergefell v. Hodges* 2015b, 2594). He stressed that the same-sex marriage advocates did not seek the right to marry to destroy the institution but rather because they recognized its transcendent importance as part of the human condition.

The outcome of the case became clear when Kennedy began by reciting the heartwarming stories that had prompted the litigation: Obergefell's wish to be recorded as the surviving spouse of his deceased partner in Ohio; DeBoer and Rowse's urgency to jointly adopt their three special needs children in Michigan; and DeKoe's desire to retain his marital rights when he returned to his home state of Tennessee.

Kennedy delved into the legal and social evolution of marriage policies, linking them to changing attitudes toward women's rights and greater acceptance of gay men and lesbians. Not limiting himself to marriage alone, he discussed the broader implications of evolving LGBT rights, including the Court's own gradual move in that direction after *Bowers v. Hardwick* (1986), in which it upheld the Georgia sodomy law. On a parallel track, he reviewed the numerous state and federal court rulings that established marriage equality for most of the LGB community.[1]

Turning to the constitutional analysis, Kennedy explained that the due process clause incorporates fundamental principles of liberty and autonomy, including respect for intimate life choices. Acknowledging the importance of the past for determining the scope of its protection, he stressed that it does not set boundaries on the acquisition of rights. In a spirited defense of an evolving Constitution, he declared that the framers "entrusted to future generations a charter protecting the right of all persons to enjoy liberty as we learn its meaning [and] when new insight reveals discord between the Constitution's central protections and a received legal stricture, a claim to liberty must be addressed" (*Obergefell v. Hodges* 2015b, 2598).

Beginning with *Loving*, Kennedy reviewed the cases based on the well-known proposition that the right to marry is enshrined in the due process clause. He conceded that prior marriage cases did not contemplate unions between individuals of the same sex but reiterated that the Court must adapt itself to societal changes. The right to marry, he said, arose from at least four enduring constitutional principles derived from past decisions that apply equally to same-sex and different-sex couples. Citing numerous rulings outlining the fundamental rights doctrine, Kennedy identified four principles that arose out of those cases: first, that the "right to personal choice regarding marriage is inherent in the concept of individual autonomy"; second, that the "right to marry is fundamental because it supports a two-person union unlike any other in its importance to the committed individuals"; third, that the right to marry "safeguards children and families and thus draws meaning from related rights of childrearing, procreation, and education"; and last, that "marriage is the keystone of our social order" (*Obergefell v. Hodges* 2015b, 2599–2602).

Aside from these ethereal truths, he also pointed to a multitude of practical reasons (taxation, property rights, survivorship, and inheritance, to name just a few) that underscore the importance of marriage. Emphasizing that same-sex couples enjoy the rights of dignity and equality, he said, in addition to excluding same-sex couples from the benefits that states provide to married couples, marriage inequality stigmatizes and demeans them and forces them to live with uncertain futures.

In presenting their arguments against marriage equality in the lower courts, the states had repeatedly attempted to characterize same-sex marriage as a new right and therefore subject to the narrow construction of fundamental rights analysis that the Court had imposed in *Glucksberg*. They cited the Court's warning that "liberty under the Due Process Clause must be defined in a most circumscribed manner, with central reference to specific historic practices" (721). Kennedy, however, distinguished *Glucksberg*, noting that its methodology was appropriate in that case, but is inappropriate when fundamental rights, such as intimacy and marriage, are at stake. He conceded that *Glucksberg* had contemplated a narrower definition of liberty, and if the Court adhered to that approach, then it would almost certainly dash these plaintiffs' efforts to cast their right to marry as a fundamental right. Advocating a dynamic view of the Constitution, Kennedy declared it unfair to limit the acquisition of rights only to those currently enjoying them, for this would preclude new groups from ever being able to exercise them in the future. He granted that marriage is a "matter of history and tradition" but insisted that fundamental rights are not static and must arise from a "better informed understanding of how constitutional imperatives define a liberty" (*Obergefell v. Hodges* 2015b, 2602).

The states had also argued that *Loving* had only established a fundamental right to interracial marriage and did not extend to same-sex marriage. Kennedy explained that the Court had asserted a wide-ranging right and held that interracial couples could not be excluded from it. Moreover, society had progressed to a greater awareness of the rights involved, and just like the plaintiffs in *Loving*, same-sex couples cannot be denied the benefits of marriage that the rest of society enjoys. "It would," he emphasized, "disparage their choices and diminish their personhood to deny them this right" (*Obergefell v. Hodges* 2015b, 2602).

Kennedy discussed the complex and symbiotic relationship between the due process and equal protection clauses of the Fourteenth Amendment, pointing out that *Loving* was decided on the dual grounds of equality and liberty.[2] He explained that, after finding that Virginia's ban on interracial marriage violated equal rights under the equal protection clause, the Court also held that it infringed on the fundamental liberties of interracial couples, a due process violation. In a statement equally applicable to state bans on same-sex marriage, Kennedy explained that the "reasons why marriage is a fundamental right became clear and compelling [in *Loving*] from a full awareness and understanding of the hurt that resulted from laws barring interracial unions" (*Obergefell v. Hodges* 2015b, 2603).[3]

The Court ended by addressing the familiar argument voiced by same-sex marriage opponents throughout the litigation, as well as by the Sixth Circuit, namely that the judiciary should refrain from preempting the political process by ruling on the constitutionality of marriage inequality. Rather, the opposition maintained, the courts should allow the issue to percolate throughout the nation and permit states to decide it according to their own values and at their own pace. Kennedy countered by pointing out that same-sex marriage had been vehemently debated in a wide array of public and private fora and thoroughly aired in the state and federal courts, in the state legislatures, in the private sector, and among the citizenry. Many "have devoted substantial attention to the question . . . [which] has led to an enhanced understanding of the issue—an understanding reflected in the arguments now presented for resolution as a matter of constitutional law" (2605).

Echoing the dissenting Sixth Circuit judge, the majority stressed that, though principles of democracy ordinarily require courts to exercise judicial restraint and defer to the decisions of the people and their elected representatives, the courts are constitutionally obligated to act when fundamental rights are at stake. "An individual can invoke a right to constitutional protection when he or she is harmed," he proclaimed, "even if the broader public disagrees and even if the legislature refuses to act" (2605).[4]

Kennedy made short shrift of the familiar argument that same-sex marriage would have a detrimental effect on different-sex marriages because it would sever the link between "natural procreation and marriage." He dismissed this line of reasoning, saying that a couple's decision to marry is based on numerous tangible and intangible factors, and it is "wholly illogical," "unrealistic," and "counterintuitive" to believe that it would be affected if the state allowed same-sex couples to marry (2607).

Careful not to denigrate people holding opposing views, Kennedy addressed the issue that would reverberate in the legislatures, in the courts, and among citizens for years to come. He respectfully acknowledged that there are people with deeply held religious beliefs who do not sanction same-sex marriage. Nevertheless, he insisted, their rights are not at issue, for the First Amendment guarantees that they can continue to adhere to their convictions. Whatever their beliefs or the beliefs of others who disapprove of marriage equality for nonreligious reasons, he said that he hoped for a civil dialogue between adherents and opponents of marriage equality. He insisted that, whether that dialogue takes place or not, the Constitution bars states from infringing on the rights of same-sex couples who wish to marry.

Quickly disposing of the Ohio and Tennessee laws, Kennedy said that, as even the attorneys for these states had conceded, if same-sex marriage is legal in all states, then there is no justification for any state to refuse to recognize valid same-sex marriages performed in other states.

He movingly ended by proclaiming marriage as one of the foundations of human relations, saying,

> No union is more profound than marriage, for it embodies the highest ideals of love, fidelity, devotion, sacrifice, and family. In forming a marital union, two people become something greater than once they were. As some of the petitioners in these cases demonstrate, marriage embodies a love that may endure even past death. It would misunderstand these men and women to say they disrespect the idea of marriage. Their plea is that they do respect it, respect it so deeply that they seek to find its fulfillment for themselves. Their hope is not to be condemned to live in loneliness, excluded from one of civilization's oldest institutions. They ask for equal dignity in the eyes of the law. The Constitution grants them that right. (2608)

The four dissenting judges, each writing a separate opinion (joined by at least two others), expressed disapproval of the majority's exercise of judicial activism that removed marriage policy-making from the people and their representatives. Roberts called the opinion "deeply disheartening," echoing the Sixth Circuit's view that it was improper for the high court to declare marriage equality a constitutional right. He said that it should have framed the asserted right more narrowly and properly applied the *Glucksberg* analysis; had it done so, the plaintiffs would have been unable to show that the right of same-sex marriage is deeply rooted in history and tradition.[5] Moreover, he warned, the majority's approach could lead to a judicial finding of a fundamental right to plural marriage in the future (see Nicolas 2016; Yoshino 2015).

Roberts sought to make clear that he was taking no position on the wisdom or fairness of marriage inequality, merely addressing himself to the legitimacy of the majority opinion. He charged that, in the midst of the nation's ongoing deliberation over same-sex marriage, with this decision, "five lawyers have closed the debate and enacted their own vision of marriage as a matter of constitutional law. Stealing this issue from the people will for many cast a cloud over same-sex marriage, making a dramatic social change that much more difficult to accept" (*Obergefell v. Hodges* 2015b, 2612). He deplored the majority's arrogance for striking laws in more than half the states and transforming an institution that existed for more than a thousand years, ending dramatically by asking, "[J]ust who do we think we are?" (2612).[6]

The other dissenters, Scalia, Thomas, and Alito, also sought to avoid the impression that they condemned same-sex couples or impugned their motives for wishing to marry. For the most part, they limited themselves to criticizing the majority for intruding into and resolving the debate over marriage equality. In their view, because the Constitution is silent on the issue, the Court should have declared itself agnostic about the outcome of the nation's debate over marriage policy and entrusted the future of marriage equality to the majoritarian decision-making process.

Scalia complained the majority departed from principles of judicial restraint by eliminating the public's role in the debate and creating liberties not contemplated in the Constitution. Calling it a "judicial putsch," he charged that it committed the unpardonable sin of depriving the people of the "freedom to govern themselves" (2627). Thomas also accused the Court of overstepping the limits of its constitutional role, for the "concept of 'liberty' [that] it conjures up bears no resemblance to any plausible meaning of that word as it is used in the Due Process Clause" (2632).

Alito echoed the others in upbraiding the majority for usurping the state's decision-making process and taking the debate over marriage away from the people and their representatives to whom it properly belonged. Unlike the other dissenters, Alito delved into the merits of the debate over same-sex marriage, citing the state's legitimate interest in furthering procreation by prohibiting same-sex couples from marrying. Finally, considering the laws already percolating in state legislatures in anticipation of limiting the effect of the high court's ruling. Alito ironically expressed concern that the majority opinion would lead to vilifying opponents of same-sex marriage and portraying them as bigots.[7] He predicted that, by imposing same-sex marriage by judicial fiat, the Court had precluded states from enacting conscience laws that would offer its detractors a safe harbor for resisting marriage equality.

The Supreme Court majority largely reflected the views of the nation. In a *Huffington Post*/YouGov poll taken immediately after the decision, 49 percent of the respondents approved of it, while 41 percent disapproved. The opposition was divided about how their political leaders should respond to the ruling, with a virtual tie between those who believed that politicians "should express their disapproval, and move onto other issues" (44 percent) and those who felt that "they should concentrate on finding ways to continue to fight against gay marriage" (45 percent). The majority of respondents did not favor a constitutional amendment that would return the issue of same-sex marriage to the states (48 percent opposed to 37 percent in favor) (Moore 2015).

Almost a year later, in May 2016, polls showed that most Americans supported marriage equality. Pew Research Center (2016) reported the results of a poll in which 55 percent of Americans supported same-sex marriage. Similarly, a Gallup poll (2016) found that 61 percent of the population agreed that marriages between same-sex couples should be legal.

Despite its stirring affirmation of equality, the Supreme Court did not put the issue of the legitimacy of same-sex marriage, nor, more generally, discrimination against the LGBT community, to rest. Opponents continued their efforts to distance themselves from marriage equality, chiefly by claiming that it interfered with the exercise of their religious beliefs. Not surprisingly, the outcry against it was strongest in the states that had maintained restrictions on marriage until the Court's ruling. Indeed, the Pew survey revealed that only 43 percent of respondents living in states where same-sex marriage had been illegal approved of it, while 68 percent of respondents living in states where same-sex marriage was legal favored it (Pew Research Center 2015).

REACTIONS TO *OBERGEFELL*

In the year following the decision, opposition to same-sex marriage was a frequent talking point in the 2016 Republican primaries. Louisiana Governor Bobby Jindal, a presidential contender, ominously predicted that

> this decision will pave the way for an all out assault against the religious freedom rights of Christians who disagree with this decision. This ruling must not be used as pretext by Washington to erode our right to religious liberty. The government should not force those who have sincerely held religious beliefs about marriage to participate in these ceremonies. That would be a clear violation of America's long held commitment to religious liberty as protected in the First Amendment.

He ended by declaring, "I will never stop fighting for religious liberty and I hope our leaders in D.C. join me" (*New Orleans Times-Picayune*, June 26, 2015).[8] Jindal vowed that Louisiana would continue to obey the state constitution that bars same-sex marriage and would not issue marriage licenses to same-sex couples until the lower courts "affirm" the Supreme Court (*New Orleans Times-Picayune*, July 2, 2015).[9]

Texas Governor Greg Abbott denounced the opinion in a press release, promising that, "despite the Supreme Court's rulings, Texans' fundamental right to religious liberty remains protected. No Texan is required by the Supreme Court's decision to act contrary to his or her religious beliefs regarding marriage" (Office of the Governor Greg Abbott 2015). The Texas and Mississippi attorneys general directed county clerks not to issue marriage licenses to same-sex couples while awaiting further instructions.[10] Within the week, the Fifth Circuit ordered an end to the delaying tactics in Louisiana, Texas, and Mississippi, declaring, "*Obergefell* . . . is the law of the land and, consequently, the law of this circuit and should not be taken lightly by actors within the jurisdiction of this court" (*Robicheaux v. Caldwell* 2015, at 4).[11]

Wisconsin Governor Scott Walker, another aspiring presidential candidate, called for a constitutional amendment to allow states to define marriage, signaling the importance of the issue in the 2016 Republican primaries. He said, "I can assure all Wisconsinites concerned about the impact of today's decision that your conscience rights will be protected, and the government will not coerce you to act against your religious beliefs" (*TalkingPointsMemo*, June 26, 2015). Senator Lindsey Graham, Republican from South Carolina, another emerging Republican candidate for president, shied away from a proposed marriage amendment but promised to commit himself "to ensuring the protection of religious liberties of all Americans" (*Politico*, June 26, 2015).

The Alabama Attorney General, who also voiced his disappointment with *Obergefell*, prophetically warned that, while the fight over the legality of same-sex marriage may have ended, the battle will continue and its "focus will now turn to the exercise of one's religious liberty" (*Washington Post*, June 26, 2016). Ironically, a Lambda Legal official echoed this view, saying, "[W]ith courts and legislatures ending bans on same-sex marriage, some who oppose it have turned to Plan B, the use of religion" (*New York Times*, March 30, 2015).

The conflict between religious liberty and same-sex marriage emerged even before *Obergefell* was announced, with lawsuits challenging the right of business owners, such as photographers, florists, caterers, and bakers, to deny their services to same-sex couples.[12]

The litigation chiefly arose in states that prohibited discrimination because of sexual orientation in places of public accommodation. Public accommodations, such as "retail stores, restaurants, parks, hotels, doctors' offices, and banks," are broadly defined as privately-owned enterprises that serve the public (Movement Advancement Project 2016b). By 2015, twenty-one states and the District of Columbia had laws against discrimination on the basis of sexual orientation in public accommodations (National Conference of State Legislatures 2015).[13]

Most of the cases revolved around wedding vendors who refused to participate—even indirectly—in same-sex marriage ceremonies, claiming they were entitled to exemptions from public accommodations laws because of their religious beliefs (see Lim and Melling 2014).[14] The nation's attention focused on a New Mexico photographer and a Colorado baker, each of whom asserted that their state's antidiscrimination law infringed on their religious liberty.[15]

The New Mexico Human Rights Act (NMHRA) prohibits discrimination because of sexual orientation in several areas, including public accommodations. When Vanessa Willock asked Elaine Huguenin, co-owner and chief photographer of Elane Photography, to photograph her commitment ceremony to her same-sex partner, Huguenin declined to do so, noting her religious beliefs against same-sex marriage. Willock filed a complaint with the state Human Rights Commission, which found in her favor; she waived her award of attorneys' fees, and the commission imposed no other fines or damages on the studio.

The lower state courts upheld the commission's finding, and the studio appealed to the state supreme court, arguing that it did not discriminate against Willock and her partner on the basis of their sexual orientation but because it did not wish to "endorse" their same-sex ceremony (*Elane Photography v. Willock* 2013, 61). The owners also argued that their refusal was not based on their status as lesbians (they said they would take pictures of them as long as they did not touch or display affection for each other) but on their conduct (the act of solemnizing their commitment).

The unanimous court rejected the distinction between status and conduct, saying, "[T]o allow discrimination based in conduct so closely correlated with sexual orientation would severely undermine the purpose of the NMHRA" (61). It added that it would be anomalous if the law protected same-sex couples against discrimination "only to the extent that they do not openly display their same-gender sexual orientation" (62).

The owners asserted that the NMHRA abridges their First Amendment right by compelling them to send a positive message about a same-sex wedding ceremony. The court observed that the law does not demand such a message but only requires that they treat all couples alike in the course of doing business.

In assessing the owners' claim that their refusal was justified by First Amendment's right of free exercise, the court put aside the question of whether a corporation possesses such a right but held that, even if it does, the NMHRA does not violate it.[16] Individuals are not excused from complying with neutral laws of general applicability, such as the NMHRA, the court said, citing *Employment Division, Department of Human Resources v. Smith* (1990), in which the Supreme Court upheld an Oregon state agency that denied unemployment benefits to two Native American drug rehabilitation counselors who were discharged for using peyote. It rejected the counselors' religious defense, ruling that the free exercise clause does not excuse individuals from obeying a "generally applicable law," such as a drug law.

Prior to *Smith*, in adjudicating free exercise claims, the Court applied strict scrutiny to laws burdening religion and obliged the government to show that it had a compelling justification for the challenged law.[17] In 1993, Congress enacted RFRA as H.R.1308 (Public Law No. 103-141) to reverse *Smith* and restore the free exercise clause to its privileged status. H.R. 1308 passed in a 97–3 vote in the Senate and a unanimous voice vote in the House; Clinton signed it on November 16, 1993 (Congress.gov 1993).[18]

In *City of Boerne v. Flores* (1997), the Supreme Court held that RFRA exceeded Congress's authority under section 5 of the Fourteenth Amendment by forcing state and local entities to show that they have a compelling reason to enact laws burdening religion.[19] Thus, unlike the federal government, under *City of Boerne*, state and local entities are not required to prove that they have a compelling interest in enforcing laws that hinder individuals from exercising their religious beliefs.[20]

The New Mexico Supreme Court avoided interpreting the parameters of the state RFRA by holding that it only applies to actions involving the government, not to lawsuits between private individuals. The US Supreme Court effectively ended the controversy by denying the owners' appeal of the state high court decision (*Elane Photography v. Willock* 2014).

The Colorado case involved Jack Phillips, owner of Masterpiece Cakeshop, who refused to design and bake a wedding cake for David Mullins and Charlie Craig because of his religious beliefs.[21] After filing a charge with the Colorado Civil Rights Division, which found probable cause of discrimination, the couple filed a formal complaint with the Colorado Office of Administrative Courts, claiming that Phillips violated the state public accommodations law by discriminating against them. He countered that he did not violate the law, for he did not discriminate against them because of their sexual orientation but because he would be "displeasing God and acting contrary to the teachings of the Bible" if he served them (*Craig v. Masterpiece Cakeshop, Inc.* 2013, at 3).

In a ruling dated December 6, 2013, Administrative Law Judge Robert Spencer found in the couple's favor. Echoing the New Mexico Supreme Court, he said, "[O]nly same-sex couples engage in same-sex weddings, therefore it makes little sense to argue that refusal to provide a cake to a same-sex couple for use at their wedding is not 'because of' their sexual orientation" (at 5). He concluded that Phillips violated the one-hundred-year-old Colorado Anti-Discrimination Act (CADA) and "any restriction on religious practices that results from the application of the law is incidental to its focus upon preventing discrimination in the marketplace" (at 11).[22]

The Civil Rights Commission upheld Spencer's order on May 30, 2014, and Phillips appealed to the Colorado Court of Appeals. The court cited *Elane*, rejecting Phillips's attempt to distinguish the couple's conduct from their status. It declared that, "but for their sexual orientation, Craig and Mullins would not have sought to enter into a same-sex marriage, and but for their intent to do so, Masterpiece would not have denied them its services" (*Craig v. Masterpiece Cakeshop, Inc.* 2015, para. 34).

The court was also not persuaded by Phillips' argument that he did not violate the CADA because he was ready to sell the couple his baked goods or serve them in his shop, reasoning that he was required to offer them the same services that he provided to the public. Guided by *Smith* and *Elane*, the court found the CADA a neutral, generally applicable law rationally related to the state's legitimate interest in eradicating discrimination in public accommodations.[23] It upheld the commission's findings.[24]

The outcomes were similar in suits against business owners in Arizona, California, Idaho, Nevada, New York, Oregon, Vermont, and Washington State. Responding to the litigation, a number of states sought to strengthen the rights of owners to assert religious defenses in antidiscrimination suits. A Pew Research Center (2015a) survey taken in September 2014 found Americans almost evenly divided over the issue, with 49 percent agreeing that wedding vendors should be obligated to serve same-sex couples and 47 percent believing that they should be able to deny their services.

STATE RFRAS

Most state officials recognized their obligation to implement marriage equality, yet at the same time, a number sought to evade it by relying on state religious freedom laws that had been enacted to counter *Smith*.[25] Like the 1993 act, a state RFRA requires the government to prove that it has a compelling interest in a law that substantially burdens an individual's exercise of religion and is the least restrictive alternative, in other words, satisfy strict scrutiny (Selznick 2014). These laws vary, with some affording greater leeway for religious beliefs than the federal version and others limiting the allowable exemptions (see Martin 2016).

States began to enact RFRAs in the immediate wake of *Smith*, but the more recent laws—mostly in states under the control of Republican governors and legislatures—privilege free exercise over equality.[26] Some laws also constrain municipalities from enacting public accommodations laws prohibiting discrimination against the LGBT community (Koppelman 2015).

By 2016, almost half the states passed RFRAs that, like their federal counterpart, required courts to apply strict scrutiny to government actions that burdened religious exercise.[27] There are two types of recently enacted RFRAs: The first wave laws do not specify opposition to marriage equality as a legitimate reason to refuse service to same-sex couples, although it seems clear from their legislative histories that they were intended to shield opponents of marriage equality from legal liability. The second wave laws, commonly known as First Amendment Defense Acts (FADA), explicitly insulate individuals and organizations that have religious objections to same-sex marriage from penalties.[28] Mathew Staver, founder and chair of Liberty Counsel, believes that the latter are more advantageous because "it's easier to focus and easier to have quick talking points and focused information so everyone knows what the issue is" (*New York Times*, March 3, 2016).[29] With the passage of such measures, it is not surprising that a year after *Obergefell*, the executive director of the National Center for Transgender Equality commented, "[O]ne of the main things we are doing is fighting against the post-marriage backlash" (*New York Times*, June 30, 2016).

Arizona was the first state to experience a negative reaction when it attempted to enhance its religious freedom law. In February 2014, the legislature sought to amend its existing state RFRA (enacted in 1999 as section 41-11493 and section 41-1493.01), which precisely mirrored the federal law. The revised version (SB 1062) would have broadened the definition of person and made the religious defense applicable in actions brought against private individuals rather than solely against the government, as in the federal RFRA.[30] Inspired by the case in neighboring New Mexico, the Arizona law would have therefore permitted business owners to assert their religious beliefs as defenses in civil suits brought by private individuals.[31] Had this version of the law been in place in New Mexico and Colorado, the outcome of the cases there would have been different.[32]

Critics called it a "license to discriminate" against gay men and lesbians, but its sponsor denied the charge, saying that it is "about preventing discrimination against people who are clearly living out their faith" (*The Advocate*, February 20, 2014). On February 26, bowing to pressure from gay and lesbian activists, scores of business leaders in the state and around the country, the National Football League (NFL), and both US senators, Governor Jan Brewer vetoed the bill.[33] She cautioned, "[T]he law has the potential to create more problems than it purports to solve" (*The Advocate*, February 26, 2014).[34]

About a year later, controversy over LGBT rights erupted in Arkansas as the state legislature became the second in the nation (after Tennessee) to approve an anti-antidiscrimination measure.[35] SB 202, barring local governments from passing measures to protect the LGBT community against discrimination, was enacted because a number of state legislators were concerned that municipalities, such as Eureka Springs, Little Rock, and Fayetteville, passed (or would pass) local antidiscrimination ordinances. Indeed, the Fayetteville City Council approved such an ordinance that was later repealed by the voters. Reflecting the experience with Colorado's Amendment 2, declared unconstitutional in *Romer*, SB 202 did not specify gay men and lesbians as the excluded group and offered a neutral explanation for the bill, saying that it advanced business interests.

SB 202 became law on February 25, 2015. Governor Asa Hutchinson resisted pleas for a veto from local and national LGBT rights groups. Allowing the bill to go into effect without his signature, Hutchinson explained that he did not sign it because he was "concerned about the loss of local control . . . [and that discrimination] was not at issue" (Arkansas State Legislature 2015a; see *Arkansas News*, February 24, 2015).[36]

Arkansas soon became embroiled in another controversy over LGBT rights as the legislature deliberated over whether to pass HB 1228, a religious freedom law. But before the bill was sent to Hutchinson, Governor Mike Pence of Indiana set off a firestorm that dwarfed the reaction to the Arizona bill by affixing his signature to Indiana's version of a religious freedom act (SB 101) on March 26, 2016; the law was scheduled to go into effect on July 1, 2015.[37]

Pence signed SB 101 at a ceremony closed to the press and the public but attended "by supportive lawmakers, Franciscan monks and nuns, orthodox Jews, and some of the state's most powerful lobbyists on conservative social issues" (*Indianapolis Star*, April 2, 2016). In signing the bill, he claimed that it is

> not about discrimination and if I thought it legalized discrimination in any way in Indiana, I would have vetoed it. In fact, it does not even apply to disputes between private parties unless government action is involved. For more than twenty years, the federal Religious Freedom Restoration Act has never undermined our nation's anti-discrimination laws, and it will not in Indiana. (Indiana Governor Mike Pence 2015a)

Despite Pence's denial of the law's discriminatory effects, there was little doubt about its intended purpose. Urging its passage, Advance America, the head of an Indiana group claiming to be the "state's largest pro-family, pro-church, pro-private and home school, and pro-tax reform organization," proclaimed that "SB 101 will help protect individuals, Christian businesses and churches from those supporting homosexual marriages and those supporting government recognition and approval of gender identity (male cross-dressers)." He said the law would benefit "Christian bakers, florists and photographers" who refused to take part in a "homosexual marriage"; a "Christian business" that refused "to allow a man to use a woman's restroom"; and a "church" that refused to "be used for a homosexual wedding" (Advance America 2015a).[38]

The reaction was swift, as LGBT activists accused the state of encouraging discrimination, leading to protests at the statehouse. Businesses and sports figures weighed in, with a great deal of publicity focusing on the National Collegiate Athletic Association (NCAA)'s Final Four Tournament, scheduled for the next week in Indianapolis. With insufficient time to move to another location, the president of the NCAA, headquartered in Indianapolis, warned, "[M]oving forward, we intend to closely examine the implications of this bill and how it might affect future events as well as our workforce" (ESPN 2016a).

Millions of dollars were at stake, with businesses, conventions, performing artists, and college and professional athletic organizations expressing their concerns about the discriminatory effects of the law and some threatening to move scheduled events out of state or to boycott it for future events.[39] The mayor of Seattle issued an executive order banning city employees from using government funds in Indiana (*Seattle Times*, March 28, 2015). Later, other states and municipalities did the same.

Caught in the maelstrom, Pence insisted that the law was not about discrimination but about protecting religious freedom, adding, "[T]here's been a lot of misunderstanding about this bill" (*Politico*, March 27, 2016). He continually asserted that it was only intended to prevent government intrusion into religion, blaming the media for causing the uproar with its "reckless" and "shameless" reporting and charging that the state was being unfairly attacked by an "avalanche of intolerance" (*Politico*, March 29, 2015).

Asked by host George Stephanopoulos on ABC's *This Week* to comment on the statement by one of the law's supporters that it would protect the "Christian florist," Pence said, "George, look, the issue here is, you know, is tolerance a two way street or not?" Subsequently questioned about whether "it should be legal in the state of Indiana to discriminate against gays or lesbians," he obfuscated, saying, "Hoosiers don't believe in discrimination. I mean the way I was raised, in a small town in Southern Indiana, is you're—you're kind and caring and respectful to everyone. Anybody that's been in Indiana for five minutes knows that Hoosier hospitality is not a slogan, it's a reality" (*ABC News*, March 29, 2015).[40]

As much as he and others attempted to defend the law by claiming that it was identical to the 1993 federal RFRA, it was clear that it was not. First, unlike the federal law (and most of the prior state RFRAs), it expressly defined person as a business entity with a right of free exercise; second, unlike the federal law, it explicitly allowed religious liberty as a defense in a private lawsuit. Indeed, the state legislature rejected an amendment that would have prohibited businesses from discriminating (Graham 2015).[41]

Insisting that he would not change the law, Pence promised instead to clarify it and correct the misunderstandings. On April 2, 2015, he issued a press release to announce a "fix," explaining,

> Last week the Indiana General Assembly passed the Religious Freedom Restoration Act raising the judicial standard that would be used when government action intrudes upon the religious liberty of Hoosiers, and I was pleased to sign it. Over the past week this law has become a subject of great misunderstanding and controversy across our state and nation. However we got here, we are where we are, and it is important that our state take action to address the concerns that have been raised and move forward. Last weekend I called upon the Indiana General Assembly to clarify that this new judicial standard would not create a license to discriminate or to deny services to any individual as its critics have alleged. I am grateful for the efforts of legislators, business and other community leaders who came together to forge this clarifying language in the law. (Indiana Governor Mike Pence 2015b)[42]

The state could have repealed the law or enacted a measure to prohibit discrimination because of sexual orientation. With respect to the latter, Pence told Stephanopoulos that he would "not push for that. That's a—that's not on my agenda and that's not been the—that's not been an objective of the people of the state of Indiana. And it doesn't have anything to do with this law. I mean, George, Bill Clinton signed the Religious Freedom Restoration Act in 1993" (*ABC News*, March 29, 2015). In the end, the publicity forced Pence and the legislature to reconsider and reformulate the offending law while continuing to insist that the reactions to it stemmed from misunderstandings and misperceptions.

The chief executive officer of Angie's List, a company headquartered in Indianapolis, called the amendment "insufficient," emphasizing that "it applies only to entities affected by the so-called religious freedom bill. . . . It does not change existing Indiana nondiscrimination law, which *does not* include protections against discrimination based on sexual orientation or gender identity in employment, education, public accommodations, or housing." HRC and the ACLU also released statements, criticizing the new law for allowing a religious liberty defense in the areas of education and health care. Additionally, they stressed, without a statewide antidiscrimination law, LGBT people are still subject to discrimination (*The Advocate*, April 2, 2015, emphasis in the original).

Pence, perhaps unwittingly, heightened their concern, stating,

> Hoosiers deserve to know, that even with this legislation, the Religious Freedom Restoration Act enhances protections for every church, non-profit religious organization or society, religious school, rabbi, priest, preacher, minister or pastor in the review of government action where their religious liberty is infringed. The law also enhances protection in religious liberty cases for groups of individuals and businesses in conscience decisions that do not involve provision of goods and services, employment and housing. (*Indianapolis Star*, April 2, 2015)

Pence's capitulation was heavily criticized by groups that had supported the original version of the law, making it clear that they had intended it "as a sword to promote discrimination against the LGBT community in the public sphere" (Southern Poverty Law Center 2016).[43] An ADF senior counsel warned that the amended version "will actively force private business owners to violate their consciences." He said Pence should not have signed it because it will put a heavy burden on business owners who never refused to serve "homosexuals" but had simply begged off from participating in their same-sex marriages because of their religious beliefs. He continued,

> Unfortunately, state lawmakers caved in quickly to pressure from activists spewing disinformation and accepted the fix, again assuming wrongly that discrimination laws are never used improperly to punish dissidents from the ascendant orthodoxy on same-sex marriage. The Indiana "fix" removes a major defense that business owners could have used to defend themselves against a coercive charge of discrimination. (Lorence 2015)

The head of Advance America also attacked Republican leaders for conceding. In a press release, he urged legislators to vote against the conference committee report on SB 50. "The proposed change to Indiana's Religious Freedom Restoration Act is not a 'fix,'" he proclaimed, "but a hammer to destroy religious freedom for Hoosiers around the state." He warned,

> [I]f the conference committee report is adopted, Christian bakers, florists and photographers would no longer have the benefit of Indiana law to help protect them from being forced by the government to participate in a homosexual wedding. Likewise, a Christian busi-

> ness owner would no longer have the benefit of Indiana law to help protect him from being forced to permit a male cross-dresser to use the women's restroom and women's shower area. (Advance America 2015c)

Benefiting from the Indiana debacle, Hutchinson and the Arkansas legislature were spared these reactions to their proposed RFRA. On March 31, 2015, less than a week after Pence signed the Indiana law, the Arkansas legislature sent HB 1228, subtitled "To Enact The Religious Freedom Restoration Act; And To Declare An Emergency," to the governor for his signature. Hutchinson, who had initially indicated that he would sign it if it were similar to other state RFRAs, sent it back to the legislature to be altered to more closely resemble the federal law.

As originally written, HB 1228 defined persons even more broadly than the Indiana law had and required the government to prove that the burden on religious freedom was "essential" to advancing a compelling state interest; it also contained an "emergency clause" expressly stating that the highest government interest was the preservation of religious liberty (Arkansas State Legislature 2015b).[44]

With protests at the state capitol, major corporations, such as Yelp, Apple, and Walmart—the state's largest employer—weighed in to urge Hutchinson to veto. In the end, he signed the modified Act 975 on April 2, 2015. There were significant changes in the law. The revised version eliminated the broad definition of person and the requirement that the burden on religion must be "essential" to furthering the government's compelling reason; it also removed the language indicating that the government does not have to be a party to the action while retaining the "Emergency Clause."[45]

During the signing ceremony, Hutchinson expressed satisfaction with the bill, observing, "[I]t protects religious freedom, it establishes a framework for the balancing act that the courts must determine these types of cases, and thirdly, I think it does recognize the diversity of our culture and our workforce" (*Arkansas Matters*, April 3, 2015). He avoided mentioning that, unlike Indiana, where more than a dozen municipalities passed antidiscrimination ordinances, Arkansas law prevented cities and towns from doing so.

Others were not as pleased as Hutchinson, pointing out that, because Arkansas's civil rights laws still excluded the LGBT community, there is no prohibition against discrimination for any reason in the state. HRC's legal director warned of the problems with the Arkansas law:

> The fact remains that the only way to ensure LGBT Arkansans are treated equally under state law is to add explicit protections for them. . . . Moving forward, Arkansas should explicitly clarify that the RFRA cannot be used to undermine non-discrimination protections at any level. In addition, all states and the federal government should provide explicit non-discrimination protections on the basis of sexual orientation and gender identity. The federal Religious Freedom Restoration Act, while well-intentioned, has been used in recent years to justify problematic behavior that harms third parties. (Human Rights Campaign 2015e)

PUBLIC OFFICIALS AND RELIGIOUS FREEDOM

Beginning in 2014, when it seemed likely that marriage equality would become a reality, officials with responsibility for issuing marriage licenses or officiating at marriage ceremonies claimed that their religious objections to same-sex marriage entitled them to refuse to perform their duties. At the same time, state legislatures considered bills to bar public officials from issuing licenses to same-sex couples or, at a minimum, insulate them from liability for declining to issue licenses or perform marriages. The Texas Preservation of Sovereignty and Marriage Act (HB 4105), prohibiting state or local governmental employees from "recogniz[ing], grant[ing], or enforc[ing] a same-sex marriage license," exemplifies the former. Although approved in committee, it went no further (Texas Legislature Online 2015).

Because it became clear that such a measure was unconstitutional, most states opted for the latter approach, freeing public officials to refuse to perform their duties without fear of consequences. The Louisiana Marriage and Conscience Act (HB 707), for example, was intended to prevent government retaliation against public officials who cited their religious beliefs as reasons to refuse to perform their duties (*New York Times*, January 28, 2015).[46] In a 10–2 vote, a House committee killed that bill as well (*New Orleans Times Picayune*, May 19, 2015). Its defeat had prompted Jindal to issue his executive order (BJ 15-8).

The outcome was different in North Carolina. The Act to Allow Magistrates and Registers of Deeds to Recuse Themselves from Performing Duties Related to Marriage Ceremonies Due to Sincerely Held Religious Objection" (SB 2) permitted public officials to recuse themselves from performing marriages. Without specifying what precipitated the law, most of the legislative debate was devoted to same-sex marriage (North Carolina General Assembly 2015).[47]

The bill handily passed the Republican-dominated legislature, but ironically, in view of his later stance on LGBT rights, Governor Pat McCrory vetoed it on May 28, 2015. He released a statement, explaining, "I recognize that for many North Carolinians, including myself, opinions on same-sex marriage come from sincerely held religious beliefs that marriage is between a man and a woman. However, we are a nation and a state of laws [and] . . . no public official who voluntarily swears to support and defend the Constitution and to discharge all duties of their office should be exempt from upholding that oath" (State of North Carolina 2015b).

By June 11, 2015, when both houses of the North Carolina legislature had voted to override his veto, McCrory expressed his regret in another press release:

> It's a disappointing day for the rule of law and the process of passing legislation in North Carolina. I will continue to stand up for conservative principles that respect and obey the oath of office for public officials across our state and nation. While some people inside the beltline are focusing on symbolic issues, I remain focused on the issues that are going to have the greatest impact on the next generation such as creating jobs, building roads, strengthening education and improving our quality of life. (State of North Carolina 2015a)

A member of the North Carolina House also voiced his disappointment, presciently warning, "[G]lobal corporations go where they want to go in the United States [and] we've sent a message that we're in favor of inequality and that we are not a tolerant state" (*Charlotte Observer*, June 11, 2015).

In December 2015, a member of the Virginia State Senate prefiled a bill (Senate Bill No. 40) that mirrored North Carolina's in allowing clerks with religious or moral objections to refuse to issue marriage licenses. It would have sent the rejected couple to the Department of

Motor Vehicles for the license (Virginia's Legislative Information System 2016).[48] The bill was later sent back to committee after its sponsor admitted that he could not definitely say it would not also protect clerks who refused to issue marriage licenses to interracial couples (*Washington Post*, January 27, 2016; *Washington Post*, January 29, 2016).

As state legislatures began to adjourn in June 2015, the LGBT community succeeded in defeating more than forty anti-LGBT bills, including religious freedom restoration laws, right of refusal laws, laws barring local antidiscrimination ordinances, laws restricting LGBT couples from adopting, and laws monitoring restroom use by transgender individuals. Many were aimed at circumventing LGBT rights by juxtaposing them with claims of religious liberty. In the end, only SB 202 in Arkansas and SB 2 in North Carolina became law (Keith 2015).

In addition to their efforts to counter marriage equality through legislative actions, opponents also carried on the fight at the personal level. The face of the opposition was Kim Davis, a county clerk in Rowan County, Kentucky, whose response to *Obergefell* attracted the nation's attention in a dispute that occupied the courts, the press, and many of the Republican candidates for president for more than a year.[49] Davis's defiance raised questions about whether public officials, sworn to uphold the law, could violate their oaths of office while retaining their government positions.[50]

Davis, then a Democrat—now a Republican—was elected to a four-year term in the $80,000-a-year position in 2014, succeeding her mother, who had been in the job for thirty-seven years; Davis served under her as deputy clerk for twenty-six of those years. Ironically, when elected, she said, "I promise to . . . follow the statutes of this office to the letter" (*Morehead News*, November 7, 2014).

The controversy in Rowan County began on June 27, 2015—the day after the Court announced *Obergefell*—when Davis, an Apostolic Christian, ordered her deputy clerks to stop issuing all marriage licenses.[51] Under Kentucky law, county clerks or their deputies issue marriage licenses, yet Davis refused because she believed that it would validate same-sex marriage. She also refused to permit her deputies to distribute them (one clerk was willing to do so), arguing that her name and title would appear on the license.[52]

On July 1, 2015, two same-sex and two different-sex couples filed a federal lawsuit against Davis, arguing that her policy substantially interfered with their right to marry by preventing them from acquiring a license in the county of their residence. They could have traveled to another county for their licenses but felt that it would not have had the same meaning. With lawyers from Liberty Counsel representing her, Davis claimed that the minimal intrusion on their right to marry was offset by her right to religious freedom.[53] Her supporters viewed her case as an important symbol of the conflict between religion and marriage equality. One of her lawyers declared, "[M]any in Christian circles believe we are only now beginning the culture wars over marriage" (*New York Times*, August 13, 2015).[54]

Kentucky Federal District Court Judge David Bunning ruled on August 12, 2015, characterizing the issue as a "conflict between two individual liberties held sacrosanct in American jurisprudence . . . [that] threaten to impinge on the opposing party's rights" (*Miller v. Davis* 2015a, 930).[55] He found that, as in *Loving* and *Zablocki*, there was a significant burden on the plaintiffs' right to marry. In applying strict scrutiny, because a fundamental right was at issue, Bunning rejected Davis's argument that the state had a compelling interest in preserving her religious liberty, citing its equally compelling reason in enforcing the establishment clause and its vital interest "in upholding the rule of law" (*Miller v. Davis* 2015a, 936). Determining that the plaintiffs would "suffer irreparable harm" if their constitutional rights were violated, he turned to the question of the harm to Davis. She contended that the governor's directive to the state county clerks substantially burdened her religious exercise without a compelling reason. As a neutral policy directive intended to ensure that county clerks complied with the high court ruling and not aimed at repressing religion, Bunning found it constitutional, without requiring the state to show a compelling reason.

He ruled that Davis's signature would not signify approval of a same-sex marriage but merely certify a couple's eligibility to marry and that carrying out her duties would not burden her religion. Bunning concluded that Davis was unlikely to prevail on any of her remaining arguments as well and held that the plaintiffs had satisfied the criteria for a preliminary injunction. He said:

> The State is not asking her to condone same-sex unions on moral or religious grounds, nor is it restricting her from engaging in a variety of religious activities. Davis remains free to practice her Apostolic Christian beliefs. She may continue to attend church twice a week,

> participate in Bible Study and minister to female inmates at the Rowan County Jail. She is even free to believe that marriage is a union between one man and one woman, as many Americans do. However, her religious convictions cannot excuse her from performing the duties that she took an oath to perform as Rowan County Clerk. (944)

He granted the plaintiffs' motion for a preliminary injunction and ordered Davis to refrain from carrying out her "no licenses" policy when these plaintiffs sought a license. She failed to report for work the next day while continuing to order her clerks not to issue licenses.[56]

Davis immediately sought a stay of Bunning's order, and two weeks later, on August 28, 2015, a unanimous Sixth Circuit panel denied it, finding little reason to think that she could successfully argue that she did not have to comply with a Supreme Court ruling (*Miller v. Davis* 2015b). She applied to the US Supreme Court for an emergency stay of the injunction pending Fourth Circuit review. On August 31, 2015, with no dissents, the high court denied her motion (*Davis v. Miller* 2015). With its ruling, the Supreme Court ended the possibility of a stay while her case was on appeal and ended, as well, any legal grounds for not issuing marriage licenses in Rowan County.

When the plaintiffs and other couples appeared at the county clerk's office on September 1, 2015, the clerk told them that the office was not issuing licenses during the appeals process. They filed another motion, asking the court to hold her in civil contempt and fine her. Bunning ordered Davis and her deputy clerks to appear before him to show cause why he should not issue a contempt citation. During the hearing, five of the six deputies agreed under oath that they would sign the necessary documents for all couples, and Bunning asked Davis if she would allow it. He ordered a recess to give her time to consult with her legal team; she did not return from the recess, her lawyer explaining that she would not grant them the authority to sign (*Washington Post*, September 3, 2015).

Bunning found her in contempt, and because he believed fines were insufficient, he had her taken into federal custody (*Miller v. Davis* 2015c). In another order dated September 3, 2015, he modified the preliminary injunction to clarify that she was obligated to provide marriage licenses to all eligible couples, not just the plaintiffs (*Miller v. Davis* 2015d).

Reacting to the decision to imprison her, one of her lawyers darkly warned, "[T]oday, for the first time in history, an American citizen has been incarcerated for having the belief of conscience that marriage is the union of one man and one woman." She will only be released, he added, if "she's willing to change her conscience about what belief is" (*New York Times*, September 3, 2015).

The next day, Staver, one of Davis's attorneys, announced that she considered the marriage licenses issued in her absence invalid because they were signed by the deputies without her authority. "They are not worth the paper that they are written on," he said (*National Public Radio*, September 4, 2015).

Beshear as well as the county attorney and judge executive insisted that the licenses were valid even though she had not signed them (*Lexington Herald-Leader*, September 8, 2015). The governor was under pressure to issue an executive order removing clerks' names from marriage licenses but declined, claiming that he lacked the authority because it required legislative action. He also refused to call a special session with a price tag of $60,000 to accommodate Davis (*Courier-Journal*, July 8, 2015; *National Public Radio*, September 1, 2015).

Five days later, Bunning lifted the contempt citation and released her from jail after the plaintiffs reported that they received a marriage license (with Davis's name removed and replaced by the words *Rowan County*); as a condition of her release, he warned her not to interfere with the issuance of licenses (*Miller v. Davis* 2015e).

Once out of jail, Davis insisted she would still not issue licenses but that she would allow her deputies to do so, warning, however, that they were invalid without her authorization (*Huffington Post*, September 8, 2015). In addition to removing her name and title from the licenses, she altered them by adding that they were issued "Pursuant to Federal Court Order #15-CV-44DLB." The plaintiffs asked Bunning to reinforce his earlier orders and, this time, impose fines to coerce her to obey; they also asked him to place the clerk's office in receivership to issue licenses if her noncompliance persisted.[57]

Davis filed an emergency motion to stay the court's September 3, 2015 order pending her appeal to the Sixth Circuit.[58] On September 23, 2015, Bunning denied the stay (*Miller v. Davis* 2015f); on November 5, 2015, the Sixth Circuit upheld Bunning's ruling (*Miller v. Davis* 2015g).

Despite losing numerous motions and appeals, Davis won in the end. Beshear's successor, Matt Bevin, acceded to her wishes and signed Executive Order 2015-048 on December 22, 2015, to remove county clerks' names from marriage licenses. "It's a great Christmas present for Kim Davis and for others like her," said Staver (*Lexington Herald-Leader*, December 22, 2015).

The legislature codified Bevin's order by passing SB 216 on April 13, 2016 (Kentucky Legislature 2016).[59] Following this, Davis returned to the Sixth Circuit, asking it to dismiss her appeals, vacate all court orders—including the contempt citation—and absolve her from court costs. On July 13, 2016, the Sixth Circuit agreed that the law had mooted the issue and vacated the August 12, 2015 and September 3, 2015 orders, leaving Bunning's contempt citation in place (*Miller v. Davis* 2016).[60]

Polls showed that most Americans disagreed with Davis's position; an *ABC News/Washington Post* poll conducted from September 7 to 10, 2015, reported that almost three-quarters of the respondents (74 percent) agreed that "equality under the law should trump religious beliefs." When asked if Davis should issue licenses notwithstanding her religious principles, 63 percent said she should (*Politico,* September 15, 2015).

TRANSGENDER RIGHTS

When the furor over Davis's rebellion had receded by the end of 2015, the nation soon became absorbed in controversy over transgender rights, this time centering almost exclusively on the use of bathroom facilities by members of the transgender community. While same-sex marriage still remains anathema to the Christian right, "by removing the last key barrier to equality under the Constitution for gay, lesbian, and bisexual people, *Obergefell* also marks the passing of the torch from 'LGB' to 'T.' The next civil rights frontier belongs to transgender people" (Barry et al. 2016, 509).

The legal status of restroom use for transgender individuals is uncertain outside the employment context, in which, according to the EEOC and OSHA, employers must allow transgender employees to access bathroom facilities based on their gender identity. The outlook for transgender students is murkier, as the Title IX litigation continues to wend its way through the federal courts. Outside the education and employment context, the public had not generally been involved in the debate over restroom access—until the referendum on the Houston Equal Rights Ordinance (HERO) on November 3, 2015.

In May 2014, with the support of Democratic Mayor Annise Parker—one of the first lesbian mayors of a major city—the Houston City Council passed an antidiscrimination ordinance in an 11–6 vote. HERO prohibited discrimination because of sex, race, color, disability, and myriad other categories, including sexual orientation and gender identity; it broadly applied to city services, employment and contracting, public accommodations, housing, and private employment, exempting religious institutions and organizations. Despite the strong support on the council, its opponents collected enough signatures for a petition to bring it to a referendum for a vote.

The opposition to HERO was largely fueled by fear. Ignoring the fact that the law served as a wide-ranging vehicle for fighting discrimination, most of the attention focused on its effect on public bathroom use—emphasizing that it would allow men to dress as women and invade women's bathrooms. One study reported that local TV stations, which often unthinkingly stoked the public's fear, devoted 40 percent of their coverage of the referendum to bathrooms and only 10 percent to the rest of its provisions (Heffernan 2016).

Proposition 1, as the ordinance appeared on the ballot, straightforwardly asked if voters were in favor of it. Parker emphasized HERO's broad application and decried the overblown attention to its effect on bathroom usage. She said, "[W]hile much of the debate has centered around the gay and transgender section of the ordinance, it is a comprehensive ordinance. It is a good step forward for the city of Houston" (*Free Press Houston*, May 29, 2014).

A coalition of Christian pastors and social conservatives, including the ADF, joined forces to defeat HERO, calling it the "Sexual Predator Protection Act." An ad by the chief opposition group, Campaign for Houston, warned, "[T]his ordinance will allow men to freely go into women's bathrooms, locker rooms and showers. That is filthy, that is disgusting and that is unsafe." Its banner read, "No Men in Women's Bathrooms" (*ThinkProgress*, August 24, 2014).[61]

The vote to repeal won handily, with 157,110 votes (60.97 percent); HERO's supporters received only 100,582 votes (39.03 percent).[62] When the results were tallied, Texas Lieutenant Governor Dan Patrick declared, "[I]t was about protecting our grandmoms, and our mothers and our wives and our sisters and our daughters and our granddaughters. I'm glad Houston led tonight to end this constant political-correctness attack on what we know in our heart and our gut as Americans is not right" (*Ballotpedia* 2015). Parker accused HERO's opponents of running a "calculated campaign of lies designed to demonize a little-understood minority, and to use that to take down an ordinance that 200 other cities across America and 17 states have successfully passed and operated under" (*Houston Press*, November 3, 2015).[63]

There had been some concern that the 2016 NCAA Final Four tournament, scheduled to be played in Houston in March, would be moved to a new location because of HERO's defeat, but the city appeared to suffer no negative consequences from the repeal vote. NCAA officials suggested the possibility that the absence of an equal rights ordinance might be a factor in their decision to return to Houston in the future. NFL officials also said that they had no plans to move the 2017 Super Bowl out of Houston (*New York Times*, November 4, 2015). Although the tourist and convention industries worried about the loss of business, no events were cancelled (*Houston Chronicle*, January 28, 2016; *Houston Chronicle*, November 4, 2016).

It is unclear why there was no adverse impact. Perhaps equal rights advocates were stymied because HERO lost in a referendum and they were unable to exert pressure to reverse it. Ironically, a *KHOU/KUHF* poll showed that a quarter of the law's opponents said that they would reassess their position if the NFL would renege on its Super Bowl commitment or the NCAA would move the Final Four tournament out of Houston (*Houston Chronicle,* November 4, 2015).

The victory in Houston, the first for the Christian right since *Obergefell*, ended the year and set the tone for the upcoming battles in 2016, when it appeared that the entire nation was obsessed with bathroom usage. Scenarios of the dangers women and children faced in public bathrooms were not novel in the United States; they had played a significant role in past civil rights struggles.[64]

The "clash over bathrooms, an issue that appeared atop no national polls . . . [had become] the next frontier in America's fast-moving culture wars" (*New York Times*, May 21, 2015). In January 2016, for example, a Tennessee bill (HB 2414 and SB 2387) would have required transgender students to use public school bathrooms according to their birth status; it was removed from the legislative calendar a few months later (LegiScan 2016).[65]

Reacting to the flurry of such bills as this, the National Taskforce to End Sexual and Domestic Violence Against Women (2016) released a statement condemning the scare tactics used to promote such laws. It affirmed that there was no "increase in sexual violence or other public safety issues due to nondiscrimination laws. Assaulting another person in a restroom or changing room remains against the law in every single state." Indeed, there is substantial evidence that the "bathroom predator" is a myth.[66] Reports from numerous experts, government officials, and school administrators around the country underscore that antidiscrimination laws and school antidiscrimination policies have not generated sexual attacks or inappropriate behavior in bathrooms (Fitzgerald 2016; Maza and Brinker 2014; see *Washington Post*, May 13, 2016). Nevertheless, in addition to Tennessee, legislators in Arizona, Florida, Georgia, Kentucky, Maryland, Mississippi, North Carolina, South Carolina, and South Dakota all introduced bills to confine transgender individuals to the bathroom of the sex that appears on their birth certificates.[67]

South Dakota captured the nation's attention early in 2016 when its legislature began to consider an "Act to restrict access to certain restrooms and locker rooms in public schools" (HB 1008) to limit transgender students to using the locker rooms and restrooms of their biological sex.[68] The bill's sponsor said that it was "entirely preventative," admitting that there was no evidence that any harm had come from allowing transgender students to use the bathrooms of their choice (*New York Times*, February 26, 2016). In a meeting in which several state legislators spoke candidly, they revealed little understanding of gender identity issues (one calling transgender students "twisted" and another implying that they were mentally unstable) and little sensitivity to the problems that the bill would cause (*ThinkProgress*, February 8, 2016).

Bill supporters claimed that its purpose was to protect students' safety and privacy, arguing that it showed "compassion for transgender students." Opponents said that having to use separate bathroom facilities, which were often inconveniently located, stigmatized transgender students. Moreover, they said, such laws would lead to inevitable lawsuits, with the federal government taking the students' side (*Washington Post*, February 16, 2016).

HB 1008 handily passed both houses and was sent to the governor, who initially said that it "seems like a good idea," for his signature. On March 1, 2015, Governor Dennis Daugaard instead vetoed the measure, explaining that it "does not address any pressing issue" and would interfere with local authority. He stressed that the bill "invites conflict and litigation . . . [and] would place every school district in the difficult position of following state law while knowing it openly invites federal litigation." Moreover, he added, the "law will create a certain liability for school districts and the state in an area where no such liability exists today" (South Dakota State News 2016).[69]

The events in South Dakota indicate that such laws are not inevitable and that public officials are aware of the likelihood of litigation that will accompany them as well as the possible loss of federal funding and business opportunities.[70] North Carolina proved to be an exception as it rushed into passage of HB 2, disregarding the experiences of other states that had enacted anti-LGBT laws.

Despite McCrory's promise to "remain focused on the issues that are going to have the greatest impact on the next generation," he signed a law—the first of its kind in the nation—that eventually led to a confrontation with the federal government and the potential loss of federal dollars and lost business.[71] HB 2 was precipitated by events in Charlotte, the state's largest city. On February 22, 2016, after a narrow defeat the previous year, the city council voted 7–4 to approve Ordinance 7056, prohibiting businesses and city contractors from discriminating on the basis of marital status, familial status, sexual orientation, gender identity, and gender expression. An accompanying document ("Frequently Asked Questions") explained that a "business may not prohibit a transgender person from using the restroom or locker room consistent with the gender identified or expressed by that person." The document stressed that the ordinance is only for the protection of transgender individuals and does not supersede harassment or "indecent exposure laws" (Charlotte City Clerk 2016; see *Charlotte Observer*, February 22, 2016). Just before its passage, McCrory warned Charlotte's leaders that the ordinance might

> create major public safety issues by putting citizens in possible danger from deviant actions by individuals taking improper advantage of a bad policy. Also, this action of allowing a person with male anatomy, for example, to use a female restroom or locker room will most likely cause immediate State legislative intervention which I would support as governor. (*Charlotte Observer*, February 22, 2016)

As with HERO, the opposition to the Charlotte ordinance primarily focused on bathroom use. Immediately following the city council vote, McCrory and the House Speaker vowed to nullify the ordinance and prevent other municipalities from following Charlotte's example (*BuzzFeed*, February 23, 2016). On March 22, 2016, legislative leaders called a special session—at a cost of $42,000 a day—to override the ordinance. Both chambers met on March 23, 2016, and approved the Public Facilities Privacy and Security Act (HB 2) the same day. It passed in the House in an 84–25 vote after only three hours of debate. The Senate vote was 32–0; Senate Democrats left the chamber before the vote to protest their exclusion from the legislative process. McCrory signed it that night (*City Lab*, March 23, 2016; *News & Observer*, March 26, 2016).[72]

The law stripped local government entities of the authority to create antidiscrimination public accommodations laws and limited protected categories in state antidiscrimination laws to race, religion, color, national origin, age, handicap, and biological sex as designated on an individual's birth certificate.[73] Although its effect on the LGBT community received the most attention, HB 2 accomplished a few of the legislature's other goals, including preventing local governments from topping the state minimum wage of $7.25 an hour and eliminating discrimination suits in state courts.[74]

HB 2 supporters defended the law and attacked the Charlotte ordinance. The lieutenant governor called the ordinance "unconstitutional" and characterized it as

> amazingly discriminatory against, especially women and girls who no longer basically had the freedom to walk into a restroom and know that they were gonna be safe and secure in that restroom, without a man walking in or a pedophile or a predator walking into that bathroom. That's really discriminatory if you want to talk about discrimination there. (*Indy Week*, April 4, 2016)

As in Indiana, the reaction was immediate: swift condemnations by LGBT rights activists; protests at the executive mansion in Raleigh; online campaigns to boycott the state; states and municipalities banning official travel to North Carolina; more than one hundred corporate leaders urging repeal; major companies threatening to leave the state or abandoning planned expansions; cancelled concerts and conventions; and sports organizations considering moving events out of the state (*Washington Post*, March 24, 2016). Additionally, a number of federal agencies weighed in, announcing that they would determine whether HB 2 violates federal law and implicates federal funding.

With economic pressure mounting, on April 12, 2016, McCrory defended HB 2 as necessary to "stop the breach of basic privacy and etiquette"; others characterized it as "common sense" (*Washington Post*, March 24, 2016). Critics questioned the law's enforcement mechanism, wondering whether police would be stationed in public bathrooms and demand to see birth certificates (see *Mother Jones*, April 7, 2016; *TownDock*, April 15, 2016).

In an attempt to pacify the critics, McCrory announced Executive Order No. 93 in a video address, saying,

> You know, after listening to people's feedback for the past several weeks on this issue, I have come to the conclusion that there is a great deal of misinformation, misinterpretation, confusion, a lot of passion, and frankly, selective outrage and hypocrisy, especially against the great state of North Carolina. But based on this feedback, I am taking action to affirm and improve the state's commitment to privacy and equality. To that end, today I have signed an executive order with the goal of achieving that balance. (*City Lab*, April 12, 2016; *National Public Radio*, April 12, 2016; *Washington Post*, April 18, 2016)

McCroy's order protected state workers from discrimination because of gender identity and sexual orientation and "encouraged" the legislature to restore a state cause of action for employment discrimination suits.[75] Much of it was not new, merely noting existing law allowing local governments and private businesses to establish employment discrimination policies and permitting private businesses to determine their own bathroom rules. It reiterated HB 2's bathroom policy for all public buildings, permitting "reasonable accommodations" when convenient, and reaffirmed that local governments cannot include LGBT protections in their public accommodations laws (NC Governor Pat McCrory 2016).[76]

Public opinion in the state was divided and contradictory; a poll commissioned by *WRAL News* showed that half the respondents disapproved of HB 2, with 38 percent approving, but more than half (56 percent) agreed with the bathroom provision. Slightly more than half (52 percent) agreed that LGBT antidiscrimination measures should be included in state law, and 36 percent disagreed (*WRAL*, April 12, 2016). Similarly, a *CNN* national poll taken a month later found 57 percent opposing laws like HB 2 and 38 percent supporting them (*CNN*, May 9, 2016).[77]

The economic consequences mounted, with more than six hundred new jobs disappearing, millions of convention and tourist dollars vanishing, and the possibility of losing billions of dollars in federal funding.[78] The National Basketball Association (NBA), that had warned of relocating the 2017 All Star game from Charlotte if the law were not changed, announced on August 19, 2016, that New Orleans, which does not have a similar law, would host the game (National Basketball Association 2016; see ESPN 2016; *Huffington Post*, August 19, 2016).

As the events in North Carolina were beginning to unfold, Georgia's Governor Nathan Deal had to decide whether to sign HB 757, an amalgam of SB 284, the First Amendment Defense Act of Georgia, and HB 757, the Pastor Protection Act, renamed the Free Exercise Protection Act.[79] The legislation promised religious leaders and institutions as well as faith-based 501(c)(3) organizations that they would face no adverse legal consequences if they acted on their religious principles about sex or marriage (Georgia General Assembly 2016; see *Atlanta Journal-Constitution*, February 20, 2016).[80]

As the controversy grew more intense, with opponents expressing concerns about the wide-ranging nature of the bill and corporate leaders warning of dire economic consequences, Deal announced his veto, saying, "I don't think we have to discriminate against anyone to protect the faith-based community in Georgia of which my family and I are a part of for all of our lives" (Governor Nathan Deal 2016).

Shortly after Deal's veto, Mississippi Governor Phil Bryant was asked to sign the Protecting Freedom of Conscience from Government Discrimination Law (HB 1523), broadly preventing the state from "discriminating" against individuals, businesses, public employees, and religious organizations that act on their "sincerely-held religious beliefs or moral convictions" toward same-sex marriage, extramarital sex, and gender identity.[81] The first law to explicitly link religion to opposition to transgender bathroom use, it applies to policies related to employment, housing, adoption, foster care, same-sex marriages, and sex-segregated facilities (Mississippi Legislature 2016).[82] Aside from LGBT advocacy groups, business organizations, like the Mississippi Economic Council and the Mississippi Manufacturer's Association, and major employers, like Toyota and Nissan, urged Bryant to veto, citing the harm to the state's business environment (*Clarion-Ledger*, April 4, 2016).

Their efforts proved futile. Bryant signed it on April 5, 2016, tweeting that it "protect[s] sincerely held religious beliefs and moral convictions of individuals, organizations, and private associations from discriminatory actions by state government," adding that it "merely reinforces the rights which currently exist to the exercise of religious freedom as stated in the First Amendment to the U.S. Constitution" (*BuzzFeed*, April 5, 2016).[83]

FEDERAL AGENCIES AND LGBT RIGHTS

The federal government soon became embroiled in the controversy over LGBT rights, primarily by asserting that HB 2 infringes on Title VII and Title IX. Most attention focused on the latter, in part because of the enormity of federal education funding involved. In the heated climate of the 2016 election, the legal arguments were subsumed in politics, with North Carolina and others states accusing Obama of overreaching.[84]

Shortly after HB 2 became law, Principal Deputy Assistant Attorney General Vanita Gupta, head of the Civil Rights Division, informed McCrory in a letter dated May 4, 2016, that DOJ "has determined" that North Carolina is violating Title VII by discriminating on the basis of sex. Citing the employment cases—*Barnes*, *Glenn*, *Macy*, *Schroer*, and *Smith*—she stated, "[F]ederal courts and administrative agencies have applied Title VII to discrimination against transgender individuals based on sex, including gender identity." Even more recently, she said that in *Lusuardi v. Department of the Army* (2015), the EEOC found in favor of a transgender woman who complained that her employer blocked her from bathroom facilities that accorded with her gender identity. The commission ruled that "equal access to restrooms is a significant, basic condition of employment . . . [and denying the complainant] a restroom that other persons of her gender were freely permitted to use . . . constitutes a harm or loss with respect to the terms and conditions of Complainant's employment."

Gupta's letter reiterated that Title VII authorizes the attorney general to ask a court to order compliance with the statute when, as here, there is a "pattern or practice of discrimination." It requested the state to "advise" DOJ by May 9, 2016 whether it "will remedy these violations" and take appropriate action with respect to HB 2. It ended by noting that DOJ had also informed the University of North Carolina and the Department of Public Safety of their violations of the Violence Against Women Reauthorization Act of 2013 (VAWA) and Title IX (US Department of Justice, Civil Rights Division 2016; see *Charlotte Observer*, May 4, 2016; *WRAL*, May 4, 2016).[85]

On May 9, 2016, the North Carolina General Assembly leadership—Phil Berger as President Pro Tem of the Senate and Tim Moore as Speaker of the House—sued DOJ, asking for a declaratory injunction "to instruct the Department in no uncertain terms that its overbearing abuse of executive authority flouts our Constitution's limitations on federal power and tramples on the sovereign dignity of the States and their citizens" (*Berger v. United States Department of Justice* 2016, at 2–3). The complaint used such extreme language as "utter unworkability," "ideological extremity" (at 3), "open-ended threat" (at 6), and "stunningly overbroad conclusory determinations" (at 17) and accused the federal government of violating constitutional principles of separation of powers and federalism as well as the Tenth Amendment and the Administrative Procedure Act (APA).

McCrory filed suit against DOJ the same day, saying that the agency's "position is a baseless and blatant overreach" (*McCrory v. United States* 2016a, at 2). The primary thrust of the lawsuit was that Title VII does not protect transgender status, and in any event, there is no discrimination because "all state employees are required to use the bathroom and changing facilities assigned to persons of their same biological sex, regardless of gender identity or transgender status" (at 5). On September 16, 2016, McCrory voluntarily dismissed the suit against the federal government, citing the "substantial costs to the State of litigating similar legal theories in two different judicial districts" (*McCrory v. United States* 2016b, at 3).

In the third lawsuit of the day (*United States of America v. North Carolina* 2016), DOJ filed a complaint against the state, the Department of Public Safety, and the University of North Carolina, challenging HB 2 as it pertains to transgender persons and seeking an injunction. It reprised much of Gupta's letter, accusing the state of violating Title VII and Title IX by discriminating because of sex and VAWA by discriminating because of sex and gender identity.

Quoting from statements made by state officials, DOJ alleged that HB 2 intentionally discriminates against transgender individuals by allowing nontransgender employees into facilities consistent with their gender identity while preventing transgender employees from doing so. It declared that HB 2 "stigmatizes and singles out transgender employees, results in their isolation and exclusion, and perpetuates a sense that they are not worthy of equal treatment and respect" (at 9).[86]

At a press conference after the federal government filed suit, Lynch proclaimed,

> [T]his action is about a great deal more than just bathrooms. This is about the dignity and respect we accord our fellow citizens and the laws that we, as a people and as a country, have enacted to protect them—indeed, to protect all of us. And it's about the founding ideals that have led this country—haltingly but inexorably—in the direction of fairness, inclusion and equality for all Americans.

Addressing the people of North Carolina—her home state—she added, "[W]hat this law does is inflict further indignity on a population that has already suffered far more than its fair share. This law provides no benefit to society—all it does is harm innocent Americans" (US Department of Justice 2016).

The controversy soon intensified with the release of a DCL from Gupta and DOE's Catherine Lhamon to all school districts in the nation. The document, dated May 13, 2016, was termed a "Significant Guidance Letter," responding to questions from school districts asking for clarification of existing law. Its key message was that the two agencies regard gender identity as sex within the statute and its regulations, meaning "that a school must not treat a transgender student differently from the way it treats other students of the same gender identity." Such a letter does not have the force of law, and they explained that it "does not add requirements to existing law, but provides information and examples to inform recipients about how the Departments evaluate whether covered entities are complying with their legal obligations" (US Department of Justice, Civil Rights Division, and US Department of Education, Office for Civil Rights 2016).[87] The directive did not contain an explicit threat but put states on notice that the government might take action against noncomplying states.

State officials across the country attacked the administration, accusing it of overstepping its authority and endangering students' lives. With billions of dollars at stake, a number of states struck back. On May 25, 2016, Texas and ten other states filed a federal lawsuit against several federal agencies, charging that they "conspired to turn workplaces and educational settings across the country into laboratories for a massive social experiment, flouting the democratic process, and running roughshod over commonsense policies protecting children and basic privacy rights" (*State of Texas v. United States* of America 2016a, at 3).[88] Recounting Title IX and ENDA's legislative histories, the plaintiffs stressed that Congress had clearly intended them to limit these laws to biological sex only. The thrust of their argument was that the federal government relied on Guidances and "Dear Colleague Letters" to rewrite the laws and threaten noncomplying states with ominous economic consequences for noncompliance. Doing so, they said, violated the APA's rule-making procedures, federalism, spending clause, and separations of power principles.[89]

The states moved for a nationwide injunction against the May 2016 Guidance, claiming that congressional intent as well as Title VII, Title IX, and 34 C.F.R., section 106.33 clearly indicate that the term sex refers to biological and anatomical differences between men and women as determined at birth. The federal defendants argued that the government's interpretation of sex in the Guidance is in accord with "the nondiscrimination mandate" embodied in these laws and should be broadly construed to effectuate them (*State of Texas v. United States of America* 2016b, at 9; see *Dallas News*, August 12, 2016; *Longview News Journal*, August 12, 2016; *Texas Tribune*, August 12, 2016). Moreover, they contended, the Guidance is a lawful construction of text and regulations that are silent on the question of transgender individuals and restroom facilities.

On August 21, 2016, Texas Federal District Court Judge Reed O'Connor issued a nationwide injunction, finding that the Guidance failed to comply with the procedural requirements of the APA and conflicted with laws and regulations currently in effect. The court broadly enjoined the federal defendants from applying the Guidance to all public schools in the country and from relying on the interpretation that sex includes gender identity in any ongoing Title IX investigation or future litigation (*State of Texas v. United States of America* 2016b).

Two months later, O'Connor rejected the federal government's motion to limit the scope of the injunction to the states that filed suit, because "the alleged violation extends nationwide." He held that the federal statutes require uniform interpretation of law and limiting the injunction to the parties in the action would risk the federal government unlawfully using the Guidance to violate the rights of other states through its authority over their school districts and workplaces (*State of Texas v. United States of America* 2016c, at 4). O'Connor's injunction left a number of questions unanswered, primarily how it would affect other jurisdictions in the nation in the absence of a definitive Supreme Court ruling on the matter.

The question about the effect of O'Connor's broad injunction came to light in another suit brought by Texas and twenty-five other states against an Obama immigration policy had led to an evenly divided Supreme Court opinion, leaving the Texas judge's anti-Obama ruling in place. In a hearing over an action by the United States Citizenship and Immigration Services, New York Federal District Court Judge Nicholas Garaufis questioned whether the Texas court's interpretation of immigration policy should apply in the case before him. Garaufis expressed concern that "somehow a court sitting in Brooklyn, New York, in the 2nd Circuit, must give full faith and credit to a decision of the Fifth Circuit which may be erroneous?" He continued, saying, "that doesn't sound like justice to me.... I don't know what's going on out there to Texas on the border but I know what's going on in New York. And I'm very concerned about it and I have absolutely no intention of simply marching behind in the parade that's going on out there in Texas, if this person has rights here" (*Politico*, October 19, 2016; *New York Times*, October 9, 2016).

Within days of McCrory signing HB 2, two transgender students and a transgender employee of the University of North Carolina filed suit against the state in *Carcaño v. McCrory* (2016a). They argued that HB 2 violated their right to due process, equal protection, and Title IX by discriminating against them on the basis of sex, broadly defined as "gender nonconformity, gender identity, transgender status, and gender transition" (at 34). They alleged that HB 2 "not only disproportionately burdens transgender people, but intentionally targets them for differential treatment" and blocks local antidiscrimination measures (at 29). Echoing Kennedy's ruling in *Romer*, they claimed that the law stems from "animus toward LGBT people" (at 36). Reversing the arguments of HB 2 supporters, they contended that it "endangers the safety, privacy, security, and well-being of transgender individuals" (at 35).

On August 1, 2016, North Carolina Federal District Court Judge Thomas Schroeder heard arguments on the plaintiffs' motion for a preliminary injunction. During argument, he quizzed the attorney for the state about whether the law makes bathrooms safer and how it is enforced. When told that there was no "enforcement mechanism," he asked, "[T]hen why have it?" (*News & Observer*, August 1, 2016).[90]

Acting quickly to reach a decision before classes started, Schroeder issued a ruling on August 26, 2016. He reserved judgment on the likelihood of the plaintiffs' success on the constitutional claims, saying that he required more briefing from the parties. But in large part because of the Fourth Circuit's ruling in *G.G. v. Gloucester County*, Schroeder issued a limited injunction preventing the University of North Carolina from enforcing the restroom provision against the three transgender plaintiffs. He stated, "[I]t is important to emphasize that this injunction returns the parties to the status quo ante as it existed in Title IX facilities prior to Part I's [the bathroom bill portion of the law] passage in March 2016. On the current record, there is no reason to believe that a return to the status quo ante pending a trial on the merits will compromise the important state interests asserted" (*Carcaño v. McCrory* 2016b, at 5).[91]

The NCAA delivered more bad news to North Carolina, announcing on September 12, 2016, that it would not host any of the seven 2016–2017 championship events planned for the state (National Collegiate Athletic Association 2016). Two days later, the Atlantic Coast Conference (ACC), home to four North Carolina schools, issued a statement saying that it would relocate all eight championship events out of the state in the coming year (Atlantic Coast Conference 2016).

Later in the week, the state's Restaurant and Lodging Association lobbying group, anxious to end the controversy, called on the Charlotte City Council to repeal its equal rights ordinance and said that the state legislature was prepared to repeal HB 2 if Charlotte did so. McCrory's office released a statement on September 16, 2016, offering to call a special legislative session to repeal HB 2 if its conditions were met. His director of communication said,

> [F]or the last nine months, the governor has consistently said state legislation is only needed if the Charlotte ordinance remains in place. If the Charlotte City Council totally repeals the ordinance and then we can confirm there is support to repeal among the majority of state lawmakers in the House and Senate, the governor will call a special session. It is the governor's understanding that legislative leaders and the lieutenant governor agree with that assessment.

An HRC official characterized the maneuver as a "cheap trick" in which Charlotte would repeal its ordinance and "trust they will hold up their end of the bargain on a full repeal of HB 2."

Sounding far from conciliatory, Moore placed the blame entirely on the city, saying, "

> [T]he legislature and governor did not create this controversy—the Mayor and City Council of Charlotte did. If the Charlotte City Council and Mayor fully and unconditionally repeal their ordinance then I believe we have something to discuss. As for the House of Representatives, any specifics to be done would be subject to discussions and a decision of the caucus. I applaud the Governor in his continued efforts to promote the economic growth of our state while ensuring basic privacy and safety protections of citizens in bathrooms, showers and changing facilities. (*WNCN/NBTV*, September 16, 2016)

Charlotte Mayor Jennifer Roberts refused to accept blame for the situation in the state, and, despite being under heavy pressure from the business community, said that there were no current plans to repeal Ordinance 7056. The city attorney released a memo, pointing out that the state can act on HB 2 without the necessity of a repeal by Charlotte (*News & Observer*, September 19, 2016).

Although estimates vary, one report of the economic damage characterized the cost to the state as "snowballing" and reported a loss of more than $200 million since HB 2 was passed in March. The number was computed by adding "fleeing businesses," the "exodus of high-profile sports events," "conventions canceled," "major performances canceled," "film companies exit[ing]," "states ban[ning] travel to North Carolina," and "court costs." The "biggest potential blow would be the loss of federal funding" (estimated at $4.8 billion a year). As its momentous effects continued to mount, some Republican state officials joined the chorus to repeal HB 2, saying that they did not realize how explosive the issue was. Others asked for a compromise, without specifying what that would be (*Facing South*, September 16, 2016).

In a later disclosure, more than fifty investment managers representing more than $2.1 trillion in managed assets released a statement calling on the state to repeal HB 2 in its entirety. Their announcement promoted the adoption of nondiscrimination policies "that are essential if we want companies—any our economy to succeed, and we can't let a hate-filled law get in the way" (*Charlotte Observer*, September 26, 2016). McCrory responded by calling it the "height of hypocrisy" for "New York hedge fund billionaires to lecture North Carolina about how to conduct its affairs." McCrory's description of the leadership behind the announcement was not quite apt, as two of the organizers were the chief executive officer of Trillum Asset Management, with an office in Durham, and the head of Croatan Institute, also based in North Carolina (*Charlotte Observer*, September 26, 2016).

NOTES

1. Only two circuit courts upheld state marriage restrictions: the Sixth Circuit in the case before the court and the Eighth Circuit in *Citizens for Equal Protection v. Bruning* (2008).

2. Chiefly focusing on the right to marry as a fundamental right, inherent in a person's liberty, Kennedy failed to answer the question about the appropriate level of scrutiny for laws based on sexual orientation (see Wolff 2015).

3. The opinion placed much greater emphasis on the plaintiffs' right to liberty than to equality, but the Court cited numerous cases holding that equality was closely linked to liberty.

4. Stripping opponents of one of the mainstays of their legal arguments in the lower courts, the Court formally overruled *Baker v. Nelson* (1972).

5. Roberts was reprising the old argument that the plaintiffs were asserting a new right of same-sex marriage rather than seeking to exercise the existing fundamental right to marry.

6. Roberts frequently compared the majority ruling to the discredited *Lochner v. New York* (1905), accusing the Court of exceeding its judicial role by legislating from the bench based on its policy preferences rather than on the Constitution.

7. Such laws would shield business owners from legal liability if they denied services to gay and lesbian customers by citing their religious beliefs.

8. There is a voluminous literature on the failure to comply with Supreme Court decisions (see, for example, Canon and Johnson 1999, one of the first to address the issue of noncompliance and evasion). See Tobias (2015) for a more recent analysis focusing on same-sex marriage.

9. On May 19, 2015, the proposed Louisiana Marriage and Conscience Act (HB 707)—a religious freedom bill—died in a Louisiana House committee (*New Orleans Times-Picayune*, May 19, 2015). Jindal issued Executive Order BJ 15-8 the same day, proclaiming that it was "of preeminent importance that government take no adverse action against a person, wholly or partially, on the basis that such person acts in accordance with his religious belief that marriage is or should be recognized as the union of one man and one woman, but that this principle not be construed to authorize any act of discrimination" (Office of the Governor of Louisiana 2015). On April 13, 2016, Jindal's successor, John Bel Edwards, rescinded Jindal's order and issued his own Executive Order JBE 2016-11, prohibiting discrimination against state employees and employees of state contractors based on sexual orientation and gender identity (Office of the Governor of Louisiana 2016).

10. State Supreme Court Chief Justice Roy Moore went a step further. Comparing it to the infamous *Dred Scott v. Sanford* (1857), Moore argued that *Obergefell* only applied to Sixth Circuit states and that Alabama probate judges were bound by an earlier state supreme court ruling that declared the marriage ban constitutional (*New York Times*, February 8, 2015; *New York Times*, June 26, 2015; *New York Times*, January 6, 2016; *New York Times*, May 6, 2016).

11. The First Circuit was also required to step in (twice) to correct the errors of Puerto Rico Federal District Court Judge Juan Perez-Gimenez, who, among other things, held that *Obergefell* did not apply to the island because it is a territory, not a state (Lambda Legal 2016).

12. Clergy are not required to perform same-sex marriage ceremonies (see Selznick 2014).

13. In March 2015, seventeen states, plus the District of Columbia, banned discrimination on the basis of sexual orientation and gender identity in public accommodations: California, Colorado, Connecticut, Delaware, Hawaii, Illinois, Iowa, Maine, Maryland, Minnesota, Nevada, New Jersey, New Mexico, Oregon, Rhode Island, Vermont, and Washington State. Four other states (Massachusetts, New Hampshire, New York, and Wisconsin) only prohibited discrimination because of sexual orientation but not gender identity (National Conference of State Legislatures 2015). By July 2016, Massachusetts and New York had included gender identity within their public accommodations protections, leaving only New Hampshire and Wisconsin as the outliers. Some state laws are more broadly aimed at discrimination in other areas, such as housing and employment. Twenty-nine states offer no protection at all for members of the LGBT community; indeed, Arkansas, North Carolina, and Tennessee prohibit local governments from passing antidiscrimination ordinances (Movement Advancement Project 2016b).

14. Koppelman (2015) believes that exemptions should be granted, stating, "[T]he gay rights movement has won. It will not be stopped by a few exemptions. It should be magnanimous in victory" (628). Willing to grant exceptions to owners of public accommodations, he would not grant religious exemptions to employers who discriminate against LGBT employees. Sanders (2016) agrees, arguing that business owners must only deny service on the basis of sincere religious beliefs, not "mere distaste for gay people or a political dissent from LGBT rights" (246). However, he cautions that the LGBT community " should recognize that facts and the motivations of persons who have allegedly discriminated can be murky and complicated, and that occasionally the better path to justice and civil peace is to forbear from using all of the weapons that law makes available to complaining parties."

15. Nejaime and Siegel (2014) refer to claims affecting third parties that are based on "religious objections to being made complicit in the assertedly sinful conduct of others [as] complicity-based conscience claims" (2519). Unlike the federal RFRA, aimed at protecting religious minorities and having minimal impact on the larger society, the complicity-based conscience claims affect society more broadly. They arise from small business owners (like the Colorado baker and New Mexico photographer) as well as privately held corporations, such as Hobby Lobby.

16. The New Mexico Supreme Court ruling preceded the US Supreme Court's decision in *Hobby Lobby*.

17. Even after *Employment Division, Department of Human Resources v. Smith* (1990), laws targeting a religion for disparate treatment received strict scrutiny.

18. Section 2(a) of RFRA states that its purposes are "(1) to restore the compelling interest test as set forth in *Sherbert v. Verner* [1963] . . . and *Wisconsin v. Yoder* [1972] . . . and to guarantee its application in all cases where free exercise of religion is substantially burdened; and (2) to provide a claim or defense to persons whose religious exercise is substantially burdened by government." Section 3(a) explains that RFRA applies to a "rule of general applicability." Section 3(b) is more stringent than the pre-*Smith* standard (as articulated in *Sherbert* and *Yoder*) by providing that the "government may substantially burden a person's exercise of religion only if it demonstrates that application of the burden to the person—(1) is in furtherance of a compelling governmental interest; and (2) is the least restrictive means of furthering that compelling governmental interest" (see Selznick 2014).

19. With some exceptions, the Eleventh Amendment grants state immunity from suit by private individuals for money damages. The Supreme Court held that section 5 of the Fourteenth Amendment, authorizing Congress to enact appropriate enforcement legislation, nullifies state immunity under the Eleventh Amendment. In *City of Boerne,* the Court specified that Congress may pass laws under the authority of section 5 only if it has evidence that the state violated the Fourteenth Amendment and that the law intends to remedy the violations. In the absence of such evidence, the Eleventh Amendment shields states from damage suits (see Mezey 2000).

20. In 2000, Congress enacted the Religious Land Use and Institutionalized Persons Act (Public Law No. 106-274), mirroring RFRA for religious bodies and prison inmates. To avoid the problem of *City of Boerne*, the law was enacted under Congress's spending power and commerce authority. The federal courts are split on its constitutionality (see Gedicks 2005).

21. Phillips also justified his action because same-sex marriages were illegal, but the judge found that was irrelevant because he would do the same with civil unions or commitment ceremonies. The couple was planning to marry in Massachusetts, with a reception in Colorado; Colorado began to recognize same-sex marriages in October 2014.

22. The Civil Rights Commission ordered Phillips to comply with the CADA and submit quarterly compliance reports for two years.

23. The appellate court noted that there was only one case—*Church of Lukumi Babalu Aye, Inc. v. City of Hialeah* (1993)—in which the high court found that the challenged law had an improper purpose of suppressing religious practices and therefore required the state to provide a compelling state interest to justify it.

24. On April 25, 2016, the Colorado Supreme Court denied Phillips's petition for a writ of certiorari (*Masterpiece Cakeshop Inc. v. Colorado Civil Rights Commission* 2016a). Calling himself a "cake artist," he filed a petition for

certiorari in the US Supreme Court on July 22, 2016 (*Masterpiece Cakeshop Inc. v. Colorado Civil Rights Commission* 2016b).

25. State RFRAs generally authorize religious waivers unless the government can provide a compelling reason in the challenged law (see Laycock 2014). Twenty-one states enacted RFRAs between 1993 and 2015: Alabama, Arizona, Arkansas, Connecticut, Florida, Idaho, Illinois, Indiana, Kansas, Kentucky, Louisiana, Mississippi, Missouri, New Mexico, Oklahoma, Pennsylvania, Rhode Island, South Carolina, Tennessee, Texas, and Virginia; the most recent are Arkansas and Indiana, in 2015. An additional seventeen states sought to amend existing religious freedom laws in 2015 (National Conference of State Legislatures 2016).

26. The September 2014 Pew survey found that 68 percent of Republicans believed that owners should be able to refuse services, while only 33 percent of Democrats did (Pew Research Center 2015a). A study by Goidel, Smentkowski, and Freeman (2016) reports that, in March 2012, 39 percent of respondents in a survey conducted by the Public Religion Research Institute believed that religious liberty was under attack; in November 2012, the number increased to 50 percent, with another jump to 54 percent by May 2014. The study shows that opposition to same-sex marriage was positively associated with believing in threats to religion.

27. On March 22, 2016, Kansas Governor Sam Brownback signed a law entitled the Exercise of Religious Freedom by Postsecondary Education Student Associations Act (SB 175) to prevent public colleges and universities from taking adverse actions against religious student groups that require "leaders or members" to "adhere to," "comply with," or "be committed to furthering" the group's "sincerely held religious beliefs" (Kansas Legislative Sessions 2016).

28. A proposed (but ultimately rejected) Kansas law, passed by the lower house, provided that the government could not compel individuals to act against their religious beliefs in offering services, goods, or employment in celebration of marriage, civil unions, or domestic partnerships (Koppelman 2015, 631–32).

At the federal level, Republicans introduced legislation to insulate from liability persons who objected to marriage equality because of their religious beliefs. On June 17, 2015, during the first session of the 114th Congress, Representative Raul Labrador, Republican from Idaho, and Senator Mike Lee, Republican from Utah, introduced identical versions of the First Amendment Defense Act as H.R. 2802 and S. 1598, respectively. Section 3(a) would prevent the federal government from "tak[ing] any discriminatory action against a person, wholly or partially on the basis that such person believes or acts in accordance with a religious belief or moral conviction that marriage is or should be recognized as the union of one man and one woman, or that sexual relations are properly reserved to such a marriage." Each was referred to committee, but no further action was taken on them (Congress.gov 2015a; Congress.gov 2015b).

29. Liberty Counsel describes itself as an "international nonprofit litigation, education, and policy organization dedicated to advancing religious freedom, the sanctity of life, and the family" (Liberty Counsel 2016).

30. Section 1(5) of the Arizona bill defined person as "any individual, association, partnership, corporation, church, religious assembly or institution or other business organization." Section 2(D) provided that a "person whose religious exercise is burdened in violation of this section may assert that violation as a claim or defense in a judicial proceeding regardless whether the government is a party to the proceeding. The person asserting such a claim or defense may obtain appropriate relief."

31. Katz (2015) argues that the law would put a heavy burden on a private citizen by requiring evidence that the "relief to which he or she is otherwise entitled would not substantially burden the opposing party's exercise. If it would, the citizen must also prove that granting relief furthers a substantial governmental interest using the least restrictive means, notwithstanding the resulting burden to the other party's exercise" (51).

32. Parsing the language of the federal RFRA, the circuits are split on whether the religious freedom defense can be asserted in private litigation, with the Second, Eighth, Ninth, and DC Circuits allowing it and the Sixth and the Seventh rejecting it. The New Mexico Supreme Court clearly aligned itself with the latter group (Chaganti 2013). The recently-enacted RFRAs remove any doubt that they are applicable in private suits.

33. Arizona's football team, the Cardinals, joined the NFL and the Arizona Super Bowl Host Committee in expressing their opposition to the bill. The Cardinals' statement declared, "[W]e do not support anything that has the potential to divide, exclude and discriminate." It did not explicitly threaten to move, but an NFL spokesperson said, "[O]ur policies emphasize tolerance and inclusiveness, and prohibit discrimination based on age, gender, race, religion, sexual orientation, or any other improper standard." With perhaps the most to lose, the local host committee reported that it has "heard loud and clear from our various stakeholders that adoption of this legislation would . . . deal a significant blow to the state's economic growth potential. We do not support this legislation." These reactions raised concerns among state business leaders that Super Bowl XLIX, scheduled for February 1, 2015, in Glendale, Arizona, would be moved to another location with a tremendous loss of revenue for the state (ESPN 2014). Arizona had already forfeited a Super Bowl in 1993 for not recognizing Martin Luther King Jr. Day as a holiday.

34. Shortly before Brewer's veto, the Maine legislature voted down a version of RFRA, a bill more closely related to the federal law than the Arizona bill (State of Maine Legislature 2014). Its sponsor defended it, saying, "This is about government. This isn't about private citizens against private citizens. It does not allow religious people to get away with anything they want to. It does not guarantee claimants a victory in government actions. It simply requires that the government has a strong justification." Despite his reassurances, an opponent characterized the bill as a "step backwards . . . as being filled with unintended consequences [and that is] . . . being used as an end run around the Maine Human Rights Act" (*Bangor Daily News*, February 18, 2014).

35. In 2011, Tennessee's Equal Access to Intrastate Commerce Act was the first anti-antidiscrimination law in the nation (not counting Colorado's Amendment 2). The Tennessee Court of Appeals dismissed the challenge to it for lack of standing on November 6, 2014 (*The Chattanoogan*, November 6, 2014).

36. Section 14-1-402 stated that the purpose of the law was to guarantee "that businesses, organizations, and employers doing business in the state are subject to uniform nondiscrimination laws and obligations." Section 14-1-403 made it illegal for local governments to "adopt or enforce an ordinance, resolution, rule, or policy that creates a protected classification or prohibits discrimination on a basis not contained in state law" (Arkansas State Legislature 2015a). Because LGBT status is not a "protected classification" under Arkansas law, this provision barred cities and counties from passing antidiscrimination ordinances.

37. Section 7 of SB 101 defined a person as "(1) An individual. (2) An organization, a religious society, a church, a body of communicants, or a group organized and operated primarily for religious purposes. (3) A partnership, a limited liability company, a corporation, a company, a firm, a society, a joint-stock company, [or] an unincorporated association." Section 9 provided that a

> person whose exercise of religion has been substantially burdened, or is likely to be substantially burdened, by a violation of this chapter may assert the violation or impending violation as a claim or defense in a judicial or administrative proceeding, regardless of whether the state or any other governmental entity is a party to the proceeding. If the relevant governmental entity is not a party to the proceeding, the governmental entity has an unconditional right to intervene in order to respond to the person's invocation of this chapter. (Indiana General Assembly 2015a)

38. In a later communication, Advance America added that the law would protect a "pro-life business owner" from government compulsion to "rent his

facility to a pro-abortion group" or to provide "abortion coverage for his employees" (Advance America 2015b).

39. The vice president of marketing for Visit Indy later announced that the law had a severe impact on the Indiana economy, saying that twelve conventions decided not to come to Indianapolis at least in part because of it, with a loss of $60 million (*Indianapolis Star*, January 26, 2016).

40. Immediately after SB 101 became law, the owners of Memories Pizza said that they would refuse to cater same-sex weddings because of their religious beliefs (*Indianapolis Star*, April 3, 2015).

41. The Indiana law defined person more broadly than the Arizona bill that Brewer vetoed. Moreover, in interpreting the federal RFRA in *Hobby Lobby*, the Court held that a "closely held for-profit corporation" is a person within the context of the law and can exercise religion (see Luchenitser 2014). The Federal Dictionary Act, the authoritative source for definitions of words in federal law, defines person broadly "unless the context indicates otherwise applies" (see Lupu 2015).

42. The RFRA Amendment (Senate Enrolled Act 50) added the following language to Section 7:

> This chapter does not: (1) authorize a provider to refuse to offer or provide services, facilities, use of public accommodations, goods, employment, or housing to any member or members of the general public on the basis of race, color, religion, ancestry, age, national origin, disability, sex, sexual orientation, gender identity, or United States military service; (2) establish a defense to a civil action or criminal prosecution for refusal by a provider to offer or provide services, facilities, use of public accommodations, goods, employment, or housing to any member or members of the general public on the basis of race, color, religion, ancestry, age, national origin, disability, sex, sexual orientation, gender identity, or United States military service; or (3) negate any rights available under the Constitution of the State of Indiana.

Section 7.5 defined a provider as

> one (1) or more individuals, partnerships, associations, organizations, limited liability companies, corporations, and other organized groups of persons. The term does not include: (1) A church or other nonprofit religious organization or society, including an affiliated school. . . . (2) A rabbi, priest, preacher, minister, pastor, or designee of a church or other nonprofit religious organization or society when

the individual is engaged in a religious or affiliated educational function of the church or other nonprofit religious organization or society. (Indiana General Assembly 2015b)

43. The Southern Poverty Law Center (2016) identifies the following as "Christian Right" groups that "have wrapped their bigotry [against the LGBT community] in the cloak of religious freedom": ADF, American Family Association, Becket Fund for Religious Liberty, Family Research Council, Focus on the Family, and Liberty Counsel. Some of these were involved in the passage of the Indiana law.

44. HB 1228 would have amended Title 16, Chapter 123 (Civil Rights) of the Arkansas code. Section 16-23-404(4) defined person as an "individual, association, partnership, corporation, church, religious institution, estate, trust, foundation, or other legal entity." Section 16-123-405(1) provided, "A state action shall not substantially burden a person's right to exercise of religion . . . unless it is demonstrated that applying the substantial burden to the person's exercise of religion in this particular instance (1) Is essential to further a compelling governmental interest." Section 16-123-407(a) stated, "Regardless of whether the state or one of its political subdivisions is a party to the proceeding, a person . . . may assert the violation or impending violation as a claim or defense in a judicial or administrative proceeding." Section 16-123-408(3) contained an "Emergency Clause," stating, "[T]here is not a higher protection offered by the state than the protection of a person's right to religious freedom; and that this act is immediately necessary because every day that a person's right to religious freedom is threatened is a day that the First Amendment to the United States Constitution is compromised." Because of the "emergency," the act would become effective immediately after the governor signed it (Arkansas State Legislature 2015b).

45. Section 16-123-404(a)(1) stated, "A government shall not substantially burden a person's exercise of religion . . . except that a government may substantially burden a person's exercise of religion only if it demonstrates that application of the burden to the person is (1) In furtherance of a compelling governmental interest." Section 16-123-404(b)(1) stated, "A person whose religious exercise has been burdened in violation of this section may assert that violation as a claim or defense in a judicial proceeding and obtain appropriate relief against a government" (Arkansas State Legislature 2015c).

46. HB 707 provided, "Notwithstanding any other law to the contrary, this state shall not take any adverse action against a person, wholly or partially, on the basis that such person acts in accordance with a religious belief or moral conviction about the institution of marriage" (Louisiana State Legislature 2015).

47. Section 1 of SB 2 gave magistrates, assistant registers of deeds, and deputy registers the "right to recuse from performing all lawful marriages . . . based upon any sincerely held religious objection." Officials who take advantage of this law cannot perform any marriages for six months. If no officials in a jurisdiction are willing to issue licenses, then the "Administrative Office of the Courts shall ensure that a magistrate is available in that jurisdiction for performance of marriages for the times required" (North Carolina General Assembly 2015).

48. The Virginia law would have amended section 20-14 of the Code of Virginia to provide that the "clerk or deputy clerk shall not be required to issue a marriage license if such clerk has an objection to the issuance of such license on personal, ethical, moral, or religious grounds" (Virginia's Legislative Information System 2016).

49. In February 2016, the Republican National Committee adopted a resolution condemning the Obama administration for interpreting Title IX to include gender identity. The resolution was based on several assertions, including (1) a "person's sex is defined as the physical condition of being male or female, which is determined at conception, identified at birth by a person's anatomy, recorded on their official birth certificate, and can be confirmed by DNA testing" and (2) "transgender policies deal with students who choose to be designated by their desired gender identity; an identity that conflicts with their anatomical sex." Based on these assumptions, the committee "encourage[d] State Legislatures to recognize that these Obama gender identity policies are a federal governmental overreach, a misinterpretation of Title IX policies, and an infringement upon the majority of students' Constitutional rights" and "enact laws that protect student privacy and limit the use of restrooms, locker rooms and similar facilities to members of the sex to whom the facility is designated" (Republican National Committee 2016). This document was not publicized but was discovered by a reporter a month later (*ThinkProgress*, February 26, 2016; see *Washington Blade*, February 25, 2016).

50. In *Brady v. Dean* (2001), the Vermont Supreme Court rejected the claims of town clerks who objected to the requirement that they issue civil union licenses (or appoint an assistant in their place) because of their religious beliefs. The court dismissed the suit because the clerks failed to show that the law substantially burdened their religion. The court was doubtful but held it unnecessary to decide whether such officials could "retain public office while refusing to perform a generally applicable duty of that office on religious grounds" (434). It also found that the act of appointing a successor did not amount to a constitutional violation because it was an "indirect and attenuated connection to the subject of the law" (435).

51. Davis claimed that she wanted to avoid discriminating against same-sex couples.

52. After *Obergefell*, Kentucky Governor Steve Beshear informed county clerks of their responsibility to issue marriage licenses, saying, "[Y]ou can continue to have your own personal beliefs but, you're also taking an oath to fulfill the duties prescribed by law, and if you are at that point to where your personal convictions tell you that you simply cannot fulfill your duties that you were elected to do, than obviously an honorable course to take is to resign and let someone else step-in who feels that they can fulfill those duties" (*Towleroad*, July 22, 2015).

53. The couples sued Davis in her individual and official capacities, making her potentially personally liable. Shortly thereafter, citing "real concerns" from clerks around the state, two Republican state legislators announced on July 15, 2015, that they would sponsor legislation to exempt county clerks from liability for denying marriage licenses to same-sex couples because of their religious beliefs (*Lexington Herald-Leader*, July 15, 2015). Introduced in 2016, the bill failed to pass.

54. As part of Miller's suit against her, Davis filed a third-party complaint against Beshear for violating her religious freedom by compelling her to issue marriage licenses to same-sex couples (*Davis v. Beshear* 2015; see *Morehead News*, August 7, 2015).

55. Davis claimed a violation of her rights under the federal and state constitutions and the state RFRA. A few days later, Bunning denied her motion to stay the injunction pending her appeal but granted a temporary stay until August 31, 2015, to allow the Sixth Circuit to review her request for a stay.

56. Elected officials cannot be discharged, only recalled or impeached.

57. In a bizarre turn of events, Davis claimed that she met with Pope Francis at the Vatican Embassy on September 24, 2015, during his visit to Washington, DC. The meeting, which the Vatican did not acknowledge until almost a week later, raised a number of questions. Staver reported it as a private meeting initiated by the Vatican; Davis said the Pope offered support for her position and "thanked her for her courage." The Vatican later confirmed that she was there but denied that it was a private meeting initiated by the Vatican. Instead, a Vatican spokesperson said that she was part of a larger group and had been invited by Archbishop Carlo Maria Vigano, the Papal Nuncio (Ambassador to the United States), who issued the invitation without informing the Pope. Vigano was known for his strong opposition to same-sex marriage. The Vatican later stated that any meeting between the Pope and Davis "should not be considered a form of support of her position" (*New York Times*, September 30, 2015; *New York Times*, October 2, 2015; *Washington Post*, October 2,

2015). On April 12, 2016, the Vatican announced that it was accepting Vigano's resignation (*CNN*, April 12, 2016).

58. Davis claimed that Bunning's modification misinterpreted Rule 62(c) of the Federal Rules of Civil Procedure.

59. On April 21, 2016, the appeals court removed Bevin from the suit.

60. On August 18, 2016, Bunning dismissed the suit against Davis (*Daily Independent*, August 19, 2016).

61. Under Texas law, it was already illegal to enter a restroom reserved for the opposite sex "in a manner calculated to cause a disturbance."

62. There was only a 27.45 percent turnout for the election (*Ballotpedia* 2015).

63. Other major Texas cities, including Arlington, Austin, Brownsville, Dallas, El Paso, and Fort Worth, already had laws against discrimination based on sexual orientation and gender identity at the time of the Houston vote (*Texas Tribune*, December 2014).

64. Since World War II, public bathrooms have figured centrally in African-American civil rights struggles for racial integration in the workplace and in schools. Integrating these spaces in the southern United States meant doing away with Jim Crow laws that mandated, among other things, separate public bathrooms for blacks and whites. Whites defended these segregated spaces with violence. And, with varying degrees of cynicism, segregationists often interpreted demands for racial equality as black male demands for interracial sexual contact with white women. (*Slate*, November 10, 2015)

65. The Tennessee bill stated that public schools and institutions of higher education must "require that a student use student restroom and locker room facilities that are assigned for use by persons of the same sex as the sex indicated on the student's *original* birth certificate" (LegiScan 2016, emphasis added).

66. According to its website, "Media Matters for America is a Web-based, not-for-profit, 501(c)(3) progressive research and information center dedicated to comprehensively monitoring, analyzing, and correcting conservative misinformation in the U.S." (see http://mediamatters.org/about).

67. In 2015, the Florida legislature considered the Single-Sex Public Facilities Act (HB 583), requiring that

> single-sex public facilities be restricted to persons of sex for which facility is designated; prohibits knowingly & willfully entering single-sex public facility designated for or restricted to persons of other sex; provides criminal penalties; requires the use of segregated facilities such as dressing rooms, locker rooms, and bathrooms according to gender identity rather than birth status.

It died in committee on April 28, 2015 (Florida Senate 2015).

68. Section 2 of HB 1008 provided that "every restroom, locker room, and shower room located in a public elementary or secondary school that is designated for student use and is accessible by multiple students at the same time shall be designated for and used only by students of the same biological sex."

Section 3 stated that,

> if any student asserts that the student's gender is different from the student's biological sex, and if the student's parent or guardian consents to that assertion in writing to a public school administrator, or if the student is an adult or an emancipated minor and makes the assertion in writing to a public school administrator, the student shall be provided with a reasonable accommodation. A reasonable accommodation is one that does not impose an undue hardship on a school district. (South Dakota Legislature, 2016)

69. Even as Daugaard vetoed HB 1008, another bill restricted transgender high school students on athletic teams.

70. The federal government has rarely withheld funding but did so in the 1960s when schools and hospitals remained segregated, making a huge impact. The threat is often enough to encourage settlement agreements (*Washington Post*, May 9, 2016).

71. After a contentious governor's race, McCrory finally conceded the election to Roy Cooper on December 5, 2016. Cooper's television ads had denounced HB 2, criticizing McCrory for his role in it and saying he wanted to repeal it. Although McCrory likely lost his bid for reelection for a number of reasons, observers believed that his strong defense of HB 2 played a large part in Cooper's victory (*News & Observer*, December 5, 2016). On December 19, 2016, the Charlotte City Council voted 10–0 to rescind the part of its nondiscrimination ordinance that HB 2 preempts. Facing accusations that she abandoned the LGBT community, Roberts justified the council's action, saying that it "should in no way be viewed as a compromise of our principles or commitment to non-discrimination." Cooper, who had worked to broker the deal, announced, "Senate Leader Phil Berger and House Speaker Tim Moore assured me that as a result of Charlotte's vote, a special session will be called . . . to repeal HB 2 in full." On Wednesday morning, the city council held an emergency meeting and jettisoned the entire ordinance in a 7–2 vote. With this action, the city's antidiscrimination protection reverted to its 1968 version. With many Republicans on record against repealing HB 2, when the state legislature met, however, instead of a full repeal, Berger introduced a bill (SB 4) to prevent local governments from enacting ordinances related to discrimi-

nation in employment, public accommodations, and bathroom and locker room facilities for six months; HB 2 would expire after the six-month period. In the end, the House ended the session without taking a vote and the Senate voted against repealing HB 2 in a 32–16 vote. Despite Charlotte's rescission, HB 2 remained in place (*Charlotte Observer*, December 19, 2016; *News & Observer*, December 19, 2016; *Charlotte Observer*, December 21, 2016; *Business Insider*, December 21, 2016; *Huffington Post*, December 21, 2016; *Washington Post*, December 21, 2016).

72. The state legislature might have forced McCrory's hand. Having vetoed SB 2, he wanted to avoid angering his base during an election year by vetoing HB 2, especially knowing that the legislature would likely override it (see *Washington Post*, April 14, 2016).

73. North Carolina residents may only request new birth certificates after sex reassignment surgery.

74. Part I of HB 2 defined biological sex as the "physical condition of being male or female, which is stated on a person's birth certificate" and required "every multiple occupancy bathroom or changing facility [in government buildings and public schools] to be designated for and only used by persons based on their biological sex" (North Carolina General Assembly 2016a).

75. On July 18, 2016, McCrory signed legislation reestablishing the right of protected classes to sue in state court for wrongful discharge (North Carolina General Assembly 2016b).

76. Section 3 of Executive Order No. 93 states, "[W]hen readily available and when practicable in the best judgment of the agency, all cabinet agencies shall provide a reasonable accommodation of a single occupancy restroom, locker room or shower facility upon request due to special circumstances." Section 4 "invited and encouraged [other state and local government agencies] to do the same" (NC Governor Pat McCrory 2016).

77. The poll found that 75 percent of respondents favored civil rights law protection for transgender people and 80 percent favored them for gays and lesbians (*CNN*, May 9, 2015).

78. On April 24, 2016, the NCAA Board of Governors adopted a policy requiring sites seeking to host NCAA events to "demonstrate how they will provide an environment that is safe, healthy, and free of discrimination, plus safeguards the dignity of everyone involved in the event." It sent out a questionnaire in July, asking potential host cities how they will deal with discrimination (*USA Today*, July 22, 2016).

79. On February 19, 2016, the Georgia Senate Rules Committee combined SB 284 with HB 757 (see *Atlanta Journal-Constitution*, February 20, 2016).

80. Section 2 of SB 757 authorized ministers "to decline to [solemnize marriages] . . . in their discretion, in the exercise of their rights to free exercise of

religion." Section 4 provided that "no faith based [501(c)(3) organization] shall be required to provide [facilities or] social, educational, or charitable services that violate such faith based organization's sincerely held religious belief" (Georgia General Assembly 2016).

81. The state RFRA, enacted in 2014, allowed businesses and individuals to refuse to serve anyone they believed would "substantially burden" their "religious exercise." It also appended the words *In God We Trust* to the state's seal.

82. Section 2 of HB 1523 specifies three protected religious beliefs: "(a) Marriage is or should be recognized as the union of one man and one woman; b) Sexual relations are properly reserved to such a marriage; and (c) Male (man) or female (woman) refer to an individual's immutable biological sex as objectively determined by anatomy and genetics at time of birth." Section 3(6) allows "sex-specific standards or policies concerning employee or student dress or grooming, or concerning access to restrooms, spas, baths, showers, dressing rooms, locker rooms, or other intimate facilities or settings" (Mississippi Legislature 2016).

83. On June 20, 2016, Mississippi Federal District Court Judge Carleton W. Reeves dismissed a constitutional challenge to HB 1523, holding that the plaintiffs could not show imminent harm if it went into effect because they did not plan to marry for three years (*Alford v. Moulder* 2016). A week later, in *Campaign for Southern Equality v. Bryant* (2016a), Reeves allowed the plaintiffs to reopen an earlier judgment and seek to amend his 2015 injunction. He reasoned that, because HB 1523 permits state agents to opt out of same-sex marriages, it interferes with *Obergefell* and the 2015 injunction against Mississippi's same-sex marriage ban. A day before it was to go into effect, Reeves issued a preliminary injunction in *Barber v. Bryant* (2016), ruling that HB 1523 violates the First and Fourteenth Amendments by privileging specified religious beliefs. He found that, "under the guise of providing additional protection for religious exercise, it creates a vehicle for state-sanctioned discrimination on the basis of sexual orientation and gender identity" (at 40). Reacting to Reeves's ruling, Bryant announced that he would file his own appeal even though the attorney general said that he was undecided about an appeal and wondered if the law were passed for political reasons. On August 12, 2016, the Fifth Circuit denied Bryant's request to stay the injunction and expedite the appeal (*Campaign for Southern Equality v. Bryant* 2016b; see *Mississippi Today*, July 7, 2016; *Mississippi Today*, August 12, 2016).

84. Most of the criticism seemed to be directed against the president personally.

85. Among other things, the 2013 VAWA (Public Law No. 113-4), signed on March 7, 2013, prohibits recipients of federal funds from discriminating in any

"program or activity" based on "actual or perceived race, color, religion, national origin, sex, gender identity, sexual orientation, or disability."

86. On May 12, 2016, the administration announced that it would not withhold funds from North Carolina during the litigation (*Washington Post*, May 12, 2016).

87. The DCL was accompanied by a twenty-five-page document discussing "practical ways to meet Title IX's requirements." It included practices already in place, like installing privacy curtains or allowing students to change clothes in bathroom stalls (US Department of Education 2016).

88. The other states, most with Republican governors, were Alabama, Arizona, Georgia, Louisiana, Maine, Oklahoma, Tennessee, Utah, West Virginia, and Wisconsin. Taking matters into its own hands, the Oklahoma Senate approved a bill (SB 1619) requiring schools to offer nontransgender students separate facilities; it failed to pass out of house committee (*Tulsa World*, May 25, 2016). Section 1(C) of SB 1619 allowed a request "for a religious accommodation based on . . . sincerely held religious beliefs that would require the school to provide bathroom and other facilities for the exclusive use of that student's sex." Section 2(D) ruled out a "single-occupancy" facility "as an allowable accommodation" (Oklahoma State Legislature 2016).

89. Another suit filed by Nebraska (with Arkansas, Kansas, Michigan, Montana, North Dakota, Ohio, South Carolina, South Dakota, and Wyoming also as plaintiffs) in July 2016 accused the federal agencies of violating the APA by creating a new law that redefines sex (*State of Nebraska v. United States of America* 2016).

90. On August 1, 2016, McCrory allowed a bill diverting $500,000 from disaster relief to defending HB 2 to pass without his signature (*News & Observer*, August 1, 2016).

91. Schroeder began by noting the parties' agreement that sex-segregated facilities advance state privacy concerns and that there was no danger to anyone in the days before HB 2 was enacted. Moreover, the state's counsel admitted that transgender people were unobtrusively using facilities that accorded with their gender identity before the law and will likely persist in doing so without anyone's knowledge. He attributed this in part to state trespassing and indecent exposure laws that further the state's legitimate concerns about privacy and security.

5

GLOBAL PERSPECTIVES

Viewing LGBT rights from a global perspective, over the last several decades, dozens of nations have enacted measures to end discrimination against their LGBT citizens by decriminalizing sexual activity, legalizing same-sex relationships, and recognizing the needs of transgender individuals (see Johnson 2013). Despite the progress and rhetorical commitment to equality of rights in international agreements and worldwide compacts, discrimination against the LGBT community remains commonplace in much of the world.

Reflecting their common law tradition of judicial decision-making that often puts courts at the forefront of equal rights struggles, the judiciary was instrumental in furthering LGBT rights in Canada and South Africa and, eventually, in the United States. Cognizant of the need to exercise judicial restraint to maintain their legitimacy, the courts in all three nations believed that their responsibility to adjudicate constitutional challenges and give effect to their country's foundational documents outweighed their duty to defer to the people's elected representatives.[1]

In part because of the absence of the common law tradition of judicial policy-making on the European continent, the quest for equal rights there achieved greater success in legislatures than in courts (Lind 2008; see McReynolds 2006). When parliaments refused to act, LGBT activists pursued their rights in the supranational European Court of Human Rights (ECtHR), claiming violations of the European Convention on Human Rights (ECHR). Consistent with the ECHR guarantees, the Court often supported challenges to discriminatory policies but refrained from imposing marriage equality on the European states. Fearful of destroying its legitimacy, the ECtHR has been unwilling to exceed the bounds of judicial restraint and override national marriage restrictions.

LGBT RIGHTS LITIGATION IN CANADA

Before embarking on a campaign against marriage inequality, Canadian LGBT rights advocates challenged sodomy laws, unfair tax and pension policies, constraints on access to public welfare benefits, and employment discrimination. In one of the first battles over LGBT rights in Canada, the gay and lesbian community unsuccessfully asked the courts to decriminalize sexual conduct by ending arrest and imprisonment for engaging in private consensual sexual acts. *Klippert v. The Queen* (1967) revealed the Canadian Supreme Court's unwillingness to interfere with parliamentary authority over the criminal justice system. In reviewing Klippert's conviction, the Court pointed out that Parliament had amended the sodomy law in 1961 to expand the definition of the crime to include consideration of the likelihood of committing future offenses. Because Klippert refused to avow that he would no longer engage in the "criminal" conduct, the Court upheld his conviction. The ruling spurred Pierre Trudeau's Liberal Party to propose to decriminalize sodomy between consenting adults over the age of twenty-one as part of the reformation of the criminal code, passed on August 26, 1969. The new law eliminated a "major political and legal obstacle for the LGBT movement in Canada" (Smith 2011, 75; Backer 1996).

The passage of the 1982 Canadian Charter of Rights and Freedoms spurred LGBT litigation, enhancing the judiciary's "legal and moral authority as the interpretor and articulator of fundamental constitutional values" (Murphy 2001, 299). In fulfilling their role of constitutional adjudication, Canadian courts determine whether a law challenged as discriminatory infringes on the Charter's equal rights guarantee, section 15(1).[2] Unlike the South African Constitution, with its explicit prohibition of discrimination based on sexual orientation and the European Charter of Fundamental Rights, the Canadian Charter does not include sexual orientation as a prohibited area of discrimination (Wintemute 2004; see Jefferson 1985).

The first obstacle for the LGBT rights advocates once the Charter was in place was to persuade the courts that sexual orientation is "analogous" to the classifications in section 15(1) and deserving of the same rigorous constitutional protection as the specified categories (see *Law v. Canada* 1999; *Miron v. Trudel* 1995). In *Canada v. Mossop* (1993), decided before the Charter was implemented, the Supreme Court considered whether the definition of family in the Canada Human Rights Act (HRA) extended to same-sex couples. Brian Mossop, a Canadian federal employee, was denied bereavement leave to attend the funeral of his partner's father, a right guaranteed by the union contract allowing leave for the death of an "immediate family" member. The contract broadly defined "family" as "spouses" (including common law spouses), parents, siblings, and in-laws, as well as permanent household residents.[3]

The lower courts were divided on whether the HRA's ban on discrimination because of family status extended to same-sex couples. In a divided vote, the Supreme Court narrowly interpreted it to exclude same-sex couples.[4] Chief Justice Antonio Lamer explained for the 4–3 majority that the framers of the act did not envision same-sex couples as a family.[5] The dissent, written by Judge Claire L'Heureux-Dubé, argued that the traditional family, as perceived by the majority, was not the exclusive model for today's family.

Two years later, the Court revisited the rights of same-sex couples in *Egan v. Canada* (1995) to determine whether the benefits of the Old Age Security Act encompass same-sex partners. James Egan began collecting benefits under the act when he turned sixty-five. When John Nesbit, his partner of forty-five years, applied for the spousal allowance available to economically deprived couples, the government rejected his claim because he did not fit the definition of spouse. The law benefitted different-sex couples in both common law marriages (who lived together for at least a year and publicly represented themselves as husband and wife) and traditional marriages. Egan argued that the statute conflicted with section 15(1) of the Charter.

The lower courts rejected his claim, but the high court handed LGBT litigants their first national victory when it unanimously declared that sexual orientation is an innate and immutable characteristic, analogous to the enumerated categories specified in section 15(1). The victory was diminished because the judges disagreed about the constitutionality of the challenged law. Speaking for four judges, Judge Gérard LaForest declared the act consistent with section 15(1) because it was based on Parliament's reasonable belief that heterosexual marriage reflected the social and biological truths that procreation and childcare were optimized in different-sex couples. Judge John Sopinka joined their opinion, finding the discrimination justified under the savings clause, section 1 of the Charter.[6] The remaining four judges, in an opinion by Judge Peter Cory, voted to strike the law, emphasizing the futility of declaring sexual orientation a protected category under section 15(1) while maintaining the prohibitions on same-sex relationships. Thus, *Egan* advanced LGBT rights by including sexual orientation as a protected classification within section 15(1) but sanctioned the discrimination against same-sex couples.

Several years later, in *Vriend v. Alberta* (1998), the Court considered an appeal from a ruling by the Alberta Human Rights Commission (AHRC).[7] Delwin Vriend, an instructor at a Christian college in Edmonton, was dismissed soon after he revealed that he was gay. The AHRC rejected his complaint because sexual orientation was not a prohibited ground of discrimination under the provincial Individual's Rights Protection Act (IRPA). The lower courts were divided on whether the Charter required the IRPA to include discrimination because of sexual orientation within its purview. In a unanimous decision announced by Lamer, the Court found that the IRPA had a disparate effect on the LGBT community by precluding them from seeking legal remedies for discrimination; it took the unusual step of curing the constitutional defect by reading sexual orientation into the law; that is, by adding it to the text.

As the "first unequivocal pro-gay and -lesbian rights ruling," *Vriend* marked a significant advance for the Canadian LGBT community (Gotell 2002, 91). A year later, *M. v. H.* (1999) was a major step forward in ending discrimination based on sexual orientation. M. and H., a lesbian couple, met the criteria for a common law marriage except for their sexual orientation. After their ten-year relationship ended, M. left the couple's home and sought spousal support from H. under the Ontario Family Law Act (FLA), a law authorizing benefits to unmarried different-sex couples who lived together for at least three years or were "in a relationship of some permanence."

M. filed suit, claiming that the FLA abridged her rights under the Charter. The lower court agreed and ordered the words of the statute changed from a man and a woman to two persons. H. appealed, with the Ontario Attorney General intervening. The Ontario Court of Appeal upheld the lower court, suspending the ruling for a year to allow the provincial legislature to revise the statute.

The provincial attorney general pursued the case in the Supreme Court, arguing that the law was intended to assist women, typically the dependent partners in dissolving relationships, and their children. A joint opinion by Cory and Judge Frank Iacobucci spoke for the 8–1 majority. Cory had no difficulty finding the law discriminatory, for, in addition to depriving individuals in same-sex couples an economic benefit, it implied that they did not have the same type of relationships as different-sex couples. Moreover, it signified that they were "less worthy of recognition and protection" (57). Iacobucci added that, because the purpose of the law was to assist dependent partners upon the dissolution of a once-interdependent relationship, the government had no valid reason to distinguish between same-sex and different-sex couples, as all individuals in economic straits could benefit from the act. There was no reasonable connection between the law's purported objectives—bolstering the finances of dependent spouses and reducing the burden on the public fisc—and withholding benefits from gay or lesbian applicants. The Court ordered section 29 struck in its entirety, delaying the implementation of its decision for six months. Iacobucci noted that the ruling might affect other laws and policies that limited benefits to different-sex couples and invited legislatures to reappraise them in light of the holding. Despite Cory's assurance that the case was not about "marriage per se" (48), the sole dissenter, Judge Charles Gonthier, cautioned that the likely outcome of the majority opinion would be an eventual declaration that the Charter required marriage equality.

In Canada, the federal government regulates the capacity to marry, while the provinces control the conditions of marriage. Reflecting this division of authority, the provincial legislatures, as well as the federal Parliament, reacted to *M. v. H.* by erasing numerous legal distinctions between different-sex and same-sex couples, the most important of which was the federal Modernization of Benefits and Obligations Act

(MBOA). The MBOA amended sixty-eight statutes (primarily dealing with pension, tax, and public welfare policy) to extend federal benefits and duties to all unmarried couples who had cohabitated in conjugal relationships for more than a year, regardless of their sexual orientation. Phrased in gender-neutral language, the amendments reserved the term spouses for married couples. To offset mounting opposition to the changes, the MBOA affirmed that these amendments did not undermine the common law definition of marriage as the "lawful union of one man and one woman to the exclusion of others."

Because it proclaimed the functional equivalency of same-sex and different-sex unions, *M. v. H.* sparked legal challenges in the provincial courts, with LGBT activists claiming that marriage inequality violated the Charter.[8] Following the ruling in *M. v. H.*, the Québec government amended its laws to equalize many of the rights of same-sex and different-sex couples, stopping short of establishing marriage equality. Determined to test the legality of the restriction on same-sex marriage, longtime gay rights activists Michael Hendricks and Rene Léboeuf filed suit when the court clerk refused to issue them a marriage license, informing them that the civil code restricted marriage to a man and a woman.

The one-week trial in a Québec courtroom began on November 8, 2001. Hendricks and Léboeuf, who had been together since 1973, challenged the provincial and federal laws, arguing that the restrictions on same-sex civil marriage violated the Charter's equality guarantee and "undermine[d] their dignity" (*Hendricks v. Québec* 2002, para. 65).[9] The court granted full-party status to the Ontario-based Catholic Civil Rights League and Evangelical Fellowships of Canada to intervene in the action to defend the ban on same-sex marriage.

On December 7, 2001, the Québec government announced that it would join the provinces of Manitoba and Nova Scotia in enacting a civil union law; six months later, it did so. Shortly thereafter, on September 6, 2002, Judge Louise Lemelin of the Québec Superior Court delivered the ruling, holding that excluding same-sex couples from the definition of marriage infringes on the Charter guarantees of "dignity" and "equality" (para. 155). Acknowledging the civil union bill, she held that it was inadequate to remedy the constitutional violation and rejected the government's contention that its interest in procreation justified the law. In the end, because she believed that the court should exercise restraint, she delayed the implementation of the ruling for two years to allow the federal government to remove the restriction on same-sex marriage. The provincial attorney declined to appeal the court's judgment, but less than a week later, the federal government announced that it would appeal to the provincial court of appeal; however, it soon withdrew, leaving the intervenors the only parties to defend the law (Robinson 2005).

Across the country, the British Columbia litigation arose when the provincial director of vital statistics refused to grant licenses to eight same-sex couples, citing the common law restriction on same-sex partners. They filed suit, asking for parliamentary action to redefine marriage as well as a declaration that the marriage restriction was inconsistent with the Charter.

On October 2, 2001, the British Columbia Supreme Court (the lower court) handed down its ruling in *EGALE v. Canada* (2001). Judge Ian Pitfield emphasized that, in asking for a change in a fundamental societal arrangement, the plaintiffs sought a remedy that was beyond the proper scope of judicial relief. Addressing the plaintiffs' constitutional argument, he agreed that marriage inequality was inconsistent with the equal rights provision of the Charter because it discriminated on the basis of sexual orientation.[10] "Opposite-sex couples," he stated, "who marry acquire immediate social approbation and legal rights and obligations as between each other and society as a whole. Same-sex couples are denied that option and, in my opinion, they are denied equal benefit of the law" (para. 165).[11] After agreeing that the plaintiffs made a compelling argument against the law, the court nevertheless upheld it because the marriage restriction reasonably furthered the government's interest in procreation. Moreover, its objective of preserving different-sex marriage outweighed the harm to same-sex couples, especially with the increasing trend toward equal rights.

In eastern Canada again, eight Toronto same-sex couples filed suit against the city clerk for refusing to issue them marriage licenses, and on July 12, 2002, Judge Heather Smith announced the judgment of a unanimous three-judge panel of the Ontario Divisional Court (the lower court) in *Halpern v. Canada* (2002). The government argued that the plaintiffs were not deprived of a benefit because federal law had established parallel rights between same-sex and different-sex couples. Their only deprivation, the attorney general argued, was that they could not represent themselves as married. The court disagreed, holding that the province violated the Charter because the prohibition on same-sex marriage was based on sexual orientation, an analogous ground under section 15(1).

The court further rejected the government's argument that its interest in procreation, an essential element of marriage, as well as its interest in family stability, justifies the marriage policy. It confessed that it was unable to understand how marriage inequality advanced the government's interest in families and procreation. In the end, the court unanimously found the law discriminatory, but only Judge Harry LaForme believed that the court should declare it immediately inoperative. The majority deemed it more appropriate to stay the ruling for two years—until July 12, 2004—to permit the legislature to cure the violation.

On May 1, 2003, almost a year after the Ontario lower court decision, the British Columbia Court of Appeal handed down its ruling in *EGALE v. Canada* (2003a).[12] Speaking for the court, Judge Jo-Ann Prowse agreed with the lower court that the prohibition on same-sex marriage violated the Charter's guarantee of equal rights. Unlike the lower court, however, the court of appeal aligned itself with *Hendricks* and *Halpern* and held that the government's interest in procreation was not a "sufficiently pressing and substantial objective" (*EGALE v. Canada* 2003a, para. 124) to justify infringing on the rights of same-sex couples. Declaring that the appropriate remedy was to redefine marriage as a union between two persons without regard to sex, the court stayed its order to allow the legislature to remedy the unconstitutionality.

On June 10, 2003, shortly after the British Columbia Court of Appeal announced *EGALE*, the Ontario Court of Appeal handed down its judgment in *Halpern v. Canada* (2003), declaring that the provincial marriage policy discriminated on the basis of sexual orientation and demeaned a vulnerable group that had historically been subject to prejudice. It emphasized that prohibiting same-sex marriage "perpetuates the view that same-sex relationships are less worthy of recognition than opposite-sex relationships [and] in doing so, offends the dignity of persons in same-sex relationships" (para. 107).[13]

The court rejected the government's argument that traditional marriage, a relationship between a heterosexual couple, encourages the birth and well-being of children. Echoing the lower court opinion, it asserted that it was unable to understand how the policy furthered the government's interests in procreation and child-rearing, for the marriage restriction had no effect on whether heterosexual couples would have children. The court agreed with the government's paean to marriage but pointed out that the same-sex couples were not striving to abolish the institution but were "merely seeking access to it" and, like heterosexual couples, would benefit from it (para. 129). Last, the court differed with the government that the MBOA established virtually equal rights for same-sex couples, stressing that the "benefits of marriage cannot be viewed in purely economic terms [and that] the societal significance surrounding the institution of marriage cannot be overemphasized" (para. 136). Unlike the lower court, the appellate court saw no reason to suspend the remedy for any length of time, ordering the province to change the common law definition of marriage to the voluntary union for life of two persons to the exclusion of all others and begin issuing marriage licenses to same-sex couples at once.

On July 8, 2003, a month after the appellate court ruling in *Halpern*, the Court of Appeal for British Columbia issued a unanimous supplementary opinion in *EGALE v. Canada* (2003b), lifting the stay and giving immediate effect to its May 1, 2003, ruling. The court expressed concern about the disparity between same-sex couples in Ontario—who would be able to marry in June 2003 because of *Halpern*—and couples in British Columbia, who would be unable to marry until July 12, 2004. It ordered the revised definition of marriage as the "lawful union of two persons to the exclusion of all others" to be implemented immediately (*EGALE v. Canada* 2003b, para. 8).

With their case still pending, in January 2004, Hendricks and Léboeuf returned to court to ask the Québec Court of Appeal to dismiss the intervenor's appeal and declare the prohibition on same-sex marriage immediately invalid. On March 19, 2004, in *Ligue Catholique pour les droits de l'homme v. Hendricks* (2004), the unanimous court noted the unusual legal posture of the case, among other things, that the government was not defending the law. It concluded that the intervenors no longer had a sufficient legal interest in the lower court decision and dismissed the appeal. The court dissolved Lemelin's stay and ordered the ban lifted immediately to allow same-sex couples to marry (see Robinson 2005). Hendricks and Léboeuf were married in Montreal on April 1, 2004, three years after the first same-sex marriage ceremony took place in Europe.

By 2005, most provincial and territorial courts had invalidated the common law definition of marriage, but marriage laws throughout the country lacked uniformity. Citing disparities among provincial policies, in June 2003, Prime Minister Jean Chrétien of the ruling Liberal Party announced that the federal government would no longer appeal lower court rulings to the Canadian Supreme Court and would draft legislation to legalize same-sex marriage throughout Canada. Following his announcement, Parliament drafted the Civil Marriage Act and referred it to the Supreme Court for review.[14] The proposed law defined civil marriage as the "lawful union of two persons to the exclusion of all others" and, to placate religious groups, specified that officials of religious groups may "refuse to perform marriages that are not in accordance with their religious beliefs."

Parliament asked the Court to address three questions:

> whether the Proposal for an Act Respecting Certain Aspects of Legal Capacity for Marriage for Civil Purposes falls within Parliament's exclusive legislative authority; whether extending marriage to persons of the same sex is consistent with the Charter; and whether religious officials who do not want to perform ceremonies contrary to their religious beliefs are protected.[15]

On December 9, 2004, the Court responded affirmatively to all questions (*Reference re: Same-Sex Marriage* 2004).

Shortly thereafter, on February 1, 2005, Prime Minister Paul Martin's government, supported by members of the New Democratic Party and the Bloc Quebecois, launched the effort to legalize same-sex marriage throughout Canada by introducing the Civil Marriage Act, C-38.[16] Polls taken at the time showed the country almost equally divided on the issue; one poll showed that 42 percent of the respondents approved of same-sex marriage, with 40 percent opposing it (*Toronto Star*, February 12, 2005). Conservative leader Stephen Harper led the opposition, supported by religious leaders and church officials, charging that the bill did not sufficiently protect the religious liberty of same-sex marriage opponents. Amid intense debate, C-38 received final approval from the House of Commons in a 158–133 vote on June 28, 2005; the Senate vote, 47–21, followed on July 19, 2005. The law went into effect when the Queen gave her royal assent on July 20, 2005, making Canada the fourth country in the world to adopt marriage equality.

LGBT RIGHTS LITIGATION IN SOUTH AFRICA

The struggle for LGBT rights in South Africa was inextricably linked to the country's effort to overcome its history of apartheid.[17] Under the leadership of Nelson Mandela, inaugurated as president on May 10, 1994, the ruling African National Congress (ANC) devoted itself to eliminating the legacy of racial oppression.[18]

Prior to 1994, when the ANC required allies in toppling the apartheid regime, it entered into a coalition with the LGBT community; when apartheid ended, the LGBT leadership persuaded government leaders to include a ban on discrimination because of sexual orientation in the new Constitution (Newstrom 2007). That document is unique in specifying sexual orientation as one of the prohibited areas of discrimination (Thoreson 2008, 681).[19] Many ANC elites accepted Mandela's coalition with the LGBT community, but others—especially those outside the country—opposed it. Mandela's commitment to eradicating vestiges of apartheid extended to gender equality, and the ANC leadership echoed his view that discrimination based on sexual orientation was inconsistent with the equal rights principles that epitomized the anti-apartheid movement.

The party's opposition to gender inequality did not reflect South African public opinion; most South Africans were at best indifferent to discrimination against the LGBT community during the struggle against racial oppression (Christiansen 2000; Croucher 2011; Johnson 1997). The prevailing view was that homosexuality was "'unAfrican' or 'Eurocentric'" (Lukoff 1999, 469) and "wrong, immoral, against God's way, et cetera" (Wing 2002, 823). In a 1987 interview with Peter Tatchell, a noted British journalist, Solly Smith, ANC's representative in Britain, commented, "[L]esbian and gay rights do not arise in the ANC. We cannot be diverted from our struggle. . . . We believe in the majority being equal. These people are in the minority. The majority must rule." More strikingly, Ruth Mompati, a member of the ANC National Executive Committee and an ardent advocate for women's rights who was exiled in London, said, "I can't even begin to understand why people want lesbian and gay rights. The gays have no problems. . . . I don't see them suffering. No one is persecuting them." She added, "Tell me, are gays and lesbians normal. No, it is not normal" (quoted in Croucher 2011, 161).

In publicizing these comments, Tatchell sought to shed light on the ANC's antipathy toward LGBT rights and to strengthen the leadership's support for LGBT equality in the emerging South Africa. He sent Mompati's comments to Thabo Mbeki, ANC director of information, who sought to reassure him, saying, "[T]he ANC is firmly committed to removing all forms of discrimination and oppression in a liberated South Africa . . . [and that] commitment must surely extend to the protection of gay rights" (Mbeki 2005, 149; Thoreson 2008).[20]

The South African Constitution has been extolled as a "monumental achievement" (Webb 1998–1999, 205). It is widely viewed as "one of the most liberal in the world" (Du Toit 2006, 681; Christiansen 2000; Lukoff 1999). Under Mandela's leadership, reflecting the government's adherence to principles of equality, tolerance, and dignity, the Republic of South Africa became "one of the most progressive human rights proponents in the international community" (Byrn 2002; Johnson 1997, 589; Lukoff 1999; Thoreson 2008; Wing 2002).[21] Ironically, despite the Constitution's explicit condemnation of gender discrimination, South Africa represents an anomaly with a judicial system that took the lead in eradicating discrimination on the basis of sexual orientation, against a backdrop of hostility toward the LGBT community (Newstrom 2007; Williams 2004; see De Vos 2007). In 2011, a Human Rights Watch report "revealed widespread ignorance [especially] about lesbians and transgender men and deep-rooted prejudice against gender and sexual non-conformity." It continued, "[W]hile the report documents the vulnerability of lesbians and transgender men, in particular, their treatment is part of a broader and chronic problem of gender-based violence in South Africa" (Human Rights Watch 2011).

In 1997, the Constitutional Court (the highest court) demonstrated its commitment to the new South Africa by eloquently stating that "at the heart of the prohibition of unfair discrimination lies a recognition that . . . all human beings will be accorded equal dignity and respect regardless of their membership of particular groups" (*President of the Republic of South Africa v Hugo* 1997, para. 41).[22] Recognizing that government regulation invariably involves differentiating among citizens, Justice Lourens Ackermann explained in *Harksen v Lane NO* (1998) that, when adjudicating claims of inequality, the Court's primary task is to distinguish "mere differentiation" from "unfair discrimination" (para. 43).

Gay and lesbian activists were aware that they would never secure equal rights unless they challenged the sodomy laws that branded them as criminals for engaging in consensual sexual activity.[23] The first case in which a South African court ruled on the constitutionality of the common law offense of sodomy was *State v Kampher* (1997). After Gordon Kampher's conviction for sodomy, the Magistrate's Court suspended his one-year sentence (as long as he received no other convictions), concluding that the framers of the Constitution had intended to decriminalize sexual contact between two males, and found the common law offense of sodomy invalid under the 1993 Constitution (see Schmid 2000). The ruling, setting aside Kampher's conviction and sentence, represented the first instance of a South African court evaluating LGBT rights. A pathbreaking opinion, *Kampher* "deserves significant credit for helping to open the doors of the High Courts to a barrage of sexual-orientation cases" (Berger 2008, 18).

The Constitutional Court ruled on the constitutionality of sodomy laws in *National Coalition for Gay and Lesbian Equality v Minister of Justice* (1999).[24] Speaking for a unanimous Court, Ackermann emphasized the discriminatory effect of the common law restriction on gay men by "reinforc[ing] already existing societal prejudices and severely increas[ing] the negative effects of such prejudices on their lives" (para. 23). He approvingly cited rulings by the ECtHR and the Canadian Supreme Court, praising their understanding of the harms caused by singling out individuals because of their sexual orientation. Further, he added, in stigmatizing them as criminals, the prohibition of sodomy was an assault on their dignity and subjected them to arrest and prosecution merely for engaging in human activities. The effect, he said, was similar to that of apartheid on racial groups: "There can be no doubt that the existence of a law which punishes a form of sexual expression for gay men degrades and devalues gay men in our broader society" (para. 28). The Court concluded that the discrimination was "unfair," abridging the equality provision of the Constitution and infringing on dignity and privacy. Moreover, it found that the law stemmed from prejudice and served no legitimate purpose. Ackermann specifically rejected religious beliefs—however sincerely held—as justification for the discrimination.

Justice Albie Sachs concurred to underscore his views on the intertwined relationship among the constitutional guarantees of equality, dignity, and privacy, stressing that the state must act affirmatively to protect all three. He concluded with the hope that the "emancipatory effects of the elimination of institutionalised prejudice against gays and lesbians will encourage amongst the heterosexual population a greater sensitivity to the variability of the human kind" (para. 138).[25]

Like their Canadian counterparts, the South African LGBT litigants aimed at eliminating economic and social inequality before focusing on marriage restrictions. In *National Coalition for Gay and Lesbian Equality v Minister of Home Affairs* (2000), the Court reviewed a challenge to a provision of the 1991 Aliens Control Act, a law allowing spouses and dependent children of legal South African residents entry into the country with eligibility for permanent residency.[26] The lower court had held that the restriction on "permanent same-sex life partners" violated the Constitution but suspended its order to allow Parliament to rectify the violation.

In the first Constitutional Court ruling on a law restricting same-sex relationships, Ackermann delivered the opinion for the unanimous Court.[27] He found the law based on "overlapping or intersecting discrimination on the grounds of sexual orientation and marital status, both being specified in s[ection] 9(3) and presumed to constitute unfair discrimination" (para. 40). The Court dismissed the government's contention that gay men and lesbians could comply with the marital status requirement by marrying persons of the opposite sex as "meaningless." Assessing the impact of the discrimination, it found that gay men and lesbians were a vulnerable minority, and denying them equality and dignity has a far-reaching effect, for it "all too quickly and insidiously degenerates into a denial of humanity and leads to inhuman treatment by the rest of society in many other ways." Such behavior, it continued, is "deeply demeaning and frequently has the cruel effect of undermining the confidence and sense of self-worth and self-respect of lesbians and gays" (para. 42). Moreover, because they are a vulnerable population, the discrimination is even more severe.

The government also argued that the law protected traditional family relationships by allowing spouses of lawful South African residents to reunite with their loved ones. Ackermann accused it of clinging to traditional notions of family and reinforcing a stereotypical view of same-sex couples that ignored the profound societal changes in family relationships. He pointed out that such nations as Canada, Israel, and the United Kingdom (UK) recognized that same-sex couples commit to family relationships, including children. Moreover, the government's message that "gays and lesbians lack the inherent humanity to have their families and family lives in such same-sex relationships respected or protected" dealt a blow to the dignity of same-sex couples (para. 54). Last, Ackermann stressed that the government's support for traditional marriage cannot come at the expense of the constitutional rights of same-sex couples, adding that allowing same-sex couples to benefit from the immigration law will not detract from the institution of marriage.

The Court overcame its concern about transgressing its proper judicial role and invading parliamentary authority and ordered the words "or partner, in a permanent same-sex life partnership" read into the law. Ironically, despite its stirring affirmation of same-sex relationships, the Court refrained from discussing the broader issue of marriage inequality (Louw 2005).

In 2002, the Constitutional Court ruled on Judge Margaret Satchwell's challenge to the Judges' Remuneration and Conditions of Employment Act of 1989, a law restricting survivor benefits, travel allowances, and medical care to married couples. She claimed that it unconstitutionally deprived her partner of these benefits because of their sexual orientation and marital status. Announcing another unanimous opinion, Justice Tholie Madala held that the law discriminated against the couple based on their sexual orientation (*Satchwell v President of the Republic of South Africa* 2002). Because the spousal benefits arose from a married couple's duty of reciprocal support, they must also be afforded to same-sex partners who have a permanent relationship that approximates marriage. The Court cured the unconstitutionality of the law by reading inclusive language into the statute.

In quick succession, the Court decided two cases revolving around family relationships in same-sex households. In *Du Toit v Minister for Welfare and Population Development* (2003), Suzanne Du Toit and Anna-Marie De Vos, permanent same-sex life partners, sought to adopt the two children they were raising. Despite the fact that Du Toit was the primary caregiver, only De Vos's adoption petition was granted. The couple challenged the 1983 Child Care Act and the 1993 Guardianship Act for violating their constitutional right to equality and dignity and failing to consider the children's best interests. The lower court agreed and found that only allowing married couples to adopt jointly and exercise joint guardianship over an adopted child discriminated on the basis of sexual orientation and marital status. It declared the statutes unconstitutional and ordered the corrective language of permanent same-sex life partnership read into them in all relevant places.

Justice Thembile Skweyiya announced the unanimous opinion, acknowledging the importance of the family in South African society but cautioning that the "legal conception of family and what constitutes family life should change as social practices and traditions change" (para. 19). The Court accepted the lower court's finding that the laws unfairly differentiated between same-sex couples and married couples by infringing on their constitutional guarantee; moreover, they invaded Du Toit's dignity by denying her status as the children's coparent. Unwilling to delay the remedy, rather than simply declaring the laws unconstitutional and waiting for Parliament to act, the Court agreed with the court below and ordered appropriate language read into the statutes.

Shortly after *Du Toit* was decided, the Court ruled in *J. v Director-General of Home Affairs* (2003) in a challenge over the parental rights of a lesbian couple whose children were conceived by artificial insemination. After one of the women gave birth to twins, the other unsuccessfully sought to register as their parent also. Their suit claimed that the Children's Status Act of 1987 abridged their constitutional rights by only allowing different-sex parents to register children born through artificial insemination.

Speaking for another unanimous Court, Justice Richard Goldstone addressed the claim that the law unfairly differentiated between married people and permanent same-sex life partners. He compared the type of discrimination in the adoption act in *Du Toit* to that in the challenged law, finding that both deprive persons of their constitutional rights because of their sexual orientation. The Court held that preventing same-sex couples from normalizing the relationships to the children conceived through artificial insemination is contrary to the myriad legal and social developments taking place in South Africa and cannot be justified. In the end, anxious to avoid accusations of overreaching, Goldstone accepted the government's request to suspend the declaration of invalidity for a year to allow Parliament to remedy the constitutional flaw. He urged Parliament to enact "comprehensive legislation regularising relationships between gay and lesbian persons . . . [because] it is unsatisfactory for the courts to grant piecemeal relief to members of the gay and lesbian community as and when aspects of their relationships are found to be prejudiced by unconstitutional legislation" (para. 23).

It was inevitable that the Court's generous reading of LGBT rights would lead to lawsuits challenging the common law definition of marriage (a "union of a man and a woman, while it lasts, to the exclusion of all others") and section 30(1) of the Marriage Act of 1961, limiting marriage to an individual taking another as his or her "lawful wife (or husband)" in a civil marriage ceremony.[28]

The first case in which the Court ruled on marriage inequality arose when Marie Adrianna Fourie and Cecilia Bonthuys sued to seek a change in the common law definition of marriage.[29] The lower court lower denied their claim, saying that the relief they sought was inconsistent with the Marriage Act; they appealed to the Supreme Court of Appeal (SCA), the second highest court in South Africa.

Writing for the majority, on November 30, 2004, Judge Edwin Cameron announced the SCA opinion, explaining that the Marriage Act does not define marriage but was "enacted on the assumption—unquestioned at the time—that the common law definition of marriage applied only to opposite-sex couples" (*Fourie v Minister of Home Affairs* 2005, para. 27). He reviewed the history of discrimination against gay men and lesbians, emphasizing the assaults on their privacy and dignity and noting that the courts were obliged to protect vulnerable minorities from the majoritarian legislative process by adjudicating claims based on the equality and dignity provisions of the Bill of Rights. Anxious to avoid the appearance of interfering with religious liberty, Cameron added that revising the common law definition of marriage would not compel clergy to perform religious wedding ceremonies. Because their suit only challenged the common law definition of marriage, the ruling did not apply to civil marriages governed by the Marriage Act.

Both sides appealed to the Constitutional Court, the government arguing that such major societal changes altering the historic definition of marriage should emanate from Parliament, not the courts. The plaintiffs claimed that the court should have read language into the Marriage Act that would allow them to marry immediately.

A few months before the SCA ruling, on July 8, 2004, the Lesbian and Gay Equality Project filed an application attacking the constitutionality of the Marriage Act as well as the common law definition of marriage, claiming that both violated their rights of equality, dignity, and privacy. They asked the court to change the common law definition to "marriage is the lawful and voluntary union of two persons to the exclusion of all others while it lasts" and to read the words "or spouse" into the Marriage Act. At the same time, they applied for direct access to the Constitutional Court to have their cases decided with *Fourie*. Rarely granted, this time the Court agreed, saying that it must address both the common law definition of marriage as well as the Marriage Act in deciding whether the marriage bans unfairly discriminated against gay men and lesbians.

The unanimous opinion in *Minister of Home Affairs v Fourie and Lesbian and Gay Equality Project v Minister of Home Affairs* (2006), delivered by Sachs broadly proclaimed four fundamental principles arising out of the Court's sexual orientation cases: First, there are many types of families; second, there is a long history of discrimination on the basis of sexual orientation; third, there is no wide-ranging family law policy for gay men and lesbians; and finally, the new South Africa was founded on principles of "tolerance and mutual respect" (para. 60).

Sachs emphasized that the marriage ceremony represents a public commitment that encompasses each partner's duty to support the other as well as to assume joint responsibility for children and the home. The ban on same-sex marriage excludes same-sex couples from assuming these rights and responsibilities and sends a clear message that they are less worthy than different-sex couples are. Moreover, he said, a policy of marriage inequality is more than simply an irritation, for it deprives same-sex couples of tangible (economic) as well as intangible (psychic) benefits.

The Court rejected the commonly voiced argument that the government's interest in procreation justified its marriage law, as well as arguments based on tradition and religion, pointing out that same-sex marriage would have no effect on different-sex couples who wished to marry according to their religious convictions. In the end, the Court declared the common law definition of marriage and section 30(1) of the Marriage Act invalid.

The government asked the Court to refrain from reading the words "or spouse" into the Marriage Act, claiming that it would intrude on Parliament's authority to alter the institution of marriage. It urged the Court to suspend its declaration of unconstitutionality to allow Parliament to determine the appropriate remedy. Citing separation of powers and judicial restraint principles, the majority agreed to suspend the order of invalidity for twelve months to allow Parliament a "free hand" to decide how to cure the defect. If Parliament failed to act by November 30, 2006 (a one-year deadline), then the words or spouse after the words wife (or husband) would automatically be read into the Marriage Act. Justice Kate O'Regan argued that the Court should have read the language into the act to give same-sex couples immediate relief, stressing that the courts are obligated to remedy constitutional violations and do not diminish the role of the legislature by doing so.

In response to the Court's ruling, on November 15, 2006, Parliament passed the Civil Union Act of 2006, making South Africa the fifth country in the world to adopt marriage equality (De Vos 2007; see Daniels and Brickhill 2006).[30] Henceforth all couples, regardless of sexual orientation, may enter into a civil union marriage and register it as either a marriage or a civil partnership; both have the same legal attributes as marriages entered into through the 1961 Marriage Act.[31] Same-sex marriage advocates achieved a substantial victory, but it was incomplete, for, with the 1961 act remaining intact, only different-sex couples were permitted to celebrate marriage in traditional civil or religious marriage ceremonies.[32]

THE INTERNATIONAL COMMUNITY

LGBT rights emerged as a global issue, part of an international community's commitment to advancing human rights. In 1981, the post–World War II Council of Europe (CoE), comprised of virtually all countries on the European continent, declared its opposition to discrimination against the LGBT community. The formation of the European Union (EU), initially created in 1958, became one of the most significant voices against discrimination in Europe.[33] The 1997 Treaty of Amsterdam, the first international human rights agreement to explicitly ban sexual orientation discrimination, broadly empowered the EU to "take appropriate action to combat discrimination based on sex, racial or ethnic origin, religion or belief, disability, age or sexual orientation."[34] More recently, the European Charter of Fundamental Human Rights (ECFHR) also placed members of the LGBT community under the protective wing of the EU.[35]

In 2006, a group of human rights experts met in Yogyakarta, Indonesia, under the auspices of the United Nations (UN); the outcome of the meeting was a draft of the *Yogyakarta Principles on the Application of International Human Rights Law in Relation to Sexual Orientation and Gender Identity* (2007). The authors intended the document to serve as a guideline for the UN as well as individual governments to expand human rights guarantees. The preamble to the *Yogyakarta Principles* broadly states, "All persons, regardless of sexual orientation or gender identity, are entitled to the full enjoyment of all human rights, [and] that the application of existing human rights entitlements should take account of the specific situations and experiences of people of diverse sexual orientations and gender identities." Upon the release of the *Yogyakarta Principles*, Michael O'Flaherty of Ireland, a member of the UN Human Rights Committee, affirmed the group's goals, stating, "Ending violence and abuse against people because of their sexual orientation or gender identity must become a global priority for governments."

On March 31, 2010, the Committee of Ministers of the CoE also adopted a statement against discrimination based on sexual orientation and gender identity. They recommended that member states "ensure that legislative and other measures are adopted and effectively implemented to combat discrimination on grounds of sexual orientation or gender identity, to ensure respect for the human rights of lesbian, gay, bisexual and transgender persons and to promote tolerance towards them" (Council of Europe 2011).

At the end of the year, the European Parliament's annual report on international human rights focused special attention on the treatment of members of the LGBT community, identifying a need for greater efforts to end discrimination and violence against them. Reacting to the report, MEP (Member of the European Parliament) Ulrike Lunacek, CoPresident of the Intergroup on LGBT Rights, stated,

> MEPs across the political spectrum sent a clear message that human rights are no bargaining token: they are universal, indivisible, and

> apply equally to lesbian, gay, bisexual and transgender people regardless of where they live. The European Parliament clearly stated that LGBT people's fundamental rights need to be closely monitored and protected. (European Parliament 2010)

In another breakthrough for LGBT rights, in 2011, the UN General Assembly's Human Rights Council adopted a resolution denouncing discrimination on the basis of gender identity and sexual orientation (United Nations 2011). A few years later, the secretary general announced that the UN would recognize same-sex marriages if they were legal where they were solemnized.[36]

The EU took another step toward equal rights for members of the LGBT community in 2013, adopting guidelines that proclaimed the organization's "commit[ment] to the principle of the universality of human rights and reaffirm[ed] that cultural, traditional or religious values cannot be invoked to justify any form of discrimination, including discrimination against LGBTI persons."[37] After condemning discrimination against them, the council stated,

> [T]he EU aims to promote and protect all human rights of LGBTI persons on the basis of existing international legal standards in this area, including those set by the UN and the CoE. Through the different tools available within its external action, including financial instruments available from both EU institutions and Member States, the EU will seek to actively promote and protect the enjoyment of these rights. (Council of the European Union 2013)

More recently, on May 15, 2015, commemorating the International Day against Homophobia and Transphobia, Thorbjorn Jagland, CoE Secretary General and former Prime Minister of Norway, declared,

> [W]e have made significant progress over the past decades. We cannot afford to backtrack. We must make every effort to respond to violence and discrimination against LGBT people. We must put solid legal and policy frameworks in place, provide training and ensure that victims are aware of their rights. These are not special rights, but universal rights guaranteed to all under the European Convention of Human Rights. (Council of Europe 2015)

Shortly after Jagland's statement, the EU voiced support for the Pride Parade in Strasbourg, France, on June 13, 2015, declaring, "[T]he issues of sexual orientation and gender identity continue to be used as a pretext for serious human rights violations of LGBTI persons in Europe. Regrettably," it continued, "LGBTI persons are still subject to persecution, discrimination and ill-treatment on the basis of their sexual orientation and gender identity" (European Union 2015).

Despite the rhetorical commitment to LGBT rights over the last several decades by international organizations, prejudices against the LGBT population often lead to violence. A grim report by the UN High Commissioner for Human Rights in 2015 warned of the

> continuing, serious and widespread human rights violations perpetrated, too often with impunity, against individuals based on their sexual orientation and gender identity. Since 2011, hundreds of people have been killed and thousands more injured in brutal, violent attacks. . . . Other documented violations include torture, arbitrary detention, denial of rights to assembly and expression, and discrimination in health care, education, employment and housing. (United Nations 2015)

As recently as April 2015, homosexual conduct remains criminalized in seventy-five countries and punishable by death in ten of these (Human Rights Campaign 2015b; International Lesbian, Gay, BiSexual, Trans, and Intersex Association [ILGA]–Europe 2015a; *Washington Post*, June 14, 2016).

The increasing authority of Islamic fundamentalists in the Mideast has been accompanied by gross violations of LGBT rights as documented by the International Human Rights Commission, reporting a timeline of public executions of women and men from 2014 to 2015. The victims, accused of committing crimes against public morals, including sodomy, were executed by a variety of means, including beheading, stoning, shooting, and being thrown off buildings. The list revealed the punishment the Islamic State meted out for "committing acts of the people of Lot [sodomy], spreading corruption on earth, and trying to change the innate nature of Muslims" (International Human Rights Commission 2015).[38]

The violence continues, with two LGBT activists, one of whom was the editor of *Roopbaan*, the sole LGBT magazine in the country, brutally murdered in Dhaka, Bangladesh, on April 25, 2016. A group affiliated with al-Qaeda, Ansar al-Islam, claimed responsibility for the attack, saying that the victims were killed for "promoting homosexuality in Bangladesh" (*Al Jazeera*, April 26, 2016).

In such countries as Nigeria and Gambia, homosexuality is not punishable by death, but the penalties for engaging in homosexual conduct and membership in LGBT organizations are severe (*New York Times*, July 21, 2015). Moreover, even in countries where members of the LGBT community are not subject to criminal penalties, there are numerous legal and social restrictions on them (*Washington Post*, June 26, 2015).

Like their counterparts in the common law countries, citizens of EU countries took the initial step in attaining equal rights for gay men and lesbians by challenging laws that criminalized consensual sexual activity between same-sex partners (see Waaldijk 2000; Waaldijk 2001).[39]

Sodomy laws were largely uncodified until the nineteenth century in Europe, but same-sex male sodomy was punishable throughout much of the continent, including by death in England and Wales.[40] The 1861 Offences Against the Person Act eliminated the death penalty there, but sexual contact between men remained a criminal offense. The 1895 trial of playwright and author Oscar Wilde, sentenced to two years of hard labor under the Criminal Offences Act, demonstrated the harmful effects of the law. Perhaps even more disturbing, in 1952, noted scientist Alan Turing, who played a leading role in deciphering the German code during World War II, was convicted under the same act and forced to choose between prison and hormone injections. Turing chose the latter and, after two years of this "therapy," committed suicide at forty-one.[41]

In 1954, the British government created the Wolfenden Commission, which issued a report three years later recommending the repeal of laws against homosexual sodomy. In response to the commission's report, Parliament amended the Sexual Offences Act in 1967 to decriminalize private consensual homosexual acts between men over twenty-one in England and Wales. France repealed its sodomy law in 1981, and a year later, same-sex sexual relations became legal for those fifteen and older (Stiener 2011; see Rabinowitz 1995).[42] In contrast, Germany did not abandon its same-sex sodomy laws at that time (Grigolo 2003). An ECtHR ruling in *Dudgeon v. UK* (1981) delivered a final blow to the remaining European sodomy laws, with the Court's statement against criminal sodomy a powerful impetus for the further reform of European sexual intimacy laws.

SAME-SEX PARTNERSHIPS

By 2014, a number of countries in the world—chiefly in northern Europe—had alleviated discrimination on the basis of sexual orientation and gender identity in marriage and family life, primarily by granting same-sex civil unions and partnerships many of the attributes of marriage without formally adopting marriage equality. But only a few countries took the final step of validating same-sex marriage, leaving civil marriage beyond the grasp of most LGBT couples in the world (Council of Europe 2014).

Compared to the rest of the world, "Europe has [had] the longest formal history of same-sex partnership recognition, and has (arguably) made more thorough progress in that respect" (Lind 2008, 285). The first signs of progress toward recognizing same-sex relationships appeared in the Scandinavian countries: Denmark granted same-sex couples most of the rights associated with marriage in the Registered Partnership Act of 1989; Norway accorded partnership rights to same-sex couples in 1993, followed by Sweden in 1995, Greenland and Iceland in 1996, and Finland in 2002 (Spencer 2010; Waaldijk 2000).

In 1998, the Netherlands created a system of registered partnerships for both same-sex and different-sex couples. A year later, France followed suit with the Pacte Civil de Solidarite (PaCS), which recognized permanent relationships between couples without regard to sexual orientation. Soon after, a Belgian partnership registration law took effect in 2000, followed by Germany's Life Partnership Act of 2001. Also in 2001, Portugal extended property rights to same-sex couples.

Over the next several years, an increasing number of countries adopted partnership recognition policies. In 2003, Austria created a status called unregistered cohabitation that gave cohabiting same-sex couples the same rights as unmarried cohabiting different-sex partners.[43] In the same year, Croatia permitted same-sex couples who had been together for at least three years to be accorded the same rights as different-sex cohabitating couples.[44] A year later, the UK passed its

Civil Partnerships Act, and in 2005, Andorra, Luxembourg, New Zealand, and Switzerland created partnership registration schemes. The Czech Republic and Slovenia authorized same-sex couples to enter into civil partnerships in 2006. And on opposite sides of the world, Hungary and Uruguay created civil partnerships in 2007 (see *Gay Star News*, September 21, 2011; Kukura 2006).[45]

The pattern continued, as Ireland (in 2010) and Lichtenstein (in 2011) allowed same-sex partners to enter into civil partnerships that mirrored some of the attributes of civil marriage. The Brazilian high court declared same-sex civil unions permissible in 2011, and three years later, the Maltese Parliament enacted a law legalizing same-sex civil unions. In October 2014, Estonia became the first former–Soviet Union nation to legalize civil unions for all couples regardless of their sexual orientation.

In 2015, the trend toward legalizing continued. In May 2015, the Cypriot Cabinet sanctioned same-sex civil partnership legislation and sent it to Parliament, which supported it in a 39–12 vote on November 26, 2015 (International Lesbian, Gay, BiSexual, Trans, and Intersex Association [ILGA]–Europe 2015b). In Japan, the city of Tokyo issued its first same-sex union certificate to a couple in November 2015 (*The Atlantic*, April 13, 2016). And in Chile, Ecuador, and Columbia, limited forms of civil unions also became legal (*New York Times*, June 14, 2015).

Same-sex couples made further progress in having their relationships legalized when Greece's Ministry of Justice announced that it planned to introduce legislation that would allow same-sex couples to enter into civil unions by amending a 2009 civil partnership law that expressly excluded them (*Pink News*, December 14, 2015). On December 22, 2015, over the intense opposition of the Greek Orthodox Church, the Greek Parliament approved the civil partnership law in a resoundingly positive vote (*euronews*, December 23, 2015; *Global News*, December 22, 2015; International Lesbian, Gay, BiSexual, Trans, and Intersex Association [ILGA]–Europe 2015c).

With the ECtHR ruling against it in 2015, Italy also moved toward recognizing same-sex civil partnerships. Passing out of the Senate committees, on January 28, 2016, the Italian Senate considered a civil union bill that would grant same-sex couples some marital rights. The bill, accompanied by numerous amendments, included a measure to relax rules on adoption by same-sex couples. Under Italian law, same-sex couples were unable to adopt even if one of the parents was the child's biological parent. Public opinion overwhelmingly favored the legislation, but the Catholic Church was adamantly opposed. Despite the intraparty and interparty disputes that threatened to doom its passage, the Italian Senate approved the civil union bill in a 173–71 vote on February 25, 2016. To secure its passage, the bill that cleared the Senate was stripped of the adoption provision (*The Advocate*, January 23, 2016; International Lesbian, Gay, BiSexual, Trans, and Intersex Association [ILGA]–Europe 2016b; *New York Times*, February 25, 2016; *Pink News*, February 13, 2016).

On May 11, 2016, Italy joined the rest of the western European countries in authorizing civil unions for same-sex couples when the Italian Parliament overwhelmingly approved the civil union bill; the vote in the Chamber of Deputies was 372–51, with 99 members abstaining. Some leaders of gay and lesbian groups expressed disappointment at the continued ban on same-sex marriage and adoptions by same-sex couples. The head of Rainbow Families Association charged that "this government will go down in history not for having passed the first law on gay unions, but for having denied children their family rights" (*The Florentine* 2016; *The Local Italy* 2016; *New York Times*, May 12, 2016).[46]

MARRIAGE EQUALITY

With the increasing recognition of same-sex relationships, it was likely that marriage equality would emerge, especially in the countries of western Europe. It began in 2001, when the Netherlands Parliament approved full marriage equality for same-sex couples—the first country in the world to do so (Waaldijk 2000; Waaldijk 2001). Two years later, in 2003, its neighbor Belgium followed its lead in legalizing same-sex marriage. Over the next decade, Canada and Spain granted marriage equality in 2005, as did South Africa in 2006; Norway and Sweden recognized same-sex marriage in 2009, with Argentina, Iceland, and Portugal following suit in 2010 (Encarnacion 2013–2014; Saez 2011).

Over the next few years, marriage equality continued to gain acceptance in other European states as well as other parts of the world.

Denmark permitted same-sex civil marriage in 2012, with France, England, New Zealand, Uruguay, and Wales legalizing it in 2013. In May 2013, the Brazilian National Council of Justice ruled that notary publics cannot refuse to perform same-sex marriages and must convert civil unions into marriages if asked; by that time, legislatures in almost a dozen Brazilian states had voted in favor of allowing same-sex marriage. Scotland permitted same-sex marriage in 2014 and Finland adopted marriage equality at the beginning of 2015 (with implementation delayed until 2017).

In June 2014, the Luxembourg Parliament overwhelmingly voted to permit same-sex couples to marry beginning in 2015, making it the seventeenth country in the world to do so. Shortly after it was legalized, Luxembourg's prime minister married his long-time partner in a ceremony held in the Luxembourg City Hall.

The Republic of Ireland, traditionally a conservative Catholic country, held a referendum on same-sex marriage on May 22, 2015, asking the electorate to vote on a proposed constitutional amendment: "Marriage may be contracted in accordance with law by two persons without distinction as to their sex." Despite the vehement opposition of the Catholic Church, voters overwhelmingly approved the amendment with 62 percent of the votes. With the success of the referendum, Ireland became the first country in the world to approve marriage equality by popular vote. The victory was accompanied by speculation that the vote reflected the waning authority of the Catholic Church in Ireland (*New York Times*, May 23, 2015; *Politico*, May 23, 2015; *Washington Post*, May 23, 2015).[47]

A few days after the Irish vote, Greenland's Parliament unanimously approved a marriage equality bill, allowing gay and lesbian marriages to take place beginning in October 2015. On March 3, 2015, the Slovenian National Parliament voted 51–28 to approve amendments to the Marriage and Family Relations Act that would grant equal status to same-sex and different-sex couples (*euronews*, March 4, 2015).

In Mexico, the right to marry or recognize same-sex marriage had varied by geographic region (Freedom to Marry 2014). In 2009, Mexico City's Legislative Assembly passed a marriage equality bill limited to Mexico City; the Mexico Supreme Court subsequently ruled that all Mexican states must recognize marriages performed in other parts of the country. Finally, in a decision published on June 19, 2015, the high court declared it discriminatory to restrict marriage to heterosexual couples, essentially extending marriage equality to the entire country. The effect of the ruling was to allow same-sex couples to wed in all states (Kahn 2015).[48] Two weeks later, on June 26, 2015, after the lower courts almost uniformly ruled in favor of plaintiffs challenging marriage restrictions, the US Supreme Court declared marriage equality the law of the land.

Finally, in a historic breakthrough for same-sex marriage, in early January 2016, a Chinese District People's Court accepted a suit against the civil affairs bureau that refused to register a marriage application when a bureau official told the couple that "marriage had to be between a man and woman" (*New York Times*, January 27, 2016; *Reuters*, January 6, 2016). Despite the initial optimism, a few months later, the court ruled against the couple, saying that "[T]he law permits only 'men and women' to wed" (*The Atlantic*, April 13, 2016; *New York Times*, April 13, 2016).

RESISTANCE TO MARRIAGE EQUALITY

Despite the growing number of countries adopting marriage equality, opposition to same sex-marriage continues, with a large segment of the world (almost two hundred countries) restricting marriage to different-sex couples (Foster 2010). Additionally, despite the success in Europe, where more than two-thirds of the countries have legalized same-sex marriage (Pew Research Center 2015b), two of the largest countries—Germany and Italy—continue to bar same-sex couples from marrying, as do most central and eastern European nations.

On April 27, 2015, a majority of Northern Ireland's Parliament voted against granting equal marriage rights to same-sex couples—for the fourth time. In a later vote, on November 1, 2015, 53 of the 105 members of the Northern Ireland Assembly voted in favor of marriage equality, yet the opposition Democratic Unionist Party was able to block the measure with a parliamentary maneuver (*New York Times*, November 2, 2015).[49] When marriage equality took effect on the Isle of Man in July 2016, Northern Ireland was the only part of the UK that did not allow same-sex couples to wed, despite polls showing a 70 percent approval rating (Amnesty International UK 2016).

In another defeat for same-sex couples, on June 28, 2015, the Austrian National Assembly overwhelmingly rejected a proposed resolution to allow same-sex marriage. The Polish Parliament has had a draft civil partnership bill before it since 2004 but has taken no action to date (International Lesbian, Gay, BiSexual, Trans, and Intersex Association [ILGA]–Europe 2015d). Despite Israel's progress in ending discrimination based on sexual orientation and recognizing same-sex marriages performed elsewhere, in July 2015, the Israeli Parliament voted down a bill that would have permitted civil marriage for all Israelis, including same-sex couples. The Knesset vote came as no surprise to observers, despite the growing support for same-sex marriage in the nation (*Times of Israel*, July 12, 2015).

The year 2015 ended with a resounding defeat for marriage equality in Slovenia, as its opponents obtained the requisite signatures to hold a referendum on the proposed amendments to the Marriage and Family Relations Act. The referendum, held on December 20, 2015, lost decisively, 63.5 percent to 36.5 percent, a virtual mirror image of the results in Ireland (International Lesbian, Gay, BiSexual, Trans, and Intersex Association [ILGA]–Europe 2015e; *New York Times*, December 21, 2015; *Politico*, December 15, 2015; *The Slovenian*, December 3, 2015).[50]

Ironically, a few months later, on April 20, 2016, the Slovenian General Assembly approved the Civil Partnership Act, according same-sex partners the same rights as married couples, with the exception of the right to adopt and reproductive assistance; the law takes effect in February 2017 (International Lesbian, Gay, BiSexual, Trans, and Intersex Association [ILGA]–Europe 2016a).

Despite the rise of marriage equality in most of the English-speaking countries, there has been only limited progress in Australia. A number of Australian states—Tasmania, New South Wales, Victoria, Queensland, and the Australian Capital Territory (ACT)—created civil partnerships, granting limited legal status to same-sex couples. In 2004, Parliament amended the 1961 Marriage Act to specify that marriage was the "union of a man and a woman to the exclusion of all others, voluntarily entered for life" (Saez 2011, 17-18).

Two years later, ACT passed a same-sex civil union bill, stating, "a civil union is different to a marriage but is to be treated for all purposes under territory law in the same way as a marriage." Prime Minister John

Howard overruled the law, claiming it was necessary "to defend the fundamental institution of marriage against radical laws." In 2009, pursuant a new Civil Partnership Act, a same-sex couple entered into a civil union in ACT (Foster, 2010). In 2011, the Tasmanian State Parliament approved a marriage equality bill, a futile gesture, as states have no authority over marriage policy (*Gay Star News*, September 21, 2011).

The national government had granted some rights to same-sex couples in 2008 and same-sex marriage advocates hoped to achieve full marriage equality in a parliamentary vote in 2015. Its success was unlikely given the opposition of Prime Minister Tony Abbott, leader of the Liberal Party (the more conservative of Australia's two major parties). Abbott refused to consent to members of his party voting their consciences on the bill and instead proposed to allow the public to vote on legalizing same-sex marriage. In a radio interview, he said, if same-sex marriage were to become legal, it should be done "by the whole people rather than simply brought about by the parliament" (*The Guardian*, August 24, 2015).

On September 14, 2015, Abbott was replaced by Malcolm Turnbull, whose views on same-sex marriage differed from the ousted leader's (*The Guardian*, September 14, 2015). Turnbull indicated he would have voted for marriage equality had there been a free parliamentary vote, but he nevertheless continued to call for a nonbinding plebiscite. Bill Shorten, leader of the opposition Labor Party, accused Turnbull of yielding to the wishes of the conservative members of his governing coalition (*Sydney Morning Herald*, September 24, 2015).

On his one-year anniversary in the leadership position, Turnbull introduced a bill to hold the plebiscite on February 11, 2017, issuing a strong statement supporting same-sex marriage and claiming the plebiscite "was the best way to decide a matter on which Australians had such deeply-held personal convictions." Shorten reacted by declaring that the vote was "unnecessary, expensive and would inflict untold hatred and harm on gay and lesbian people" (*Sydney Morning Herald*, September 14, 2016). A month later Labor announced it would oppose the plebiscite bill, saying Parliament should decide the matter because debate over the referendum would unleash homophobic views in the country (*International Business Times*, October 11, 2016). Parliament rejected the bill, dooming any possibility of legalizing same-sex marriage in the near future. Ironically, supporters of marriage equality joined conservatives in voting against the referendum, calling it wasteful and divisive (*The Guardian*, November 10, 2016).

THE ECTHR AND LGBT RIGHTS

The ECHR, "widely regarded as the most successful experiment in the transnational, judicial protection of human rights in the world," serves as the primary international accord guaranteeing rights of the people of Europe (Greer 2008, 680).[51] Borrowing from the Universal Declaration of Human Rights, adopted by the UN General Assembly on December 10, 1948, the ECHR was signed on November 4, 1950, and went into effect on September 3, 1953. Its signatories agreed to apply the Convention within their borders; most countries equate its provisions with national legislation, some even elevating it to constitutional or semiconstitutional status that supersedes national law (Beeson 2011).[52] Today, by virtue of their membership in the CoE, almost all European states are signatories to the Convention, encompassing hundreds of millions of people (Greer 2008, 680–81). The ECtHR, established in 1959 as the CoE's judicial organ is responsible for enforcing the ECHR.

The ECHR is primarily concerned with protecting the civil and political rights of the individuals in its signatory states, including respect for private and family life and the right to be free from discrimination, but observers have charged that, despite its sweeping equal rights guarantees, the ECtHR is reluctant to override the social and cultural norms of the member states (Murray 2010; Van de Heyning 2011). They maintain that by failing to do so, it has "diluted the special protection" the Convention accords to minority groups (Beeson 2012, 171). In appraising the role of the ECtHR in adjudicating rights claims, critics point to the Court's reliance on the margin of appreciation doctrine, which tends to favor the state over the individual in deciding cases of conflicting moral principles, such as those involving complaints of discrimination because of sexual orientation and gender identity (see Cooper 2011; Murray 2010).

In *Kozak v. Poland* (2010), the Court explained that "contracting states enjoy a margin of appreciation in assessing whether and to what extent differences in otherwise similar situations justify a different treatment in law" (para. 91). In according a margin of appreciation to the state when adjudicating claims of discrimination by LGBT applicants, the Court "balance[s] . . . the need to apply the European Convention on Human Rights' equal treatment provisions to homosexuals with the need to avoid the political third rail of full same-sex marriage legalization" (Oppenheimer, Oliveira, and Blumenthal 2014, 211). Some argue that the Court has granted the state a wider margin in LGBT rights cases "because it regarded homosexuality as antithetical to social morality and public health" (Johnson 2013, 71; see Van de Heyning 2011). The Court's rulings, however, show that, with the exception of marriage inequality, it does not accord the state a wide margin in adjudicating LGBT claims (see Spencer 2010).

LGBT litigants must also overcome the hurdle presented by the consensus doctrine, which, together with the margin of appreciation doctrine, determines the extent to which judges defer to member states. The principles of judicial restraint and democratic decision-making—frequently invoked by the courts of Canada, South Africa, and the United States—are not often expressly articulated by the ECtHR, yet the Court appears mindful of its obligation to avoid overreaching in interpreting ECHR guarantees.

The Court explained the relationship between the two doctrines in *Oliari v. Italy* (2015), saying,

> [I]n the context of "private life" the Court has considered that where a particularly important facet of an individual's existence or identity is at stake the margin allowed to the State will be restricted [citations omitted]. Where, however, there is no consensus within the member States of the Council of Europe, either as to the relative importance of the interest at stake or as to the best means of protecting it, particularly where the case raises sensitive moral or ethical issues, the margin will be wider. (para. 162)

Critics contend that the two doctrines afford judges the opportunity to achieve desired outcomes based in part on their own values (see Beeson 2011; Murray 2010; Spencer 2010).

In pursuing equal rights claims in the ECtHR, LGBT applicants primarily rely on Articles 8, 12, and 14—chiefly Article 8, either alone or in conjunction with Article 14.[53] Most claims of discrimination on the basis of sexual orientation complain of laws criminalizing same-sex sexual conduct, denying equal benefits to same-sex couples, prohibiting same-sex marriage, and restricting opportunities for adoption and child custody; claims of discrimination based on gender identity stem from the state's refusal to recognize an individual's transgender status, provide access to surgical procedures, and allow transgender individuals to adopt (see Bell 2012; Johnson 2013).

The ECtHR and Sexual Orientation Claims

Applicants complaining of discrimination based on sexual orientation commonly cite Article 8, asking the European Court to interpret its guarantee of "respect for private and family life" to declare laws interfering with bodily integrity and personal autonomy inconsistent with the ECHR. The Court first interpreted Article 8 to encompass laws restricting male sexual behavior in its 1981 ruling in *Dudgeon*. The case began in the late 1970s, when police raided Jeffrey Dudgeon's home to search for illegal drugs. They found homosexual writings and questioned him about his homosexual activities, but even though the government filed no charges against him, he challenged the Northern Ireland criminal sodomy law in the ECtHR.

The Court explained that the state may regulate homosexual activity in the interest of public morality but must have a "pressing social need" to justify interference with the individual's private life. It ruled against the state, finding that moral considerations were insufficient to justify the ban on private sexual relations between consenting adults.

Subsequent victories in the cases challenging sodomy laws illustrate the force of Article 8 in advancing LGBT rights.[54] With a few exceptions, the Court held that restrictions on private same-sex sexual conduct between consenting adults violate the command to respect private life guaranteed by the ECHR. Following *Dudgeon*, the Court relied on Article 8 (at times in conjunction with Article 14) to invalidate various sodomy laws in *Norris v. Ireland* (1988); *Modinos v. Cyprus* (1993); *Sutherland v. United Kingdom* (1997); *Smith and Grady v. United Kingdom* (1999); and *A. D. T. v. United Kingdom* (2000). These decisions decriminalized sodomy, prohibited exclusion from the military because of sexual orientation, and barred states from imposing different ages of consent for engaging in same-sex sodomy.[55]

In contrast, the Court has been more hesitant in ruling on claims of discrimination on the basis of sexual orientation in family relations, allowing states a wider margin of appreciation in reviewing such laws. In *Salgueiro Da Silva Mouta v. Portugal* (1999), *E.B. v. France* (2008), *P.B. and J.S. v. Austria* (2010), and *J.M. v. United Kingdom* (2010), for example, the ECtHR interpreted Articles 8 and 14 to invalidate restrictions on adoption, custody, and child visitation, as well as access to social welfare benefits. But in *Frette v. France* (2002) and *Gas and Dubois v. France* (2012), the Court held that restricting adoption on the basis of sexual orientation was in the child's best interests and consistent with Articles 8 and 14 (see Stone 2003).

Relationship Rights

The Court has been more favorable to applicants seeking economic and social equality under Articles 8 and 14. In *Karner v. Austria* (2003) and *Kozak*, it invalidated laws infringing on the property rights of same-sex partners. In *Vallianatos v. Greece* (2013), it held that excluding same-sex couples from the Greek civil union law contravened their rights under Articles 8 and 14. It also favored the same-sex couple in *Pajic v. Croatia* (2016), overruling the Croatian government's refusal to allow the applicant to be reunited with her Croatian partner.

The applicant in *Karner* challenged the Austrian law that prevented one member of the same-sex couple to claim their jointly held property upon the death of the other. The Court rejected the state's appeal to the "traditional family unit," holding that it could not lawfully deny same-sex couples the benefits granted to different-sex couples because, despite its legitimate interest in protecting the traditional family, it had not demonstrated the need to restrict life companionships to different-sex couples.

Similarly, in *Kozak*, the Court ruled on a policy that barred the applicant from succeeding to the tenancy of a flat—in which they both lived—upon his partner's death. The government rejected the applicant's argument that he had lived with his partner in a "de facto marital relationship" (one of the requirements for succeeding to a tenancy) because that arrangement can only be between a man and a woman. The ECtHR, held that, because the government's policy was chiefly motivated by the applicant's sexual orientation, it was inconsistent with the guarantees of Articles 8 and 14.

The Court reviewed the 2008 Greek Civil Union law in *Vallianatos* when eight Greek nationals challenged the law, charging that it violated Articles 8 and 14 by excluding them from the benefits of civil unions. It found that there was no consensus among the CoE countries on civil unions but that there was a growing trend toward legalizing same-sex relationships; of the nineteen signatory countries that authorized domestic partnerships, the Court noted that only Greece and Lithuania restricted them to different-sex couples. Reiterating that there was no prescribed type of family in current times, it emphasized that the applicants in the case are as capable of forming "stable committed relationships" and are in the same position as different-sex couples to benefit from "legal recognition and protection of their relationship" (para. 78). In the end, the ECtHR ruled that the government failed to meet its burden of showing that only different-sex civil unions fulfil its goal of protecting the family and children born outside of marriage.

In *Oliari*, the Court ruled on a challenge to Italian law, which allowed neither civil unions, domestic partnerships, nor any other quasi-marriage alternatives. Individuals had been recently permitted to enter into "cohabitation agreements"—specifically forbidden to married couples—but these were largely intended to regulate financial arrangements among people already living together.[56]

After losing in the Italian national court, a number of same-sex couples filed a claim with the ECtHR, alleging that the state violated their rights under Article 8, with some citing Article 14, as well. They asked the Court "to impose on States a positive obligation to ensure that same sex-couples have access to an institution, of whatever name, which was more or less equivalent to marriage" (*Oliari v. Italy* 2015, para. 111). The government responded by pointing out that the "Court had acknowledged that the State had no obligation to provide for same-sex marriage, [and] so it also had no obligation to provide for other same-sex unions" (para. 122).[57]

In the view of the ECtHR, the state should enjoy a wider margin of appreciation when contentious moral principles are at stake, particularly when there is no consensus among the signatory states. Nevertheless, the Court held that the "Italian Government have overstepped their margin of appreciation and failed to fulfil their positive obligation to ensure that the applicants have available a specific legal framework providing for the recognition and protection of their same-sex unions" (para. 185).

A year later, in *Pajic*, the Court overturned the state's decision to deny a residence permit to allow the applicant to rejoin her partner in Croatia. Pajic, a Bosnian-Herzegovinian national, sought a residence permit in 2011 to return to Croatia to live and start a business with her partner of two years. The government refused to issue one, citing the Aliens Act, the law that excluded same-sex couples from family reunification. After the Croatian Constitutional Court dismissed her complaint, the ECtHR agreed to rule on her claim that the state discriminated against her because of sexual orientation in violation of Articles 8 and 14. Rejecting the state's procedural arguments, the Court noted that Article 14 requires states to treat similarly situated people equally and to justify any differential treatment by citing a "legitimate aim" or a "reasonable relationship" between the "means employed and the aim sought to be realized" (para. 55). It agreed that the state enjoys a wide margin of appreciation in certain matters (like immigration), but there is a narrower margin in others so that, "just like differences based on sex, differences based on sexual orientation require 'particularly convincing and weighty reasons' by way of justification" (paras. 58–59).

Turning to its analysis of Article 8, the Court stated that it had long held that the relationship between a same-sex couple falls within its right to privacy. While it had initially excluded same-sex couples from the concept of "family" in Article 8, with changes in the laws of member states as well as in EU law, the Court now recognizes that same-sex families are within the scope of Article 8. Because the state was unable to justify the difference between unmarried different-sex couples and same-sex couples, the ECtHR found that the disparate treatment was prompted solely by the couple's sexual orientation and illegal under Articles 8 and 14.

Marriage Equality

Notwithstanding the breadth of the Court's interpretation of Article 8, it has refused to expand the meaning of family in Article 12 to include same-sex marriages (Graupner 2005). Indeed, in *Rees v. UK* (1986), it stated the "right to marry guarantee by Article 12 (art. 12) refers to the traditional marriage between persons of opposite biological sex" (para. 49).

In *Schalk and Kopf v. Austria* (2010), the only ECtHR case to mount a direct challenge to marriage inequality, the Court again explicitly declined to interpret Article 12 to guarantee the right of same-sex couples to marry.[58] The applicants argued that the ECtHR should recognize the growing acceptance of same-sex marriage in the signatory states. But while it agreed that the definition of family within Article 8 encompassed both same-sex and different-sex cohabiting couples, it gave literal meaning to the references to men and women in Article 12, explaining it is the only article in the ECHR that refers to the sexes individually. It clarified,

> All other substantive Articles of the Convention grant rights and freedoms to "everyone" or state that "no one" is to be subjected to certain types of prohibited treatment. The choice of wording in Article 12 must thus be regarded as deliberate. Moreover, regard must be had to the historical context in which the Convention was adopted. In the 1950s marriage was clearly understood in the traditional sense of being a union between partners of different sex. (para. 55)

Observing that registered partnerships were now legal in Austria, the Court conceded that there was an "emerging European consensus towards legal recognition of same-sex couples . . . [that] has developed rapidly over the past decade." But because the majority of CoE states had not legally recognized same-sex couples, the issue "must therefore still be regarded as one of evolving rights with no established consensus, where States must also enjoy a margin of appreciation in the timing of the introduction of legislative changes" (paras. 105–6). Given the deep-rooted social and cultural significance of marriage in the contracting countries, the Court believed that the margin of appreciation must permit national authorities to determine the "exact status conferred by alternative means of recognition" (para. 108).[59]

The ECtHR's unwillingness to override Austrian law caused speculation that it may have feared that a ruling in favor of marriage equality would have met resistance from a host of CoE members, especially Latvia, Lithuania, Russia, and Turkey, possibly leading to their withdrawal from the multinational organization (Oppenheimer, Oliveira, and Blumenthal 2014).

Gender Identity Claims

The Court initially rebuffed claims of discrimination based on gender identity under Articles 8 and 12, but eventually recognized that societal changes indicated it should narrow the state's margin of appreciation when ruling in these cases. Beginning with *X, Y and Z. v. United Kingdom* (1997), it held that the state may refuse to list a transgender man as the father of his adopted child because he was not the biological father. Similarly, in *Rees* and *Cossey v. UK* (1990), it ruled against two transgender men who sought to alter their birth certificates to record their sex as male to allow them to marry the women they wished to marry. In these cases, the Court accorded the states a wide margin of appreciation and accepted the UK's legal restrictions on transgender persons. In *Sheffield and Horsham v. United Kingdom* (1998), it similarly upheld a policy against a challenge that refusing to acknowledge their postoperative gender identity violated the applicants' rights.

The Court adopted a new approach to transgender claims in *Goodwin v. UK* (2002). Christine Goodwin, a postoperative transgender woman, complained that the government's refusal to alter her birth certificate to reflect her gender identity was discriminatory. Citing numerous incidents of discrimination against her because her legal documents depicted her as a man, she sought a new birth certificate reflecting her status as a woman. Explaining its departure from its earlier rulings on transgender rights, it stressed that "since the Convention is first and foremost a system for the protection of human rights, the Court must have regard to the changing conditions within the respondent state and . . . respond" (para. 74). Pointing to a new awareness of transgender people in the UK, as well as an "emerging consensus within contracting states in the Council of Europe on providing legal recognition following gender re-assignment," it held that the state was not entitled to a wide margin of appreciation simply because of differences among the contracting states in the face of "clear and uncontested evidence of a continuing international trend" (para. 85). The Court also cited Australian and New Zealand laws recognizing an individual's postoperative gender, as well as principles in the ECFHR (Murray 2010; see Defeis 2007).

In relatively quick succession, in *Van Kuck v. Germany* (2003), *L. v. Lithuania* (2008), and *Schlumpf v. Switzerland* (2009), the Court ruled that the government's refusal to provide access and financial support for sex reassignment surgery violated the right of privacy in Article 8. However, in *Hamalainen v. Finland* (2014), perhaps because it revolved around marriage, it found no violation of Articles 8 and 14 in the state's refusal to recognize the applicant's gender identity to allow his marriage to be annulled.

The ECtHR has removed many of the vestiges of discrimination on the basis of sexual orientation by requiring countries within its jurisdiction to legitimate quasi-marital arrangements, such as civil unions and domestic partnerships, yet has been unwilling to declare civil marriage equality a fundamental right under the Convention. The Court's justification for drawing the line at marriage is the lack of consensus among the signatory countries in accepting marriage equality. In waiting for a consensus to emerge, however, it forgoes its obligation to enforce human rights guarantees.

In contrast, initially slow to accept claims of discrimination on the basis of gender identity, the Court began to recognize a shifting international climate on transgender issues and was unwilling to wait for a consensus among the states to enforce the equal rights guarantees of the ECHR. Perhaps because it views transgender claims as akin to issues of health and welfare and less disruptive of the social order than same-sex marriage, it shows less restraint in adjudicating claims of discrimination by transgender applicants.

NOTES

1. There is a veritable cottage industry of literature on the litigation for equal rights in Canada and South Africa. For literature on Canada, see, for example, Davies 2008; Elliott 2006; Guitierrez 2004; Larocque 2006; Nicol and Smith 2008; and Pierceson 2005. For literature on South Africa, see, for example, Byrn 2002; and Wright 2006.

2. Section 15(1), effective in April 1985, provides, "Every individual is equal before and under the law and has the right to the equal protection and equal benefit of the law without discrimination and, in particular, without

discrimination based on race, national or ethnic origin, color, religion, sex, age or mental or physical disability."

3. At the time, a common law marriage was defined as a conjugal living arrangement between members of a different-sex couple for at least a year. Provincial laws determined the extent to which the rights and responsibilities in common law marriages resembled those in traditional marriages.

4. Because the complaint did not allege a Charter violation, the Court based the ruling on statutory interpretation, limited to interpreting the legislative intent of the law.

5. There are nine judges on the Supreme Court of Canada; at least five must hear an appeal, but more frequently, seven or nine rule on a case.

6. Section 1 allows the government to defend a discriminatory law as justified. It provides, "The Canadian Charter of Rights and Freedoms guarantees the rights and freedoms set out in it subject only to such reasonable limits prescribed by law as can be demonstrably justified in a free and democratic society" (see *Andrews v. Law Society of British Columbia* 1989; *R. v. Oakes* 1986).

7. Bavis (1999) discusses the evolution of the Court's posture toward equality under the Charter from *Andrews* to *Vriend*.

8. The ban on same-sex marriage emanated from the common law definition of marriage between a man and a woman, but the prohibition did not appear in the statutes. Because homosexuality was subject to criminal penalties until 1969, no same-sex marriages were possible.

9. Because page numbers cannot be precisely determined given the variety of case reporters, in 1995, the Canadian courts began to cite to paragraphs rather than page numbers. Other courts have also adopted this practice.

10. Walters (2003) discusses the complex relationship between common law and constitutional law and the role of the courts in Canada.

11. The opinion departed from *Layland v. Ontario* (1993), the first provincial ruling on same-sex marriage after the Charter came into effect. The three-judge panel of the Ontario Divisional Court held in *Layland* that the common law definition of marriage that restricted same-sex marriage was not discriminatory because a gay man and a lesbian had the right to marry a person of the opposite sex; it said that the law merely forbids a person from marrying someone of the same sex.

12. One of the plaintiffs in the case was Dawn Barbeau; the case is also cited as *Barbeau v. British Columbia* (2003).

13. The Massachusetts high court cited the Ontario Court of Appeal decision in *Halpern* approvingly.

14. Unlike in the United States, Parliament may seek an advisory opinion from the Supreme Court on the constitutionality of proposed legislation.

15. Parliament also submitted a fourth question to the Court, asking whether the "opposite-sex requirement" was consistent with the Charter; the Court refused to answer this question.

16. Martin replaced Chrétien as prime minister on December 12, 2003.

17. Officially established in 1948 under the ruling National Party, apartheid enforced complete separation of the races and insured white dominion for almost fifty years (Gerber 2000).

18. The Union of South Africa, established in 1910, became a republic in 1961 and withdrew from the British Commonwealth in 1968, rejoining it in 1994. In the early 1990s, following a deadly protest at Sharpeville, the government banned the ANC and other liberation groups, with many, including Mandela, imprisoned. In 1990, a year after President F.W. de Klerk assumed the office of the presidency, Mandela was finally released from prison on Robbins Island, where he had been held for twenty-seven years. The apartheid laws were repealed in 1991, and a year later, a vote to end apartheid succeeded. The all-white Parliament approved the Interim Constitution in December 1993, and it went into effect on April 27, 1994, the same day democratic elections were held. Following lengthy negotiations among constituent groups, the Constitutional Assembly ratified the Constitution on October 11, 1996. Signed into law in December 1996, it went into effect in February 1997 (Christiansen 2000; Daniels and Brickhill 2006; Gerber 2000; Luckoff 1999).

19. Section 9(1) provides, "Everyone is equal before the law and has the right to equal protection and benefit of the law." Section 9(3) provides, "The state may not unfairly discriminate directly or indirectly against anyone on one or more grounds, including race, gender, sex, pregnancy, marital status, ethnic or social origin, colour, sexual orientation, age, disability, religion, conscience, belief, culture, language and birth." Section 9(4) applies these guarantees to private acts of discrimination. Sections 10 and 14 guarantee the individual's "dignity" and "privacy," respectively. Under section 36, the limitations clause, a law is struck if based on one of the categories listed in—or analogous to—section 9(3). Section 36 provides,

> (1) The rights in the Bill of Rights may be limited only in terms of law of general application to the extent that the limitation is reasonable and justifiable in an open and democratic society based on human dignity, equality and freedom, taking into account all relevant factors, including—(a) the nature of the right; (b) the importance of the purpose of the limitation; (c) the nature and extent of the limitation; (d) the relation between the limitation and its purpose; and (e) less restrictive means to achieve the purpose.

20. Thabo Mbeki was president of South Africa for nine years, succeeding Mandela in 1999. His statement appeared in a telex sent to Tatchell on November 24, 1987 (Thoreson 2008; see Croucher 2011).

21. In addition to including gender equality, the Constitution reflected a commitment to socioeconomic rights, such as the right to adequate housing, health, and education (Kende 2003).

22. The Constitutional Court consists of eleven justices, requiring at least eight to participate in a case (Webb 1998–1999).

23. South African sodomy laws arose in the 1600s, brought by the Dutch. While arrests for consensual sodomy were rare after 1970, same-sex male sodomy was illegal under the common law as well as section 20A of the Sexual Offenses Act. Sodomy was also listed as a Schedule 1 offense in the Criminal Procedure Act, placing it in the same category as rape and murder and authorizing warrantless arrests, refusal of bail, and killing fleeing suspects (Lukoff 1999; Schmid 2000).

24. In *National Coalition for Gay and Lesbian Equality v Minister of Justice* (1998), a Witwaterand court found that the sodomy laws discriminated on the basis of gender and sexual orientation.

25. The Court did not rule on the disparity between the ages of consent. Following a decision in *Geldenhuys v The State* (2008), the laws were revised to establish sixteen as the uniform age of consent, regardless of gender or sexual orientation.

26. The National Coalition Gay and Lesbian Equality persuaded the Department of Home Affairs to exempt some same-sex couples as "special circumstances" under the law. Initially successful, the department ended the practice in 1998 (Motara 2000).

27. *Langemaat v Minister of Safety and Security* (1998) was the first ruling by a South African court to address restrictions on same-sex relationships. A Transvaal court held that the definition of dependent in a government medical policy was discriminatory because it excluded a couple in a long-term, stable relationship.

28. South Africa has a mix of legal systems: common law, derived from the British; civil law, drawn from Roman–Dutch law; and customary law, encompassing African legal traditions.

29. The Marriage Act of 1961 specified procedures for solemnizing marriage ceremonies and appointing marriage officers. Both religious and secular officials may perform marriages; the act permits religious officials to decline to participate in marriages that are contrary to their religious principles.

30. A draft version of the act would have preserved marriage for different-sex couples while allowing same-sex couples to call their relationship a civil partnership or a marriage (De Vos 2007; Yarbrough 2006).

31. A civil union is the "voluntary union of two persons . . . which is solemnised and registered by way of either a marriage or a civil partnership . . . to the exclusion, while it lasts, of all others." A "civil union partner" is a "spouse in a marriage or a partner in a civil partnership." South Africans may also enter into marriages under the Recognition of Customary Marriages Act.

32. The new law allows state marriage officers to refuse to perform same-sex marriages if it interferes with their religion, belief, or conscience. Religious marriage officers remain excused from performing ceremonies that offend their religious beliefs.

33. The EU began as the European Economic Community in 1958, with its membership comprised of six countries: Belgium, France, Germany, Italy, Luxembourg, and the Netherlands. By June 30, 2016, there were twenty-eight member states, with Croatia the last to join in 2013 (European Union 2016). On June 23, 2016, the UK, which became a member in 1973, held a referendum on its continued membership in the EU. The "leave" position won, with 52 percent of the vote to 48 percent for the "remain" side (*BBC News*, June 24, 2016). There is a great deal of uncertainty about the future relationship between the EU and the UK.

34. The European Committee on Social Rights of the CoE is responsible for monitoring state compliance with the European Social Charter (ESC). The ESC, a treaty entered into in 1961 and modified in 1996, aims at improving the standard of living and social well-being of citizens of the signatory states. Its guarantees include education, health, and nondiscrimination. See Beeson 2012 for differences between the ESC and the ECHR.

35. The ECFHR, proclaimed in Nice in 2000, became legally binding on EU institutions and national governments with the entry into force of the Treaty of Lisbon on December 1, 2009. Article 21 explicitly includes sexual orientation as a forbidden area of discrimination, the first international agreement to expressly prohibit discrimination on these grounds (Mos 2013).

36. The UN is a strong voice against LGBT discrimination. Secretary General Ban ki-Moon strongly advocates for LGBT rights, including announcing that the UN would recognize their employees' legal same-sex marriages, even if the employees' country would not (see *New York Times*, June 14, 2016). In June 2016, over the objections of Muslim and African countries, the UN Human Rights Council narrowly approved a measure proposed by the Latin American countries to appoint a monitor to report on violence and discrimination against members of the LGBT community (*New York Times*, June 30, 2016).

37. All EU members are in the CoE, but there are nineteen CoE members, such as Norway, Russia, Switzerland, and Turkey, that do not belong to the EU.

38. The organization was unable to verify all details on the list.

39. Waaldijk (2000; 2001) argues that virtually all countries follow a pattern of legal changes beginning with decriminalizing same-sex sodomy, enacting antidiscrimination laws, and finally legalizing same-sex partnerships.

40. The sodomy laws did not specify same-sex sexual conduct between women as illegal.

41. In 2009, British Prime Minister Gordon Brown offered a formal apology for Turing's treatment (Stiener 2011).

42. See Waaldijk (2000) for a discussion of decriminalization in Europe. Many countries retained different ages of consent for same-sex and different-sex couples.

43. In 2010, Austria enacted the Registered Partnership Act to extend some of the aspects of civil marriage to same-sex couples.

44. In 2013, Croatian voters overwhelmingly approved to amend the constitution to define marriage as a union between a woman and a man.

45. In Hungary, passage of the Unregistered Cohabitation Amendment to the Civil Code in 1996 extended the benefits of common law marriage to same-sex couples.

46. Prime Minister Matteo Renzi's call for a vote of confidence tied to the pending bill succeeded in a 369–193 vote; this paved the way for Parliament to approve the civil union bill (*The Local Italy* 2016).

47. The Irish Marriage Act 2015 [5] was signed into law on October 29, 2015, amending the Civil Registration Act of 2004 that restricted marriage to a woman and a man. The first marriage ceremony took place on November 17, 2015 (*New York Times*, November 17, 2015).

48. In May 2016, Mexico's president proposed that Congress formally legalize same-sex marriage (*Reuters*, May 18, 2016).

49. The Democratic Union Party invoked the peace agreement's petition of concern clause, designed to operate during political emergencies to protect minority rights (*New York Times*, November 21, 2015). When marriage equality took effect on the Isle of Man in July 2016, all parts of the UK (England, Scotland, and Wales), except Northern Ireland, permitted same-sex marriage.

50. In 2012, opponents succeeded in reversing a law at the ballot box that would have given registered same-sex partners the rights of married couples (*Politico*, December 15, 2015; *The Slovenian*, December 3, 2015).

51. The ECHR was originally known as the Convention for the Protection of Human Rights and Fundamental Freedoms.

52. The European Court of Justice (ECJ), sitting in Luxemburg, is the judicial organ of the EU. The judges (one from each EU member state) serve on the ECJ for a six-year term. Established in 1951 under the Treaty of Paris to enforce agreements of the European Coal and Steel Community, the ECJ

became the Court of the European Community under the Treaty of Rome in 1957. The ECJ's powers were expanded when the EU was created under the Maastricht Treaty in 1992; its authority was again augmented by the 2007 Lisbon Treaty. Today, the ECJ ensures the uniform interpretation and application of EU law and determines whether member states are compliant with EU policies. The court's rulings reinforce the supremacy of EU law to the laws of the member states; they are binding on the member states and individuals, and the court may penalize noncompliant states (Beeson 2011; Van De Heyning 2011). Additionally, national courts must recognize EU law. Both the ECJ and ECtHR rely on the ECHR as well as international agreements in determining standards for human rights protection; with the ECJ and the ECtHR both empowered to adjudicate cases involving EU states, conflicts occasionally arise between the two, yet more recently, they have acted in tandem (Beeson 2011; Defeis 2007; De Witte 2011). The Court's initial rulings largely revolved around discrimination in pensions and benefits to LGBT couples or individuals (Carolan 2005; Spencer 2010).

53. Article 8 provides,

> Everyone has the right to respect for his private and family life, his home and his correspondence. There shall be no interference by a public authority with the exercise of this right except such as is in accordance with the law and is necessary in a democratic society in the interests of national security, public safety or the economic well-being of the country, for the prevention of disorder or crime, for the protection of health or morals, or for the protection of the rights and freedoms of others.

Article 12 provides, "Men and women of marriageable age have the right to marry and to found a family, according to the national laws governing the exercise of this right." Article 14 provides, "The enjoyment of the rights and freedoms set forth in this Convention shall be secured without discrimination on any ground such as sex, race, colour, language, religion, political or other opinion, national or social origin, association with a national minority, property, birth or other status."

54. The Court seemed persuaded in part by the decriminalization laws that had been sweeping Europe for a number of decades.

55. The Nazi's notorious war on homosexuality led to at least 100,000 arrests and imprisonments, many in concentration camps. After World War II, almost 50,000 men were convicted of sodomy, and the law remained in place until 1994, when the German government finally rescinded it. In 2002, the government overturned the Nazi-era convictions, and in 2016, Justice Minister

Heiko Maas announced that the German government will pay reparations to those imprisoned and expunge the records of the 50,000 men convicted under the law (*The Advocate*, October 10, 2016; *New York Times*, May 12, 2016).

56. The Court commented that the civil unions allowed in such municipalities as Pisa and Milan were "purely symbolic" (*Oliari* 2015, para. 44).

57. According to the Court, eleven countries (Belgium, Denmark, France, Iceland, Luxembourg, the Netherlands, Norway, Portugal, Spain, Sweden, and the UK) fully recognized same-sex marriage. Eighteen member countries (Andorra, Austria, Belgium, Croatia, the Czech Republic, Finland, France, Germany, Hungary, Ireland, Liechtenstein, Luxembourg, Malta, the Netherlands, Slovenia, Spain, Switzerland, and the UK) allowed same-sex couples to register as civil partners (*Oliari* v. Italy 2015, para. 54).

58. The family is protected by numerous international agreements, such as the Universal Declaration of Human Rights; the International Covenant on Economic, Social, and Cultural Rights; and the Convention on the Elimination of All Forms of Discrimination against Women, yet none of these have been interpreted to require signatories to allow same-sex couples to marry (Wardle 2013, 512–13).

59. In 2010, when *Schalk* was decided, six of the forty-seven signatory states of the CoE permitted same-sex marriage (Bribosia, Rorive, and Van den Eynde 2014, 18).

CONCLUSION

It is difficult to write a conclusion for a book the subject of which is an ongoing saga. This volume shows that the lot of the LGBT community has improved over time—in the United States, as well as in the rest of the world. The steps taken toward eliminating oppressive sodomy laws, recognizing the legitimacy of same-sex relationships, and advancing transgender rights are evidence of this change.

As with past litigation efforts by minority groups, plaintiffs strove to persuade the courts that their obligation to protect minority rights outweighed their commitment to defer to majoritarian policy-making institutions. The rulings in the cases discussed here demonstrate that the outcome of the litigation was more likely to favor the LGBT plaintiffs when judges were persuaded to subordinate their duty of judicial restraint to their responsibility to adjudicate claims seeking validation of their constitutional and statutory rights.

The primary purpose of this book was to assess the effect of litigation, largely in the federal courts, on the rights of the LGBT community in the United States. Because such an analysis would have been incomplete without considering the courts' interactions with other branches of government, it also examined LGBT policy-making by institutions at the state and national levels of government. Additionally, the book added a comparative dimension by appraising LGBT rights policies in other parts of the world, focusing on the role of the courts there in advancing LGBT equality, especially in relationship recognition policies.

EMPLOYMENT OPPORTUNITY

In the United States, the courts were thrust into litigation over employment discrimination even before the passage of Title VII when they were asked to adjudicate claims that gay men and lesbians were being singled out for unfair treatment in the federal civil service. Judges invariably deferred to the government, especially in national security matters, explaining that the policies of denying security clearances to gay and lesbian employees or subjecting them to extensive investigation were justified by the national interest and did not violate due process. By the end of the 1990s, primarily because of Clinton's executive order against unfair treatment in national security investigations—the first presidential act to remove sexual orientation as a consideration in federal employment policy—this manifestation of employment discrimination in the federal workforce was greatly diminished. Later, LGBT federal workers also benefited from Obama's executive order that made it illegal for federal contractors to discriminate against their employees because of sexual orientation.

Although members of the LGBT community have become more accepted in the workplace, gay and lesbian employees have continued to face an uphill battle in convincing the courts that federal law, specifically Title VII, protects them from employment discrimination. The problem is enhanced by the fact that the decades-old Title VII was enacted at a time when discrimination on the basis of sexual orientation was neither grounds for moral outrage nor legal action. Courts looking to legislative intent or the statutory language found little support in expanding Title VII. The EEOC, the federal agency charged with combatting employment discrimination in the nation, has been in the forefront, attempting to persuade the courts that the reference to sex in Title VII applies to sexual orientation.

Congress could have resolved the debate over the interpretation of Title VII by enacting federal legislation prohibiting employment discrimination against the LGBT community; none succeeded, despite repeated attempts to pass such a law. The first attempt to include sexual orientation as a protected classification occurred with the introduction of the Equality Act in 1974, followed by the National Lesbian and Gay Civil Rights Bill and, eventually, ENDA. Since the initial consideration of antidiscrimination legislation more than four decades ago, there have been persistent efforts in almost every legislative session to place sexual orientation on a par with race, sex, and religion. Congress twice appeared on the verge of enacting a version of ENDA, yet the bills were defeated both times. At the subnational level, a number of states and municipalities have included sexual orientation and gender identity within their employment antidiscrimination laws—providing varying degrees of protection—but most have not.

The opposition to protecting gay men and lesbians from employment discrimination may arise from a number of reasons, but lately it has been primarily fueled by concern over the scope of a religious exemption in the law. Religious adherents argue that religious and quasi-religious institutions must be granted immunity from compliance with the nondiscrimination principles of the law.

TRANSGENDER RIGHTS

Taking a leading role in promoting equality for the transgender community, Biden called discrimination against transgender individuals the "civil rights issue of our time." As Biden correctly observed, the transgender community is a frequent target of discrimination because its members do not conform to the gender roles based on their biological sex.

Despite their unwillingness to apply Title VII to claims of employment discrimination because of sexual orientation, the courts have been more accepting of claims of discrimination by transgender plaintiffs. Their success can be largely traced to the Supreme Court's interpretation of Title VII in its 1989 ruling in *Price Waterhouse.* Since then, most courts have agreed that, in equating sex with gender in *Price Waterhouse*, the Supreme Court opened the door for litigants to argue that individuals complaining of employment discrimination based on gender nonconformity stated a valid Title VII claim because their appearance and conduct varied from society's binary gender norms. The transgender plaintiffs have been assisted by federal agencies, such as the EEOC and OSHA, that played key roles in convincing the courts to expand the protections in federal law to include discrimination based on gender identity.

Congress has paid scant attention to issues of discrimination against transgender persons. Although ENDA eventually included a prohibition against discrimination based on gender identity, it was a pyrrhic victory for transgender employees because the law failed to clear Congress. With some exceptions, state and local governments have also been hesitant to bar discrimination against transgender employees, leaving most transgender plaintiffs dependent on Title VII and hoping to persuade the courts of their interpretation of the law.

In addition to employment discrimination, transgender individuals are also subject to unfair treatment in at least two other important policy-making arenas: prisons and schools. The litigation over prison policies has primarily has revolved around inmates' complaints that correctional departments violate the Eighth Amendment by failing to provide health care for their medical needs and by housing them in unsafe facilities where they are vulnerable to physical attack. Although the courts have been reluctant to rule in the prisoners' favor and override the prison officials' security concerns, in some cases, the litigation ended when the state released the prisoner before providing the needed medical care, leading to dismissal of the Eighth Amendment action.

Litigation over transgender rights in schools has become one of the most hotly litigated matters in the United States. Such cases typically arise when transgender students claim that they are being discriminated against by being forced to use restroom and locker room facilities that correspond to their anatomical sex at birth rather than the gender with which they identify. The transgender litigants most often cite their school's obligation not to discriminate because of sex under Title IX. However, although most courts have acknowledged that Title IX case law is governed by Title VII case law (primarily relying on *Price Waterhouse* and its progeny), no court has explicitly held that discrimination based on gender identity violates Title IX.

DOE and DOJ have played leading roles in advancing the rights of transgender youth by issuing guidelines supporting a broad interpretation of Title IX and concluding that the statute's ban on discrimination on the basis of sex encompasses gender identity. Based on DOE's analysis, a Fourth Circuit panel ruled in favor of a student who complained that his school's restroom policy violated his rights under Title IX. The victory in the circuit court was short-lived, as the Supreme Court stayed the lower court order and then agreed to review the ruling.

With the nation divided, the courts must resolve the controversy over whether the rights of transgender individuals—as employees, students, and members of the general public—are being denied. With litigation involving states as plaintiffs and defendants, the federal government as plaintiff and defendant, and private individuals as plaintiffs, however, it is unlikely that the resolution will be swift.

MARRIAGE EQUALITY

Perhaps the most dramatic change in LGBT policy has been the shift in the judiciary's posture on the constitutional right to same-sex marriage. The first glimmer of hope for marriage equality advocates emerged in a 1993 ruling by the Hawaii Supreme Court. It took another decade for the Massachusetts high court to negate the state's restriction on same-sex marriage. In what would become a familiar refrain, the court noted that, despite its obligation to defer to democratic decision-making, judicial restraint was inappropriate when the litigation revolved around claims of the deprivation of constitutional rights.

Over the next decade, same-sex marriage became legal in much of the nation through judicial rulings and legislative policy-making. In 2013, the Supreme Court, which had been silent on same-sex marriage, struck DOMA, perhaps in part persuaded by the federal government's refusal to defend DOMA in court.

The *Windsor* majority strongly affirmed the principle of equal rights for same-sex couples and paved the way for a far-ranging assault on marriage inequality in the federal courts. Yet the opinion refrained from resolving the debate over the proper level of scrutiny to apply in cases involving discrimination based on sexual orientation, leaving it to the lower courts to interpret its ambiguous language. In the inevitable litigation that resulted from *Windsor*, the lower federal courts followed the lead of the high court in furthering equality for same-sex couples without resolving the impact of the scrutiny doctrine. The courts were virtually unanimous in ruling for the plaintiffs in these cases, dutifully discussing the matter of scrutiny but dismissing its importance to the resolution of the case. The marriage equality advocates proved remarkably successful—prevailing in almost all legal challenges to state marriage restrictions—as the courts held that the states violated their Fourteenth Amendment rights.

The judges were careful to avoid comments on the wisdom or morality of same-sex marriage, but the rulings showed that they found the states' arguments for restricting same-sex marriage barely rational and bore little, if any, relationship to the states' interests in procreation, children's welfare, and preserving the sanctity of traditional marriage and two-parent families. Moreover, many derided the states' positions, suggesting that they were, at best, illogical. The opinions demonstrated that most judges were uneasy about striking state laws that reflected majoritarian decision-making but, in the end, overcame their concern about potential judicial overreach, persuaded that their obligation to counter inequality outweighed their duty of judicial restraint.

The courts have been the dominant force in resolving the clash over marriage equality in the nation. Because of federalism principles and the states' wide-ranging authority to regulate marriage, Congress was constrained in its ability to intervene in same-sex marriage policy-making. When it did interpose itself, it supported marriage inequality by enacting DOMA and, with the support of the Bush administration, frequently proposing constitutional amendments to bar same-sex couples from marrying.

CONTINUING STRUGGLES

Gay men and lesbians achieved a momentous victory when the Supreme Court declared same-sex marriage a fundamental right protected by the Fourteenth Amendment. However, the post-*Obergefell* nation soon became embroiled in battles over the effect of the ruling, revolving around whether the First Amendment shielded business owners who opposed marriage equality from complying with state and local antidiscrimination laws because of their religious beliefs. A bevy of bakers, photographers, and florists soon achieved national prominence because of their refusal to participate, albeit indirectly, in same-sex marriage ceremonies. State courts in Colorado, New Mexico, and Washington State, among others, rejected their arguments that their religion entitled them to turn away same-sex couples, holding that state public accommodations laws required them to treat their customers equally.

The courts also played a key role in the effort to require public officials who cited their Christian beliefs in refusing to issue marriage licenses to same-sex couples to follow the law. However, although the court ordered a county clerk to perform her duty, she ultimately was able to evade her responsibility when the newly elected governor acquiesced to her position and accommodated her religious beliefs.

Last, under the rubric of promoting religious freedom, state legislatures have enacted laws requiring the government to justify policies that allegedly infringed on religious exercise. Ostensibly modeled after the federal RFRA—intended to protect vulnerable religious minorities from government overreach—many of the state RFRAs were designed to shield private individuals, business entities, and charitable organizations from liability for discriminatory conduct against the lesbian, gay, bisexual, and transgender communities.

As these laws proliferated, states came under fire from several directions, with critics strongly arguing for their repeal. Following a veto of such a law by the governor of Arizona, Indiana enacted a version of RFRA that brought negative publicity and huge pecuniary losses to the state. Eventually, as Indiana and other states realized the high price they were paying for such policies, the laws began to decline in popularity.

While the opposition to same-sex marriage on religious grounds occupied much of the nation's attention, controversy over the role of gender identity in public policy-making soon took center stage. The North Carolina legislature set off a firestorms that dwarfed the reaction in Indiana with a law to confine transgender people to the bathroom facility consistent with the gender shown on their birth certificates. The state was likely emboldened by the recent defeat of a civil rights ordinance in Houston, also driven largely by fears of transgender individuals in the "wrong" bathrooms.

North Carolina soon began to feel the consequences of its action, losing millions of dollars and facing threats from the federal government to withhold billions of dollars in federal education funding. Despite the intense opposition that resulted from the North Carolina law, Mississippi soon followed with a statute allowing businesses and individuals to refuse service to same-sex couples and deny transgender persons access to the facilities of their choice if they have a religious objection. A dozen other states are currently also considering following in their paths, apparently unconcerned about the likely firestorms that would ensue. Predictably, the federal courts were inundated with lawsuits revolving around the North Carolina and Mississippi statutes, with the federal government arguing that discrimination based on gender identity fell within the parameters of the federal laws prohibiting sex discrimination.

GLOBAL PERSPECTIVES

Within a decade, litigants in Canada and South Africa had successfully challenged outdated sodomy laws, inequality in employment benefits and entitlements, and restrictions on family relationships. Although their progress was not always smooth, within a relatively short period of time, the courts extended constitutional guarantees to individuals in same-sex relationships, including the right to marry. After the judiciary paved the way by striking the marriage restrictions, the national parliaments cemented the victory for the advocates by enacting marriage equality laws to legitimate the rulings.

The rulings in these cases were remarkably similar, with the courts in both countries recognizing that their responsibility to interpret their country's foundational documents required them to strike the challenged badges of inequality. While not explicitly using the language of heightened scrutiny or judicial restraint, judges of the Canadian and South African courts viewed the plaintiffs as vulnerable minorities in need of judicial protection from majoritarian decision-makers. The litigation resolved many of their legal problems; it has, however, left other forms of discrimination intact, especially in South Africa, where cultural norms have hindered equality for members of the LGBT community.

LGBT activists in Europe followed the same approach to litigation in the ECtHR as the plaintiffs in the national courts of Canada and South Africa, beginning with cases seeking to decriminalize same-sex sexual conduct. Once they accomplished this goal, they challenged social and economic inequality and sought judicial validation of same-sex relationships, including civil marriage. More recently, the ECtHR litigation has encompassed various claims of discrimination based on gender identity, from demands for medical treatment to requests to alter official documents to reflect the individual's gender identity.

Despite the growing acceptance of same-sex relationships over time, however, only about two dozen countries—chiefly in western Europe—have permitted same-sex marriage. In part, because of the absence of the common law tradition of judicial policy-making on the European continent, most activists achieved greater success in their national legislatures in western Europe than in the courts in pursuing their goal of marriage equality. But in countries where parliaments refused to act, applicants turned to the ECtHR, claiming violations of the ECHR. Although many succeeded in convincing the Court to remove vestiges of discrimination based on sexual orientation, they failed to persuade it to declare same-sex marriage a fundamental right under the ECHR.

There are myriad structural, institutional, and historical reasons that the ECtHR has not followed the lead of the Canadian, South African, and US judiciary in declaring same-sex marriage a fundamental right. The primary reason for the divergence among them is the ECtHR's apprehension that, if it overrode state marriage restrictions, the lack of a consensus on same-sex marriage within the CoE would threaten its legitimacy and lead to open defiance of its rulings. In contrast, recognizing the changing consensus of attitudes in CoE nations toward the transgender community, beginning in 2002, the Court became more willing to rule against laws and policies depriving transgender individuals of equal rights.

INSTITUTIONAL COMPARISONS

This book confirms that the LGBT community in the Unites States correctly assessed the efficacy of mounting a litigation strategy in pursuing its quest for equality. Acknowledging their duty to protect minority rights, the courts largely proved to be more receptive to LGBT demands for equal rights than legislatures.

As the rulings showed, the LGBT rights cases reflected judges' uneasiness about the potential harm to democratic decision-making principles if they overruled policies enacted by the representative institutions. In most of the cases involving LGBT plaintiffs, both majority and minority opinions acknowledged that judges must be careful not to stray over the line between deference to the legislature and support for vulnerable members of society. The difference between the majority and the dissents revealed that, despite their shared concern about the proper role of the judiciary, the majority believed that a court's greater duty lay in advancing the egalitarian principles reflected in their founding documents.

In contrast, although the ECtHR moved the countries of Europe toward accepting a number of the LGBT community's equal rights claims, it has refrained from taking the ultimate step of approving marriage equality as a right arising from the ECHR. As demonstrated in these cases, the primary barrier to declaring the right to same-sex marriage was the ECtHR's awareness of the absence of consensus on marriage equality in the CoE countries. Unwilling to threaten its legitimacy by exceeding its self-imposed limit of judicial restraint, the Court declared marriage equality beyond the purview of the ECHR.

Over the years, the US Congress has for the most part opposed efforts to expand LGBT rights. It has rejected legislation to prohibit employment discrimination because of sexual orientation and gender identity and refused to include them as protected classifications within existing civil rights laws, such as Title VII and Title IX. At the subnational level, a number of state and local legislative bodies enacted laws banning employment discrimination, barring discrimination in public accommodations and schools, and adopting marriage equality. Although, the efficacy of these laws in preventing and punishing discriminatory conduct has varied, they represented significant advances for the LGBT community. Despite some measure of success at the state and municipal levels, absent federal legislation, significant obstacles remain in fighting against discrimination in employment, housing, education, public accommodations, and health care. Moreover, by enacting laws that privilege religious freedom over LGBT equality and adopting policies that constrict the expression of gender nonconformity, states have actively thwarted LGBT demands for equality.

The civil rights of the LGBT community were greatly advanced by the Obama administration, which has taken the most effective measures to propel LGBT rights forward. Obama's refusal to defend DOMA in court; his support of the Don't Ask, Don't Tell repeal legislation; and his executive order barring discrimination by federal contractors has added to a greater record of achievement in furthering LGBT rights than any of his predecessors. In his administration, executive branch agencies—the EEOC, OSHA, DOE, DOD, and DOJ—have actively pursued policies to combat the inequalities that constrain the lives of the LGBT population in employment, health care, and education. Ultimately, the courts will determine the effectiveness of their efforts, but their compelling legal arguments made the federal government an indispensable ally in the struggles for LGBT rights.

WHAT LIES AHEAD?

The election of Donald Trump and Pence was very disquieting for the LGBT community, worried about whether the advances it has made will come to a halt or even be reversed, confining its members once again to a "separate and unequal" world by turning back the accumulated gains in LGBT civil rights.

Even before the results of the election were known, they had cause for concern, for the Republican Party platform advocated a sharp reversal of most of the progress that the LGBT community had made over the past several years. The platform condemned the high court's opinions in *Windsor* and *Obergefell*, pledging to return decision-making over such social issues to the states. It committed itself to enacting federal legislation aimed at protecting opponents of same-sex marriage in educational institutions, businesses, and charitable organizations from antidiscrimination laws when they act on their religious beliefs that marriage must be restricted to one man and one woman. It also objected to the recent efforts to include gender identity within civil rights laws, especially Title IX, and expressed support for state efforts to combat the administration's attempts to augment transgender rights. Finally, the party called for the appointment of judges who would strictly interpret the Constitution according to its original meaning and avoid legislating from the bench. Even the usually supportive Log Cabin Republicans proclaimed it as the "most anti-LGBT platform in the party's 162-year history" (*New York Times*, July 18, 2016).

Although Trump acknowledged the LGBT community in his convention speech, he did nothing to separate himself and his running mate from the excesses of the party's platform. There is little to be learned from Trump's campaign statements about LGBT rights, as he has given contradictory signals about his views. In a television interview in April, Trump said that transgender people should use the bathroom in which they feel comfortable. At a subsequent town hall event, he criticized North Carolina's controversial law, urging the state to "leave it the way it is," adding, "[T]here have been very few complaints the way it is" (*Daily News*, April 28, 2016; *Politico*, April 21, 2016; *Politico*, June 16, 2016). Later, however, he inexplicably reversed himself, saying that the issue should be left to the states to decide (*CBS News*, April 22, 2016).

Following the tragedy at the Pulse nightclub in Orlando in June, Trump offered support for the victims, promising to protect them from future acts of violence. However, it appeared that he chiefly used the event to promote his pro-gun and anti-Muslim agenda (*Huffington Post*, June 13, 2016). Additionally, he took advantage of it to attack his opponent for failing to support LGBT rights, claiming that he was the only real advocate for the LGBT community and declaring that barring Muslims from the United States would prevent such massacres in the future. Indeed, ostensibly to show his support for the LGBT community, although there was little or no evidence that the killer was motivated by anti-LGBT sentiments, he later stated that he wanted to ban Muslims who support the death penalty for gay men and lesbians from entering the United States (*The Advocate*, August 15, 2016; *The Advocate*, October 3, 2016).

Finally, in another policy shift, although he expressed opposition to the Court's ruling on same-sex marriage during the campaign and promised to appoint judges who would overturn it, more recently, when asked about it on national television after the election, he said, "[I]t—it's irrelevant because it was already settled. It's law. It was settled in the Supreme Court. I mean it's done. It's done. It—you have—these cases have gone to the Supreme Court. They've been settled. And, I'm fine with that" (*CBS News*, November 13, 2016). Other than these brief mentions, there has been no indication of specific policies that he would support with respect to LGBT rights or the direction his administration would take.

Aside from his personal beliefs, Trump's vow to appoint a Supreme Court judge "in the mold of Scalia" likely represents the greatest threat to the future of LGBT rights. Speaking to an audience during the second televised debate at Washington University, Trump called Scalia, who had consistently opposed LGBT rights, a "great judge" and vowed that he would appoint a justice who will follow in his footsteps in faithfully interpreting the Constitution (*The Advocate*, October 10, 2016).

Buoyed in part by this promise, exit polls showed that more than three-quarters of white Evangelicals in the country voted for Trump. In addition to expecting him to appoint judges whose views they favor, they also believe that he will promote religious liberty by supporting legislation that shields business owners who object to same-sex marriage because of their religious beliefs from antidiscrimination laws (*New York Times*, November 11, 2016; *Washington Post*, November 9, 2016).

Pence was in the House of Representatives from 2001 to 2013, when he assumed the office of governor of Indiana, in which he served until his election as vice president. Unlike Trump, Pence's views on LGBT rights are well documented from the positions he took in the House as well as his actions as Indiana's governor. Shortly before the 2016 election, critics observed that Pence would "arguably be the most openly anti-LGBT Vice-President in history if elected" (*Towleroad*, October 4, 2016).

When Pence ran for Congress, his campaign website stated that he favored diverting funds intended for HIV and AIDS care to organizations that perform conversion therapy (a discredited type of "therapy" that seeks to change an individual's sexual orientation). Other statements on his website encouraged Congress to oppose legalizing same-sex marriage and refrain from viewing sexual orientation as a protected classification in antidiscrimination laws (*BuzzFeed*, July 14, 2016; *TowleRoad*, July 15, 2016).

During his time in the House, he voted against expanding hate crime legislation to include persons victimized because of their sexual orientation, against passing ENDA, and against the repeal of Don't Ask, Don't Tell. He voted for constitutional amendments limiting marriage to a man and a woman (*On The Issues*, August 22, 2016).

As governor, Pence supported passage of the state RFRA in 2015, a law welcomed by LGBT rights opponents in the state. He argued that it merely preserved the religious liberty of people who opposed same-sex marriage. He defended the law, saying that it was not discriminatory because it was modeled on the 1993 federal RFRA (which, he noted, was signed by Clinton) and was intended to prevent state and local governments from burdening the exercise of religion. After the furor caused by the law, especially the economic damage to the state, Pence was forced to retreat and send a revised version to the legislature, insisting that the law was misunderstood but that he accepted the need for clarification.

None of Trump's cabinet nominees is known for supporting LGBT rights; on the contrary, a number of them, chiefly Senator Jefferson Sessions of Alabama, have a long history of opposing LGBT equality. As one critic stated, "Pick Any LGBTQ Rights Issue [and] Jeff Sessions Has Voted Against It" (*Huffington Post*, November 22, 2016). Not surprisingly, Trump's choice of Sessions for the post of attorney general, a position of crucial importance in the continuing struggles over LGBT rights, has created apprehension within the LGBT community.

Sessions was first elected to the Senate in 1996 and most recently reelected in 2014. In 1996, when serving as the state attorney general before moving to the Senate, he exerted his influence in an attempt to block the Southeastern Lesbian, Bisexual College Conference from taking place on the University of Alabama campus. He cited a 1992 state law making it illegal for public universities to fund any group promoting "actions prohibited by the sodomy and sexual misconduct laws" (*CNN*, December 2, 2016). Sessions's efforts were thwarted when the university president repudiated his position, saying that the group had a constitutional right to gather at the university; the law was declared unconstitutional by the federal court shortly thereafter (*The Advocate*, December 2, 2016; *CNN*, December 2, 2016).

Like Pence, Sessions supported constitutional amendments to ban same-sex marriage. In March 2014, following the high court's ruling in *Windsor*, Sessions was one of only ten cosponsors of the State Defense of Marriage Act of 2014, a bill to replace the federal definition of marriage with the state definition. Additionally, he characterized *Obergefell* as an "effort to secularize by force and intimidation" (*CNN*, December 2, 2016; *Daily News*, December 2, 2016).

His other anti-LGBT votes included opposing repeal of Don't Ask, Don't Tell and objecting to including sexual orientation in federal hate crime legislation. Moreover, he voted against reauthorizing the 2013 VAWA to extend federal protection to gay men and lesbians victimized by violence (*On The Issues*, April 24, 2016).

As attorney general, Sessions will be in a position to determine the future of transgender rights policy (*Politico*, November 18, 2016). One of his first decisions will be how to proceed in DOJ's suit against North Carolina over HB 2 (*Huffington Post*, November 22, 2016). Another immediate issue for his attention will be to determine DOJ's role in laws shielding religious adherents from the consequences of discriminatory acts against the LGBT community.

Representative Tom Price of Georgia, Trump's choice for his HHS Secretary is likely less well-known for his record on LGBT rights, but his longstanding opposition to promoting equal rights for the LGBT community puts him on a par with Pence and Sessions. Serving in the House of Representatives from 2005 until the present, Price also opposed marriage equality and supported constitutional amendments to define marriage only as between a man and a woman; he characterized the day *Obergefell* was announced as "not only a sad day for marriage, but a further judicial destruction of our entire system of checks and balances" (*The Advocate*, November 28, 2016; *On The Issues*, March 9, 2016: *On The Issues*, December 2, 2016). He voted against including sexual orientation within federal hate crime legislation; against repealing Don't Ask, Don't Tell; and against reauthorizing VAWA.

Most disturbing for the transgender community was his statement on the DOE and DOJ guidelines. He called it "absurd that we need a 'federal restroom policy' for our nation's schools. This is yet another abuse and overreach of power by the Obama Administration, and a clear invasion of privacy. Schools should not have to fear retaliation for failure to comply" (*On The Issues*, December 2, 2016; *Towleroad*, November 29, 2016). Finally, Price opposed the firing of Atlanta Police Chief Kevin Cochran for his comments characterizing "homosexuality as a 'sexual perversion.'" Price claimed that firing Cochran abridged his First Amendment rights (*Towleroad*, November 29, 2016).

Trump's selection for DOE, Betsy DeVos, has also raised concerns for LGBT groups. DeVos and members of her family have a long history of donating large sums of money to anti-LGBT rights organizations, such as Focus on the Family, the Family Research Council, and the National Organization for Marriage. They have also contributed funds to oppose efforts to legalize same-sex marriage in California, Florida, and Michigan (*New York Magazine*, November 30, 2016; *On The Issues*, December 2, 2016; *Politico*, November 25, 2016). As head of

DOE, DeVos would supervise OCR and be able to exert enormous influence over the agency's interpretation of Title IX. In doing so, she could play a decisive role in determining the future of transgender rights in the nation's public schools.

By the nature of their positions, if confirmed, these officials will likely have a great effect on the LGBT community, but other Trump nominees—Ben Carson, James Mattis, Rick Perry, and Mike Pompeo, for example—have all expressed unfavorable views toward LGBT rights claims at various times (see *The Advocate*, December 2, 2016; *Towleroad*, December 1, 2016; *The Advocate*, October 29, 2015; *The Advocate*, December 14, 2016; *The Advocate*, December 12, 2016; *the pride*, November 30, 2016).

By placing individuals such as these in positions of authority over issues crucial to the LGBT population, Trump has almost certainly increased the likelihood of a rollback of equal rights during his administration.

REFERENCES

Advance America. 2015a. "Help Protect Religious Freedom in Indiana." March 24. Available at http://www.advanceamerica.com/blog/?p=1846

———. 2015b. "Indiana's New Religious Freedom Law Is under Attack." March 30. Available at http://www.advanceamerica.com/blog/?p=1854

———. 2015c. "Advance America Opposes Destruction of Religious Freedom Restoration Act." April 2. Available at http://www.advanceamerica.com/pdf/RFRAPressRelease.pdf

Ali, Russlynn. 2010. "Dear Colleague Letter: Bullying and Harassment." *US Department of Education, Office for Civil Rights*, October 26. Available at http://www2.ed.gov/about/offices/list/ocr/letters/colleague-201010.pdf

———. 2011. "Dear Colleague Letter." *US Department of Education, Office for Civil Rights*, April 4. Available at http://www2.ed.gov/about/offices/list/ocr/letters/colleague-201104.html

Almeida, Joanna, Renee M. Johnson, Heather L. Corliss, Beth E. Molnar, and Deborah Azrael. 2009. "Emotional Distress among LGBT Youth: The Influence of Perceived Discrimination Based on Sexual Orientation." *Journal of Youth and Adolescence* 7: 1001–14.

American Civil Liberties Union. 2015. "Know Your Rights: Transgender People and the Law." Available at https://www.aclu.org/know-your-rights/transgender-people-and-law

American Medical Association House of Delegates. 2008. "Removing Financial Barriers to Care for Transgender Patients." Available at http://www.tgender.net/taw/ama_resolutions.pdf

American Psychiatric Association. 2013. "Gender Dysphoria." Available at http://www.dsm5.org/documents/gender%20dysphoria%20fact%20sheet.pdf

American Psychological Association. 2015. "Answers to Your Questions about Transgender People, Gender Identity, and Gender Expression." Available at http://apa.org/topics/lgbt/transgender.aspx?item=10.

Amnesty International UK. 2016. "Amnesty Hails New Marriage Equality in Isle of Man." July 22. Available at https://www.amnesty.org.uk/press-releases/amnesty-hails-new-marriage-equality-law-isle-man

Arkansas State Legislature. 2015a. "SB202—To Amend the Law Concerning Ordinances Of Cities And Counties By Creating The Intrastate Commerce Improvement Act And To Declare An Emergency." February 25. Available at http://www.arkleg.state.ar.us/assembly/2015/2015R/Bills/SB202.pdf

——— 2015b. "HB1228." April 2. Available at http://www.arkleg.state.ar.us/assembly/2015/2015R/Pages/BillInformation.aspx?measureno=hb1228

———. 2015c. "SB975." April 2. Available at http://www.arkleg.state.ar.us/assembly/2015/2015R/Pages/BillInformation.aspx?measureno=SB975

Atlantic Coast Conference. 2016. "Statements from the Atlantic Coast Conference." September 14. Available at http://www.theacc.com/news/statements-from-the-atlantic-coast-conference-09-14-2016.

Backer, Larry Cata. 1996. "Constructing a 'Homosexual' for Constitutional Theory: Sodomy Narrative Jurisprudence, and Antipathy in United States and British Courts." *Tulane Law Review* 71: 529–96.

Badash, David. 2015. "Obama Administration Announces Support for Amending Civil Rights Act to Protect LGBT People." *New Civil Rights Movement*, November 10. Available at http://www.thenewcivilrightsmovement.com/davidbadash/obama_administration_announces_support_for_amending_civil_rights_act_to_protect_lgbt_people

Badgett, M. V. Lee. 2012. "The Impact of Extending Sexual Orientation and Gender Identity Non-Discrimination Requirements to Federal Contractors." *Williams Institute*, February. Available at http://williamsinstitute.law.ucla.edu/wp-content/uploads/Badgett-EOImpact-Feb-20121.pdf

Badgett, M. V. Lee, Holning Lau, Brad Sears, and Deborah Ho. 2007. "Bias in the Workplace: Consistent Evidence of Sexual Orientation and Gender Identity Discrimination." *Williams Institute*, June. Available at http://williamsinstitute.law.ucla.edu/wp-content/uploads/Badgett-Sears-Lau-Ho-Bias-in-the-Workplace-Jun-2007.pdf

Ballotpedia. 2015. "City of Houston Anti-Discrimination HERO Veto Referendum, Proposition 1 (November 2015)—Ballotpedia." November. Available at https://ballotpedia.org/City_of_Houston_Anti-Discrimination_HERO_Veto_ReferendumProposition_1_(November_2015).

Barker, Matthew. 2009. "Employment Law—Antidiscrimination—Heading toward Federal Protection for Sexual Orientation Discrimination?" *University of Arkansas at Little Rock Law Review* 32: 111–33.

Barry, Kevin M., Brian Farrell, Jennifer L. Levi, and Neelima Vanguri. 2016. "A Bare Desire to Harm: Transgender People and the Equal Protection Clause." *Boston College Law Review* 57: 507–82.

Bartrum, Ian. 2014. "The Ninth Circuit's Treatment of Sexual Orientation: Defining 'Rational Basis Review with Bite.'" *Michigan Law Review First Impressions* 112: 142–50.

Bavis, Craig D. 1999. "*Vriend v. Alberta, Law v. Canada, Ontario v. M. and H.*: The Latest Steps on the Winding Path to Substantive Equality." *Alberta Law Review* 37: 683–714.

Beck, Allen J. 2014. "Sexual Victimization in Prisons and Jails Reported by Inmates 2011–12." *US Department of Justice, Bureau of Justice Statistics*, December. Available at http://www.bjs.gov/content/pub/pdf/svpjri1112_st.pdf

Beeson, Samantha. 2011. "European Human Rights, Supranational Judicial Review and Democracy." In *Human Rights Protection in the European Legal Order: The Interaction between the European and the National Courts*, edited by Patricia Popelier, Catherine Van de Heyning, and Piet Van Nuffel, 97–145. Cambridge, UK: Intersentia.

———. 2012. "Evolutions in Non-Discrimination Law within the ECHR and the ESC Systems: It Takes Two to Tango in the Council of Europe." *American Society of Comparative Law* 60: 147–79.

Bell, Mark. 2012. "A Gender Identity and Sexual Orientation: Alternative Pathways in EU Equality Law." *American Journal of Comparative Law* 60: 127–46.

Bendlin, Susan S. 2013. "Gender Dysphoria in the Jailhouse." *Cleveland State Law Review* 61: 957–82.

Berg, Nate. 2012. "Mapping Acceptance of Same-Sex Marriage." *City Lab*,
September 21. Available at http://www.citylab.com/politics/2012/09/mapping-acceptance-same-sex-marriage/3356/

Berger, Jonathan. 2008. "Getting to the Constitutional Court on Time: A Litigation History of Same-Sex Marriage." In *To Have and to Hold*, edited by Melanie Judge, Anthony Manion, and Shaun deWaal, 17–28. Auckland Park, South Africa: Fanele.

Berman, Russell. 2014. "Gay Rights Bill 'Unnecessary,' Says Speaker Boehner." *The Hill*, November 14. Available at http://thehill.com/blogs/blog-briefing-room/news/190295-gay-rights-bill-unnecessary-says-boehner

———. 2015. "Will Congress Protect Gay Rights Beyond Marriage?" *The Atlantic*, July 24. Available at http://www.theatlantic.com/politics/archive/2015/07/the-next-big-fight-for-gay-rights/399488/

Bialik, Carl. 2011. "Reliable Tally of Gay Population Proves Elusive." *Wall Street Journal*, April 16.

Bissinger, Buzz. 2015. "Caitlyn Jenner: The Full Story." *Vanity Fair*, July.

Bossin, Phyllis. 2005. "Same Sex Unions: The New Civil Rights Struggle or an Assault on Traditional Marriage?" *Tulsa Law Review* 40: 381–420.

Bribosia, Emmanuelle, Isabelle Rorive, and Laura Van den Eynde. 2014. "Same-Sex Marriage: Building an Argument before the European Court of Human Rights in Light of the US Experience." *Berkeley Journal of International Law* 32: 1–43.

Brown, George R., and Everett McDuffie. 2009. "Health Care Policies Addressing Transgender Inmates in Prison Systems in the United States." *Journal of Correctional Health Care* 15: 280–91.

Brydum, Sunnivie. "New Defense Secretary 'Open-Minded' on Transgender Military Ban," *The Advocate* , November 17, 2015. Available at http://www.advocate.com/transgender-military-ban/2015/02/23/new-defense-secretary-open-minded-transgender-military-ban

Burns, Crosby, and Jeff Krehely. 2011. "Gay and Transgender People Face High Rates of Workplace Discrimination." *Center for American Progress*, May. Available at https://cdn.americanprogress.org/wp-content/uploads/issues/2011/06/pdf/workplace_discrimination.pdf

Buzuvis, Erin E. 2011. "Transgender Student-Athletes and Sex-Segregated Sport: Developing Policies of Inclusion for Intercollegiate and Interscholastic Athletics." *Journal of Sports an Entertainment Law* 21: 1–58.

———. 2013. "On the Basis of Sex: Using Title IX to Protect Transgender Students from Discrimination in Education." *Wisconsin Journal of Law, Gender, and Society* 28: 219–43.

Byrn, Mary Patricia. 2002. "Same-Sex Marriage in South Africa: A Constitutional Possibility." *Minnesota Law Review* 87: 511–42.

Cain, Patricia A. 1993. "Litigating For Lesbian and Gay Rights: A Legal History." *Virginia Law Review* 179: 551–1641

Canon, Bradley C., and Charles A. Johnson. 1999. *Judicial Policies: Implementation and Impact*. 2nd ed. Washington, DC: Congressional Quarterly Press.

Carolan, Bruce. 2005. "Judicial Impediments to Legislating Equality for Same-Sex Couples in the European Union." *Tulsa Law Review* 40: 527–58.

Carter, Ashton. 2015b. " Remarks at LGBT Pride Month Ceremony." *US Department of Defense*, June 9. Available at http://www.defense.gov/News/Speeches/Speech-View/Article/606678/remarks-at-lgbt-pride-month-ceremony

Case, Mary Ann. 2014. "Legal Protections for the 'Personal Best' of Each Employee: Title VII's Prohibition on Sex Discrimination, the Legacy of *Price Waterhouse v. Hopkins*, and the Prospect of ENDA." *Stanford Law Review* 66: 1333–80.

Catalyst. 2015. "Quick Take: Lesbian, Gay, Bisexual & Transgender Workplace Issues." New York: Catalyst.

Chaganti, Shruti. 2013. "Why the Religious Freedom Restoration Act Provides a Defense in Suits by Private Plaintiffs." *Virginia Law Review* 99: 343–74.

Charlotte City Clerk. 2016. "Charlotte's Non-Discrimination Ordinance and N.C. House Bill 2." May 4. Available at http://charmeck.org/city/charlotte/CityClerk/Documents/NDOrdinance.pdf

Christiansen, Eric C. 2000. "Ending the Apartheid of the Closet: Sexual Orientation in the South African Constitutional Process." *New York University Journal of International Law and Politics* 32: 997–1058.

Clancy, Shawn. 2011. "The Queer Truth: The Need to Update Title VII to Include Sexual Orientation." *Journal of Legislation* 37: 119-41.

Clark, Matthew. 2003. "Stating a Title VII Claim for Sexual Orientation Discrimination in the Workplace: The Legal Theories Available After *Rene v. MGM Grand Hotel*." *UCLA Law Review* 51: 313-38.

Clinton Bill. 1995a. "Executive Order No. 12968—Access to Classified Information." *Weekly Compilation of Presidential Documents*, August 2. Available at https://www.gpo.gov/fdsys/pkg/WCPD-1995-08-07/pdf/WCPD-1995-08-07-Pg1365.pdf

———. 1995b. "Letter to Senator Edward M. Kennedy on the "Employment NonDiscrimination Act." *Weekly Compilation of Presidential Documents,* October 19. Available at https://www.gpo.gov/fdsys/pkg/WCPD-1995-10-23/pdf/WCPD-1995-10-23-Pg1881.pdf

———.1996. "Debate Transcript." October 16. Available at http://www.debates.org/index.php?page=october-16-1996-debate-transcript#1996

———. 1997. "Statement on the Proposed 'Employment Non-Discrimination Act.'" *Weekly Compilation of Presidential Documents*, April 24. Available at https://www.gpo.gov/fdsys/pkg/WCPD-1997-04-28/pdf/WCPD-1997-04-28-Pg577-3.pdf

———. 1998. "Further Amendment to Executive Order 11478, Equal Employment Opportunity in the Federal Government." May 28. Available at https://www.federalregister.gov/articles/1998/06/02/98-14689/further-amendment-to-executive-order-11478-equal-employment-opportunity-in-the-federal-government

Colby, Sandra L., and Jennifer M. Ortman. 2015. "Projections of the Size and Composition of the U.S. Population: 2014 to 2060." *US Census Bureau*, March. Available at https://www.census.gov/content/dam/Census/library/publications/2015/demo/p25-1143.pdf

Congress.gov. 1993. "H.R. 1308—Religious Freedom Restoration Act of 1993." November 16. Available at https://www.congress.gov/bill/103rd-congress/house-bill/1308/all-actions?overview=closed#tabs

———. 2015a. "H.R.2802—First Amendment Defense Act." June 17. Available at https://www.congress.gov/bill/114th-congress/house-bill/2802

———. 2015b. "S.1598—First Amendment Defense Act." June 17. Available at https://www.congress.gov/bill/114th-congress/senate-bill/1598

Congressional Record. 1990. 101st Cong., 2d sess., vol. 136.

Congressional Record. 1994. 103d Cong., 2d sess., vol. 140.

Congressional Record. 1995. 104th Cong., 1st sess., vol. 141.

Congressional Record. 1996. 104th Cong., 2d sess., vol. 142.

Cooper, Sarah Lucy. 2011. "Marriage, Family, Discrimination and Contradiction: An Evaluation of the Legacy and Future of the European Court of Human Rights' Jurisprudence." *German Law Journal* 12: 1746–63.

Council of Europe. 2011. "Recommendation CM/Rec (2010)5 of the Committee of Ministers to Member States on Measures to Combat Discrimination on Grounds of Orientation or Gender Identity." June. Available at http://www.coe.int/t/dghl/standardsetting/hrpolicy/Publications/LGBT_EN.pdf

———. 2014. "Malta Recognizes Same-Sex Civil Partnerships." June 6. Available at http://www.coe.int/t/dg4/lgbt/default_en.asp

———. 2015. "All Efforts Must Be Made to Eradicate Hate and Violence against LGBT People in Europe, Says Secretary General." May 17. Available at https://wcd.coe.int/ViewDoc.jsp?p=&Ref=DC-PR072(2015)&Language=lanEnglish&Ver=original&Site=DC&BackColorInternet=F5CA75&BackColorIntranet=F5CA75&BackColorLogged=A9BACE&direct=true#Top

Council of the European Union. 2013. "Guidelines to Promote and Protect the Enjoyment of All Human Rights by Lesbian, Gay, Bisexual, Transgender and Intersex (LGBTI) Persons." June 24. Available at http://www.consilium.europa.eu/uedocs/cms_Data/docs/pressdata/EN/foraff/137584.pdf

Cox, Daniel. 2016. "Gay Marriage Won, but Other Liberal Causes Will Probably Struggle to Copy Its Success." *FiveThirtyEight*, May 16. Available at http://fivethirtyeight.com/features/gay-marriage-won-but-other-liberal-causes-might-struggle-to-copy-its-success

Croucher, Sheila. 2011. "South Africa: Opportunities Seized in the Post-Apartheid Era." In *The Lesbian and Gay Movement and the State: Comparative Insights into a Transformed Relationship*, edited by Manon Tremblay, David Paternotte, and Carol Johnson, 153–66. Farnham, UK: Ashgate.

Dabrowski. Julie. 2014. "The Exception That Doesn't Prove the Rule: Why Congress Should Narrow ENDA's Religious Exemption to Protect the Rights of LBGT Employees." *American University Law Review* 63: 1957–84.

Dane County Youth Commission. 2015. "2015 Dane County Youth Assessment Overview Report." September. Available at https://danecountyhumanservices.org/yth/dox/asmt_survey/2015/2015_exec_sum.pdf?version=meter+at+0&module=meter-Links&pgtype=article&contentId=&mediaId=&referrer=&priority=true&action=click&contentCollection=meter-links-click

Daniels, Reynaud N., and Jason Brickhill. 2006. "The Counter-Majoritarian Difficulty and the South African Constitutional Court." *Penn State International Law Review* 25: 371–404.

Davies, Christine. 2008. "Individual Rights, Community Strategy." *University of Toronto Faculty of Law Review* 66: 101–34.

Defeis, Elizabeth. 2007. "Dual System of Human Rights: The European Union." *Journal of International and Comparative Law* 14: 1–8.

De Vos, Pierre. 2007. "The 'Inevitability' of Same-Sex Marriage in South Africa's Post-Apartheid State." *South African Journal on Human Rights* 23: 432–65.

De Witte, Bruno. 2011. "The Use of the ECHR and Convention Case Law by the European Court of Justice." In *Human Rights Protection in the European Legal Order: The Interaction between the European and the National Courts*, edited by Patricia Popelier, Catherine Van de Heyning, and Piet Van Nuffel, 17–34. Cambridge, UK: Intersentia.

du Toit, Cornel W. 2006. "Religious Freedom and Human Rights in South Africa after 1996: Responses and Challenges." *Brigham Young University Law Review* 2006: 677–98.

Elders, Jocelyn, and Alan M. Steinman. 2014. "Report of the Transgender Military Service Commission." *Palm Center*, March. Available at http://archive.palmcenter.org/files/Transgender%20Military%20Service%20Report.pdf

Elliott, Douglas. 2006. "Secrets of the Lavender Mafia: Personal Reflections on Social Activism and the Charter." *Journal of Law and* Equality 5: 97–123.

Ellis, Taylor Alyse Pack. 2014. "Why the EEOC Got It Right in *Macy v. Holder*: The Argument for Transgender Inclusion in Title VII Interpretation." *The Scholar* 16: 375-416.

Encarnacion, Omar. 2013–2014. "International Influence, Domestic Activism, and Gay Rights in Argentina." *Political Science Quarterly* 128: 687–719.

Endean, Steve. 2006. *Bringing Lesbian and Gay Rights into the Mainstream: Twenty Years of Progress,* edited by Vicki Eaklor. New York: Harrington Park Press.

ESPN. 2014. "Cards, NFL Respond to Controversial Bill." February 25. Available at http://espn.go.com/blog/arizona-cardinals/post/_/id/4773/cards-nfl-respond-to-controversial-bill

———. 2016a. "Indiana's New Law Concerns NCAA." March 30. Available at http://espn.go.com/college-sports/story/_/id/12563363/ncaa-concerned-indiana-new-law-religious-objections

———. 2016b. "NBA Moving All-Star Game from North Carolina." July 22. Available at http://www.espn.com/nba/story/_/id/17120170/nba-moving-all-star-game-charlotte-north-carolina-bill

European Court of Human Rights. 1950. "European Convention on Human Rights." November 4. Available at http://www.echr.coe.int/Pages/home.aspx?p=basictexts&c=#n1359128122487_pointer

European Parliament. 2010. "European Parliament Calls for Protection of LGBT People's Human Rights Worldwide." December 16. Available at http://www.lgbt-ep.eu/press-releases/european-parliament-calls-for-protection-of-lgbt-peoples-human-rights-worldwide

European Union. 2015. "EU Statement on Drawing Attention to the Need for Improvement of Human Rights of LGBTI Persons in Europe." June 17. Available at http://www.eeas.europa.eu/delegations/council_europe/documents/press_corner/lgtbi_statement.pdf

———. 2016. "The EU in Brief." April 13. Available at http://europa.eu/about-eu/basic-information/about/index_en.htm

Faithful, Richael. 2009. "Transitioning Our Prisons toward Affirmative Law: Examining the Impact of Gender Classification Policies on U.S. Transgender Prisoners." *Modern American* 5: 3–8.

Feldblum, Chai R. 2000. "The Federal Gay Rights Bill: From Bella to ENDA." In *Creating Change: Sexuality, Public Policy, and Civil Rights*, edited by John D'Emilio, William B. Turner, and Urvashi Vaid, 149–87. New York: St. Martin's Press.

Fidas, Deena, Liz Cooper, and Jenna Raspanti. 2014. "The Cost of the Closet and the Rewards of Inclusion: Why the Workplace Environment for LGBT People Matters to Employers." *Human Rights Campaign Foundation*, May. Available at http://hrc-assets.s3-website-us-east-1.amazonaws.com//files/assets/resources/Cost_of_the_Closet_May2014.pdf

Fitzgerald, Erin. 2016. "A Comprehensive Guide to the Debunked 'Bathroom Predator' Myth." *Media Matters*, May 5. Available at http://mediamatters.org/research/2016/05/05/comprehensive-guide-debunked-bathroom-predator-myth/210200

Fleischaker, Eric T. 2014. "The Constitutionality of Prolonged Administrative Segregation for Inmates Who Have Received Sex Reassignment Surgery." *Hastings Constitutional Law Quarterly* 41: 903–25.

The Florentine. 2016. "Italian Parliament Approves Civil Unions for Same-Sex Couples." May 12. Available at http://www.theflorentine.net/news/2016/05/italian-parliament-approves-sam

Flores, Andrew R., Jody L. Herman, Gary J. Gates, and Taylor N. T. Brown. 2016. "How Many Adults Identify as Transgender in the United States?" *Williams Institute*, June. Available at http://williamsinstitute.law.ucla.edu/wp-content/uploads/How-Many-Adults-Identify-as-Transgender-in-the-United-States.pdf

Florida Senate. 2015. "CS/CS/HB 583: Single-Sex Public Facilities." July 1. Available at https://www.flsenate.gov/Session/Bill/2015/0583/Category

Foster, S. Elizabeth. 2010. "The World after Proposition 8: A Global Survey of the Right to Marry." *California International Law Journal* 18: 4–15.

Freedom to Marry. 2014. "Freedom to Marry Internationally." Available at http://www.freedomtomarry.org/landscape/entry/c/International

Frye, Phyllis Randolph. 2003. "Transgenders Must Be Brave While Forging This New Front on Equality." *Georgetown Journal of Gender and the Law* 4: 767–79.

Gallup. 2012. "Special Report: 3.4% of U.S. Adults Identify as LGBT." October 18. Available at http://www.gallup.com/poll/158066/special-report-adults-identify-lgbt.aspx

Gallup. 2015. "Americans Greatly Overestimate Percent Gay, Lesbian in U.S." May 21. Available at http://www.gallup.com/poll/183383/americans-greatly-overestimate-percent-gay-lesbian.aspx?version=print

Gallup. 2016. "Americans' Support for Gay Marriage Remains High, at 61%." May 19. Available at http://www.gallup.com/poll/191645/americans-support-gay-marriage-remains-high.aspx

Gates, Gary J. 2011. "How Many People Are Lesbian, Gay, Bisexual, and Transgender?" *Williams Institute*, April. Available at http://williamsinstitute.law.ucla.edu/wp-content/uploads/Gates-How-Many-People-LGBT-Apr-2011.pdf

Gates, Gary J., and Jody L. Herman. 2014. "Transgender Military Service in the United States." *Williams Institute*, May. Available at http://williamsinstitute.law.ucla.edu/wp-content/uploads/Transgender-Military-Service-May-2014.pdf

Gay, Velma Cheri. 2015. "50 Years Later . . . Still Interpreting the Meaning of 'Because of Sex' within Title VII and Whether It Prohibits Sexual Orientation Discrimination." *Air Force Law Review* 73: 61–109.

Gay & Lesbian Advocates & Defenders . 2011. "Federal Bureau of Prisons Makes Major Change in Transgender Medical Policy." September 30. Available at http://www.glad.org/current/pr-detail/federal-bureau-of-prisons-makes-major-change-in-transgender-medical-policy/

Gay & Lesbian Alliance Against Defamation. 2014. "Transgender FAQ." Available at http://www.glaad.org/transgender/transfaq

———. 2015. "New GLAAD Report Maps Long Road To Full LGBT Acceptance, Despite Historic Legal Advances." February 9. Available at http://www.glaad.org/releases/new-glaad-report-maps-long-road-full-lgbt-acceptance-despite-historic-legal-advances

Gedicks, Frederick Mark. 2005. "On the Permissible Scope of Legal Limitations on the Freedom of Religion or Belief in the United States." *Emory International Law Review* 19: 1187–1275.

Georgia General Assembly. 2016. "2015–2016 Regular Session—HB 757." March 28. Available at http://www.legis.ga.gov/Legislation/en-US/display/20152016/HB/757

Gerber, Paula. 2000. "South Africa: Constitutional Protection for Homosexuals—A Brave Initiative, but Is It Working?" *Australasian Gay and Lesbian Law Journal* 2000, no. 9: 37–57.

Givens, Laura R. 2013. "Why the Courts Should Consider Gender Identity Disorder a Per Se Serious Medical Need for Eighth Amendment Purposes." *Journal of Race, Gender and Justice* 16: 579–606.

Goidel, Kirby, Brian Smentkowski, and Craig Freeman. 2016. "Perceptions of Threat to Religious Liberty." *PS: Political Science and Politics* 49: 426–32.

Gotell, Lise. 2002. "Queering Law: Not by *Vriend*." *Canadian Journal of Law and Society* 17: 89–113.

Governor Nathan Deal. 2016. "Transcript: Deal HB 757 Remarks." March 28. Available at http://gov.georgia.gov/press-releases/2016-03-28/transcript-deal-hb-757-remarks-0

Graham, David A. 2015. "Why Is Indiana's Religious Freedom Different from All Other Religious Freedom Laws?" *The Atlantic*, March 30.

Grant, Jaime M., Lisa A. Mottet, and Justin Tanis. 2011. *Injustice at Every Turn: A Report of the National Transgender Discrimination Survey*. Washington, DC: National Center for Transgender Equality and National Gay and Lesbian Task Force. Available at http://www.thetaskforce.org/static_html/downloads/reports/reports/ntds_full.pdf

Graupner, Helmut. 2005. "Sexuality and Human Rights in Europe." *Journal of Homosexuality* 48: 107–39.

Greer, Steven. 2008. "What's Wrong with the European Convention of Human Rights?" *Human Rights Quarterly* 30: 680–702.

Greytak, Emily A., Joseph G. Kosciw, and Elizabeth M. Diaz. 2009. *Harsh Realities: The Experiences of Transgender Youth*. New York: Gay, Lesbian and Straight Education Network. Available at http://files.eric.ed.gov/fulltext/ED505687.pdf

Grigolo, Michael. 2003. "Sexualities and the ECHR: Introducing the Universal Sexual Legal Subject." *European Journal of International Law* 14: 1–19.

Guitierrez, Deborah. 2004. "Gay Marriage in Canada: Strategies of the Gay Liberation Movement and the Implications It Will Have on the United States." *New England Journal of International and Comparative Law* 10: 175–227.

Hansen, Simon P. 2013. "Whose Defense Is It Anyway? Redefining the Role of the Legislative Branch in the Defense of Federal Statutes." *Emory Law Journal* 62: 1159–1204.

Harris, Benjamin Cerf. 2015. "Likely Transgender Individuals in U.S. Federal Administrative Records and the 2010 Census." CARRA Working Paper No. 2015-03. Center for Administrative Records Research and Applications, US Census Bureau, May 4.

Harris, Zenobia V. 2010. "Breaking the Dress Code: Protecting Transgender Students, Their Identities, and Their Rights." *The Scholar: St. Mary's Law Review on Minority Issues* 13:149–200.

Harris Poll. 2015. "Majority of Americans Agree: Businesses and Government Officials Should Not Discriminate against LGBT People." October 6. Available at http://www.theharrispoll.com/politics/Businesses-Govt-Should-Not-Discriminate-against-LGBT.html

Hart, Lindsay. 2014. "With Inadequate Protection under the Law, Transgender Students Fight to Access Restrooms in Public Schools Based on Their Gender Identity." *Northern Kentucky Law School* 41: 315–37.

Havlik, Gwen. 2012. "Equal Protection for Transgendered Employees? Analyzing the Court's Call for More Than Rational Basis in the *Glenn v. Brumby* Decision." *Georgia State University Law Review* 28: 1315–40.

Heffernan, Dani. 2016. "Debunking the 'Bathroom Bill' Myth." *Gay & Lesbian Alliance Against Defamation*, February 25. Available at https://www.glaad.org/blog/debunking-bathroom-bill-myth-glaad-releases-new-resource-journalists

Holder, Eric. 2014. "Treatment of Transgender Employment Discrimination Claims under Title VII of the Civil Rights Act of 1964." *Office of the Attorney General*, December 15. Available at https://www.justice.gov/file/188671/download

Human Rights Campaign. 2014a. "An Important Step toward Workplace Equality: An Executive Order on Federal Contractors." Available at http://www.hrc.org/resources/an-important-step-toward-workplace-equality-an-executive-order-on-federal-c

———. 2014b. "With Executive Order, Obama Takes Place in History." July 21. Available at http://www.hrc.org/blog/with-executive-order-obama-takes-his-place-in-history

———. 2015a. "Cities and Counties with Non-Discrimination Ordinances That Include Gender Identity." January 28. Available at http://www.hrc.org/resources/cities-and-counties-with-non-discrimination-ordinances-that-include-gender

———. 2015b. "Criminalization around the World." April. Available at http://hrc-assets.s3-website-us-east-1.amazonaws.com//files/assets/resources/Criminalization-Map-042315.pdf

———. 2015c. "Finding Insurance for Transgender-Related Healthcare." August 1. Available at http://www.hrc.org/resources/entry/finding-insurance-for-transgender-related-healthcare

———. 2015d. "A History of Federal Non-Discrimination Legislation." Available at http://www.hrc.org/resources/a-history-of-federal-non-discrimination-legislation

———. 2015e. "New Arkansas RFRA Still Empowers Discrimination." April 2. Available at http://www.hrc.org/blog/new-arkansas-rfra-still-empowers-discrimination

———. 2016. "Statewide Employment Laws and Policies." January 7. Available at www.hrc.org/state_maps

Human Rights Campaign Foundation. 2009. "Degrees of Equality: A National Study Examining Workplace Climate for LGBT Employees." Available at http://hrc-assets.s3-website-us-east-1.amazonaws.com//files/assets/resources/DegreesOfEquality_2009.pdf

Human Rights Watch. 2011. "South Africa: LGBT Rights in Name Only?" December 5. Available at https://www.hrw.org/news/2011/12/05/south-africa-lgbt-rights-name-only

Indiana General Assembly. 2015a. "Senate Bill 101." March 26. Available at https://iga.in.gov/legislative/2015/bills/senate/101#document-92bab197

——— 2015b. "Senate Bill 50." April 2. Available at https://iga.in.gov/legislative/2015/bills/senate/50#document-1bdf457b

Indiana Governor Mike Pence. 2015a. "Governor Pence Issues Statement Regarding the Religious Freedom Restoration Act." March 26. Available at http://www.in.gov/activecalendar/EventList.aspx?view=EventDetails&eventidn=214653 information_id=212489&type=&syndicate=syndicate

———. 2015b. "Governor Pence Signs Religious Freedom Restoration Act Clarification Bill." April 2. Available at https://secure.in.gov/activecalendar/EventList.aspx?fromdate=4/2/2015&todate=4/2/2015&display=Day&type=public&eventidn=215938&view=EventDetails&information_id=212917

International Human Rights Commission. 2015. "Timeline of Publicized Executions for 'Indecent Behavior' by IS [Islamic State] Militias." August 2. Available at https://www.outrightinternational.org/dontturnaway/timeline

International Lesbian, Gay, BiSexual, Trans, and Intersex Association (ILGA)–Europe. 2015a. "Annual Review of the Human Rights Situation of Lesbian, Gay, Bisexual, Trans and Intersex People in Europe 2015." May. Available at http://www.ilga-europe.org/sites/default/files/01_full_annual_review_updated.pdf

———. 2015b. "Civil Unions to Become a Reality in Cyprus." November 26. Available at http://www.ilga-europe.org/print/resources/news/latest-news/civil-unions-realty-cyprus

———. 2015c. "Greece Becomes 26th European Country to Recognise Same-Sex Partnerships." December 22. Available at http://www.ilga-europe.org/resources/news/latest-news/greece-becomes-26th-european-country-recognise-same-sex-partnerships

———. 2015d. "New Coalition for Civil Partnerships in Poland." December 16. Available at http://www.ilga-europe.org/resources/news/latest-news/new-coalition-civil-partnerships-poland

———. 2015e. "Slovenian Referendum Rejects Marriage Equality." December 20. Available at http://www.ilga-europe.org/print/resources/news/latest/slovenian-referendum-rejects-marriage-equality

———. 2016a. "Greater Equality Is on the Way for Same-Sex Couples in Slovenia." July 22. Available at http://www.ilga-europe.org/resources/news/latest-news/greater-equality-same-sex-couples-slovenia

———. 2016b. "The Journey towards Civil Unions for Same-Sex Couples in Italy." January 27. Available at http://www.ilga-europe.org/resources/news/latest-news/journey-towards-civil-unions-same-sex-people-italy

Jasiunas, J. Banning. 2000. "Is ENDA the Answer? Can a 'Separate but Equal' Federal Statute Adequately Protect Gays and Lesbians from Employment Discrimination?" *Ohio State Law Journal* 61: 1529–57.

Jefferson, James E. 1985. "Gay Rights and the Charter." *University of Toronto Faculty of Law* 43: 70–89.

Johnson, Paul. 2013. *Homosexuality and the European Court of Human Rights*. New York: Routledge.

Johnson, Voris E. 1997. "Making Words on a Page Become Everyday Life: A Strategy to Help Gay Men and Lesbians Achieve Full Equality under South Africa's Constitution." *Emory International Law Review* 11: 583–632.

Jones, Joshua. 2010. "Section 504 of the Rehabilitation Act of 1973: A Double-Edged Sword for the Protection of Students with Gender Identity Disorder." *Wisconsin Journal of Law, Gender, and Society* 25: 353–89.

Kahn, Carrie. 2015. "How Mexico Quietly Legalized Same-Sex Marriage." *NPR*, June 16. Available at http://www.npr.org/sections/parallels/2015/06/16/414964843/how-mexico-quietly-legalized-same-sex-marriage

Kansas Legislative Sessions. 2016. "SB 175." March 23. Available at http://www.kslegislature.org/li/b2015_16/measures/documents/sb175_enrolled.pdf

Kaplan, Roberta A., and Julie E. Fink. 2012. "The Defense of Marriage Act: The Application of Heightened Scrutiny to Discrimination on the Basis of Sexual Orientation." *Cardozo Law Review De Novo* 2012: 203–15.

Karimi, Faith, and Michael Pearson. 2016. "The 13 States That Still Ban Same-Sex Marriage." *CNN*, February 13. Available at http://www.cnn.com/2015/02/13/us/states-same-sex-marriage-ban

Katz, Robert. 2015. "Indiana's Flawed Religious Freedom Law." *Indiana Law Review* 49: 37–55.

Keisling, Mara. 2016. "Mara Keisling Really Just Did Say That." *National Center for Transgender Equality*, June 18. Available at http://www.transequality.org/blog/mara-keisling-really-just-did-say-that

Keith, Jarod. 2015. "Wave of Anti-LGBT Proposals across the South Dead as Legislatures Adjourn." *Campaign for Southern Equality*, June 23. Available at http://www.southernequality.org/wave-of-anti-lgbt-proposals-across-the-south-dead-as-legislatures-adjourn

Kende, Mark. 2003. "The South African Constitutional Court's Embrace of Socio-Economic Rights: A Comparative Perspective." *Chapman Law Review* 60: 137–60.

Kentucky Legislature. 2016. "SB 216." April 13. Available at http://www.lrc.ky.gov/lrcsearch

Koch, Katie, and Richard Bales. 2008. "Transgender Employment Discrimination." *UCLA Women's Law Journal* 17: 243–67.

Koppelman, Andrew. 1996. "Same Sex Marriage and Public Policy: The Miscegenation Precedents." *Quinnipiac Law Review* 16: 105–34.

———. 2015. "Gay Rights, Religious Accommodations, and the Purposes of Antidiscrimination Law." *Southern California Law Review* 88: 619–59.

Kosciw, Joseph G., Mark Bartkiewicz, and Emily A. Greytak. 2012. "Promising Strategies for Prevention of the Bullying of Lesbian, Gay, Bisexual, and Transgender Youth." *Prevention Researcher* 19: 10–13.

Kosciw, Joseph G., Emily A. Greytak, Neal A. Palmer, and Madelyn J. Boesen. 2014. *The 2013 National School Climate Survey: The Experiences of Lesbian, Gay, Bisexual and Transgender Youth in Our Nation's Schools.* New York: Gay, Lesbian and Straight Education Network. Available at https://www.glsen.org/sites/default/files/2013%20National%20School%20Climate%20Survey%20Full%20Report_0.pdf

Kukura, Elizabeth. 2006. "Finding Family: Considering the Recognition of Same-Sex Families in International Human Rights Law and the European Court of Human Rights." *Human Rights Brief* 13: 17–24.

Lambda Legal. 2016. "New Judge Strikes Down Puerto Rico Marriage Ban Hours after Lambda Legal Victory." April 8. Available at http://www.lambdalegal.org/blog/20160408_new-judge-strikes-down-pr-marriage-ban-hours-after-victory

Larocque, Sylvain. 2006. *Gay Marriage: The Story of a Canadian Social Revolution.* Toronto: Lorimer.

Laycock, Douglas. 2014. "Religious Liberty and the Culture Wars." *University of Illinois Law Review* 2014: 839–80.

Lederman, Josh. 2015. "Biden Backs Transgender Military Service." *Military Times*, October 4. Available at http://www.militarytimes.com/story/military/2015/10/04/biden-backs-transgender-military-service/73332168

Lee, Alvin. 2008. "Trans Models in Prisons: The Medicalization of Gender Identity and the Eighth Amendment Right to Sex Reassignment Therapy." *Harvard Journal of Law and Gender* 31: 447–71.

Lee, Jason. 2012. "Lost in Transition: The Challenges of Remedying Transgender Employment Discrimination under Title VII." *Harvard Journal of Law and Gender* 35: 423–61.

LegiScan. 2016. "Tennessee House Bill 2414." April 19. Available at https://legiscan.com/TN/drafts/HB2414/2015

Lewis, Marion Halliday. 1990. "Unacceptable Risk or Unacceptable Rhetoric? An Argument for a Quasi-Suspect Classification for Gays Based on Current Government Security Clearance Procedures." *Journal of Law and Politics* 7: 133–76.

Liberty Counsel. 2016. "Advancing the Mission through Three Pillars of Ministry." Available at https://www.lc.org/about-liberty-counsel

Lim, Marvin, and Louise Melling. 2014. "Inconvenience or Indignity? Religious Exemptions to Public Accommodations Laws." *Journal of Law and Policy* 22: 705–25.

Lind, Craig. 2008. "Queering Marriage: The Legal Recognition of Same-Sex Relationships around the World." In *To Have and to Hold: The Making of Same-Sex Marriage in South Africa*, edited by Melanie Judge, Anthony Manion, and Shaun de Waal, 284–99. Auckland Park: Fanele.

The Local Italy. 2016. "Italy Says 'Yes' to Civil Unions in Historic Vote." May 11. Available at http://www.thelocal.it/20160511/breaking-italy-says-yes-to-gay-civil-unions-gay-rights-marriage.

Lorence, Jordan. 2015. "Indiana's 'Fix' Gives Religious-Liberty Haters a New Weapon." *The Federalist*, April 3. Available at http://thefederalist.com/2015/04/03/indianas-fix-gives-religious-liberty-haters-a-new-weapon

Louisiana State Legislature. 2015. "HB 707." May 19. Available at https://www.legis.la.gov/legis/BillInfo.aspx?&i=227415

Louw, Ronald. 2005. "Advancing Human Rights through Constitutional Protection for Gays and Lesbians in South Africa." *Journal of Homosexuality* 48: 141–62.

Luchenitser, Alex J. 2014. "Hobby Lobby's Illusory Limits, and Justice Kennedy's Injudicious Joinder." *American Constitution Society for Law and Policy*, June 30. Available at http://www.acslaw.org/acsblog/hobby-lobby%E2%80%99s-illusory-limits-and-justice-kennedy%E2%80%99s-injudicious-joinder

Lukoff, Jennifer C. 1999. "South Africa Takes the Initial Step towards a Brilliant Twenty-First Century: A Comparative Study of *State v. Kampher* and *Bowers v. Hardwick*." *New York Law Journal of International and Comparative Law* 18: 459–81.

Lupu, Ira. C. 2015. "*Hobby Lobby* and the Dubious Enterprise of Religious Exemptions." *Harvard Journal of Law and Gender* 38: 35–101.

Malloy, S. Elizabeth. 2011. "What Best to Protect Transsexuals from Discrimination: Using Current Legislation or Adopting a New Judicial Framework?" *Women's Rights Law Reporter* 32: 283–322.

Maravilla, Christopher Scott. 2001. "Judicial Review of Security Clearances for Homosexuals Post–*U.S. Department of the Navy v. Egan*." *St. Thomas Law Review* 13: 785–801.

Martin, Hanna. 2016. "Race, Religion, and RFRA: The Implications of *Burwell v. Hobby Lobby Stores, Inc.* in Employment Discrimination." *Cardozo Law Review De Novo* 2016: 1–39.

Maza, Carlos, and Luke Brinker. 2014. "15 Experts Debunk Right-Wing Transgender Bathroom Myth." *Media Matters for America*, March 20. Available at http://mediamatters.org/research/2014/03/20/15-experts-debunk-right-wing-transgender-bathro/198533

Mbeki, Thabo. 2005. "Letter to Peter Tatchell." In *Sex and Politics in South Africa*, edited by Neville Hoad, Karen Martin, and Graeme Reid, 149. Cape Town: Double Storey.

McGowan, Miranda Oshige. 2012. "Lifting the Veil on Rigorous Rational Basis Scrutiny." *Marquette Law Review* 96: 376–460.

McKay, Heather L. 2011. "Fighting for Victoria: Federal Equal Protection Claims Available to American Transgender Schoolchildren." *Quinnipiac Law Review* 29: 493–549.

McReynolds, Anjuli Willis. 2006. "What International Experience Can Tell U.S. Courts about Same-Sex Marriage." *UCLA Law Review* 53: 1073–1105.

Merkley, Jeff. 2015. "Historic, Comprehensive LGBT Non-Discrimination Legislation Introduced in Congress." July 23. Available at https://www.merkley.senate.gov/news/press-releases/historic-comprehensive-lgbt-non-discrimination-legislation-introduced-in-congress

Mezey, Susan Gluck. 2000. "The U.S. Supreme Court's Federalism Jurisprudence: *Alden v. Maine* and the Enhancement of State Sovereignty." *Publius: The Journal of Federalism* 30: 21–38.

———. 2007. *Queers in Court: Gay Rights Law and Public Policy*. Lanham, MD: Rowman & Littlefield.

———. 2011. *Elusive Equality: Women's Rights, Public Policy, and the Law*. 2nd ed. Boulder, CO: Lynne Rienner.

Miller, Hayley. 2015. "Report: Ban on Transgender Military Service to End May 2016." *Human Rights Campaign*, August 26. Available at https://www.hrc.org/blog/report-ban-on-transgender-military-service-to-end-may-2016.

———. 2016. "DOJ Answers Complaint; Recognizes Sexual Orientation Discrimination under Federal Law." January 29. Available at http://www.hrc.org/blog/doj-answers-complaint-recognizes-sexual-orientation-discrimination-under-fe

Miller, William H. 2004. "Position of Trust: Security Clearance Decisions after September 11, 2001." *George Mason University Civil Rights Law Journal* 14: 229–54.

Mississippi Legislature. 2016. "House Bill 1523." April 5. Available at http://billstatus.ls.state.ms.us/2016/pdf/history/HB/HB1523.xml

Moore, Peter. 2015. "Poll Results: Gay Marriage." YouGov, June 29. Available at https://today.yougov.com/news/2015/06/29/poll-results-gay-marriage

Mos, Michael. 2013. "Conflicted Normative Power Europe: The European Union and Sexual Minority Rights." *Journal of Contemporary European Research* 9: 78–93.

Motara, Shireen. 2000. "Focus: The Constitutional Court's 1999 Term." *South African Journal on Human Rights* 16: 344–50.

Movement Advancement Project. 2016a. "Local Employment Non-Discrimination Ordinances." February 2. Available at http://www.lgbtmap.org/equality-maps/non_discrimination_ordinances/policies

———. 2016b. "Non-Discrimination Laws." July 12. Available at http://www.lgbtmap.org/equality-maps/non_discrimination_laws

Movement Advancement Project, Center for American Progress, and Human Rights Campaign. 2013. "A Broken Bargain: Discrimination, Fewer Benefits and More Taxes for

LGBT Workers (Full Report)." June. Available at http://www.lgbtmap.org/file/a-broken-bargain-full-report.pdf

Murphy, Jason. 2001. "Dialogic Responses to *M. v. H.*: From Compliance to Defiance." *University of Toronto Faculty of Law* 59: 299–317.

Murray, John L. 2010. "The Influence of the European Convention on Fundamental Rights on Community Law." *Fordham International Law Journal* 33: 1388–1422.

Myers, Richard S. 2014. "The Implications of Justice Kennedy's Opinion in *United States v. Windsor.*" *Elon Law Review* 6: 323–35.

National Basketball Association. 2016. "New Orleans Selected to Host NBA All-Star 2017." August 19. Available at http://www.nba.com/2016/news/08/19/new-orleans-to-host-the-nba-all-star-2017

National Center for Lesbian Rights. 2011. "Complaint to OCR." October 10. Available at http://www.nclrights.org/wp-content/uploads/2013/09/Arcadia_Redacted_OCR_Complaint_07.24.2013.pdf

———. 2015. "Federal Government Approves School Policy That Affirms and Respects Transgender Students." July 13. Available at http://www.nclrights.org/press-room/press-release/federal-government-approves-school-policy-that-affirms-and-respects-transgender-students

National Center for Transgender Equality. 2015. "Safe Schools Nondiscrimination Laws." January 30. Available at http://www.transequality.org/issues/resources/map-state-schools-nondiscrimination-laws

National Coalition of Anti-Violence Programs. 2015. "National Report on Hate Violence against Lesbian, Gay, Bisexual, Transgender, Queer and HIV-Affected Communities." June 9. Available at http://www.avp.org/storage/documents/Reports/MEDIARELEASE_2014_NCAVP_HVREPORT.pdf

National Collegiate Athletic Association. 2016. "NCAA to Relocate Championships from North Carolina for 2016–17." September 12. Available at http://www.ncaa.org/about/resources/media-center/news/ncaa-relocate-championships-north-carolina-2016-17

National Conference of State Legislatures. 2015. "State Public Accommodations Laws." March 13. Available at http://www.ncsl.org/research/civil-and-criminal-justice/state-public-accommodation-laws.aspx

———. 2016. "2015 Religious Freedom Restoration Act Legislation." Available at http://www.ncsl.org/research/civil-and-criminal-justice/state-rfra-statutes.aspx#RFRA

National LGBTQ Task Force. 2014. "State Nondiscrimination Laws in the U.S." May 21 Available at http://www.thetaskforce.org/static_html/downloads/reports/issue_maps/non_discrimination_5_14_new.pdf

National Taskforce to End Sexual and Domestic Violence against Women. 2016. "National Consensus Statement of Anti-Sexual Assault and Domestic Violence Organizations in Support of Full and Equal Access for the Transgender Community." April 21. Available at http://www.4vawa.org

NC Governor Pat McCrory. 2016. "Executive Order No. 93 to Protect Privacy and Equality." April 12. Available at http://governor.nc.gov/document/executive-order-no-93-protect-privacy-and-equality

Neily, Clark. 2012. "Judicial Engagement Means No More Make-Believe Judging." *George Mason Law Review* 19: 1053–70.

Nejaime, Douglas, and Reva B. Siegel. 2014. "Conscience Wars: Complicity-Based Conscience Claims in Religion and Politics." *Yale Law Journal* 124: 2516–91.

Newstrom, Lisa. 2007. "The Horizon of Rights: Lessons from South Africa for the Post-*Goodridge* Analysis of Same-Sex Marriage." *Cornell International Law Journal* 40: 781–804.

New York State. 2015. "Governor Cuomo Introduces Regulations to Protect Transgender New Yorkers from Unlawful Discrimination." October 22. Available at https://www.governor.ny.gov/news/governor-cuomo-introduces-regulations-protect-transgender-new-yorkers-unlawful-discrimination

Nicol, Nancy, and Miriam Smith. 2008. "Legal Struggles and Political Resistance." *Sexualities* 11: 667–87.

Nicolas, Peter. 2016. "Fundamental Rights in a Post-*Obergefell* World." *Yale Journal of Law and Feminism* 27: 331–61.

North Carolina General Assembly. 2015. "Senate Bill 2/S.L. 2015-75." June 11. Available at http://www.ncleg.net/gascripts/BillLookUp/BillLookUp.pl?Session=2015&BillID=s2

———. 2016a. "House Bill 2." March 23. Available at www.ncleg.net/Sessions/2015E2/Bills/House/PDF/H2v4.pdf

———. 2016b. "House Bill 169/S.L. 2016-99." July 18. Available at http://www.ncleg.net/gascripts/BillLookUp/BillLookUp.pl?Session=2015&BillID=h169v8.html

Obama, Barack. 2014a. "Executive Order—Further Amendments to Executive Order 11478, Equal Employment Opportunity in the Federal Government, and Executive Order 11246, Equal Employment Opportunity." *White House, Office of the Press Secretary*, July 21. Available at https://www.whitehouse.gov/the-press-office/2014/07/21/executive-order-further-amendments-executive-order-11478-equal-employmen

———. 2014b. "Remarks by the President at Signing of Executive Order on LGBT Workplace Discrimination." *White House, Office of the Press Secretary*, July 21. Available at https://www.whitehouse.gov/the-press-office/2014/07/21/remarks-president-signing-executive-order-lgbt-workplace-discrimination

Office of the Governor Greg Abbott. 2015. "Governor Abbott Statement on Supreme Court Ruling on Same-Sex Marriage." June 26. Available at http://gov.texas.gov/news/press-release/2113

Office of the Governor of Louisiana. 2015. "Executive Order BJ 15-8." May 19. Available at http://www.doa.la.gov/osr/other/bj15-8.htm

———. 2016. "Executive Order JBE 2016-11." April 13. Available at http://gov.louisiana.gov/assets/ExecutiveOrders/JBE16-11.PDF

Office of Personnel Management, Equal Employment Opportunity Commission, Office of Special Counsel, and Merit Systems Protection Board. 2015. "Addressing Sexual Orientation and Gender Identity Discrimination in Federal Civilian Employment: A Guide to Employment Rights, Protections, and Responsibilities." June. Available at https://www.opm.gov/policy-data-oversight/diversity-and-inclusion/reference-materials/addressing-sexual-orientation-and-gender-identity-discrimination-in-federal-civilian-employment.pdf

Oklahoma State Legislature. 2016. "Bill Information for SB 1619." May 23. Available at http://www.oklegislature.gov/BillInfo.aspx?Bill=sb%201619

Oppenheimer, David B., Alvaro Oliveira, and Aaron Blumenthal. 2014. "Religiosity and Same-Sex Marriage in the United States and Europe." *Berkeley Journal of International Law* 32: 195–238.

Out & Equal. 2014. "LGBT Executive Order." July 21. Available at http://www.outandequal.org/connect/about/media-announcements/lgbt-executive-order

Peebles, Burton F. 2015. "Blurred Lines: Sexual Orientation and Gender Nonconformity in Title VII." *Emory Law Journal* 64: 911–54.

Peek, Christine. 2004. "Breaking Out of the Prison Hierarchy: Transgender Prisoners, Rape, and the Eighth Amendment." *Santa Clara Law Review* 44: 1211–48.

Pepper, Stacy. 2013. "The Defenseless Marriage Act: The Legitimacy of President Obama's Refusal to Defend DOMA §3." *Stanford Law and Policy Review* 24: 1–34.

Perez, Thomas. 2014. "DIRECTIVE (DIR) 2014-02." June 30. Available at https://www.dol.gov/ofccp/regs/compliance/directives/Directive_2014-02.pdf

Pew Research Center. 2014. "A Survey of LGBT Americans: Social Acceptance." September 18. Available at http://www.pewsocialtrends.org/2013/06/13/chapter-2-social-acceptance/#social-acceptance

Pew Research Center. 2015a. "Americans split over whether businesses must serve same-sex couples." March 30. Available at http://www.pewresearch.org/fact-tank/2015/03/30/businesses-serving-same-sex-couples/

Pew Research Center. 2015b. "Where Europe stands on gay marriage and civil unions." June 9. Available at http://www.pewresearch.org/fact-tank/2015/06/09/where-europe-stands-on-gay-marriage-and-civil-unions/

Pew Research Center. 2015c. "5 Facts about same-sex marriage." June 26. Available at http://www.pewresearch.org/fact-tank/2015/06/26/same-sex-marriage/

Pew Research Center. 2016. "Changing Attitudes on Gay Marriage." May 12. Available at http://www.pewforum.org/2016/05/12/changing-attitudes-on-gay-marriage/

Pierceson, Jason. 2005. *Courts, Liberalism, and Rights: Gay Law and Politics in the United States and Canada.* Philadelphia: Temple University Press.

———. 2014. *The Road to the Supreme Court and Beyond: Same-Sex Marriage in the United States.* Lanham: Rowman & Littlefield.

Pike, Jennifer. 2015. "Congressional LGBT Equality Caucus Announces Transgender Equality Task Force." *Human Rights Campaign,* November 17. Available at https://www.hrc.org/blog/congressional-lgbt-equality-caucus-announces-transgender-equality-task-force

Pinello, Daniel R. 2009. "Location, Location, Location: Same-Sex Relationship Rights by State." *Law Trends and News*, Fall. Available at http://www.americanbar.org/newsletter/publications/law_trends_news_practice_area_e_newsletter_home/bl_feat5.html

Pizer, Jennifer C., Brad Sears, Christy Mallory, and Nan D. Hunter. 2012. "Evidence of Persistent and Pervasive Workplace Discrimination against LGBT People: The Need for Federal Legislation Prohibiting Discrimination and Providing for Equal Employment Benefits." *Loyola of Los Angeles Law Review* 45: 715–79.

Posner, Richard. 1997. "Sex, Law, and Equality: Should There Be Homosexual Marriage? And If So, Who Should Decide?" *Michigan Law Review* 95: 1578–87.

Rabinowitz, Clarice B. 1995. "Proposals for Progress: Sodomy Laws and the European Convention on Human Rights." *Brooklyn Journal of International Law* 21: 425–69.

Raflo, Amanda. 2010. "Evolving Protection for Transgender Employees under Title VII's Sex Discrimination Prohibition: A New Era Where Gender Is More Than Chromosomes." *Charlotte Law Review* 2: 217–50.

Rao, Devi M. 2013. "Gender Identity Discrimination Is Sex Discrimination: Protecting Transgender Students from Bullying and Harassment Using Title IX." *Wisconsin Journal of Law, Gender and Society* 28: 245–70.

Rapport, Adele. 2015. "OCR Case No. 05-14-1055." *US Department of Education, Office for Civil Rights*, November 2. Available at http://www2.ed.gov/documents/press-releases/township-high-211-letter.pdf

Reed, Alex. 2013. "A Pro-Trans Argument for a Transexclusive Employment Non-Discrimination Act." *American Business Law Journal* 50: 835–74.

———. 2014. "Abandoning ENDA." *Harvard Journal on Legislation* 51: 277–314.

———. 2015. "Redressing LGBT Employment Discrimination via Executive Order." *Notre Dame Journal of Law, Ethics and Public Policy* 29: 133–67.

Republican National Committee. 2016. "Resolution Condemning Governmental Overreach Regarding Title IX Policies in Public Schools." February 25. Available at https://prod-static-ngop-pbl.s3.amazonaws.com/media/documents/Resolution_Title_IX%20_Overreach.pdf

Rezabek, Rachael. 2014. "(D)Evolving Standards of Decency: The Unworkability of Current Eighth Amendment Jurisprudence as Illustrated by *Kosilek v. Spencer*." *Southern California Law Review* 87: 420–50.

Robinson, B. A. 2005. "Homosexual (Same-Sex) Marriages in Canada: Québec: *Hendricks and Léboeuf* Case." *Religious Tolerance*, November 20. Available at http://www.religioustolerance.org/hom_msrb4.htm

Rotondo, Stephanie. 2014. "Employment Discrimination against LGBT Persons." *Georgetown Journal of Gender and the Law* 16: 103–39.

Rubenstein, William B. 2001. "Do Gay Rights Laws Matter? An Empirical Assessment." *Southern California Law Review* 75: 65–120.

Sachs, Michael. 2004. "The Mystery of Title VII: The Various Interpretations of Title VII as Applied to Homosexual Plaintiffs." *Wisconsin Women's Law Journal* 19: 359–80.

Saez, Macarena. 2011. "Same-Sex Marriage, Same-Sex Cohabitation, and Same-Sex Families around the World: Why 'Same' Is So Different." *American University Journal of Gender, Social Policy and the Law* 19: 1–54.

Samar, Vincent J. 2015. "Interpreting *Hobby Lobby* to Not Harm LGBT Civil Rights." *South Dakota Law Review* 60: 47–62.

Sanders, Steven. 2014. "Mini-DOMAs as Political Process Failures: The Case for Heightened Scrutiny of State Anti-Gay Marriage Amendment." *Northwestern University Law Review Colloquy* 109: 12–26.

———. 2016. "RFRAs and Reasonableness." *Indiana Law Journal* 91: 243–66.

Schaefer, Agnes Gereben, Radha Iyengar, Srikanth Kadiyala, Jennifer Kavanagh, Charles C. Engel, Kayla M. Williams, and Amii Kress. 2106. "The Implications of Allowing Transgender Personnel to Serve Openly in the U.S. Military." Santa Monica, CA: RAND Corporation. Available at http://www.rand.org/pubs/research_briefs/RB9909.html

Schmid, Heidi Joy. 2000. "Decriminalization of Sodomy under South Africa's 1996 Constitution: Implications for South African and U.S. Law." *Cardozo Journal of International and Comparative Law* 8: 163–204.

Schwin, Kevin. 2009. "Toward a Plain Meaning Approach to Analyzing Title VII: Employment Discrimination Protection for Transsexuals." *Cleveland State Law Review* 57: 645–70.

Sears, Brad, and Christy Mallory. 2011. "Documented Evidence of Employment Discrimination and Its Effects on LGBT People." *Williams Institute*, July. Available at http://williamsinstitute.law.ucla.edu/wp-content/uploads/Sears-Mallory-Discrimination-July-20111.pdf

Selznick, Loren F. 2014. "Running Mom and Pop Businesses by the Good Book: The Scope of Religious Rights of Business Owners." *Albany Law Review* 78: 1353–92.

Shay, Giovanna. 2014. "In the Box: Voir Dire on LGBT Issues in Changing Times." *Harvard Journal of Law and Gender* 37: 407–57.

Shields, John, Rebekah Jill Glassman, Kelly Whitaker, Heather Franks, and Ilsa Bertolini. 2013. "Estimating Population Size and Demographic Characteristics of Lesbian, Gay, Bisexual, and Transgender Youth in Middle School." *Journal of Adolescent Health* 52: 248–50.

Shuki-Kunze, Jennie R. 1998. "The 'Defenseless' Marriage Act: The Constitutionality of the Defense of Marriage Act as an Extension of Congressional Power under the Full Faith and Credit Clause." *Case Western Reserve University Law Review* 48: 351–79.

Simopoulos, Eugene F., and Eindra Khin Khin. 2014. "Fundamental Principles Inherent in the Comprehensive Care of Transgender Inmates." *Journal of the American Academy of Psychiatry and the Law* 42: 26–36.

Skinner-Thompson, Scott, and Ilona M. Turner. 2013. "Title IX's Protections for Transgender Student Athletes." *Wisconsin Journal of Law, Gender and Society* 28: 271–300.

Smith, Miriam. 2011. "Canada: The Power of Institutions." In *The Lesbian and Gay Movement and the State: Comparative Insights into a Transformed Relationship*, edited by Manon Tremblay, David Paternotte, and Carol Johnson, 73–88. Farnham, UK: Ashgate.

Smith, Whitney E. 2009. "In the Footsteps of *Johnson v. California*: Why Classification and Segregation of Transgender Inmates Warrants Heightened Scrutiny." *Journal of Race, Gender and Justice* 15: 689–727.

South Dakota Legislature. 2016. "House Bill 1008." March 7. Available at http://sdlegislature.gov/legislative_session/bills/Bill.aspx?Bill=1008&Session=2016

South Dakota State News. 2016. "Gov. Daugaard Vetoes HB 1008." March 1. Available at http://news.sd.gov/newsitem.aspx?id=19926

Southern Poverty Law Center. 2016. "'Religious Liberty' and the Anti-LGBT Right." February 11. Available at https://www.splcenter.org/20160211/religious-liberty-and-anti-lgbt-right

Spencer, Kate. 2010. "Same Sex Couples and the Right to Marry: European Perspectives." *Cambridge Student Law Review* 6: 155–76.

State of Maine Legislature. 2014. "Actions for LD 1428." February 20. Available at http://legislature.maine.gov/LawMakerWeb/subjects.asp?ID=280048537

State of North Carolina. 2015a. "Governor McCrory Releases Statement on Senate Bill 2." June 11. Available at http://governor.nc.gov/press-release/governor-mccrory-releases-statement-senate-bill-2

———. 2015b. "Governor Pat McCrory Defends Constitution." May 28. Available at http://governor.nc.gov/press-release/governor-mccrory-defends-constitution

Stiener, Jason. 2011. "A Survey of the Protections Afforded to the Rights of Gay and Lesbian Individuals." *International Journal of Civil Society Law* 9: 74–84.

Stone, Thomas Willoughby. 2003. "Margin of Appreciation Gone Awry: The European Court of Human Rights' Implicit Use of the Precautionary Principle in *Frette v. France* to Backtrack on Protection from Discrimination on the Basis of Sexual Orientation." *Connecticut Public Interest Law Journal* 3: 218–36.

Strasser, Mark. 2012. "DOMA, the Constitution, and the Promotion of Good Public Policy." *Albany Government Law Review* 5: 613–33.

Sung, William C. 2011. "Taking the Fight Back to Title VII: A Case for Redefining 'Because of Sex' to Include Gender Stereotypes, Sexual Orientation, and Gender Identity." *Southern California Law Review* 84: 487–539.

Szwalbnest, Olivia. 2010. "Discriminating Because of 'Pizzazz': Why Discrimination Based on Sexual Orientation Evidences Sexual Discrimination under the Sex-Stereotyping Doctrine of Title VII." *Texas Journal of Women and the Law* 20: 75–94.

Tarzwell, Sidney. 2006. "The Gender Lines Are Marked with Razor Wire: Addressing State Prison Policies and Practices for the Management of Transgender Prisoners." *Columbia Human Rights Law Review* 38: 167–219.

Texas Legislature Online. 2015. "HB4105." May 12. Available at http://www.legis.state.tx.us/BillLookup/History.aspx?LegSess=84R&Bill=HB4105

Thompson, Erik S. 2015. "Compromising Equality: An Analysis of the Religious Exemption in the Employment Non-Discrimination Act and Its Impact on LGBT Workers." *Boston College Journal of Law and Social Justice* 35: 284–318.

Thoreson, Ryan Richard. 2008. "Somewhere over the Rainbow Nation: Gay, Lesbian and Bisexual Activism in South Africa." *Journal of Southern African Studies* 34: 679–97.

Tieger, Ethan Z. 2014. "Transsexual Prisoners and the Eighth Amendment: Reconsidering *Kosilek v. Spencer* and Why Prison Officials May Not Be Constitutionally Required to Provide Sex-Reassignment Surgery." *Suffolk University Law Review* 47: 627–57.

Tobias, Carl. 2015. "Implementing Marriage Equality in America." *Duke Law Journal* 65: 25–49.

Tobin, Harper Jean, Raffi Freedman-Gurspan, and Lisa Mottet. 2015. "A Blueprint for Equality." *National Center for Transgender Equality*, June. Available at http://www.transequality.org/sites/default/files/docs/resources/NCTE_Blueprint_June2015.pdf

Tobin, Harper Jean, and Jennifer Levi. 2013. "Securing Equal Access to Sex-Segregated Facilities for Transgender Students." *Wisconsin Journal of Law, Gender, and Society* 28: 301–30.

Transgender Law Center. 2012. "Vice President Joe Biden: Transgender Discrimination 'Civil Rights Issue of Our Time.'" October 30. Available at http://transgenderlawcenter.org/archives/2312

———. 2013. "ENDA: Our Support and Concerns." April 25. Available at http://transgenderlawcenter.org/archives/7729

———. 2014. "Joint Statement on Withdrawal of Support for ENDA and Call for Equal Workplace Protections for LGBT People." July 8. Available at http://transgenderlawcenter.org/archives/10702

———. 2015. "TLC celebrates Groundbreaking CA prison Policy Ensuring Access to Gender-Affirming Medical Care." October 21. Available at http://transgenderlawcenter.org/archives/12109

Trans Policy News. 2009. "DOJ Will Not Appeal Federal District Court Ruling (*Schroer v. Library of Congress*)." July 1. Available at https://transpolicynews.wordpress.com/2009/07/01/doj-will-not-appeal-federal-district-court-ruling-schroer-v-library-of-congress

United Nations. 2011. "17/19 Human Rights, Sexual Orientation and Gender Identity." June 17. Available at https://documents-dds-ny.un.org/doc/UNDOC/GEN/G11/148/76/PDF/G1114876.pdf

———. 2015. "Discrimination and Violence against Individuals Based on Their Sexual Orientation and Gender Identity." May 4. Available at http://www.un.org/en/ga/search/view_doc.asp?symbol=A/HRC/29/23&referer=/english/&Lang=E

US Department of Defense. 2011. "Repeal of 'Don't Ask, Don't Tell' (DADT) Quick Reference Guide." October 28. Available at http://archive.defense.gov/home/features/2010/0610_dadt

———. 2015. "Remarks by Secretary Carter at a Troop Event in Kandahar, Afghanistan." February 22. Available at http://www.defense.gov/News/News-Transcripts/Transcript-View/Article/607016/remarks-by-secretary-carter-at-a-troop-event-in-kandahar-afghanistan

———. 2016. "Secretary of Defense Ash Carter Announces Policy for Transgender Service Members." June 30. Available at http://www.defense.gov/DesktopModules/ArticleCS/Print.aspx?PortalId=1&ModuleId=764&Article=821675

US Department of Education. 2015a. "Agreement to Resolve between Township High School District 211 and the U.S. Department of Education, Office for Civil Rights." December 2. Available at http://www2.ed.gov/documents/press-releases/township-high-211-agreement.pdf

———. 2015b. "Settlement Reached with Palatine, Ill., Township High School District 211 to Remedy Transgender Discrimination." December 3. Available at http://www.ed.gov/news/press-releases/settlement-reached-palatine-ill-township-high-school-district-211-remedy-transgender-discrimination

———. 2016. "Resources for Transgender and Gender-Nonconforming Students." July 8. Available at http://www2.ed.gov/print/about/offices/list/ocr/lgbt.html

US Department of Education, Office for Civil Rights. 2001. "Revised Sexual Harassment Guidance: Harassment of Students by School Employees, Other Students, or Third Parties." January. Available at http://www2.ed.gov./about/offices/list/ocr/docs/shguide.pdf

———. 2014. "Questions and Answers on Title IX and Sexual Violence." April 29. Available at http://www2.ed.gov/about/offices/list/ocr/docs/qa-201404-title-ix.pdf

———. 2015. "Letter from James A. Ferg-Cadima, OCR Acting Deputy Assistant Secretary of Policy, January 7, 2015, *G. G. v. Gloucester County School Board*, Brief For The United States As *Amicus Curiae* Supporting Plaintiff-Appellant And Urging Reversal." October 28. Available at http://blogs.edweek.org/edweek/rulesforengagement/transgenderstudentbrief.pdf

US Department of Justice. 2011. "Statement of the Attorney General on Litigation Involving the Defense of Marriage Act." February 23. Available at https://www.justice.gov/opa/pr/statement-attorney-general-litigation-involving-defense-marriage-act

——. 2013. "Resolution Agreement between the Arcadia Unified School District, the U.S. Department of Education, Office for Civil Rights, and the U.S. Department of Justice, Civil Rights Division." July 24. Available at http://www.justice.gov/sites/default/files/crt/legacy/2013/07/26/arcadiaagree.pdf

———. 2014a. "Statement by Attorney General Eric Holder on Federal Recognition of Same-Sex Marriages in Michigan." March 28. Available at http://www.justice.gov/opa/pr/2014/March/14-ag-320.html

———. 2014b. "Statement by Attorney General Eric Holder on Federal Recognition of Same-Sex Marriages in Utah." January 10. Available at http://www.justice.gov/opa/pr/2014/January/14-ag-031.html

———. 2015a. "Statement of Interest of the United States, *Diamond v. Owens*. Case No. 5:15-cv-50-CHW." April 3. M.D. Ga.

———. 2015b. "Statement of Interest of the United States, *G.G. v. Gloucester County School Board*, Civil No. 4:15cv54." June 29. Available at http://www.justice.gov/sites/default/files/crt/legacy/2015/07/09/gloucestersoi.pdf

———. 2015c. "Statement of Interest of the United States, *Tooley v. Van Buren Public Schools*, Case No. 2:14-cv-13466-AC-DRG." February 24. Available at http://www.justice.gov/sites/default/files/crt/legacy/2015/02/27/tooleysoi.pdf

———. 2016. "Attorney General Loretta E. Lynch Delivers Remarks at Press Conference Announcing Complaint against the State of North Carolina to Stop Discrimination against Transgender Individuals." May 9. Available at https://www.justice.gov/opa/speech/attorney-general-loretta-e-lynch-delivers-remarks-press-conference-announcing-complaint

US Department of Justice, Civil Rights Division. 2016a. "Letter from Vanita Gupta to Pat McCrory." May 4. Available at http://www.wral.com/read-the-justice-department-letter-regarding-house-bill-2/15682478/

US Department of Justice, Civil Rights Division, and US Department of Education, Office for Civil Rights. 2016. "Dear Colleague Letter on Transgender Students." May 13. Available at https://www.justice.gov/opa/file/850986/download

US Department of Labor, Occupational Safety and Health Administration. 2015. "A Guide to Restroom Access for Transgender Workers." June 1. Available at https://www. osha .gov/Publications/ OSHA 3795.pdf

US General Accounting Office. 2004. "Defense of Marriage Act: Update to Prior Report," GAO-04353R, January 23. Available at http://www.gao.gov/assets/100/92441.pdf

US House Committee on the Judiciary. 1996. H. Rep. No. 104-664

US Office of Management and Budget. 2007. "Final Bulletin for Agency Good Guidance Practices." January 25. Available at https://www.whitehouse.gov/sites/default/files/omb/fedreg/2007/012507_good_guidance.pdf

US Senate. 2013. Report 113-105. 1st session, 113th Cong. September 13.

Van de Heyning, Catherine. 2011. "No Place Like Home." In *Human Rights Protection in the European Legal Order: The Interaction between the European and the National Courts*, edited by Patricia Popelier, Catherine Van de Heyning, and Piet Van Nuffel, 65–96. Cambridge, UK: Intersentia.

Virginia's Legislative Information System. 2016. "SB 40 Marriage licenses; Issuance of License by State Registrar of Vital Records, Conscience Clause." January 13. Available at https://lis.virginia.gov/cgi-bin/legp604.exe?161+sum+SB40

Waaldijk, Kees. 2000. "Civil Developments: Patterns of Reform in the Legal Position of Same-Sex Partners in Europe." *Canadian Journal of Family Law* 2000 17: 62–88.

———. 2001. Small Change: How the Road to Same-Sex Marriage Got Paved in the Netherlands. In *Legal Recognition of Same-Sex Partnerships*, edited by Robert Wintemute and Mads Andenaes, 437–64. Oxford: Hart.

Walters, Mark D. 2003. "Incorporating Common Law into the Constitution of Canada: *EGALE v. Canada* and the Status of Marriage." *Osgoode Hall Law Journal* 41: 75–114.

Wardle, Lynn D. 1998. "*Loving v. Virginia* and the Constitutional Right to Marry, 1790–1990." *Howard University Law Journal* 41: 289–347.

———. 2013. "Equality Principles as Asserted Justifications for Mandating the Legalization of Same-Sex Marriage in American and Intercountry-Comparative Constitutional Law." *Brigham Young University Journal of Public Law* 27: 489–527.

———. 2014. "'Sticks and Stones': *Windsor*, the New Morality, and Its Old Language." *Elon Law Review* 6: 411–46.

Webb, Hoyt. 1998–1999. "The Constitutional Court of South Africa: Rights Interpretation and Comparative Constitutional Law." *University of Pennsylvania Journal of Constitutional Law* 1: 205–83.

Williams, Kerry. 2004. "'I Do' or 'We Won't': Legalising Same-Sex Marriage in South Africa." *South African Journal of Human Rights* 20: 32–63.

Williams Institute. 2009. "Documenting Discrimination on the Basis of Sexual Orientation and Gender Identity in State Employment." September. Available at http://williamsinstitute.law.ucla.edu/wp-content/uploads/ExecutiveSummary1.pdf

———. 2014a. "Evidence of Discrimination: LGBT Employees in the Workplace." March. Available at http://williamsinstitute.law.ucla.edu/uncategorized/infographic-envidence-of-discrimination-march-2014

———. 2014b. "Executive Order Will Protect 34 Million Federal Contractor Employees from Sexual Orientation and Gender Identity Discrimination." July 18. Available at http://williamsinstitute.law.ucla.edu/press/press-releases/18-july-2014

Wilson, Bianca D. M., Khush Cooper, Angeliki Kastanis, and Sheila Nezhad. 2014. "Sexual and Gender Minority Youth in Foster Care: Assessing Disproportionality and Disparities in Los Angeles." *Williams Institute*. Available at http://williamsinstitute.law.ucla.edu/wp-content/uploads/LAFYS_report_final-aug-2014.pdf

Wing, Adrien Katherine. 2002. "The Fifth Anniversary of the South African Constitution: A Role Model on Sexual Orientation." *Vermont Law Review* 26: 821–27.

Wintemute, Robert. 2004. "Sexual Orientation and the Charter: The Achievement of Formal Legal Equality." *McGill Law Journal* 49: 1143–80.

Wolff, Tobias Barrington. 2015. "The Three Voices of *Obergefell*: In a Profound Review of Case Law, Substantive Due Process, and the Social Virtues of Marriage, the U.S. Supreme Court Made Marriage Equality a Reality." *Los Angeles Lawyer* 38: 28–32.

World Professional Association for Transgender Health (WPATH). 2011. *Standards of Care for the Health of Transsexual, Transgender, and Gender Nonconforming People*. 7th ed. Available at http://www.wpath.org/site_page.cfm?pk_association_webpage_menu=1351&pk_association_webpage=4655

Wright, Wade K. 2006. "The Tide in Favour of Equality: Same-Sex Marriage in Canada and England and Wales." *International Journal of Law, Policy and the Family* 20: 249–85.

Yarbough, Michael W. 2006. "South Africa's Wedding Jitters: Consolidation, Abolition, or Proliferation?" *Yale Journal of Law and Feminism* 18: 497–521.

The Yogyakarta Principles on the Application of International Human Rights Law in Relation to Sexual Orientation and Gender Identity. 2007. March. Available at http://www.yogyakartaprinciples.org/wp/wp-content/uploads/2016/08/principles_en.pdf

Yoshino, Kenji. 2015. "A New Birth of Freedom: *Obergefell v. Hodges*." *Harvard Law Review* 129: 147–79.

INDEX OF CASES

INDEX

ABOUT THE AUTHOR

Susan Gluck Mezey is a professor emeritus of political science at Loyola University Chicago; she holds a Ph.D. from Syracuse University and a J.D. from DePaul University. Her publications include *Elusive Equality: Women's Rights, Public Policy, and the Law*, 2nd ed. (2011); *Gay Families and the Courts: The Quest for Equal Rights* (2009); *Queers in Court: Gay Rights Law and Public Policy* (2007); *Disabling Interpretations: Judicial Implementation of the Americans with Disabilities Act in Federal Court* (2005); and *Pitiful Plaintiffs: Child Welfare Litigation and the Federal Courts* (2000).